Competition Law of the EC and UK

Competition Law of the EC and UK

Fourth Edition

Mark Furse

OXFORD
UNIVERSITY PRESS

OXFORD
UNIVERSITY PRESS

Great Clarendon Street, Oxford OX2 6DP

Oxford University Press is a department of the University of Oxford.
It furthers the University's objective of excellence in research, scholarship,
and education by publishing worldwide in

Oxford New York

Auckland Bangkok Buenos Aires Cape Town Chennai
Dar es Salaam Delhi Hong Kong Istanbul Karachi Kolkata
Kuala Lumpur Madrid Melbourne Mexico City Mumbai Nairobi
São Paulo Shanghai Taipei Tokyo Toronto

Oxford is a registered trade mark of Oxford University Press
in the UK and in certain other countries

Published in the United States
by Oxford University Press Inc., New York

British Library Cataloguing in Publication Data
Data available

Library of Congress Cataloging in Publication Data
Data available
ISBN 0–19–925880–5

1 3 5 7 9 10 8 6 4 2

Typeset in ITC Stone Serif and ITC Stone Sans
by RefineCatch Limited, Bungay, Suffolk
Printed in Great Britain by
Ashford Colour Press Ltd,
Gosport, Hampshire

OUTLINE CONTENTS

DETAILED CONTENTS

PREFACE

Never put anything in writing, its highly illegal and it could bite you right in the arse!!!!
(email sent by Mike Brighty, a Sales Director at Hasbro, to a colleague)

After changes upon changes, we are more or less the same.
(Paul Simon, *The Boxer*)

In May 2002, in the preface to the third edition of this work, I wrote that I intended to be working on the new edition within a year. At that time it was anticipated that a substantial reform of the way in which competition law was applied within the EC would be completed in early 2003. It is now May 2004, and that reform process is just coming to fruition, the EC Commission having published all relevant Community material, although the Office of Fair Trading in the UK has been particularly slow to produce promised new materials. It remains to be seen whether these extensive changes will in fact result in a fundamental difference in the application of competition law in the future, and my suspicion is that they will not.

The changes in competition law over the past two years have been numerous. From the top down, the EC has fundamentally redefined the relationship between Community and national law (a development dealt with here in Chapter 3—and reflected in the change in title of the book). As part of this process the application of the law relating to agreements has been substantially changed, the investigative procedure has been updated, and new rules have been introduced in relation to the penalties and remedies. A new EC Merger Control regulation has been produced, and other instruments, including the block exemption regulation of technology transfer, have been revised. All of these developments are dealt with here. In the UK the Competition Act 1998 has begun to bite, and there have been a number of decisions and appeals, some of which have received substantial publicity. At the time of writing the OFT is engaged in a high-profile investigation of alleged price fixing within the private schools sector. In 2002 the Enterprise Act 2002 was enacted (a move only presaged in the last edition of this book). This has resulted in changes to some aspects of the Competition Act, and to the institutional structure of competition law enforcement in the UK. It also brought into place new regimes in relation to merger control, and to the investigation of markets wherein com-petitive failures might be identified. More controversially a new cartel offence has been created, and for the first time in the modern era people may be imprisoned for anti-competitive activity implemented in the UK.

All of these developments have necessitated substantial rewriting of much of this book. There are two entirely new chapters, and merger control has been expanded and split into two chapters, both of which are in effect also new. Another six chapters have been substantially rewritten and some of the material has been reordered. The scheme of the book now is to deal with basic issues and jurisdiction in the first four chapters. This means that international issues are dealt with earlier than has been the case before, although this seems to be their logical position in the text. Procedural matters are dealt with in Chapters 5 through 8, and the 'new Regulation 17', Regulation 1/2003, is prominently dealt with here. Agreements, including the cartel offence, are dealt with in Chapters 8–12, while Chapters 13–17 deal with dominance, and market failure. Merger control is dealt with in Chapters 18–20, and finally the common law of competition in England and Wales is discussed in Chapter 21. In each of the three substantive areas discussion of the law is preceded by an introduction of some of the relevant economics. My guiding principle throughout the preparation of this new edition has been to present a picture of the law as it is today, not a full historical discourse. This book is, as has always been the case, designed primarily for those coming to competition law for the first time, and is not intended to be the final word in any area, although I hope that it is more than sufficient for the purposes of undergraduate students or those committed to private study of this vibrant area of law. I hope also that the emphasis on economics, an understanding of which I believe to be essential for those studying the subject, will not be off-putting to students of law.

I owe thanks to a number of people, and to three groups in particular. First, to former colleagues and students at the University of Westminster where I worked from 1986 to 2002, and the Nicolas Copernicus University, Torun, Poland, where I was employed in 2003, and in particular Dr Malgorzata Nesterowicz. Professor Susan Nash has contributed indirectly to Chapter 12, which deals with the new cartel offence, and her generosity in sharing expertise is much appreciated. In the village of Ebrington, my home in the Cotswolds, I must thank for their fellowship over the last two years Jeromy, Colin, Andy, Lynn, Joan, and Graham—thanks guys. Finally I am happy to acknowledge the support of my new colleagues at the University of Glasgow, and the exceptional students with whom I have been privileged to share my first year of what I hope will be many here. While it is unfair to single out some to the exclusion of others I must in particular acknowledge the help, support, and companionship of Professor Noreen Burrows, and Maria Fletcher. Both have read parts of this book and their comments have improved it. Jonathan Galloway has improved Chapter 4 with his comments on an earlier draft. The staff at OUP have been exceptionally patient, and, as usual, helpful and professional. As is always the case, any errors and omissions are my sole responsibility. I would welcome comments on the text in this book, which may be addressed to me at: m.furse@law.gla.ac.uk.

All author royalties from this edition are being paid to the Saraswati Project, which is based in Bhaktapur in Nepal. As well as being breathtakingly beautiful, Nepal is desperately poor, and has been ravaged by a long-running insurgency. The last time I returned from the country I was fortunate to meet, during the course of a long delay, Ms Gerd Baetens, a Belgian teacher, who in the best tradition of individual charity has established a programme to assist in particular children, by giving them, and their parents, a chance to study, supporting their educational needs and where necessary providing assistance with food, shelter, and healthcare.

As with the best of such programmes the ultimate aim is to provide recipients with the skills to live independently.

The law in this edition is intended to be up to date as at 1 May 2004.

Mark Furse
The University of Glasgow
May 2004

TABLE OF CASES

TABLES OF DECISIONS AND REPORTS

UK Decisions

EC Decisions

Reports

EC Commission

Monopolies and Mergers Commission

TABLES OF LEGISLATION

FOREIGN LEGISLATION

United States

LIST OF ABBREVIATIONS

ATC	Average total cost
AVC	Average variable cost
CA 98	Competition Act 1998
CAT	Competition Appeals Tribunal
CBI	Confederation of British Industry
CC	Competition Commission
CCAT	Competition Commission Appeals Tribunal
CDDA	Company Directors Disqualification Act 1986
CDO	Competition disqualification order
CDU	Competition disqualification undertaking
CFI	Court of First Instance
DG Comp	Director General of Competition
DGFT	Director General of Fair Trading
DOJ	Department of Justice (USA)
DTI	Department of Trade and Industry
EA 02	Enterprise Act 2002
EAEC	European Atomic Energy Community (Euratom)
EC	European Community
ECHR	European Convention on Human Rights 1950
ECJ	European Court of Justice
ECMR	European Community Merger Regulation/European Community merger regime
ECN	European Competition Network
ECSC	European Coal and Steel Community
ECU	European Currency Unit (now replaced by the Euro, €)
EEA	European Economic Area
EEC	European Economic Community (now the EC)
EFTA	European Free Trade Area
EU	European Union
EUCAR	European Council for Automotive Research and Development
FTA	Fair Trading Act 1973
FTC	Federal Trade Commission (USA)
GATT	General Agreement on Tariffs and Trade
GCI	Global Competition Initiative
GISC	General Insurance Standards Council
HHI	Herfindahl–Hirschman Index
ICN	International Competition Network
ICPAC	International Competition Policy Advisory Committee
IIB	Institute of Insurance Brokers
IPR	Intellectual property right
JV	Joint Venture
MMC	Monopolies and Mergers Commission
NAFTA	North American Free Trade Agreement
NCA	Network of Competition Authorities
NCC	National Consumer Council
PCIJ	Permanent Court of International Justice
OECD	Organization for Economic Cooperation and Development

OFT	Office of Fair Trading
OPEC	Organization of Petroleum Exporting Countries
RPC	Restrictive Practices Court
RPM	Resale price maintenance
RTPA	Restrictive Trade Practices Act 1976
SCP	Structure–Conduct–Performance model
SFO	Serious Fraud Office
SIEC	Significantly impeding effective competition
SLC	Substantial lessening of competition/Substantially lessen competition
SSNIP	Small but significant non-transitory increase in price
TEU	Treaty on European Unity ('Maastricht Treaty')
UNCTAD	United Nations Conference on Trade and Development
USTR	United States Trade Representative
WTO	World Trade Organization

1

Introduction to competition law

1.1 Introduction

The primary purpose of competition law is to remedy some of the situations in which the free market system breaks down. The point was well made in the House of Lords debate during the passage of the Competition Act 1998 that 'competition law provides the framework for competitive activity. It protects the process of competition. As such it is of vital importance' (Hansard (HL) 30 October 1997, col. 1156).

The 'invisible hand' that Adam Smith identified in 1776 ensures in most situations that free market economies left to their own devices will produce results more beneficial than can be realized by intervening in the markets. This conclusion has been supported by evidence put forward by economists over the last 200 years, and, since the collapse of East European planned economies, forms the basis for most of the world's economic systems. The process of competition is seen as being of value and meriting protection. In its White Paper *Productivity and Enterprise* (Cm. 5233, July 2001), the UK Government argued that

The importance of competition in an increasingly innovative and globalised economy is clear. Vigorous competition between firms is the lifeblood of strong and effective markets. Competition helps consumers get a good deal. It encourages firms to innovate by reducing slack, putting downward pressure on costs and providing incentives for the efficient organisation of production. As such, competition is a central driver for productivity growth in the economy, and hence the UK's international competitiveness. (para. 1.1)

Similar sentiments, albeit on a less grand scale, were expressed by the UK Competition Commission ('CC') in a recent report into the contemplated merger (examined under the now defunct merger provisions of the Fair Trading Act 1973) between Safeway plc and any one of a number of supermarket chains:

When working effectively, competition involves a process of rivalry between firms that strive to win customers' business by achieving the lowest level of costs and prices, developing new products or services or exploiting particular strengths, skills or other advantages to meet customer needs more effectively than competitors. (*Safeway plc and Asda Group Limited (owned by Wal-Mart Stores Inc); Wm Morrison Supermarkets PLC; J Sainsbury plc; and Tesco plc: A report on the mergers in contemplation* (Cm. 5950, September 2003), at para. 2.88)

It is often said, however, that 'competition sows the seeds of its own destruction'; encouraged to compete, successful entrepreneurs may achieve positions where they are able to prevent others from competing and thereby damage the process as a whole. A variant on this problem is that there may be some situations in which there is only room for a single firm in a market, and, unless steps are taken to regulate the conduct of this firm, it too may act to the detriment of the economy. The fact that in both the EC and the UK a competitor harmed by another's unlawful anti-competitive conduct may go to court to seek damages or another suitable remedy also serves to place stress on the right of business people to conduct their affairs in a fair and reasonable commercial environment. Competition law is not, directly, about consumer protection, or trading standards, although both may benefit from the application of competition law (see, however, Averitt, N. W., and Lande, R. H., 'Consumer Sovereignty: A Unified Theory of Antitrust and Consumer Protection Law', (1997) *Antitrust Law Journal* 713).

In the United Kingdom there are two systems of competition law: domestic law and the law of the European Community (EC). The relationship between these two regimes is examined in Chapter 3. With the passage of the Competition Act 1998 the domestic regime was strengthened and, following the demands of both the business community and consumer groups, brought into much closer alignment with EC law. An examination of these two regimes forms the basis of this book. Most of the law dealt with here is based on statutes or other public enactments. In both systems lawyers and regulators are likely to look for guidance to the operation of the antitrust law of the United States, which is briefly introduced later in this chapter, and then considered in relation to specific cases throughout the book. The common law of England and Wales remains applicable in a small class of cases, which are considered further in Chapter 21.

To the frustration of many lawyers competition law is heavily reliant on economics, and it is not only those new to the subject who may be hesitant when dealing with a different discipline with its own language and 'rules'. In practice lawyers handling the more complex cases are likely to rely on expert witnesses and documentation provided either by companies themselves or by firms of economic consultants. However, without some understanding of what questions should be raised, and what significance the answers then have, such communication becomes difficult and inefficient. It is for this reason that the reader of this book is faced with economics both later in this introduction, and in Chapters 8, and 18. It might be possible to pass these by, but the case law that is discussed elsewhere will be clearer if they are read, and then returned to as necessary. These sections are not intended to serve as a complete guide to the subject of industrial economics, and the interested reader is referred to specialist texts. Particularly useful is Bishop, S., and Walker, S., *The Economics of EC Competition Law*, London, Sweet & Maxwell, 2nd edn, 2002.

1.2 **The development of competition law**

The American Sherman Act 1890 is taken as the starting point of modern competition (or in America, 'antitrust') law but the roots of competition law lie much deeper. Senator Sherman himself told the Senate that his bill did 'not announce a new principle of law, but applies old and well-recognized principles of the common law to the complicated jurisdiction of our State and Federal Government'. It has even been suggested, unconvincingly, that the Act is based in part on the Constitution of Zeno, Emperor of the East from 474 to 491, promulgated in 483. Roman legislation dealing with some aspects of competition predates the Constitution by over 500 years.

In England competition law has developed in fits and starts since before legal memory, and only in the last half of the twentieth century was it subjected to rigorous economic analysis. At present there is no satisfactory single history of the early competition laws, and much of the best work has been done by those researching the circumstances surrounding the creation of the Sherman Act in 1890 (see, e.g., Thorelli, H. B., *The Federal Antitrust Policy*, Stockholm (1954); see also Lord Wilberforce, Campbell, A., and Elles, N., *The Law of Restrictive Trade Practices and Monopolies*, London, Sweet & Maxwell (2nd edn, 1966)). Various Saxon kings had taken action against a range of trading practices, including, for example, the purchase of commodities before they reached their designated market place in order to enhance the price, and make a profit on a later sale, known as the crime of foresteel, or forestalling, which is referred to in the Domesday Book (1086). Other laws set out punishments for ingrossers, who similarly obtained agricultural produce with the intention of reselling it at a profit; regrators, who purchased products in one market place to resell them in either the same or a neighbouring market at a higher price; and travelling salesmen, known as 'badgers', who dealt mainly in foodstuffs, purchasing in one place and reselling at a premium in another. At the time of the Magna Carta (1215) legislation provided that all monopolies were to be contrary to the law because of their pernicious effect on individual freedom.

The great plagues that swept across Europe in the late medieval period resulted in shortages of both labour and commodities. Although it is now believed that contemporary accounts tended to exaggerate the impact of the plagues, and of the Black Death in particular, there is no reason to doubt that 'there was such a scarcity of labourers that women and even small children could be seen at the plough and leading the waggons' (Keen, M., *Medieval Europe*, London, Penguin Books (1968), p. 234). The various statutes which aimed to fix both prices and wages at pre-plague levels in order to prevent labourers moving to seek better-paid employment, thereby damaging the interests of landowners, were a response in part to problems created by these shortages. The 1349 Statute of Labourers is notable by virtue of its introduction of the requirement that merchants overcharging should pay multiple damages to injured parties, which is followed today in the American treble-damages suit (see Chapter 6).

It has also been suggested that the common law doctrine of 'restraint of trade' (which is defined in Chapter 21) emerged in response to the pressures caused by labour shortages. *John Dyer's* case (1414) YB 2 Hen 5 (of. 5, pl. 26) appears to be the first recorded case of restraint of trade. John, the Dyer, had sought to enforce a writ against a colleague who had covenanted not to practise the craft of dyeing in the same town as John Dyer for half a year. Fortunately for Dyer he was not in court when the case was heard, for the judge held that the provision was against the common law 'and by God, if the plaintiff were here, he should go to prison'. The rule that covenants in restraint of trade were not enforceable remained in place until the beginning of the seventeenth century, at which time added flexibility was introduced to accommodate changing circumstances (see, e.g., *Rogers* v *Parrey* (1613) 80 ER 1012). By the middle of the nineteenth century the courts had introduced, and had begun to expand on, the relationship of the public interest to the operation of the doctrine. In *Horner* v *Graves* (1831) 131 ER 284, the judge brought the doctrine close to the modern day when he held that 'we do not see how a better test can be applied to the question whether reasonable or not, than by considering whether the restraint is not so large as to interfere with the interests of the public'. The extent to which restraint of trade was concerned with the issue of monopoly per se is a question that has not been fully resolved. It appears that judges were at least as swayed by arguments as to individual liberty, and as to the cost to the public purse of the support, however rudimentary, that might be available to the worker who was not able to secure employment because of the restraint's operation. More recent developments, discussed at 21.2.3, appear to bring the doctrine into the mainstream of competition law, and to link it directly with EC competition law.

There was little the common law could do to combat arrangements between businesses, and this area was left largely to various statutes. However, the doctrine of conspiracy crept into the area of trade regulation from the seventeenth century onwards, particularly in relation to the attempts of working people to organize themselves. The doctrine was applied to business situations in the eighteenth century, but then fell into disuse. It was confirmed in *Mogul SS Co. Ltd* v *McGregor Gow & Co.* [1892] AC 25, that it would be applied only where the objective of the conspiracy was illegal, and that it was not illegal to seek to improve a business position.

1.2.1 Monopolies and the Crown

The word 'monopoly' was probably first used in England by Thomas More in *Utopia* (1516). It carried a specific meaning:

A Monopoly is an Institution, or allowance by the King, by His Grant, Commission, or otherwise, to any person or persons, bodies politic or corporate, of or for the sole buying, selling, making, working or using of any thing, whereby any person or persons, bodies politic or corporate are sought to be restrained of any freedom, or liberty that they had before or hindered in their lawful trade. (The US Supreme Court in *Standard Oil Co. of New Jersey* v *US* (1911) 221 US 1, citing Sir Edward Coke, *Institutes*)

Such monopolies were increasingly granted from the mid-1300s. In Elizabethan England (1558–1603) the system of Industrial Monopoly Licences was heavily abused as a mechanism for raising funds for the monarch without the inconvenience of consulting Parliament. Although Parliament protested, the Queen was able to persuade it to drop a Bill that would have curbed the practice. It was therefore left to the courts in 1602 to rule that a grant of a monopoly for the making of playing cards to one Darcy was illegal and void (*Darcy* v *Allin* (1602) 11 Co Rep 84b—also known as the *Case of the Monopolies*). Even at this time the arguments against monopoly practices were becoming well rehearsed, and the court found that there were inevitable and unwelcome consequences of all monopolies: an increase in price; a reduction in quality; and a reduction in the incentive to work. The position in the early 1600s was such that Ben Jonson, in *The Devil is an Ass* (1616), was able to satirize for his audiences the practice of granting monopolies and those who negotiated them: the character of Merecraft, 'The Great Projector', promoted and sold increasingly fantastical monopoly schemes, including an inventive scheme to monopolize the market in toothpicks.

The conflict between Crown and Parliament was resolved in 1623 with the passing of the Statute of Monopolies, which declared that 'All Monopolies . . . are altogether contrary to the Laws of this Realm, and so are and shall be utterly void and of none effect and in no wise to be put into use or execution'. In making an exception for patents for a period not exceeding 21 years save where these operated to raise prices or to damage trade, the statute also formed the basis for the modern law of patents. Monopolies could still be granted to trading corporations and guilds, a practice much used by Charles I. In the 'Great Case against Monopolies', *East India Company* v *Sandys* (1685) 10 St Tr 371, it was held that a distinction could be drawn between monopolies operating *within* the realm, and those established in order to compete *outside* the realm. In the latter situation it was accepted that only a firm in a strong position could trade successfully in the difficult conditions prevailing. This argument finds a modern counterpart in the debate on the relationship between competition and national industrial policy, in particular the promotion of 'national champions': 'Competition can be enormously beneficial in many cases, but where it involves the destruction of strong interests in a wider context, it could be weakening from UK PLC's point of view' (Graeme Odgers, MMC Chairman, *Evening Standard*, 5 May 1993).

In 1772, following a House of Commons committee report, most of the old laws were repealed, and by 1844 all earlier Acts were repealed, it then being considered that the prohibitions had effects contrary to that intended, and were partly responsible for inhibiting trade and raising prices. From that time till now monopolies have not been prevented in the United Kingdom, and the modern law of competition deals with issues of the *abuse* of monopoly power, not with its existence per se.

The United Kingdom, with a belief in the benefits of economic laissez-faire, did not return to competition law until after the Second World War, when in 1948 legislation was introduced that established a domestic structure for the examination and control of anti-competitive competitive conduct. The domestic regime now is found primarily in two statutes, the Competition Act 1998 ('CA 98'), and the Enterprise Act 2002 ('EA 02').

1.2.2 Competition law and the EC

According to the European Court of Justice the provisions of EC law dealing with competition constitute 'a fundamental provision . . . essential for the accomplishment of the tasks entrusted to the Community and, in particular, for the functioning of the internal market' (*Eco Swiss China Time Ltd* v *Benetton International NV* case C–126/97 [2000] 5 CMLR 816, para. 36).

Provisions relating to competition law were included in the Treaty of Rome of 1957, which formed the legal basis for the European Economic Community, from the outset. Thus:

From the inception of this process, there seems to have been little doubt that the Treaty would have to include provisions aimed at combating restraints on competition. Not only had such provisions been included in the ECSC treaty, but there seems to have been general agreement that the elimination of tariff barriers would not achieve its objectives if private agreements or economically powerful firms were permitted to be used to manipulate the flow of trade.   (Gerber, D. J., *Law and Competition Policy in Twentieth Century Europe—Protecting Prometheus*, Oxford, Clarendon Press (1998), p. 343)

Articles 85 and 86 of the Treaty (now arts 81 and 82) related to the control of anti-competitive agreements and dominant firm abuses. Similar provisions had been placed in the earlier European Coal and Steel Community Treaty of 1951. There has been a substantial and interesting debate as to the policy pressures that underlay the inclusion of these provisions. David Gerber's seminal work, quoted above, deals in part with this question and the argument is made persuasively that rather than slavishly adopting an American-style model based on sections 1 and 2 of the Sherman Act (see below) the relevant Treaty provisions reflected a distinctly European approach to the issue of anti-competitive conduct. In particular the German ordo-liberals are cited as a key influence in the determination of the European policy. Some commentators have attacked Gerber's thesis, and it may be argued that whatever the roots of the policy, its operation in practice remains heavily influenced by American practices.

1.3 The experience of the United States

It is generally presumed that the Sherman Act, which ushered in the 'modern' era of competition law, was a response to irresistible pressures exerted from the agricultural heartland of the United States: prices and wages were rising, yet farmers, faced with disproportionately higher freight costs set by the railway companies which combined to set standard rates, were not benefiting from the trend.

Section 1 of the Sherman Act prohibits 'every contract, combination . . . or conspiracy in restraint of trade' at a federal level (that is where inter-state trade would be affected). Decisions of the US Supreme Court have restricted these words, which would, if taken at face value, condemn nearly all business conduct to apply only to 'unreasonable' restraint of trade (*Standard Oil Co. of New Jersey* v *United States* (1911) 221 US 1). This 'rule of reason' is at the heart of American law, and there is intense debate as to the place of such a rule in EC law (see further at 9.7 below). Section 2 of the Act is in the following terms: 'Every person who shall monopolize, or attempt to monopolize . . . any part of the trade or commerce among the several States . . . shall be guilty of a misdemeanor'. It is possible to argue that it is the legitimate goal of any businessman to 'monopolize' his industry, and in *United States* v *Grinnel Corp.* (1966) 384 US 563, a distinction was drawn between the 'wilful' acquisition of monopoly power, which fell to be condemned, and monopoly arising from better commercial practices which would escape the Act's application. Although it has been supplemented by other legislation over the last century, which is discussed elsewhere in this book as appropriate, the Sherman Act remains central to antitrust policy in the United States (see generally Sullivan, E. T. (ed.), *The Political Economy of the Sherman Act: The First One Hundred Years*, New York, OUP (1991)). Given that economic principles do not, unlike law, vary from country to country, there are often good reasons to look to the large body of American case law to illuminate competition cases brought elsewhere. There are, however, significant divergences in the underpinning philosophies of the American and European regimes, and principles from one regime should not be slavishly applied to the other without good justification:

Many valuable ideas for the interpretation of Community law can be derived from the discussions going on on the other side of the Atlantic and from the solutions found by the American courts. However, prudence must be counseled in transferring concepts and theories from one legal system to the other. There are substantial differences between the various elements going to make up US law and those going to make up Community law, with the result that not every problem confronting one of the two systems finds a counterpart in the other legal system.   (Advocate General Kirschner in *Tetra Pak Rausing SA* v *Commission* case T–51/89 [1991] 4 CMLR 334 at 343–4)

1.4 Economics and competition law

Economics can be employed in two main ways in relation to competition law. First, because competition law is aimed in part at remedying market failure a general macro-economic argument can be made as to the existence of such market failure and the costs imposed by it. Secondly, micro-economic arguments are likely to be relied upon in each individual case to justify intervention or to defend a company's position. Attempts to avoid the 'problem' of economics are likely to result in bad law—as was the case with the Restrictive Trade Practices Act 1976, which adopted an overly legalistic approach in an attempt to disregard economic issues. In Chapters 8 and 13 specific issues relating to collusion between firms and to actions by individual firms are considered in more detail and in Chapter 18 the economics of mergers is discussed. This section introduces the general argument advanced to support intervention and some standard economic terms.

For readers who are interested in developing their economic expertise further a good accessible text that deals with competition strategy is Besanko, D., Dranove, D., and Sharley, M., *Economics of Strategy*, New York, John Wiley & Sons (2nd edn, 2000). Specific references later in this text are given to Bishop and Walker, *The Economics of EC Competition Law*, because of its direct connection to the subject matter of this book. A recent American text, Hylton, K. M., *Antitrust Law: Economic Theory and Common Law Evolution*, Cambridge, Cambridge University Press (2003) superbly links the substantive application of US law to economic theory.

1.4.1 The problem of standards

As was noted above, it is the presumed goal of entrepreneurs to maximize their profits, and to be as successful as possible. While Bill Gates probably did not envisage 25 years ago that Microsoft would become one of the largest and most profitable corporations in the world, if asked he would probably have said that he would like it to. Now that it has assumed such a strong position Microsoft's commercial practices have been scrutinized by competition authorities around the world, and practices that might be pursued legitimately by smaller firms may be condemned if followed by Microsoft. The managers of a business may determine a strategy for all the 'right' reasons as far as that business is concerned, and yet, on the basis of a test related to society's welfare, be attacked. To what standards then are businesses to conform? Competition law is often contrasted with environmental regulation. For any given standard in environmental law (e.g., 'mercury content to be no more than three parts per million') it is a relatively easy matter to test for any given sample whether the standard is indeed being broken. It is much harder to set similar tests in the area of competition law.

In the United States 'monopolization' is condemned (see above); in the European Community the standard of conduct for a monopolist is that it should not 'abuse' its 'dominant position' (see Chapter 14). It will be impossible to determine whether this standard is being breached without recourse to economic analysis. Amongst other things the regulator or plaintiff must consider: what the relevant market is (e.g., is the market for bananas discrete, or is it part of the market for soft fruit, or all fruit?—*United Brands Co.* v *Commission* case 27/76 [1978] 1 CMLR 429); is the firm a monopolist?; is the alleged 'abuse' in fact a legitimate business tactic?; what effect is the alleged abuse having?

1.4.2 **Industrial economics and markets**

The area of economics that is most important for competition law is industrial economics, which is the branch of the science that applies micro-economic tools, such as an individual's preferences for apples over pears, or the costs of making a chair instead of a table, to wider market situations. Markets are where producers and consumers interact, and in a theoretical world of 'perfect' competition a market will produce an efficient result. Efficiency has a particular meaning in economics. An efficient position is one in which the only way to make anyone better off is to make someone else worse off. This is to say it refers to a situation in which no more mutually advantageous bargains or contracts can be made. In any situation in which A can be made better off, with B being no worse off, it will be efficient for that transaction to take place. Such a situation is referred to as one of *pareto optimum*. This theoretical ideal permits an examination of the extent to which observed market structures diverge from 'perfect competition' and the resulting harm. The requirements of perfect competition are that there must be very large, tending to infinite, numbers of producers and of consumers. The product is homogenous so that there are no significant differences between one producer's product and the next. Both producers and consumers are perfectly informed about the market and are motivated by the desire to maximize profits and satisfaction. When added to various assumptions made about the costs of production, the result is that no consumer or producer is able to influence the price of the product, and that the price at which the item is sold exactly matches the cost of making it. In observed markets these assumptions break down: consumers and producers will be able to influence the price of products, which are not homogenous, and neither group is likely to have perfect information about the market place. The antithesis of perfect competition is monopoly, with 'monopolistic', or imperfect, competition lying somewhere between the two.

When an economist uses the term 'monopoly' it has a specific meaning, different from that put forward by Coke's *Institutes* (above). A monopoly market is one in which there is only one producer. It is frequently pointed out by those questioning the basis of much of competition regulation that the most common situation in which monopoly arises is where it is the product of government action (e.g., by legal controls limiting entry into an industry, in particular where the state regulates an industry). Empirical observation suggests, in particular, that monopolies, even where they do exist, are unable to remain monopolies in the long run unless they are protected by legislative barriers to entry.

A monopolist, unlike a firm in a perfectly competitive market, has the power to determine the price at which the product is sold. Adam Smith, whose *The Wealth of Nations* (1776) serves as the basis of modern economics, suggested that 'the price of monopoly is upon every occasion the highest which can be got'. The monopolist can achieve this by choosing how much of the product to supply.

1.4.2.1 *The adverse consequences of monopolies*

Ceteris paribus ('all other things being equal') prices are higher, and output less, in markets which are monopolistic than in markets which are perfectly competitive. A consequence of the steps taken to achieve this is that it results in a non-optimal allocation of resources, by sending the 'wrong' signals as to the value/cost of products. The monopolist, by raising prices above the production cost of an item, denies consumers who are in fact prepared to pay that cost the opportunity of doing so. The monopolist has, by raising the price of the product, sent the consumer a false signal about the true value of the product in relation to other products and less consumer demand is therefore satisfied under these conditions. Further, the money that would have been spent on the monopoly product is instead spent on other products thereby raising *their* prices and the market becomes distorted.

Another issue is that of 'consumer surplus'. If a monopolist can set only one price for a product, as is the usual case in competitive market conditions, a given number of consumers will buy the product. For one of these consumers the decision has been a marginal one, and had the price been any higher the purchase would not be made. Some of the other consumers might have been prepared to pay for more, and have, in effect, achieved savings on the purchase. Consider, for example, an item in a sale—one consumer might buy it only because it has been reduced in price, while another might have been quite happy to pay the full price and feel that they have got a bargain. The total amount of this 'saving' is known as the consumer surplus. If the monopolist could force each consumer to pay their maximum price the total revenue to the monopolist rises and the consumer surplus vanishes, which represents a transfer of income from the consumers to the monopolist. This issue is often dealt with in competition law under the heading of 'price discrimination' (see Chapter 16). It is not directly a matter that impinges upon the efficiency of the situation, but it is nevertheless of legitimate interest to a regulator concerned with the distribution of income.

In 1954, in an article which has assumed seminal importance but has led to a somewhat difficult and convoluted debate, Arnold Harberger attempted to quantify the total loss to American society from the monopolistic industries in the United States (Harberger, A. C., 'Monopoly and Resource Allocation', (1954) 44 *American Economic Review* 77). Harberger estimated the difference between the total consumer demand satisfied under competitive conditions, and the reduced demand satisfied under monopoly conditions (the 'welfare triangle', or 'Harberger triangle'). In fact Harberger's estimate was only 0.1 per cent of the national income. More recent studies, however, point to figures of between 4 per cent and 20 per cent, suggesting that Harberger's estimate is an understatement and may be seen as a lower boundary.

The strategic activity undertaken to achieve, or reinforce, a monopoly position ('rent seeking') may also represent a cost of monopolies. This might include excessive advertising that has no benefit in terms of increased sales, and aggressive competition that does not increase either consumer or producer welfare. The intense British Airways/Virgin Atlantic competition of the mid- to late 1990s is sometimes cited as an example of such conduct.

1.4.3 The policy debate—Harvard *v* Chicago, and the new industrial economics

Until the mid-1980s competition economists, regulators, and to a certain extent lawyers, could be placed into two broad camps: the Harvard school and the Chicago school. Although the crude divisions these labels suggest have largely broken down under the influence of more modern economic analysis, there remains some value in the distinction, and it is still common to find these labels applied either to personalities or to approaches. The debate is not an abstract one as the policy implications of the ideas advanced by each school are very different. As will be seen in Chapter 13, if the Chicago school adherents are correct there is no need for regulators to consider anti-competitive conduct such as 'predation'; if the Harvard school supporters are correct, it may be right for regulators to intervene in such situations.

The first major school of thought to develop emerged at Harvard University when, in the 1930s, researchers conducted analyses of specific industries. Their conclusions led to the Structure–Conduct–Performance model (SCP): performance is determined by firms' conduct, which is in turn determined by the market structure. Kaysen and Turner, for example, consistent with the general distrust of corporate America and large business that was widely shared at the time, argued that the limitation of market power should be the central focus of competition policy and that market power should be reduced wherever this could be done without a corresponding cost in the performance of the industry (Kaysen, C., and Turner, D. F., *Antitrust Policy: An Economic and Legal Analysis*, Cambridge, Mass., Harvard UP (1959)).

One of the first practices that the Chicago school and notably Stigler examined, was that of the welfare implications of the structure of an industry, and of barriers to entry into that industry. Where the Harvard economists had argued that higher barriers enabled incumbents to increase prices, and were therefore prima facie to be condemned, the Chicagoans are concerned to examine the nature of the barrier, tolerating those which are the result of efficiency considerations. The SCP, Harvard model is replaced by one in which performance dictates market structure—the 'reverse causation' argument. In other words, monopolistic industries are the result of efficiency and superior performance, and should not then be attacked precisely because the firms in them have succeeded. Thus Bork has argued that the real question for competition policy is whether 'artificial' barriers, not being the result of more efficient production or economies of scale, prevent the effective operation of the market (Bork, R. H., *The Antitrust Paradox*, New York, The Free Press (1993)). More generally it is the tendency of the Chicago school to accept that, in the real world, the model of perfect competition can be used to explain most business behaviour, which is to say that all companies are constrained by competition.

Alongside this sits the general assumption of the school that the only concern of competition policy should be the attainment of efficiency, and that ancillary 'non-economic' goals such as the equitable distribution of income, or the socio-political problems of a concentration of economic power should not be a part of any competition policy. For a recent text following a Chicagoan line see Gordon, R. L., *Antitrust Abuse in the New Economy*, Cheltenham, Edward Elgar, 2002.

The Chicagoan assumption that real-world behaviour will tend to match that forecast by the perfect competition model is now being subject to increasingly rigorous challenges with the emergence of the new (or 'modern') industrial economics, which is informed in part by the empirical evidence provided in various antitrust actions. It appears to be now well established that the competitive assumptions made by some of the more extreme Chicagoans are incorrect, and are not supported by evidence. The standard-bearers of the Chicagoan viewpoint in America over more recent years have been R. H. Bork and R. A. Posner, both of whom were appointed to the bench under the Republican presidencies, and who remain in a position to exercise some considerable influence over the debate in America. Bork's *The Antitrust Paradox* (above) is a highly entertaining polemic, and provokes much debate, although it now lags behind contemporary economic argument. Posner's record in adjudicating antitrust actions in his time on the bench has been examined by American commentators and found lacking. Again it has been noted that he has disregarded strong evidence, characterized by some economists as incontrovertible, to the effect that concentration in any industry is almost inevitably damaging to consumer welfare.

The more pragmatic line taken by the new industrial economics is that in a monopolistic market, where the expected benefits outweigh the likely costs, a profit-maximizing firm will engage in strategic behaviour. For adherents to the new industrial economics one of the roles of competition policy is to make the expected costs of such strategic behaviour sufficiently great to outweigh the expected benefits, thereby deterring such conduct.

Broadly, the aims of competition policy are in line with the new industrial economics, although generalizations as to the aims of the various regimes are dangerous (see further Chapter 2). As was noted above, the aim of competition policy is not to achieve perfect competition as an alternative to monopoly. The definition of competition more usually accepted by regulatory authorities is that of the 'workable competition' first discussed by J. M. Clark in 1940 (30 *American Economic Review* 241). Workable competition accepts that there are elements of monopoly in virtually all markets, and has, as its goal, making such structures compatible with strong competition. It therefore contains an element of pragmatism that courts find more attractive than more rigorous economic models (see, e.g., *Metro-SB-Grossmärkte GmbH & Co. KG* v *Commission* case 26/76 [1978] 2 CMLR 1).

It should be noted, too, that an increasing emphasis on the impact of technology on industrial development is leading to some new approaches to markets and industry being developed (see, e.g., Sutton, J., *Technology and Market Structure*, Boston, MIT Press (1999)).

1.4.4 **Basic tools of economic analysis**

There is less controversy surrounding the basic tools of economics than there is about the policy implications of different market structures. The Harvard and Chicago schools alike are in agreement as to these components. Markets represent the aggregation of individual elements, and there will be situations in competition law where these individual elements become important in determining the existence of anti-competitive behaviour, and in resolving other economic issues, such as the ability of a monopolist to raise prices, or the existence of other products that restrict the monopolist's power.

1.4.4.1 *Demand, supply, and price*

In a free market economy the price of any product is set by the relationship between the demand for the product and the supply of the product. *Ceteris paribus*, the greater the supply, and the less the demand, the less the price of the product will be. The demand for a product is the sum of the demand of individual consumers. In all save a few cases a consumer's individual demand for a product will be inversely related to its price, and can be represented diagrammatically as a 'curve' that slopes downwards from left to right (see Figure 1.1). The 'elasticity of demand', references to which are often encountered in competition cases, is the extent to which demand is sensitive to price. An inelastic demand curve denotes that consumers are unresponsive to changes in price: if price rises by 10 per cent demand falls by *less* than 10 per cent. The more inelastic demand is, therefore, the

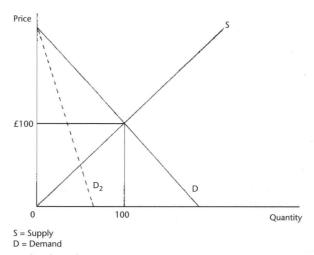

S = Supply
D = Demand

Figure 1.1 Demand and supply curves

Note: The price at which the product is sold, and the quantity sold, will be that where the demand and supply curves intersect. Demand curve D_2 is less elastic than D; if these two curves are looked at in isolation it will be seen that a change in price (from, e.g., £100 to £150) will have a bigger effect on D than on D_2.

more a monopolist will be able to raise prices and still increase their income. It may be presumed that petrol has an inelastic demand. If the demand for petrol was in fact elastic the government would not be able to raise significant revenue by taxation on petrol, for any increase in tax would be more than matched by a drop in sales. An elastic demand curve denotes that consumers are very responsive to changes in price: if price rises by 10 per cent demand falls by *more* than 10 per cent, and in such a situation a monopolist raising prices will find that income will fall. Any product that has many substitutes is likely to have an elastic demand. The demand for compact discs is probably inelastic, but the demand for any individual disc will be more elastic. Thus if the price of all discs were to rise by 10 per cent, sales would probably not fall by as much as 10 per cent, but if The Sugababes' new CD was priced at 20 per cent more than any other disc, consumers might prefer to purchase an alternative from the wide range stocked by any music store. Supply curves slope upwards left to right, showing that the relationship between supply and price is that, *ceteris paribus*, the higher the price the greater the level of supply. The price of the product, the quantity supplied, and the quantity bought will be that set where demand and supply curves intersect.

As suggested above, the demand for a product will also be affected by the prices of *other* products, which is termed 'cross-elasticity of demand' or 'substitutability'. An examination of substitutability is almost essential in determining the boundaries of any given product market. If demand for one product is highly sensitive to the price of another (e.g., clementines and mandarins) it is probably unwise to treat the market for clementines as being a separate one distinct from the market for mandarins. Producers and retailers of clementines will have to be always considering what is happening in the market for mandarins. Analysis of substitutability accordingly features prominently in many competition cases. This is just one area in which the language of business may differ from the language of competition law. The sales or marketing director of any business may have a very clear view of the market that is being targeted by that business, but, if subject to a competition investigation, a very different definition of the market (often but not always a wider one) may be adopted.

1.4.4.2 Costs

Certain competition law issues cannot properly be resolved without an analysis of the costs faced by the company concerned. This is true of allegations of predation, where the charge is that the business is making losses or acting primarily with the intention of driving a competitor out of the market, or of preventing entry into the market, and of allegations of 'profiteering' where the company is accused of making too much profit (see Chapters 13 and 16).

Costs of production can be separated out in various ways. The primary divisions made by economists are between fixed and variable costs; marginal, average, and total costs; and short-run and long-run costs. Consider the example of a mass-produced motor car. In the short run fixed costs are those that stay constant whatever the level of production (e.g., the rent on the factories and perhaps

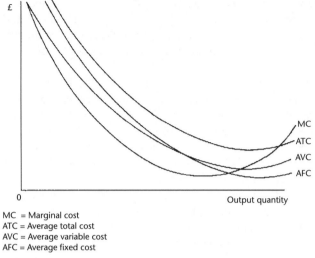

MC = Marginal cost
ATC = Average total cost
AVC = Average variable cost
AFC = Average fixed cost

Figure 1.2 Cost curves
Note: This figure assumes that there are economies of scale, so marginal and variable cost fall first. Once these economies are exhausted costs will begin to rise again.

research and development); variable costs alter according to the level of production (e.g., the cost of steel, plastics, and labour). Marginal costs are those of the additional unit of production (the cost of making one extra car). Generally marginal costs fall as production rises through the operation of 'economies of scale'. Economies of scale are the benefits that arise from producing more of any item. It is, for example, cheaper to produce the tenth motor car in a mass-production plant than it is to produce the first, and the 10,000th will be considerably cheaper still. Where there are economies of scale, the average cost, which is the total cost divided by the quantity produced, will fall as output rises. In the long run there may be significant differences and the concept of fixed costs in particular becomes less definite, for even factories can be disposed of. The various cost curves are shown in Figure 1.2. Supply of a product will be determined by the costs of production and the demand for the product.

1.4.4.3 *Markets*

The definition of a 'relevant market' is essential to several aspects of competition law. Markets are where consumers and suppliers of a product or service interact. As was mentioned above (at 1.4.4.1) it may, for the purposes of rigorous analysis, be necessary to determine whether product A competes with product B. This is particularly important in the case of investigations into abuses of a dominant position, as we need to know in respect of what the undertaking is believed to be dominant. For example, is there a market for bus services? If there is it might be possible to apply the laws of dominance to a bus company that has a strong market position in a given area. On the other hand, if bus services compete strongly with rail and taxi services, with walking, and with the use of private cars, then it would probably not be possible to apply the law. As indicated above the most important factor here is that of the extent to which products are interchangeable one for the other.

The test favoured by competition authorities is the SSNIP test (which is discussed further at 14.2.4). This asks what the effect would be on product A of a Small but Significant Non-transitory Increase in Price of product A by a hypothetical monopolist. To put this another way: if all of A were to be produced by one supplier, and the price of A were to rise by 5–10 per cent, and the price of all other products stayed constant, what would happen to the demand for A? In all save the most extreme circumstances *some* customers at least will switch to another product as they would be at the margin of the demand for product A. Other customers would accept a substantial price rise, while still remaining loyal to A. The question is whether the income lost from those customers who defect is more than compensated for by an increase in income from those remaining. Or to put it more simply still, would the price rise be profitable? If such a price rise would be profitable we assume that there is a market for A. If it would not be we need to determine to which products customers are switching most readily, and include those in the SSNIP test (i.e., run the same hypothetical exercise on the assumption that products A and B are controlled by the same supplier). This exercise can be more than merely hypothetical as sales data may provide many answers. For example, if there is an unexpected heat wave in October, and sales of ice cream rise, it might be possible to determine whether sales of cold canned drinks have fallen—which might imply a degree of substitutability between the two products. In other circumstances this exercise can be more difficult, and the SSNIP test may fail to produce an accurate result. This is most clearly the case where there is an existing monopolist who has behaved intelligently. A monopolist is expected to raise the price of their product to the highest profitable level. Were the price to rise any further in such a case it would lead to losses, and might suggest to the unwary that the market was wider than for the monopolist's product. If there was a single supplier of bicycles and the price was raised to the maximum profitable level it might be that a further price rise would push some customers towards purchasing motorcycles, although it is highly unlikely that these are in the same relevant market. Such a mistake was made by the US Supreme Court in the case of *United States v E I duPont* 351 US 377 (1956). Here the court found that there was not a market for cellophane, as were the price to rise profits would fall. It is widely accepted that the court was wrong, as it started from a position where prices had *already* risen above the competitive level to the monopoly level. This danger is now known as the 'cellophane fallacy', or 'cellophane trap'.

Further factors in defining relevant markets, and the importance of doing so in the areas of agreements, single firm conduct, and mergers, are dealt with as appropriate throughout this text.

1.4.5 **Barriers to entry**

The implications of barriers to entry are that their existence reinforces monopolistic tendencies in a market. Theoretical models of market structure focus only on *actual* competition facing producers, and make no reference to *potential* competition. It has long been recognized that potential competition serves as a restraint on the conduct of incumbents (those already in the market) in just the same way as does the actual competition faced. The higher the barriers that exist, the greater is the ability of the incumbent to ignore the potential competition.

While the existence of barriers to entry in any given situation may be a matter of some concern to those investigating the market, there is intense debate between the Harvard and Chicago schools as to the policy implications of barriers to entry, and even as to what a barrier to entry is. The issue is of such importance that it should be dealt with at this early stage. At its very broadest, a barrier to entry is any factor that operates as a cost of a new entrant into a market. By this definition it might include such factors as: lack of knowledge about the market; any premium rate paid for capital to compensate for the risk this lack of knowledge results in; the cost of acquiring the necessary physical capacity (plant and raw materials); the cost of establishing brand recognition with consumers, and a distribution system, etc.

Whether all barriers to entry should be a matter of concern to competition regulation is contested. Some barriers are the result of the success of the incumbent (e.g., the need to develop brand loyalty) and it may be argued that if the incumbent has had to overcome this hurdle it is, or has been over time, in no better a position than any potential entrant. In fact these still reinforce the power of the incumbent, but some (notably Chicagoans) argue that such barriers should be of no concern to regulators and are merely evidence of the efficiency of the incumbent. Adherents of the Harvard school would permit competition policy to examine *any* barrier, and in some circumstances to impose positive obligations on incumbents to reduce barriers. In an extreme case this could, for example, take the form of restricting their product lines so as to allow a niche for the entrant, or to allow entrants access to the incumbent's established distribution network. Such policies are likely to face severe resistance from businesses that have led the way into a market and succeeded, and whose officers are often perplexed at the demands made on them by the law.

All commentators would accept that barriers that result from governmental action are a source of legitimate concern, although such barriers will often be justified on the grounds of health and safety, or may be accompanied by ongoing industry regulation that will ameliorate the consequence of the market power granted to the incumbent.

1.4.6 **Conclusion**

Unfortunately the analysis conducted by the various regulatory authorities is often somewhat lacking in formal rigour, and the EC Commission decisions have in particular been criticized for lacking in-depth economic analysis. In its *Green Paper on Vertical Restraints* (see Chapter 9) the EC Commission argued that

economic theory is just one of the sources of policy. In practice, the application of economic theory must take place in the context of the existing legal texts and jurisprudence. Secondly, economic theories are necessarily based on simplifying assumptions often obtained in the context of stylised theoretical models that cannot take into account all the complexities of real life cases. (para. 86)

It might plausibly be argued that, if an economic theory based on simplifying assumptions has been tested and refined against empirical data, that theory could serve as a legal test and is at least as likely to produce reliable results as is a pragmatic individual analysis of each case.

Care should be taken over the way in which economic 'evidence' is used in competition cases. While economic consultants will regularly be employed to advance arguments in competition cases, and in many cases their evidence will be determinative of the issues, there are some dangers with constructing elaborate economic 'stories' to explain observed conduct. An illustration of the problems may be found in the UK case of *Napp Pharmaceutical Holdings Ltd* v *The Director General of Fair Trading* [2002] CompAR 13. Napp was condemned for discriminatory predatory pricing in one sector of its market (the case is discussed in full in Chapter 16). Its economic consultants, Nera, produced an argument to the effect that the undertaking was rationally pricing low in one sector as this ensured follow-through sales in another sector, and that this 'portfolio' pricing was a legitimate and profitable strategy that was available to all its competitors as well. The Competition Commission Appeals Tribunal (CCAT), which heard the case, found no suggestion in the documents produced by Napp that it had in fact been consciously following such a strategy. The Tribunal noted that 'Napp does not strike us as a naïve or badly managed company', and argued that 'if its pricing policy had in fact been seen by Napp in the way that its economic consultants suggest, we would have expected the company's internal documents to demonstrate that' (para. 252).

2

The European Community and United Kingdom regulatory regimes

2.1 Introduction

The enactment of the Sherman Act in the United States of America in 1890 was a major development in competition law, and the American regime has had a pervasive influence on the development of the law elsewhere. In part this is because the success of the American economy was attributed, amongst other factors, to the efficacy of the US antitrust law. The UK and Community regimes arose independently although the story since the UK's accession to the EC on 1 January 1973 has been that of pressure on the domestic regime to adapt to the dominant EC system. The impetus for change has come largely from industry in the UK whose interests would be likely to be served by a 'one-stop' shop. On 1 May 2004 substantial changes to the EC regime further refined the relationship between the two systems. This chapter serves as an introduction to the two regimes.

2.2 Undertakings—the subjects of competition law

Throughout this chapter, and throughout the rest of this book, references are made to 'undertakings', which are the sole subjects of the substantive law relating to agreements, and to the abuse of dominant positions. This is the word used in the EC Treaty and in Community secondary legislation, and has been adopted in the UK Competition Act 1998. For the EC undertakings are the sole subjects of competition law, although in certain narrowly defined circumstances individual persons may be involved in investigation procedures. In the UK the cartel offence extends only to individuals. In the early years of the application of competition law the word 'undertaking' caused some difficulties, and attempts to provide a precise definition were largely unsuccessful. The better course is to argue by analogy with past decisions and cases, and to look to the intent underlying the legislation itself. A broad understanding of the concept may be clear from the words used by the ECJ in *Hofner and Elser* v *Macrotron GmbH* case C–41/90 [1993] 4 CMLR 306, where the Court held that 'the concept of an undertaking encompasses every entity engaged in economic activity, regardless of the legal status of the entity and the way in which it is financed' (para. 21).

In defining the undertaking in any particular circumstance it is necessary to look to the economic and factual reality of the situation, and not to legal structure. A single individual may be an undertaking in circumstances where they have an impact on the market in a capacity other than that of a consumer. Thus in *Reuter/ BASF* 76/743/EEC (1976) OJ L254/40, an inventor was held to be an undertaking and therefore subject to art. 81. In *UNITEL* 78/516/EEC (1978) OJ L157/39 opera singers were brought within the scope of the law. Parent and subsidiary companies may be held to be part of the same undertaking, and not to be their separate legal constituents. This can have the benefit of removing arrangements between them from the provisions of art. 81 and the Chapter I Prohibition, which require that 'two or more undertakings' be implicated in the practice (see, e.g., *Re Christiani & Nielsen* 69/165/EEC [1969] CMLR D36 and more recently, *Viho Europe BV v Commission* case T–102/92 [1995] 4 CMLR 299; and see further Chapter 9). Undertakings do not have to be making profits nor even be engaged in profit-making activity: in the course of a proceeding relating to the 1990 football World Cup, the EC Commission expressly stated that organizations did not have to be profit making as long as they were engaged in economic activity (*Distribution of Package Tours During the 1990 World Cup* 92/521/EEC (1992) OJ L326/31). In restricted circumstances commercial activities carried out by arms of the state may not fall within the definition of 'undertaking', although this cannot serve as a broad exemption. For example, in the case of *Coapi* 95/188 (1995) OJ L122/37, the Commission condemned a decision of an association of industrial property agents in Spain. Coapi argued that as it was responsible for the discharge of functions assigned to it by virtue of Spanish law (Law No. 2/1974), and was governed by public law, it could not be regarded as an undertaking for the purposes of Community competition law. The Commission, relying on the definition given by the Court in *Hofner* (above), held that these facts did not prevent Coapi from being regarded as an undertaking subject to the provisions of art. 81.

State undertakings that are *purchasing* goods on the market for use in the provision of services are *not* undertakings for the purposes of competition law. In the case of *Federacion Nacional de Empresas de Instrumentacion Cientifica, Medica, Tecnica y Dental (FENIN) v Commission* case T–319/99 [2003] 5 CMLR 1 the CFI upheld a Commission decision finding that the national health service of Spain was not acting as an undertaking when it purchased services from the market place, even though it was a monopsony (monopolistic purchaser). The Court held, at paras 36–37 that

it is the activity consisting in offering goods and services on a given market that is the characteristic feature of an economic activity, not the business of purchasing as such. Thus, as the Commission has argued, it would be incorrect, when determining the nature of that subsequent activity, to dissociate the activity of purchasing goods from the subsequent use to which they are put. The nature of the purchasing activity must therefore be determined according to whether or not the subsequent use of the purchased goods amounts to an economic activity.

Consequently, an organisation which purchases goods—even in great quantity—not for the purpose of offering goods and services as part of an economic activity, but in order to use them in the context of a different activity, such as one of a purely social nature, does not act as an undertaking simply because it is a purchaser in a given market. Whilst an entity may wield very considerable economic power, even giving rise to a monopsony, it nevertheless remains the case that, if the activity for which that entity purchases goods is not an economic activity, it is not acting as an undertaking for the purposes of Community competition law and is therefore not subject to the prohibitions laid down [in arts 81 and 82 EC].

In *Cisal* (*Cisal di Battistello Venanzio & Co Sas* v *Istituto Nazionale Per L'Assicurazione Contro Gli Infortuni Sul Lavoro (INAIL)* case C–218/00 [2002] 4 CMLR 24) the ECJ, on a reference from an Italian tribunal, considered the position of 'INAIL', a body 'entrusted by law with the management of a scheme providing insurance against accidents at work and occupational diseases' (para. 21). It has been accepted in a number of cases that *any* activity consisting in offering goods or services on a market is an economic activity (see, e.g., joined cases C–180–184/98 *Pavlov and others* v *Stichting Pensioenfunds Medische Specialisten* [2000] ECR I-6451, at para. 75). In the present case it was argued that services provided by the alleged undertaking were fully comparable to those provided by a private insurer. The Court found, however, that the insurance scheme operated with a clear social, rather than commercial, purpose. For example, the effect of the way the scheme was arranged, and contributions were collected, was to subsidize poorer-paid workers by contributions from better-paid workers. It was also clear that the activity of INAIL was subject to close supervision and control by the State. In this instance, therefore, the ECJ held that INAIL was not, for the purposes of EC competition law, an undertaking.

The question of the extent to which professional associations—for example the Bar, or the British Medical Association (BMA)—are undertakings whose conduct and decisions may be subject to the constraints of competition law has been a matter of some discussion for a number of years. In February 2002 the ECJ shed some light on this issue in a case relating to the Dutch Bar (*Wouters, Savelbergh and Price Waterhouse Belastingadviseurs BV* v *Algemene Raad Van de Nederlandse Orde Van Advocaten* case C–309/99 [2002] 4 CMLR 27). First, the Court held that individual members of the Bar carried out economic activities in that they offered 'for a fee, services in the form of legal assistance consisting in the drafting of opinions, contracts and other documents and representation of clients in legal proceedings. In addition, they bear the financial risks attaching to the performance of those activities' (para. 48). It was irrelevant, the Court said, that these activities were complex and technical. Secondly, the association of individual members in the Bar would constitute an '*association of undertakings* within the meaning of Art 81(1)' (para. 64), although the Bar *itself* would not be classed as an undertaking for the purposes of art. 82. In particular when the Bar adopted regulations governing the activities of its members in some cases these regulations would be neither of a social function, nor the exercise of special powers typically held by a public authority. Rather the Bar 'acts as the regulatory body of a profession, the practice of which constitutes an economic activity' (para. 58). It should be noted at this stage that this does not automatically mean that the conduct of such professional associations will be condemned. Rather it is the position that because the conduct attaches to an 'undertaking', or 'association of undertakings' its (anti-) competitive impact can be examined in the light of the appropriate legislation and standards. Note that in *Arduino* v *Compagnia Assicuratrice RAS SpA* case C–35/99 [2002] 4 CMLR 25 the ECJ held, on an art. 234 reference from an Italian court, that the adoption by the state of a national rule approving fees set by the Italian Bar Council was not caught by art. 81.

Apart from providing a test as to the application of art. 81(1), the limits of the undertaking can be relevant to the fact-finding procedure of Regulation 1/2003 (see Chapter 5), and to the penalties imposed under that Regulation.

For the purposes of United Kingdom law the same approach is taken under the terms of the Competition Act 1998 as is taken under Community law. In the case of *The Institute of Independent Insurance Brokers* v *The Director General of Fair Trading* [2001] CompAR 62 the CCAT held that the Office of Fair Trading (OFT) had been incorrect to dismiss a complaint on the grounds that the entity, the activity of which formed the basis of the complaint, was not an undertaking. The Director was called upon to look at various rules relating to insurance set by the General Insurance Standards Council (GISC). This described itself as 'an independent, non-profit making organisation, funded entirely by membership fees, whose main purpose is to make sure that general insurance customers are treated fairly'. In the decision the Director concluded that 'in light of European case law' GISC's regulatory function 'does not constitute an economic activity' (*Application by the Institute of Insurance Brokers ('IIB') under s. 47(1)* [2001] UKCLR 838, para. 18). Considering all the facts, including the fact that GISC was set up as a private company, existing solely by contract, and was run by a board of directors, the CCAT found that it could see 'no compelling reason why GISC should not be regarded itself as an undertaking' (para. 258).

The OFT has also held that a health care trust purchasing social care services is not acting as an undertaking (*The North & West Belfast Health and Social Services Trust* CA/98/11/2002). On appeal the Competition Appeals Tribunal (CAT) held that the Trust *was* acting as an undertaking when it purchased services, and remitted the case to the OFT (*BetterCare Group Limited* v *Director General of Fair Trading* [2002] CompAR 226) which made a new decision on other grounds. Following the ruling of the CFI in *FENIN* the OFT issued *Policy note 1/2004: The Competition Act 1998 and public bodies* (OFT 443, January 2004). In essence this summarizes the EC case law, and seeks to depart from the ruling of the CAT—which in the light of *FENIN* does appear to be incorrect in law. The conclusion of the OFT is set out at para. 27 of the policy note:

Having regard to the above legal position, the OFT considers that generally where a public body is only a purchaser of goods or services in a particular market and is not involved in the direct provision of any goods or services in that market or a related market, that body will not be an undertaking for the purposes of the CA98.

2.3 **The European Community**

2.3.1 **The legal order**

The Community legal order is governed by the primary legislation of the relevant treaties, to which all 25 Member States have acceded. For the purposes of competition law the most important treaty is the European Community (EC) Treaty. This treaty, which was originally the European Economic Community (EEC) Treaty, has been amended on a number of occasions, both in response to the accession of new Member States, and to pressures for institutional reform. The most significant recent development in the life of the EC has been the accession of 10 new Member States on 1 May 2004. This created a pressure on the application of competition law that led to a major reform, or modernization programme, designed to make the system more manageable. These developments permeate the text throughout this book. At the same time as the accession arrangements were being implemented discussion was under way on the development of a draft constitution for the European Community that would make further significant changes. The draft constitution, if enacted in its current form, would not impact on the substance of the provisions relating to competition law, but does, for example, specify in art. 12(1) that 'the Union shall have exclusive competence to establish the competition rules necessary for the functioning of the internal market' (Draft Treaty Establishing a Constitution for Europe, submitted to the European Council meeting in Thessaloniki, 20 June 2003). The constitution, if adopted, would replace the current European Treaties and create a single legal order known as the European Union (EU). Were that the case it would be correct to call EC competition law 'EU competition law', an appellation which is, at present, inaccurate. Even if the draft constitution were signed in the near future it would not come into force until it had been ratified by all 25 Member States in accordance with their constitutional methods of ratification. This process would be likely to take some time.

As with other Community policy areas, EC competition law is established and developed via a variety of legal sources. At the top of the legal hierarchy is the EC Treaty. By itself the Treaty does not provide sufficient detail to permit the existence of a fully and completely functioning legal order, and a considerable quantity of secondary legislation has been made. Article 249 EC lists the types of secondary legislation that may be adopted by the EC: regulations, decisions, and directives. European Community competition law may be enforced by way of decisions made by the EC Commission, and art. 249 provides that: 'A decision shall be binding in its entirety upon those to whom it is addressed.' Both the primary and secondary legislation may be interpreted by the European courts: the Court of Justice (ECJ), and the Court of First Instance (CFI). The judgments of the courts can, therefore, be said to form a third relevant legal source of competition law. In the arena of competition law, so-called 'soft-law' is also important. This takes the form of notices and guidance published by the EC Commission, which explain and clarify the law, and which although not formally legally binding may in certain circumstances create legitimate expectations in those subject to the application of the relevant law.

Competition law featured as part of the Community regime from its inception as provisions in this respect were made in the European Coal and Steel Community (ECSC) Treaty, signed by the original six members in 1951. The ECSC Treaty has now expired (see Expiry of the ECSC Treaty (Antitrust) (Merger Control) Communication 2002 (2002) OJ C152/03, and the Communication from the Commission concerning certain aspects of the treatment of competition cases resulting from the expiry of the ECSC Treaty, 26 June 2002). The inclusion of these provisions arose in part from the 'absence of, or at least the major imperfections of, competition readily visible in the [relevant] markets' (Goyder, D. G., *EC Competition Law*, Oxford, OUP (1993), p. 19) and in part from the example of the USA whose economic success was perceived to be based partly on its free competition policies (for a challenging and distinctive view of the impact of US law on the development of EC competition policy, see Gerber, D. J., *Law and Competition in Twentieth Century Europe: Protecting Prometheus*, Oxford, Clarendon Press (1998)). The 1957 Treaty of Rome (entry into force 1 January 1958), which created the EEC, provided the blueprint for a much greater economic integration than that envisaged in the ECSC Treaty, and the various amendments to the Treaty since then have left its competition regime intact. One of the effects of the Treaty on European Union (Maastricht; TEU) 1992 (entry into force 1 November 1994) was to amend the EEC Treaty to become the European Community Treaty. Those seeking a fuller discussion of the nature of Community law and of the 'new legal order' that is the Community (*NV Algemene Transport-en Expeditie Onderneming Van Gend en Loos* v *Nederlandse Belastingadministratie* case 26/62 [1963] 1 CMLR 105) should refer to a current edition of a specialist Community law textbook, such as Steiner, J., and Woods, L., *Textbook on EC Law*, Oxford, OUP (8th edn, 2003).

2.3.2 Key Treaty provisions

2.3.2.1 *Articles 2 and 3—the tasks of the Community*

Article 2 of the EC Treaty sets a very broad set of objectives of the EC. This includes 'a high degree of competitiveness and converging economic performance'. While this is primarily an expression of industrial policy, competition law is one of the means by which this object may be achieved. Article 3 sets out more specific tasks or activities which are to be undertaken for the purposes of achieving the objectives set out in art. 2. Article 3(g) provides that one of these activities is the development of 'a system ensuring that competition in the internal market is not distorted'. This provision has frequently been referred to by the ECJ when setting out the functions of competition law in response to particular challenges, and it has often held that arts 81 and 82 EC should be interpreted in the light of arts 2 and 3(g) EC.

2.3.2.2 *Articles 81 and 82—the key substantive provisions*

Article 81 introduces a prohibition against 'agreements, decisions by associations of undertakings and concerted practices which may affect trade between Member States and which have as their object or effect the prevention, restriction or distortion of competition within the common market' (and see Chapter 9). Article 82 prohibits the 'abuse by one or more undertakings of a dominant position within the common market or a substantial part of it . . . in so far as it may affect trade between Member States' (and see Chapter 14). Conduct falling within the scope of the prohibitions is prohibited without the need for further investigation.

2.3.2.3 *Articles 83 and 85—implementation of arts 81 and 82*

Article 83 made provision for the enactment of 'any appropriate regulations or directives to give effect to the principles set out in Articles [81] and [82]'. The major regulation made under this authority is Regulation 1 of 2003, which is discussed in detail in Chapter 5. Various other procedural regulations and, in particular, block exemption regulations have been enacted: the former are largely dealt with in Chapter 5, the latter in Chapter 10. Although not expressly provided for in the Treaty, the Community has also introduced a regime to control large merger situations in the EC. This now finds expression in Regulation 139/2004, which is discussed in Chapter 19.

Article 85 places the Commission at the heart of the EC competition law regime, as it 'shall ensure the application of the principles laid down in arts 81 and 82'. The Commission is required to investigate infringements of the law, and if it finds that the law has been breached it 'shall propose appropriate measures to bring it to an end'. The arm of the Commission with responsibility for the development, application, and supervision of EC competition law is the Directorate General Competition, which will be referred to as DG Comp throughout this text. Although much of the day-to-day enforcement of competition law has been delegated to the national competition authorities of the Member States, and to national courts in the case of private actions, the Commission still retains a key role. The relationship between the powers of the Commission and of national authorities is examined later in this chapter, and in Chapter 3.

2.3.2.4 *Articles 86–89—public undertakings and state aids*

Outside of arts 81 and 82, other aspects of Community policy have an impact upon competition regulation. Most obviously art. 86 applies to public undertakings and undertakings 'to which Member States grant special or exclusive rights'. The requirement of the article is that 'Member States shall neither enact nor maintain in force any measure contrary to the rules contained in this Treaty', which is to say that state-owned or state-established or regulated undertakings are in no better position in relation to EC competition law than their private sector, market-regulated counterparts. However, undertakings falling within art. 86(2) may be placed in a more favourable position, being given the leeway to operate outside of the usual rules where these rules would 'obstruct the performance, in law or in fact, of the particular tasks assigned to them'.

Articles 87–89 EC relate to the control of state aids. Article 87(1) sets out the primary rule that

any aid granted by a Member State or through state resources in any form whatsoever which distorts or threatens to distort competition by favouring certain undertakings or the production of certain goods shall, in so far as it affects trade between Member States, be incompatible with the common market.

DG Comp has as one of its central tasks the review and control of state aids. This is an area that brings its staff into frequent conflict with the Member States. State aids are not dealt with in this book, and the interested reader is referred instead to one of the specialist texts dealing with the area.

2.3.3 The function of Community competition law

There is no clear statement in the Treaty as to the function of competition law. Limited guidance only may be obtained from the words of arts 2 and 3(g) (see 2.3.2.1). Article 81 emphasizes that consumers' interests are to be taken into account in deciding whether the legal exception of art. 81(3) applies and that consumers must be allowed 'a fair share of the resulting benefit'; and art. 82 is silent, save in its pejorative reference to 'abuse'. Valentine Korah has written that, in the EC, 'there is no agreement as to what objectives should be pursued by competition policy' ('EEC Competition Policy—Legal Form or Economic Efficiency' (1986) *Current Legal Problems* 85). The ECJ and the Commission have both indicated what the primary objectives of Community competition policy *might* be. In *Metro-SB-Grossmärkte GmbH & Co. KG v Commission* case 26/76 [1978] 2 CMLR 1 at 2, the ECJ held that

The requirement contained in Articles 3 and [81] EEC that competition shall not be distorted implies the existence on the market of workable competition, i.e., the degree of competition necessary to ensure the observance of the basic requirements and attainment of the objectives of the Treaty, in particular the creation of a single market achieving conditions similar to those of a domestic market.

Thus the position appears to be that competition policy is just one area that will be balanced alongside other objectives of Community policy as the need requires, and is not, exclusively, a tool to achieve efficiency maximization. It is the case therefore that, as other policy requirements change over time, so too might the application of competition law.

The Commission has made various claims for the operation of the law in its annual reports. The widest are those made in the 1972 Report which places stress on the general benefits of the policy:

Competition is the best stimulant of economic activity since it guarantees the widest possible freedom of action to all. An active competition policy . . . makes it easier for the supply and demand structures continually to adjust to technological development . . . Through the interplay of decentralised decision-making machinery, competition enables enterprises continuously to improve their efficiency . . . competition is an essential means for satisfying . . . the individual and collective needs of our society.   (p. 11)

In the same report the Commission also emphasized the importance of consumer interests—'Such a policy encourages the best possible use of productive resources for the greater possible benefit of the economy as a whole and for the benefit, in particular, of the consumer' (p. 12)—and the effects of anti-competitive actions on individual undertakings. In its ninth report the Commission set out its goals at the time with some clarity:

The first fundamental objective is to keep the common market open and unified . . . There is . . . a continuing need—and this is the primary task of the Community's competition policy— to forestall and suppress restrictive or abusive practices of firms attempting to divide up the market again so as to apply artificial price differences or impose unfair terms on their consumers . . .

It is an established fact that competition carries within it the seeds of its own destruction. An excessive concentration of economic, financial and commercial power can produce such far-reaching structural changes that free competition is no longer able to fulfil its role as an effective regulator of economic activity. Consequently, the second fundamental objective of the Community's competition policy must be to ensure that at all stages of the common market's development there exists the right amount of competition in order for the Treaty's requirements to be met and its aims attained. The desire to maintain a competitive structure dictates the Commission's constant vigilance over abuses by dominant firms . . .

Thirdly, the competition system instituted by the Treaty requires that the conditions under which competition takes place remain subject to the principle of fairness in the market place. [These principles are] . . .

First, equality of opportunity must be preserved for all commercial operators in the common market.

A second aspect of the principle of fairness in the market place is the need to have regard to the great variety of situations in which firms carry on business . . . this factor makes it necessary to adapt the Community competition rules so as to pay special regard in particular to small and medium [size] firms that lack strength.

Finally, equity demands that the Commission's competition policy takes account of the legitimate interests of workers, users and consumers. (*Ninth Report on Competition Policy* (1980), pp. 9–11)

For many years it was clear that a fundamental aim of the Community was to integrate the economies of the Member States, and this had an impact on the application of competition law. This dominant concern has been continually restated in decisions and cases, and is evidenced in the continuing rule that territorial protection in distribution agreements is not permitted where parallel imports are excluded. The ECJ has held, in *Etablissements Consten SA RL and*

Grundig-Verkaufs-GmbH v *Commission* cases 56 and 58/64 [1966] 1 CMLR 418 at 471, that

an agreement between a producer and a distributor which might tend to restore the national divisions in trade between member-states might be such as to thwart the most basic objects of the Community. The Treaty, whose preamble and text aim at suppressing the barriers between States . . . could not allow undertakings to restore such barriers.

The expansion of the EC in May 2004 will also, undoubtedly, have an impact on the way competition law will be applied. Thus, in its *White Paper on Modernisation of the Rules Implementing Articles [81] and [82]* (1999) OJ C132/1, hereinafter cited as the *Modernisation White Paper*, the Commission recognized that

Economic and monetary union is certain to have major consequences for competition policy. It will first entail further economic integration and, in the long term, will strengthen the effects of the internal market by helping to remove the last economic barriers between Member States. It also will help to cut the overall costs of intra-Community trade by reducing transaction costs. Such factors will encourage undertakings to develop trade and thus increase competition throughout the Union. A single currency will also increase price transparency and thus highlight price differences still existing between Member States. Economic operators may, when faced with stronger competition, be tempted to take a protectionist attitude to avoid the constraints of adapting to the new conditions, thereby compensating for their lack of competitiveness in a new environment. Lastly, the fact that some member states are, at least for the time being, not part of the monetary union may encourage undertakings to partition markets (para. 6).

As part of the modernization programme the EC Commission has emphasized repeatedly its move to a system of competition law which is clearly related to economic criteria and analysis. This policy is reflected in the block exemption regulations, which were adapted so as to reduce the reliance on legal formalism which had attracted so much criticism, and in guidelines relating to horizontal and vertical agreements (see Chapter 9 generally). In its notice *Guidelines on the application of Article 81(3) of the Treaty*, at para. 13 the Commission states that

The objective of Article 81 is to protect competition on the market as a means of enhancing consumer welfare and of ensuring an efficient allocation of resources. Competition and market integration serve these ends since the creation and preservation of an open single market promotes an efficient allocation of resources throughout the Community for the benefit of consumers.

This is a more focused statement of a 'pure' economic approach, with the efficient allocation of resources at centre stage, than has previously been found in official material. One of the key elements of modernization is that the application of competition law has been substantially devolved. It will certainly be easier for the 25 national competition authorities to produce consistent results in applying the law if the focus is economic efficiency, rather than the 'workable competition' referred to in *Metro*.

2.3.4 **The regulatory organs**

2.3.4.1 *The EC Commission*

As we have seen, art. 85 EC confers upon the EC Commission the primary role in the enforcement of Community competition law. This is consistent with the broad function of the Commission as 'guardian of the Treaty', or 'watchdog of the Community'. Rules relating to the Commission are set out in the Treaty at arts 211–19, art. 211 providing that the Commission should ensure compliance with EC law, and exercise specific powers given to it by the Council of Ministers. The Council has exercised these powers in relation to competition law in enacting Regulation 1/2003. The Commission consists of 20 Commissioners, nominated by the Member States, and accepted en masse by the European Parliament. Administratively the Commission is divided into Directorates General, with one Directorate General having responsibility for competition policy, which includes the contentious areas of state aids, and merger policy as well as 'antitrust'. A list of the Directorate's personnel and their areas of responsibility is set out at the Commission's web site (the address of which is given below).

Following modernization of the enforcement and application of EC competition law the relationship between the Commission and other actors involved in its application underwent a significant change. The Commission's role is now to supervise the operation of competition policy—it occupies a central role in the European Competition Network (see below)—and to play the lead role in the formulation of that policy as change is needed. Some of the secondary legislation gives the Commission powers that only it can apply—this is particularly the case in respect of the EC Merger Regulation discussed in Chapter 19. Under Regulation 1/2003, discussed in Chapter 5, the Commission has the power to investigate infringements of the law, and to take appropriate action, on its own initiative, or in response to complaints. However, each Member State is also required to apply the law in specific cases with the use of appropriate national procedures applied by the relevant national competition authority.

The Commission produces an annual report for the European Parliament detailing its activities in competition law over the year. DG Comp also publishes a multilingual quarterly newsletter (*Competition Policy Newsletter*). Press releases, current decisions, and developments may be found on the Commission's web site at: **http://europa.eu.int/comm/competition/index_en.html**.

2.3.4.2 *The Advisory Committee*

Article 14 of Regulation 1/2003 makes provision for an Advisory Committee on Restrictive Practices and Dominant Positions, which must be consulted before the Commission takes various decisions, in particular those which have an adverse affect on those to whom they are addressed. The Committee shall be composed of 'representatives of the competition authorities of the Member States' (art. 14(2)) and the Committee is therefore an important link between the Commission and the Member States. The Commission is required to 'take the utmost account of the opinion delivered by the Advisory Committee' (art. 14(5)). The Advisory Committee can also discuss cases under consideration by NCAs, but cannot deliver a formal opinion in respect of these (art. 14(7) and see part 4 of the Commission *Notice on cooperation within the Network of Competition Authorities* (2004) OJ C101/43).

2.3.4.3 *National competition authorities, the European Competition Network, and national courts*

The relationship between EC and national competition law is explored in the following chapter, but it is necessary at this point to introduce the roles of the relevant national competition authorities (NCAs), and the European Competition Network (ECN) in relation to the enforcement of EC competition law. In Regulation 1/2003 the basic role of the national competition authorities is set out at art. 5:

The competition authorities of the Member States shall have the power to apply arts 81 and 82 of the Treaty in individual cases. For this purpose, acting on their own initiative or on a complaint, they may take the following decisions:

— requiring that an infringement be brought to an end,

— ordering interim measures,

— accepting commitments,

— imposing fines, periodic penalty payments or any other penalty provided for in their national law.

They may also decide that there are no grounds for action. The application of this provision is considered in more detail in Chapter 5. Prior to May 2004 most NCAs did not have the power to apply arts 81 and 82 EC, and because of the legal structure of the EC regime were precluded absolutely from applying the legal exception of art. 81(3). Every Member State is now required to designate a relevant authority as an NCA. In the UK the OFT, and sector regulators with concurrent powers (see 2.4.4.1) have been designated.

While this new system is expected to lead to a faster resolution of competition cases than had been the case in the past it also raises the prospect of inconsistent enforcement of the law, and the hope is that the ECN will address these problems. Thus art. 11(1) of Regulation 1/2003 provides that 'the Commission and the competition authorities of the Member States shall apply the Community competition rules in close cooperation'. Article 11 therefore imposes the following conditions. The Commission is required to send the NCAs copies of important documents in its possession, and the NCAs are required to tell the Commission whenever they commence formal investigative measures. Likewise, when NCAs intend to take any infringement decision, or to accept commitments, or to withdraw the benefit of a block exemption regulation (see Chapter 10), they shall inform the Commission, and provide it with a summary of the case and a copy of the proposed decision. This information may also be made available to the other members of the ECN. The use to which information can be put is restricted by virtue of art. 12 of Regulation 1/2003 (see Chapter 5).

The Commission has produced a *Notice on cooperation within the Network of Competition Authorities* (2004) OJ C101/43, and the OFT, the UK's NCA, published a draft competition law guideline, *Modernisation: The Office of Fair Trading's application of EC Regulation 1/2003 and the United Kingdom legal exception regime* in April 2004 (OFT 442).

The role of national courts in the application of the law is considered as appropriate throughout this book, and in particular in Chapter 7. Generally the position is that both arts 81 and 82 EC may be invoked before national courts because both articles are said to be 'directly effective'. Both obligations and rights flow from them, and although the majority of the case law up to 2004 had been based around defensive measures, an increasing tendency to use the law as a sword (i.e., to seek damages, an injunction, or some form of specific performance) was becoming evident. (The principle of 'direct effect' is considered below at 2.3.5.3.) Both the Commission and the NCAs are entitled in some cases to reject complaints made to them on the grounds that an investigation of the complaint would not accord with their administrative and enforcement priorities, and that a national court may be a better forum for the dispute to be resolved in.

National courts ruling on directly effective Community law may also have recourse to the procedure set out in art. 234 EC. This provides a formal link between any court or tribunal in a Member State and the ECJ, giving the latter the ability to 'give preliminary rulings concerning', *inter alia*, '(a) the interpretation of this Treaty'; and '(b) the validity and interpretation of acts of the institutions of the Community'. The purpose of the article is to restrict the scope for divergence in the application of EC law by national courts. To that end, national courts or tribunals 'against whose decision there is no judicial remedy . . . shall bring the matter before the Court of Justice' (art. 234(3)), whereas lower courts or tribunals have discretion to refer (art. 234(2)). The article does not serve as an appeal process—questions must be asked in the abstract and the answers provided by the ECJ are unlikely to be such as to determine the outcome of the case on the facts, although they may often be conclusive on the point of law in question. The jurisdiction of the CFI does not extend to art. 234 references (art. 225(1)), and all references must therefore be made directly to the ECJ. Although national courts may be reluctant to involve themselves in areas of law in which they have little expertise, such as is the case with competition issues and the United Kingdom courts, the reference procedure should assist them with such matters. The relationship between national courts and the EC Commission was explored in the case of *Masterfoods Ltd* v *H B Ice Cream Ltd*; *HB Ice Cream Ltd* v *Masterfoods Ltd* case C–344/98 [2001] 4 CMLR 14 (see 3.2).

The UK Competition Appeals Tribunal (CAT) is classed as a Tribunal and is competent to refer matters to the ECJ.

2.3.4.4 *The European Court of Justice and the Court of First Instance*

Article 220 EC provides that the 'Court of Justice shall ensure that in the interpretation and application of this Treaty the law is observed'. Recognizing that the ECJ was overstretched, with cases frequently taking two years or more to be heard, the CFI was created by Council Decision 88/591, following amendments made to the EC Treaty by the Single European Act 1986 (entry into force 1 July 1987). The CFI is now governed by art. 225 EC, which provides in part that the court has 'jurisdiction to hear and determine at first instance, subject to a right of appeal to the Court of Justice on points of law only . . . certain classes of action'. Cases brought under art. 230 by individuals and undertakings (see 2.3.4.4.1) are included in the CFI's jurisdiction, and it is consequently heavily involved in determining matters of competition law, and has insisted in particular that the Commission respect the rights of undertakings against which it brings proceedings.

Article 225a EC, inserted into the EC Treaty by the Treaty of Nice (which entered into force on 1 February 2003) makes provision for the possibility of establishing judicial panels to hear and determine at first instance certain classes of action or proceedings brought in specific areas. Although this has not yet happened it is possible that there may be a competition panel in order to speed up cases in this area.

The numbers of judges to be appointed to each of the courts, and the qualifications they are required to possess, are set out in the EC Treaty. Both the CFI and the ECJ function by way of chambers which must contain at least three judges, thus giving the courts the ability to hear several cases simultaneously. The role of the Advocate General, who has no direct equivalent in domestic law, is to 'assist the court' (art. 220). This function is fulfilled by way of the opinions delivered to the court at the penultimate stage of the proceedings. The opinion is not binding on the court, which delivers only a single unanimous judgment, but is very often followed, and may be of interest as it is likely to be both more wide ranging and more speculative than the final judgment, which is often terse and focused directly to the point at issue.

As well as its specific roles in relation to arts 230, 232, and 288 (see 2.4.4.4.1) the ECJ has, in accordance with art. 229 EC, 'unlimited jurisdiction . . . to review decisions whereby the Commission has fixed a fine or periodic penalty payment', and 'may cancel, reduce or increase the fine or periodic penalty payment imposed' (Regulation 1/2003, art. 31). At the time of writing there have been no cases in which the ECJ has increased the fine imposed by the Commission, but many in which it has reduced the fine (see Chapter 6).

Appeals from the CFI to the ECJ can only be made on points of law, within two months of the CFI notifying the parties of its decision. Three specific grounds are set out in the Protocol on the Statute of the ECJ (art. 51):

(a) lack of competence of the CFI;

(b) breach of procedure before the CFI; and

(c) breach of Community law by the CFI.

The ECJ will not, therefore, review the CFI's own review of the facts of the case (*Hilti AG* v *Commission* case C–53/92P [1994] 4 CMLR 614, and *Deutsche Bahn AG* v *Commission* case C–436/97P [1999] 5 CMLR 775) and neither will it interfere in the CFI's assessment of fines where the latter has in turn considered the penalties imposed by the Commission (*BPB Industries plc and British Gypsum Ltd* v *Commission* case C–310/93P [1997] 4 CMLR 238). Were such a further review permitted the benefit of a quicker process offered by the creation of the CFI would be lost, with the effect being merely that of adding yet another judicial stage to an already drawn-out process.

The CFI and ECJ have jurisdiction to review acts taken by the EC Commission, or failures to act by the EC Commission, as well as to rule on claims based on non-contractual liability.

2.3.4.4.1 *Challenges to the Commission—arts 230, 232, and 288 EC*

Like all the institutions of the EC, the Commission is governed by the law as set out in the Treaty and in secondary legislation. Any secondary legislation is also subject to the superior law of the Treaty, and to the general principles of law developed by the ECJ. Articles 230 and 232 provide a procedure akin to judicial review: under the former, acts of the institutions which produce legal effects may be challenged; under the latter, the failure to act may be challenged. Article 288 sets out rules relating to a quasi-tortious liability of the Community for the acts of its servants.

Article 230 provides in part that

> The Court of Justice shall review the legality of acts . . . of the Commission, other than recommendations and opinions . . .
>
> It shall for this purpose have jurisdiction . . . on grounds of lack of competence, infringement of an essential procedural requirement, infringement of this Treaty or of any rule of law relating to its application, or misuse of powers.
>
> . . .
>
> Any natural or legal person may . . . institute proceedings against a decision addressed to that person or against a decision which, although in the form of a regulation or decision addressed to another person, is of direct and individual concern to the former.
>
> The proceedings provided for in this article shall be instituted within two months of the publication of the measure, or of its notification to the plaintiff . . .

While the protection of the article obviously extends to the decisions with which the Commission imposes penalty payments, which also fall within art. 229, and otherwise enforces the law under Regulation 1/2003 (see Chapter 5), the ECJ has held that the article will also apply to a range of other actions relating to competition policy, and can be invoked in circumstances other than where a formal decision has been made. Thus the ECJ, in *IBM* v *Commission* case 60/81 [1981] 3 CMLR 635, held that an act is open to review where 'it is a measure definitively laying down the position of the Commission . . . and not a provisional measure intended to pave the way for a final decision'. It has held, therefore, that the rejection of a complaint may be reviewed (*CICCE* v *Commission* case 298/83 [1986] 1 CMLR 486), as may a decision to allow a party to proceedings to examine documents obtained by the Commission (*AKZO Chemie BV* v *Commission* case 53/85 [1987] 1 CMLR 231).

While it might be difficult for parties other than those to whom the decisions are addressed to establish the necessary *locus standi* to mount a challenge under the article it would appear that any complainant under art. 7(1) of Regulation 1/2003 whose complaint leads to a decision will be able to mount a challenge, as they may be presumed to have 'direct and individual concern'. Such an expansive approach to *locus standi* follows from the analogous case of *Timex Corporation* v *EC Council and Commission* case 264/82 [1985] 3 CMLR 550, an anti-dumping case where the applicant had been the source of the initial complaint to which the Commission responded. However, the Court has held that the Commission is not required to respond to all complaints by launching a full investigation, and is allowed to determine its own priorities (*Automec srl* v *Commission* case T–24/90 [1992] 5 CMLR 431, see 7.2.1).

The most fruitful grounds for challenge under art. 230 EC tend to be that an essential *procedural* requirement has been breached, and both the ECJ and the CFI would appear now to require scrupulous observance of the correct procedures on the part of the Commission. Thus in *BASF AG* v *Commission* cases T–80/89, etc. [1995] ECR II-729, the CFI struck down a decision which had not been correctly transposed into all official Community languages.

The ECJ will not inquire into the matters of economic fact on which the Commission has based its decision, but will

limit its review . . . to verifying whether the relevant procedural rules have been complied with, whether the statement of the reasons for the decision is adequate, whether the facts have been accurately stated and whether there has been any manifest error of appraisal or a misuse of powers.   (*Remia BV* v *Commission* case 42/84 [1987] 1 CMLR 1, at para. 34)

However, it will be noted that this formula leaves significant room for the Court to go over the factual grounds relied on by the Commission, and in practice the distinction between a review of the application of the law, and of the factual evidence, can become blurred. In the 'wood pulp' cases (*A Ahlström oy* v *Commission* cases C–89/85, etc. [1993] 4 CMLR 407) the CFI, for example, relied heavily upon economic evidence in rejecting a Commission decision (see further Chapter 9). It does in fact appear to be the case that the CFI is more prepared to consider the detail of the facts of the case than is the ECJ, which is required to take a somewhat more formal legal approach.

The effect of a successful challenge under art. 230 is, according to art. 231, to render the decision, or the affected parts of it, void. The Commission is not prevented in these circumstances from re-examining the matter.

Article 232 provides in part that

Should the . . . Commission, in infringement of this Treaty, fail to act, the Member States and the other institutions of the Community may bring an action before the Court of Justice to have the infringement established.

The action shall be admissible only if the institution concerned has first been called upon to act. If, within two months of being so called upon, the institution concerned has not defined its position, the action may be brought within a further period of two months.

Any natural or legal person may, under the conditions laid down in the preceding paragraphs, complain to the Court of Justice that an institution of the Community has failed to address to that person any act other than a recommendation or an opinion.

Article 232 is less likely to form the basis of successful applications to the ECJ. In part this is because there are fewer situations in which it is likely to be invoked in practice, and in part because the obligation on the Commission is only to define its position. The Commission may define its position by an action that falls some way short of a decision reviewable under art. 230 (see, e.g., *Spijker Kwasten* v *Commission* case 231/82 [1984] 2 CMLR 284). The Court has held that the Commission does not owe a complainant the duty to take a final decision (*GEMA* v *Commission* case 125/78 [1980] 2 CMLR 177). The effect of a successful action is to require the Commission to take the necessary steps to define its position, not to compel the Commission to take a decision to any particular effect (see further Chapter 7).

Article 288 provides in part that

In the case of non-contractual liability, the Community shall, in accordance with the principles common to the laws of the Member States, make good any damage caused by its institutions or by its servants in the performance of their duties.

Although this provision is rarely invoked it would cover, for example, the situation in which Commission officials exceeded their powers in the process of carrying out any investigations authorized by Regulation 1/2003 and caused damage in the process. Article 235 provides that any disputes founded on art. 288(2) shall be heard by the ECJ. One case in which the applicant was successful was that of *Adams* v *Commission* case 145/83 [1986] 1 CMLR 506. This arose from a notorious incident in which Stanley Adams, an Englishman working in Switzerland, had provided to the Commission evidence of infringements of competition law by his employer. When the Commission returned documents to the undertaking they were so labelled as to reveal the identity of the informant, who subsequently faced prosecution under Swiss domestic law. The Court held that the Commission was liable to Mr Adams for its negligence in revealing the source of the complaint. The case became famous following the broadcast of a TV film, *A Song For Europe*, starring David Suchet as Stanley Adams.

2.3.5 Subsidiarity, the duties of the Member States, and conflicts between domestic and Community law

The relationship between EC law and the national legal regimes is governed by various constitutional principles. Some of these are set out in the EC Treaty, and others have been developed by the ECJ in its jurisprudence.

2.3.5.1 *Article 5 EC—subsidiarity*

Article 5 of the EC Treaty, introduced by the TEU, provides that

In areas which do not fall within its exclusive competence, the Community shall take action, in accordance with the principle of subsidiarity, only if and in so far as the objectives of the proposed action cannot be sufficiently achieved by the Member States and can therefore, by reason of the scale or effects of the proposed action, be better achieved by the Community.

When the concept of subsidiarity, the definition of which is uncertain at best, was introduced many commentators pointed out that, at least with respect to competition law, the principle had been in operation from the inception of the Treaty. Community jurisdiction is established only where trade between Member States is likely to be affected by the conduct in question, and, although this test has been interpreted expansively (see, e.g., *La Technique Minière* v *Maschinenbau Ulm GmbH* case 56/65 [1966] 1 CMLR 357), it serves to curtail greatly the circumstances in which the Commission is able to act. This, in turn, leaves a large measure of discretion to national governments in the structure and operation of their domestic competition law regimes. The concept of 'trade between Member States' is explored more fully in the following chapter, as is the refined relationship between the EC Commission and the Member States in the application of EC competition law. Perhaps the clearest expression of the principle of subsidiarity may be found in Regulation 139/2004 relating to the control of mergers under EC law. Here the powers of the EC Commission and of the Member States are exclusive save in tightly defined circumstances. In essence, where mergers are likely to have substantial cross-border impacts they are more likely to be subject to the jurisdiction of the Commission. Where they are more likely to affect primarily a single state they are likely to fall within the jurisdiction of that state.

2.3.5.2 *Article 10 and the principle of supremacy*

Article 10 EC provides that Member States shall:

take all appropriate measures, whether general or particular, to ensure fulfilment of the obligations arising out of this Treaty or resulting from action taken by the institutions of the Community. They shall facilitate the achievement of the Community's tasks.

They shall abstain from any measure which could jeopardise the attainment of the objectives of this Treaty.

This duty of sincere cooperation applies equally to the measures relating to competition law as to any other obligation, although in this context art. 85 (see 2.3.2.3) is also relevant in defining the roles of the Commission and the Member States as, of course, is Regulation 1/2003.

Where Community law exists it is supreme in relation to national law (*Costa* v *ENEL* case 6/64 [1964] CMLR 425), and will prevail in the event of there being any conflict. This principle of the supremacy of EC law, developed by the ECJ, extends even to provisions of national constitutions (*Internationale Handelsgesellschaft mbH* case 11/70 [1972] 1 CMLR 255; and in relation to Acts of Parliament, see, for example, *R* v *Secretary of State for Transport ex parte Factortame Ltd* case C–213/89 [1990] 3 CMLR 1). The ECJ ruled on the matter specifically in relation to competition law in *Wilhelm* v *Bundeskartellamt* case 14/68 [1969] CMLR 100, holding that where the German cartel laws conflicted with Community law the latter must take precedence.

The relationship between EC and national competition law has been clearly spelled out in Regulation 1/2003, art. 3 (see Chapter 3).

2.3.5.3 *Direct effect*

It was established by the ECJ, in the landmark case of *NV Algemene Transport-en Expeditie Onderneming Van Gend en Loos* v *Nederlandse Belastingadministratie* case 26/62 [1963] 1 CMLR 105, that where articles of the Treaty are clear, precise and unconditional they are capable of creating rights vested in individuals which can be enforced against Member States ('vertical direct effect') in national courts. In *Defrenne* v *Sabena (No. 2)* case 43/75 [1976] 2 CMLR 98, the principle was extended to allow such rights to be enforced against other persons not being part of the state ('horizontal direct effect'). The principle applies equally to regulations, which are, by the wording of art. 249 'binding in [their] entirety and directly applicable in all Member States'. Articles 81 and 82 both have direct effect.

The first competition case in the UK in which this principle was clearly recognized was that of *Garden Cottage Foods Ltd* v *Milk Marketing Board* [1983] 2 All ER 770, HL, where Lord Diplock suggested that a breach of EC law may give rise to a remedy for damages for breach of statutory duty. It has been suggested that the judgment of the ECJ in the case of *Francovich* v *Italian Republic* cases C–6 and 9/90 [1993] 2 CMLR 66, in which it was established that a Member State becomes liable for its breaches of Community law to those who can show harm as a result of the breach where an identifiable right has been infringed, further increases the pressure for national courts to find remedies for those injured by breaches of directly effective competition provisions. Thus far there has been limited private litigation in respect of competition matters (see Chapter 7). While some commentators have called for the Commission to promulgate a directive on remedies, introducing a welcome level of harmonization and certainty, this proposal has been resisted by the DG Comp.

2.4 **The United Kingdom**

2.4.1 **Introduction**

Although the UK has a rich history of competition law (see Chapter 1), there is a clean break between earlier laws, and the post-war system of competition control. This post-war system has itself been almost completely replaced by the two key statutes, the Competition Act 1998 (CA 98) and the Enterprise Act 2002 (EA 02). These apply competition law to most sectors of the economy, and even where some sectors—such as utilities—operate under special regimes, the competition rules of these Acts are generally applicable to them, although the body applying the law may vary. For discussion of the earlier law—including the Restrictive Trade Practices Acts 1976 and 1977 which may still be invoked in rare circumstances—refer to older competition law texts.

2.4.2 **The Competition Act 1998**

The Competition Act 1998 relates primarily to the control of agreements between two or more undertakings, for which provision is made in the 'Chapter I Prohibition', and to abuses committed by dominant firms, the 'Chapter II Prohibition'. The Act also provides the necessary investigative and enforcement powers, although these are supplemented by statutory instruments. The Act repealed much of the then existing competition law legislation—the Restrictive Trade Practices Acts 1976 and 1977, the Resale Prices Act 1976, and the Restrictive Practices Court Act 1976, along with much of the Competition Act 1980. The prohibitions of the Act came into force on 1 March 2000, subject to certain transitional provisions. At the time of the Act's enactment the Government made clear that its overriding objective was to reduce the burdens on industry by aligning domestic law with Community law:

To ensure smooth interaction between the EC legal and business environment and the UK prohibitions, we intend that the UK prohibitions would be interpreted in a manner consistent with the equivalent provisions under EC law. Clause 58 of the Bill [s. 60] has this effect. Such consistency would be of great benefit to so many of our businesses that currently have to worry about two different approaches to competition policy. It delivers a level playing field for our business community in the UK as firms become more and more engaged in European home markets.   (Lord Simon, Hansard (HL) 30 October 1997, col. 1145)

The substantive provisions of the Act are intended to operate in much the same way as is the case in the application of EC competition law, and to this end s. 60 of the Act requires those enforcing it to follow EC law unless there is a 'relevant difference'. This provision is discussed fully in the following chapter. The Chapter I and II Prohibitions are discussed in detail at Chapters 11, 15, and 16, and procedure is dealt with in Chapters 5–8. The Office of Fair Trading (OFT) has published a number of guides to the operation of the Act, which are available on its website, **www.oft.gov.uk**.

Amendments to the Competition Act were made by the Enterprise Act 2002 (see below), and further amendments were made in 2004 to accommodate the EC modernization process by way of the Competition Act 1998 and Other Enactments (Amendment) Regulations 2004 SI 2004/1261.

2.4.3 **The Enterprise Act 2002**

The Enterprise Act 2002 reformed those areas of law which had been largely untouched by the Competition Act 1998: merger control is dealt with in Chapter 20, and market investigation references which replaced the monopoly investigations of the Fair Trading Act 1973 are discussed in Chapter 17. The Act also introduced a new cartel offence, which stands apart from the rest of competition law in that it is directed to individuals, and permits the imposition of gaol sentences and very high fines. This is discussed in Chapter 12.

2.4.4 **The regulatory organs**

2.4.4.1 *The Office of Fair Trading*

The Office of Fair Trading (OFT) existed prior to the introduction of the Competition Act 1998, but it was put on to a new footing by the Enterprise Act 2002. The provisions relating to the OFT are ss. 1–8 of and Sch. 1 to the Enterprise Act. Section 1 of the Act puts the OFT on a firm statutory footing. Thus the OFT becomes a Non-ministerial Government Department, and is a Crown body. Section 2 abolished the office of the Director General of Fair Trading (the Director), and earlier case law and decisions will still refer to the Director rather than to the OFT, which was a body supporting the Director.

The general functions of the OFT, set out in ss. 5–8, are: the acquisition of information; the provision of information to the public (for example the OFT is required to publish an annual plan and an annual report); and the provision of information and advice to ministers. In relation to the acquisition of information, for example, the OFT has the power to 'carry out, commission or support (financially or otherwise) research' (s. 5(3)). This is for the purpose of ensuring that it has sufficient information to take informed decisions. It may also carry out educational functions to inform the public of 'the ways in which competition may benefit consumers', or may support such activities (s. 6).

More detailed rules relating to the constitution of the new OFT are set out in Sch. 1, of which para. 1 provides that the OFT itself 'shall consist of a chairman, and no fewer than four other members appointed by the Secretary of State'. The terms of appointment are to be determined by the Minister, but shall not exceed five years, although this may be renewable. Once the Chairman and other members are appointed, they may be removed by the Minister only on grounds of 'incapacity or misbehaviour'. John Vickers, the last person to hold the post of Director, was the first Chairman, supported by the Executive Director, Penny Boys. The members of the Board, at the time of writing, are: Allan Asher, Lord Blackwell, Christine Farnish, Richard Whish, and Rosalind Wright.

Internal rules of procedure, including matters such as setting a quorum, are to be determined by the OFT.

The primary roles of the OFT in the sphere of competition law are: to act as the lead NCA in the UK, applying arts 81 and 82 or assisting the EC Commission as appropriate; to enforce the Chapter I and II Prohibitions of the Competition Act 1998; to review mergers and possibly to refer them to the Competition Commission (CC—see 2.4.4.2); to conduct reviews of markets and possibly to make market investigation references to the CC; and to act as the body with primary responsibility for investigating breaches of the cartel offence, although in the investigation and prosecution of such offences it will act in partnership with the Serious Fraud Office in England and Wales, and with the Procurator Fiscal in Scotland (see Chapter 12).

In relation to a number of industries—water, gas and electricity, rail transport, communications, civil aviation, and the postal service—the special sector regulators appointed to manage competition in those industries have the power to apply the Competition Act and other provisions, including arts 81 and 82 EC as appropriate. These are referred to as the 'concurrent regulators'. In relation to telecommunications 'Ofcom' took over the role of Oftel in 2004, and very shortly after announced that it was considering the break-up of BT (*Financial Times*, 26 April 2004). Previously Oftel had made a very large number of decisions relative to activity under the Competition Act 1998 as a whole in relation to BT. A concurrency working group exists to coordinate the work of these bodies with that of the OFT.

Following the modernization of EC competition law, and the change in the relationship between EC and national law the OFT prepared a number of guidelines, which replaced earlier versions. These are as follows: *Modernisation; The major provisions; Article 81 and the Chapter I Prohibition; Article 82 and the Chapter II Prohibition; Market definition; Powers of investigation; Concurrent application to regulated industries; Enforcement; Trade associations, professional bodies and self-regulating organisations; Assessment of conduct; Assessment of market power; Vertical agreements; Land agreements; Services of general economic interest exclusion;* and *OFT's guidance as to the appropriate amount of a penalty.* These are a useful and free resource that explain relevant EC law, as well as the operation of the principles in the UK under domestic law. As appropriate they are referred to throughout this text, although at the time of writing only draft versions were available.

2.4.4.2 *The Competition Commission*

It is vitally important that the UK Competition Commission (CC—amongst competition professionals the CC is often referred to as 'CoCo') *not* be confused with the EC Commission. The CC was a creation of the Competition Act 1998, and replaced the earlier Monopolies and Mergers Commission (MMC). The CC is the body charged, under the general competition legislation, with investigating and enforcing mergers and market investigation references when these are referred to it by the OFT. It does not have the power to initiate its own actions. The CC also has a role in relation to certain specific sector regulations, but this is not dealt with in this text. For a broad discussion of the role of the CC, see the CC's publication, *General Advice and Information Guidance*, September 2002. The CC has also published its rules of procedure. All CC documents are available on the CC web site, **www.competition-commission.org.uk**.

The CC rules of procedure set out the rules applicable to references under the Enterprise Act 2002. In each case reference groups are established (i.e., merger reference groups, and market reference groups). Each group must consist of at least three persons, one of whom may, but need not necessarily, be the Chairman of the CC. The Chairman of the CC or, in his or her absence, a Deputy Chairman, may attend meetings of any group and offer advice, which the group is bound to have regard to. However, the Chairman or the Deputy may not vote unless they are serving on the relevant group. The role of the CC in relation to the specific areas of competition law is set out in each of the relevant chapters.

2.4.4.3 *The Competition Appeals Tribunal*

The Competition Appeals Tribunal (CAT) takes over the functions of the Competition Commission Appeals Tribunal (CCAT) established under the Competition Act 1998. For the sake of simplicity, in this text the name CAT is used, even where this may be historically inaccurate. The CAT is a completely independent tribunal, and hears appeals in relation to the Chapter I and II Prohibitions, and decisions taken by both the OFT and CC in relation to market investigation references and mergers, as well as in relation to the application of EC competition law by the OFT in the UK. It may also hear claims brought under provisions set out in the Enterprise Act for damages where there has been an infringement decision made by the OFT, or other appropriate body (see 7.3.1.2). The CAT has no role in relation to the cartel offence. In the case of *Napp Pharmaceutical Holdings Ltd* v *The Director General of Fair Trading* [2002] EWCA Civ 796, [2002] UKCLR 726 the Court of Appeal recognized that the CAT was 'an expert and specialist tribunal, specifically constituted by Parliament to make judgments in an area in which judges have no expertise' (per Buxton LJ at para. 34). As such it fell into the category identified in *Cooke* v *Secretary of State for Social Security* [2002] All ER 279 as being a body whose judgments the Court of Appeal would be reluctant to interfere with.

The provisions relating to the CAT, and the Competition Service, which supports it (see below), are to be found in ss. 12–16 of and in Schs 2–5 to the Enterprise Act 2002. The CAT was created by s. 12, and consists of a President appointed by the Lord Chancellor, and further members. The first President was Sir Christopher Bellamy who had formerly been a judge at the Court of First Instance, and an expert competition lawyer. Members may be either appointed to form a panel of Chairmen, or appointed as ordinary members. The terms of appointment in both cases shall not exceed eight years. The Lord Chancellor is responsible for the appointment of the President and the panel of Chairmen, while ordinary members are appointed by the Secretary of State. Appointments are made on a part-time basis, and ordinary members will be able to continue with their 'day jobs'. Detailed rules relating to the appointments to the CAT are set out in Sch. 2.

In any proceeding before the Tribunal, it shall consist of a Chairman, who must be either the President or a member of the panel of Chairmen, and two other members. Decisions are to be made by majority vote, in any case where there is not unanimous agreement (s. 14).

Decisions of the CAT may be enforced by the High Court in England and Wales (Sch. 4, para. 2), or may be recorded for execution in the Books of Council and Session in Scotland (Sch. 4, para. 3). In Northern Ireland, decisions may be enforced with the leave of the High Court in Northern Ireland (Sch. 4, para. 5).

Part 2 of Sch. 4 makes provision for the Tribunal Rules which may be adopted by the Tribunal. The matters covered include, *inter alia*: the institution of proceedings (including the setting of time limits for actions to be commenced, and the power to reject proceedings in certain cases); the possibility of holding pre-hearing reviews; the conduct of the hearing; quorum of the Tribunal; fees to be chargeable 'in respect of specified costs of proceedings'; and interim orders.

The CAT is supported by the Competition Service, whose role is 'to fund, and provide support services to' the CAT (s. 13). Schedule 3 puts a little more detail on the bare bones of s. 13. The Competition Service consists of the President and the Registrar of the CAT, and at least one member appointed by the Secretary of State in consultation with the President of the CAT.

2.4.4.4 *The Secretary of State for Trade and Industry*

One of the most significant aspects of the reform of domestic competition law in the 1998 and 2002 Acts was to greatly reduce the role of the Secretary of State for Trade and Industry who had previously played an important function in the application of the regime. Following the changes to the system made by the Enterprise Act the role of the Secretary of State is largely limited to making special interventions in merger and market reference investigations on public interest grounds. These are tightly defined in the legislation, and are explained in the relevant chapters.

2.4.4.5 *The national courts*

As well as having a role in applying arts 81 and 82 in disputes brought before them the relevant national courts may also apply the Chapter I and II Prohibitions, and may hear certain claims based on damage following breaches of orders made or undertakings given in relation to merger and market investigation references. These are dealt with primarily in Chapter 7, but also as appropriate in the text.

3

The relationship between European Community and United Kingdom competition law

3.1 Introduction

The relationship between EC competition law and national competition law is a complex one. The relationship has been at least clarified by recent legislation (Regulation 1/2003 on the implementation of the rules of competition laid down in arts 81 and 82 of the Treaty (2003) OJ L1/1) but the position is not simple, although a straightforward statement of basic principles may make it seem so. Articles 81 EC and 82 EC (which are discussed fully in Chapters 9 and 14 respectively) apply only in situations in which trade between Member States may be affected (this requirement is discussed below). In such situations national competition law may also be applied, but may not reach a result which frustrates the application of EC law. In any situation where anti-competitive agreements are made, or where there is an abuse of a dominant position and trade is not affected, the matter is exclusively one for national law. In practice Member States have aligned their competition laws with the laws of the EC so as to clarify and simplify the position for companies subject to the law. This tendency has been particularly pronounced in the UK where the Competition Act 1998 was introduced expressly to bring the domestic system into line with that of the EC, although some differences remained. In the case of merger control (dealt with in Chapters 19 and 20) the EC and domestic systems are stark alternatives—a merger may be evaluated under either, but not both, of the regimes, and if the EC asserts jurisdiction this is exclusive.

3.2 General principles governing the relationship between EC and national competition law

In any case where there is a conflict between Community law and national law, Community law takes precedence. This duty on Member States, which is not specifically set out in the Treaty, has been clarified by the ECJ in a number of cases, starting with *Costa* v *ENEL* case 6/64 [1964] CMLR 425, and is implicit in the concept of direct effect, which recognizes that duties are owed by Member States to their citizens on the basis of Community law. If the United Kingdom had needed this to be made any clearer the matter was resolved beyond all doubt in *R* v *Secretary of State for Transport, ex parte Factortame Ltd (Factortame II)* [1990] 3 CMLR 1, in which the ECJ confirmed, as in the light of its own previous case law it was bound to do, that the operation of even Acts of Parliament should be set aside where they would conflict with Community obligations. The judiciary have accepted that this means that 'the Treaty of Rome is the supreme law of this country, taking precedence over acts of parliament' (*Stoke-on-Trent City Council* v *B&Q plc* [1990] 3 CMLR 31, *per* Hoffmann L.J.). This principle is applied particularly in the light of art. 10 EC, which has been widely interpreted by the Court and been used as the foundation for a range of duties imposed on the Member States and authorities which are emanations of the state. Article 10 provides that

Member states shall take all appropriate measures, whether general or particular, to ensure fulfilment of the obligations arising out of this Treaty or resulting from action taken by the institutions of the Community. They shall facilitate the achievement of the Community's tasks.

They shall abstain from any measure which could jeopardise the attainment of the objectives of this Treaty.

In relation to competition law, in the landmark case of *Wilhelm* v *Bundeskartellamt* case 14/68 [1969] CMLR 100, the ECJ accepted the possibility of divergence between Community and national law, but held that 'parallel application of the national system should only be allowed in so far as it does not impinge upon the uniform application, throughout the Common Market, of the Community rules' (para. 6). This conclusion followed inevitably from the imperative force of Community law over national law, and from the application of art. 10: it would be incompatible with the Treaty to allow national laws to obstruct the aims of the Treaty. However, national authorities would be acting within their powers where they

intervene against an agreement, in application of their internal law, even when the examination of the position of that agreement with regard to the Community rules is pending before the Commission, subject, however, to the proviso that such application of the national law may not prejudice the full and uniform application of the Community law. (para. 7)

A similar position was reached in *GB-INNO-BM NV* v *Vereniging van de Kleinhandelaars in Tabak* case 13/77 [1978] 1 CMLR 283, concerning the relationship of a provision of Belgian law with aspects of EC competition and trade rules. Here the Court held, *inter alia*, that the

Treaty imposes a duty on member-states not to adopt or maintain in force any measure which could deprive [art. 82] of its effectiveness ... [and] Member States may not enact measures enabling private undertakings to escape from the constraints imposed by art. [81]. (paras 31 and 33)

Where a practice has been condemned at Community level it cannot be allowed to continue on the grounds that it is not condemned under national law (see, e.g.,

Vereniging van Samenwerkende Prijsregelende Organisaties in de Bouwnijverheid (SPO) v *Commission* case I–29/92, [1995] ECR–II 289, in which a cartel operating in the Dutch building industry was condemned by the Commission despite having been expressly approved by the Dutch Minister of Economic Affairs).

In the case of *Masterfoods Ltd* v *HB Ice Cream Ltd; HB Ice Cream Ltd* v *Masterfoods Ltd* case C–344/98 [2001] 4 CMLR 14, which demonstrates clearly problems that could arise in relation to the application of two legal situations to the same conduct, the administrative relationship between the application of EC competition law by the Commission and by the national courts was explored in some detail. In this case, which arose out of challenges to ice cream freezer cabinet exclusivity in Ireland, the Irish courts and the Commission were, independently, considering the same agreements in the light of the application of art. 81. The Irish High Court had found that the freezer exclusivity agreements were not restrictive of competition, and had injuncted another undertaking from placing its products in HB's freezers. The Commission, on the other hand, found that HB's agreements were in breach of art. 81(1) (in *Van den Bergh Foods Ltd* 98/531 (1998) OJ L246/1), although at the time at which the case was heard the operation of the Commission decision had been suspended by the Court of First Instance (*Van den Bergh Foods* v *Commission* case T–65/98R [1998] 5 CMLR 475). The fact that the Commission decision was contested before the CFI was clearly a factor that made the waters even more muddy than they were to begin with.

As Advocate General Cosmas recognized, the question of how to avoid inconsistent application of competition law between national courts and the EC institutions was 'the central issue' in the case (para. A14). The Advocate General first noted that the facts examined by the Commission and the national court were not the same, as they related to different time periods, and it was theoretically possible (although on a reading of the case unlikely) that the agreements could have not been restrictive of competition at one time, but been restrictive at another. In *Stergio Delimitis* v *Henninger Brau* case C–234/89 [1992] 5 CMLR 210 the Court had held that the handing down of conflicting decisions was contrary to the principle of legal certainty, and 'must therefore be avoided when national courts give decisions on agreements or practices which may subsequently be the subject of a decision by the Commission' (at para. 47). In the present case however, the *Delimitis* principles had already been breached as there was 'not merely a potential, but a clear and imminent, conflict between the decision of the first instance Irish court and a decision of the Commission that has already been adopted' (para. A25). The risk was that the Irish Supreme Court, from which the reference was taken, might also produce a decision that was in conflict with that of the Commission.

The Court held that,

> where a national court is ruling on an agreement or practice the compatibility of which with articles 81(1) and 82 of the Treaty is already the subject of a Commission decision, it cannot take a decision running counter to that of the Commission, even if the latter's decision conflicts with a decision given by a national court of first instance. (para. 60)

Regulation 1/2003 has now made express provision for the relationship between national courts and the Commission in the application of arts 81 and 82 EC. In particular, art. 16(1) of the Regulation provides that

When national courts rule on agreements, decisions or practices under art. 81 or art. 82 of the Treaty which are already the subject of a Commission decision they cannot take decisions running counter to the decision adopted by the Commission. They must also avoid giving decisions which would conflict with a decision contemplated by the Commission in proceedings it has initiated.

Article 15 of the Regulation provides for a cooperative approach between the courts and the Commission: courts may ask the Commission for information in its possession, or for opinions; copies of judgments made by national courts are to be forwarded to the Commission by the NCAs; and NCAs may make observations to the courts in writing, and, with the permission of the court, orally. The Commission also may, 'where the coherent application of art. 81 or art. 82 of the Treaty so requires ... acting on its own initiative, submit written observations to courts of the member states' (art. 15(3), and see generally *Commission Notice on the cooperation between the Commission and the courts of the EU Member States in the application of articles 81 and 82 EC* (2004) OJ C101/65). However, there is no procedure by which the Commission will be automatically informed of procedures before the national courts prior to the making of any judgment. While opinions of the Commission are only that, the requirements of art. 16, plus the inexperience of most national courts with the application of competition law, is likely to ensure that these opinions are, at the least, highly persuasive.

3.3   Regulation 1/2003

Regulation 1/2003 made a number of significant changes to the application of competition law in the EC. The two most important of these are to some extent interlinked: conferring direct effect upon all of art. 81, and setting out clear rules on the relationship between national and Community law. Recitals (8) and (9), and art. 3 are the key provisions in this latter respect. Article 3 is set out here in its entirety given its importance:

(1)   Where the competition authorities of the member states or national courts apply competition law to agreements, decisions by associations of undertakings or concerted practices within the meaning of art. 81(1) of the Treaty which may affect trade between member states within the meaning of that provision, they shall also apply art. 81 of the Treaty to such agreements, decisions or concerted practices. Where the competition authorities of the member states or national courts apply national competition law to any abuse prohibited by art. 82 of the Treaty, they shall also apply art. 82 of the Treaty.

(2)   The application of national competition law may not lead to the prohibition of agreements, decisions by associations of undertakings or concerted practices which may affect trade between member states but which do not restrict competition within the meaning of art.

81(1) of the Treaty or fulfil the conditions for the application of art. 81(3) of the Treaty or which are covered by a Regulation for the application of art. 81(3) of the Treaty. Member states shall not under this Regulation be precluded from adopting and applying on their territory stricter national laws which prohibit or sanction unilateral conduct engaged in by undertakings.

(3) Without prejudice to general principles and other provisions of Community law, paras (1) and (2) do not apply when the competition authorities and the courts of member states apply national merger control laws nor do they preclude the application of provisions of national law that predominantly pursue an objective different from that pursued by arts. 81 and 82 of the Treaty.

The core elements of this article are, therefore, as follows: (1) in any situation in which art. 81 applies it shall be applied, even if national law is also being applied; (2) national law may not reach a different result, and in particular it *may not* prohibit an agreement that is permitted under art. 81; (3) where art. 82 applies it shall be applied, even if national law is also being applied, *but* national law may be stricter than art. 82; (4) where objectives which are not competition objectives are being applied, such as for example the social objectives that accompany a universal provision requirement, it is not necessary to apply arts 81 or 82. There is uncertainty at present within the UK as to what legislation specifically would be considered to predominantly pursue an objective different from that pursued by arts 81 and 82 EC. There is also an implication that the objectives of arts 81 and 82 are primarily 'competition' based, although as we saw in the previous chapter there has in the past been a recognition from both the EC Commission and the EC courts that competition law serves wider Community objectives than would be suggested by a 'pure competition' test. The sector-specific regulators in the UK are to publish guidance which deals, *inter alia*, with this aspect.

The full ramifications of art. 3 can be seen in a recent case brought in England in which the complainant relied in part on the operation of the restraint of trade doctrine (see Chapter 21). This is an ancient part of the common law of England and Wales, and has traditionally been seen as being less about competition than about the liberty of the subject. In that case, however, the court held that its ability to apply the doctrine was restricted—or would have been restricted had the case been heard later in the year—by the requirements of art. 81 that the court felt obliged to apply by virtue of art. 3 of Regulation 1/2003 (*Days Medical Aids Limited* v *Pihsiang Machinery Manufacturing Co Ltd* [2004] EWHC 44 (Comm) at paras 265–6).

It will be noted that although a stricter approach can be applied by a national authority under national law to conduct which is an abuse of a dominant position falling within art. 82 EC, it cannot apply a stricter approach to agreements falling within art. 81. The logic underpinning this is that the application of art. 81 implies an assessment of both the advantages and disadvantages of an agreement, and that if there are no disadvantages then the agreement may be presumed to be beneficial. This is very strongly the case in respect of the third paragraph of art. 81—the 'legal exception'—as here there is an express authorization, on the grounds that benefits will flow, of a practice that would otherwise be illegal. Therefore, it might be argued that to condemn an agreement that passes these hurdles would be equivalent to frustrating one of the aims of EC competition policy. In the case of art. 82, however, there is no such reasoning. The article deals exclusively with 'abuse', a loaded term, necessarily pejorative in nature, and the fact that something is not an abuse says little about its value. Above all, there is no express permissive part of the article. It is also the case, less logically, but equally importantly, that some Member States lobbied to retain the power to control further dominant firm conduct at the time the Regulation was being drafted.

The OFT has set out its response to the requirements of art. 3 in its draft *Modernisation Guideline* published in April 2004. The thrust of the UK's response is set out at para. 4.18 which is in the following terms:

In practice, where the OFT considers that an agreement or conduct under investigation may have an effect on trade between member states, it will usually apply art. 81 as well as the Chapter I Prohibition and/or art. 82 as well as the Chapter II Prohibition.

Wherever the OFT is applying a penalty in respect of breaches of arts 81 or 82 it will take into account any penalties imposed in relation to breaches of the Chapter I Prohibition and the Chapter II Prohibition (the issue of penalties is dealt with in Chapter 6).

3.4 Trade between Member States

3.4.1 Case law

The boundary line between EC and domestic law is determined according to whether the practice in question may affect trade between Member States. Thus, art. 81(1) EC prohibits anti-competitive agreements 'which may affect trade between member states'; and art. 82 EC prohibits any abuse of a dominant position 'in so far as it may affect trade between member states'. The purpose of the provision is

to define, in the context of the law governing competition, the boundary between the areas respectively covered by Community law and the law of the Member States. Thus Community law covers any agreement or any practice which is capable of constituting a threat to freedom of trade between Member States in a manner which might harm the attainment of the objectives of a single market between the Member States, in particular by partitioning the national markets or by affecting the structure of competition within the Common Market. On the other hand conduct the effects of which are confined to the territory of a single Member State is governed by the national legal order. (*Hugin Kassaregister AB and Hugin Cash Registers Ltd* v *Commission* case 22/78 [1979] 3 CMLR 345, at 373)

In practice it will not be difficult to show that most transactions of any real size are capable of affecting trade between Member States, and the ECJ's definitive statement of the meaning of the requirement in *Société Technique Minière* v *Maschinenbau Ulm* case 56/65 [1966] ECR 235 does not provide a very satisfactory clarification: 'it must be possible to foresee with a sufficient degree of probability on the basis of a set of objective factors of law or of fact that the agreement in question may have an influence, direct or indirect, actual or potential, on the pattern of trade between the Member States' (at 249; the problems with translation of cases become apparent if the alternative report, [1966] CMLR 357, at 375, is referred to, as the wording is substantially different, although the sense is not altered).

An extreme reading of this report ('possible to foresee an indirect potential influence on the pattern of trade') would permit the application of EC law to almost any situation.

3.4.2 The Commission Notice

As part of the modernization package the EC Commission published its *Guidelines on the effect of trade concept contained in articles 81 and 82 of the Treaty* (2004) OJ C101/97. For EC jurisdiction to apply there must be an effect on trade, and that effect must be appreciable. It is made clear that the requirement 'is an autonomous Community law criterion, which must be assessed separately in each case' (para. 12). The concept of trade does not refer only to the flow of goods, but covers 'all cross-border economic activity including establishment' (para. 19). Thus, for example, an abuse which prevented a new undertaking entering a market held by the abuser might fall within the rubric, even though the entrant was not actually providing goods at the time. Any practice which affects the competitive structure of the market will, according to the existing case law, affect trade between Member States. It is also the case that a practice extending to the entire territory of only one state may by its very nature affect trade between Member States by compartmentalizing the market (see, e.g., *Dutch Acceptance Giro System* 1999/687 (1999) OJ L271/28, paras 61–3).

Although the wording of the test in *Société Technique Minière* implied a very broad interpretation of the principle, the Commission accepts in the notice that any effect must be sufficiently probable in order for EC jurisdiction to be invoked. However, 'there is no obligation or need to calculate the actual volume of trade between member states affected by the agreement or practice' (para. 27). This means, for example, that where an agreement restricts parallel trade it is not necessary to establish what trade levels would have taken place in the absence of the agreement. The test exists not to quantify harm, but merely to delimit jurisdiction. It was already clear from the cases of *Consten and Grundig*, and others, that an increase in the pattern of trade as a result of an agreement would fall within the rubric, and this is made clear in the notice where the Commission indicates that the term 'pattern of trade is neutral' (para. 34).

For an effect on trade to be appreciable, which is a requirement, it is again necessary to evaluate each situation. The broad position, set out in para. 45 of the notice, is that

When by its very nature the agreement or practice is capable of affecting trade between member states, the appreciability threshold is lower than in the case of agreements and practices that are not by their very nature capable of affecting trade between member states. The stronger the market position of the undertakings concerned, the more likely it is that an agreement or practice capable of affecting trade between member states can be held to do so appreciably.

While market share is important, and the Commission makes reference to the roughly consistent 5 per cent applied by the ECJ, it 'has not always been a decisive factor' (para. 46). In particular, the Commission says, it is important to take into account the turnover of the undertakings in the products concerned. In support of this proposition the Commission cites the ECJ ruling in *Musique Diffusion Française* v *Commission*, cases 100–103/80 [1983] 3 CMLR 221 in which the court held that although the products subject to the unlawful agreement accounted for just 3 per cent of the sales in national markets, the agreements were capable of appreciably affecting trade due to the high turnover of the relevant parties. A further clarification of this principle is made in the Commission notice on agreements of minor importance (2001) OJ C368/13, at para. 3. Here the Commission indicated that agreements between small and medium-sized undertakings, as defined in the notice, would not be likely to be found to affect trade between Member States. At para. 52 of the trade notice the Commission sets out some quantitative criteria which it suggests 'in principle' show that agreements do not affect trade. These are that (a) the aggregate market share of the parties does not exceed 5 per cent; (b) in the case of horizontal agreements the aggregate turnover of the parties does not exceed €40m, and that in the case of vertical agreements the turnover of the supplier of the products does not exceed this figure. A short-term safe harbour exists under which the Commission will allow these figures to be exceeded by 10 per cent in the case of turnover and 2 per cent in the case of market share for two years. In the case of agreements which may by their very nature be thought to effect trade the Commission's view is that where these turnover figures are exceeded there is a rebuttable presumption that there is indeed an effect on trade. The same principle will apply in the case of an agreement which affects more than a part of one state where the market share of the parties is in excess of 5 per cent. Part 3 of the notice applies these criteria to common forms of agreements and abuses.

3.5 The response in the UK to EC competition law

3.5.1 The Competition Act 1998

When the Competition Act 1998 was brought forward the government made it very clear that one of its key reasons in doing so was to align domestic law with that of the EC. Thus:

'I cannot over-emphasise that the purpose of the Bill is to ensure as far as possible a consistency with EC approach and thereby to ease burdens for business' (Lord Haskel, Hansard (HL), 17 November 1997, col. 417).

It should be stressed that the Competition Act 1998 was introduced at a time when there was no positive obligation on any Member State to align its law to that of the EC, and only the general principles of EC law, and the *Walt Wilhelm* judgment were required to be followed. However, it was abundantly clear that EC competition law was in many respects, although not all, more effective than was domestic competition law, and that for undertakings to operate within two legal regimes which were, prior to the enactment of the Competition Act 1998, very different, was expensive.

The fact that Community law was taken as a given meant that the pressure to reform was placed on the national system. These pressures, coming from a range of sources, were made very clear in the Trade and Industry Committee Fifth Report, *UK Policy on Monopolies* (HC 249, 1995). The Committee found itself persuaded that the benefits of alignment, and steps already announced but not pursued by the government of the day, made it inevitable that alignment would follow.

This alignment was substantially achieved by the introduction of two prohibitions that mirrored those of art. 81 EC and art. 82 EC. At the same time procedures were also made more similar than had been the case previously. Under Regulation 1/2003 it is national procedures that will be used—as will be discussed in Chapters 5, 6, and 7—to enforce the law in the vast majority of cases. Some differences in the substance of the law that did remain have, following the modernization programme, been removed. In the case of the law of mergers and market investigation references, and the cartel offence (see 3.5.2 below) differences do remain.

The clearest indication of the move to consistency underlying the enactment of the Competition Act 1998 is found in s. 60 of that Act. This is, for UK law, a remarkable provision, and is set out here in its entirety:

60.—(1) The purpose of this section is to ensure that so far as is possible (having regard to any relevant differences between the provisions concerned), questions arising under this Part in relation to competition within the United Kingdom are dealt with in a manner which is consistent with the treatment of corresponding questions arising in Community law in relation to competition within the Community.

(2) At any time when the court determines a question arising under this Part, it must act (so far as is compatible with the provisions of this Part and whether or not it would otherwise be required to do so) with a view to securing that there is no inconsistency between—
   (a) the principles applied, and decision reached, by the court in determining that question; and
   (b) the principles laid down by the Treaty and the European Court, and any relevant decision of that Court, as applicable at that time in determining any corresponding question arising in Community law.

(3) The court must, in addition, have regard to any relevant decision or statement of the Commission.

(4) Subsections (2) and (3) also apply to—
   (a) the Director; and

(b) any person acting on behalf of the Director, in connection with any matter arising under this Part.

(5) In subsections (2) and (3), 'court' means any court or tribunal.

(6) In subsections (2)(b) and (3), 'decision' includes a decision as to—

    (a) the interpretation of any provision of Community law,

    (b) the civil liability of an undertaking for harm caused by its infringement of Community Law.

In the view of the Director General, 'relevant decision or statement of the Commission' (s. 60(3)) means

decisions or statements which have the authority of the European Commission as a whole, such as, for example, decisions on individual cases under art. 81 and art. 82 of the Treaty. It would also include any clear statements which the European Commission has published about its policy approach in the *Annual Report on Competition Policy*. (See e.g., *The Chapter I Prohibition Guidelines*, para. 2.1.)

It is clear from the application of the Competition Act 1998 in the first four years since its prohibitions began to bite that the OFT and the Competition Appeals Tribunal (CAT) have taken great efforts to refer to Community law, and to ensure consistency with it. Although s. 60 was referred to at the time of the Act's passage by certain lawyers as 'the Klondike clause', or 'the El Dorado clause', in anticipation of a large amount of litigation as to the meaning of the term 'relevant difference', there has in fact been little such substantive debate.

3.5.2 The Enterprise Act 2002

The Enterprise Act 2002 applies to both competition law and insolvency law. In relation to the former three main substantive areas were addressed: merger control (see Chapter 20); market investigation references (see Chapter 17); and the introduction of the cartel offence (see Chapter 12). It was noted early on in this chapter that the merger control regimes of the EC and UK are largely exclusive, although there is some small overlap between them in certain respects.

Market investigation references are distinct to the UK, and allow an examination of an entire market which appears not to be functioning competitively, with the possibility of a range of remedies being imposed. The OFT accepts that art. 3 of Regulation 1/2003 *might* apply to such investigations but that 'the obligation under art. 3(1) to apply arts. 81 and 82 as well as national competition law would arise only at the stage at which the Competition Commission imposed remedies following a reference' (draft *Modernisation Guideline*, para. 4.24). The OFT does not believe that merely making such a reference, or holding an investigation, would invoke this obligation.

In the case of the cartel offence, under which individuals may be imprisoned if they have dishonestly engaged in activity condemned in s. 188 of the Enterprise Act, there is an express provision in Regulation 1/2003. Recital (8) of the Regulation provides in part that 'this Regulation does not apply to national laws which impose criminal sanctions on natural persons except to the extent that such sanctions are the means whereby competition rules applying to undertakings are enforced'. As the OFT points out in its draft *Modernisation Guideline*, 'the offence is aimed at dishonest activity by individuals . . . the cartel offence is not a means whereby competition rules applying to undertakings are enforced' (para. 4.28).

3.6 **Conclusion**

As far as the application of arts 81 and 82 is concerned the modernization process has clarified some important principles. There was, prior to the enactment of the Regulation, genuine debate, for example, as to whether a Member State could condemn, under its national law, a practice that appeared to fall within the legal exception of art. 81(3) (for a now historical perspective on this issue see Galinsky, R., 'The Resolution of Conflicts between UK and Community Competition Law' [1994] *ECLR* 16). It is now clear that this cannot happen.

The importance of the test of whether trade between Member States may be affected by an agreement or by an abuse is now enhanced, for in relation to art. 81 where trade is affected national competition law cannot go further than the application of that article, and in some respects undertakings may benefit from this. It is therefore possible that some may paradoxically be encouraged to structure conduct *so as* to affect trade. As long as the effect is not hypothetical, and is appreciable, EC competition law may be invoked.

However, some new problems have been created. There will be some discussion inevitably over what constitutes law that is not considered to be 'national competition law', such that it may be applied to the conduct of undertakings without the need to consider the application of arts 81 and 82 if there is also an effect on trade. The absolute obligation to apply EC law will also impact on national courts considering disputes where national competition law, but not EC competition law, is being argued. As was noted above at 3.3 this may have far-reaching, and perhaps unintended, consequences indeed.

4

International issues and the globalization
of competition law

4.1 Introduction

In a world where commerce is increasingly globalized, competition law inevitably raises issues that cut across national and regional boundaries. Both those enforcing the law, and those subject to its enforcement, are affected by issues relating to territoriality and jurisdiction. This is particularly the case in respect of larger mergers, which are very likely to affect more than one jurisdiction, and which will certainly do so where the merger in question is between firms from two or more different states, in respect of agreements entered into between undertakings based in more than one state, and in large monopoly cases. Freyer made the point elegantly when he wrote that 'the enforcement of antitrust laws bears directly upon the conduct and competitiveness of business firms experiencing the technological, political, and cultural challenges of converging local, national, and global markets' (Freyer, T. A., 'Antitrust and Bilateralism: The US, Japanese and EU Comparative and Historical Relationships', in Jones, C. A., and Matsushita, M. (eds), *Competition Policy in the Global Trading System*, Kluwer Law International (2002), p. 3). In its submission in a recent case before the US Supreme Court (see 4.3.2 below), the UK Government, amongst others, argued that

Effective antitrust enforcement in an increasingly global economy depends on close governmental cooperation and coordination as well as respect for the decisions of other nations. Neither commercial transactions nor anti-competitive behaviour by private firms is constrained by national boundaries.

Many cases demonstrate the tensions that may arise, and two more recent ones illustrate the issues clearly. In *General Electric/Honeywell* (decision of the EC Commission in case No. COMP/M.220 of 3 July 2001, unpublished) the EC Commission blocked a merger between two companies based in the USA notwithstanding that the same merger had been cleared by the USA authorities (the law of merger control in the EC is discussed fully in Chapter 19). This exacerbated tensions between the two regimes that had already been heightened when the Commission threatened to, although it ultimately did not, block a merger between McDonnell Douglas and Boeing in 1997. However, no situation better demonstrates the issues than that of the chain of actions taken against Microsoft Corpn. In 1994

EC/US cooperation had worked well in securing a settlement of one dispute with the company (see below). The EC authorities did not pursue matters at the heart of the case brought against the Corporation by the US Department of Justice that ran from the late 1990s through to the beginning of the new millennium, but in 2004 it made an infringement decision in respect of a similar, but different, course of conduct, and imposed both a substantial penalty of €497.2 million as well as conduct remedies (*Microsoft*, 24 March 2004, not yet published). A Commission memorandum was published to coincide with the announcement of the decision (Memo 04/70, 24 March 2004), and three extracts from this are instructive:

Microsoft is a US company. What gives the European Commission authority to decide whether its behaviour is legal or not?
Microsoft sells its products globally including in the European Union, which is one of its main markets together with the United States. It must therefore respect EU competition rules in the same way that European companies must respect US law when operating on the other side of the Atlantic.

Does this go beyond what was agreed between Microsoft and the US Department of Justice?
The US case presents certain similarities with the EU case, and the Commission did take on board those points where the US settlement had addressed its own concerns. But the EU case also presented different facts, and given the European Commission's duty to uphold EU law in the European single market, the remedies are designed to fit with the specifics of the EU case. As regards interoperability, the Commission requires, *inter alia*, the disclosure of certain server-to-server protocols not covered by the US case. As regards tying, the US remedy did not contain provisions on code removal as it was designed for a monopoly maintenance and not a tying liability.

Did the Commission cooperate with the United States on this case?
The Commission and the United States Department of Justice have kept each other regularly informed on the state of play of their respective Microsoft cases, including holding meetings at regular intervals. These meetings have been held in a cooperative and friendly atmosphere, and have been substantively fruitful in terms of sharing experiences on issues of common interest.

The US authorities, however, have protested against the decision, and the US assistant attorney-general for antitrust criticised the application of art. 82 EC, arguing that: 'rules for uprooting state monopolies are hardly suited for companies that have grown up through their own efforts'. At the same time the US administration insisted that the co-operation between the US and the EC was 'extremely strong and . . . has never been stronger' (*Financial Times*, 8 June 2004, p. 26).

Within federal systems, such as the United States, or quasi-federal systems such as the EC, the conflicts that would arise between the component entities, states, and countries respectively are dealt with largely by the creation of the central rules which will generally take precedence over the state or national law. The creation of structures to manage conflicts between states that may lack a common interest, or to deal with, for example, activity that is permitted in one state but considered harmful in or to another, is more difficult. In its *2001 Annual Report on*

Competition Policy the EC Commission noted that 'in times of globalisation, international cooperation must not be limited ... we have to find means of linking together on a global level competition authorities, but also competition policy concepts' (p. 5). The extent to which such cooperation is effective and the mechanisms by which such cooperation may be facilitated form the subject of this chapter.

There are several reasons why disparities in national laws are a cause of concern. First, they represent a cost to companies that increasingly operate in more than one state. These costs can relate both to learning the newly encountered law and to adapting a method of operation acceptable in one state to another state which may insist upon different commercial arrangements. Disparate laws may also lead to the erection of secondary import barriers by states that are, prima facie, committed to free market access and to the principles of the WTO which has assumed responsibility for the operation of the trade agreements concluded under the auspices of the General Agreement on Tariffs and Trade (the GATT). There is also a problem with the territorial effects of commercial decisions, which may impact upon more than one state with differing legal consequences in each state. This can lead to conflicts between national authorities competing for jurisdiction and, in the worst cases, either to multiple, conflicting actions taken against companies, or to companies avoiding actions altogether. Such a situation could lead also to the raising of the difficult problems posed by private international law, 'conflicts of laws'. If private litigants are involved this scenario is quite likely to arise, and it may also arise where a public authority proceeds on the basis of the 'effects' doctrine (discussed below). In this chapter a distinction will be drawn between public, institutional enforcement of competition law, which may raise issues of public international law, and private actions before national courts, which will be considered later.

The EC Commission has responded to the concerns raised by these issues by engaging in bilateral agreements with the United States, Canada, and Japan; multilateral agreements with the EEA; and by engaging in multilateral discussions via the WTO, the Organisation for Economic Cooperation and Development (OECD), and the United Nations Conference on Trade and Development (UNCTAD). Many other agreements entered into by the EC include competition provisions, including agreements with the African, Caribbean, and Pacific countries, and Euro-Mediterranean countries, along with association and cooperation agreements entered into with parties as disparate as Chile and Kazakhstan. For a recent snapshot of some of these developments see *Law in transition 2004: Competition law and policy* (European Bank for Reconstruction and Development, **www.ebrd.com/law**).

In 1995 a group of experts convened by the Commissioner in charge of competition policy delivered its report, recommending that there should be an extension of the existing bilateral arrangements and a gradual move to multilateral forms of cooperation ('Competition Policy in the New Trade Order: Strengthening International Cooperation and Rules', COM(95) 395 final). In the United States the increasing focus on international enforcement in antitrust law has led to the appointment of a special Deputy Assistant Attorney General for International

Affairs, and regular symposia are held between Japanese competition officials and their United States and Community counterparts. Other countries too are interested and involved in such dialogues and developments. Amongst others, Australia is very active, and Korea is also recognizing the international aspects of competition law enforcement. More recently competition authorities have created the International Competition Network (ICN) (discussed below). For a substantial survey of various issues relating to international developments in this area see *The Antitrust Bulletin* (2003) vol. XLVIII, Nos 2–4.

4.2 **Public enforcement**

In most competition regimes, whether in the major trading blocs or in developing countries, the enforcement of the law is largely left in the hands of the relevant public authorities. There will obviously be situations in which it will be in the interests of these bodies to cooperate with each other. Such cooperation might result, for example, in only one state taking action against a particular company where the result will remedy the wrongful conduct in all the affected states. It might lead also to the exchange of information gathered in one state that is needed to assist the relevant authority in another to press its case. It is equally possible to envisage, and find examples of, situations in which it is not obvious that it is in the authorities' interests to cooperate, or even where the authorities are in conflict. This will especially be the case where one country is seeking to protect a 'national champion', or is in no way harmed by activity undertaken by a company in its jurisdiction when that activity has effects only in another territory. A notorious example of such an approach applied generally is that of the Webb–Pomerene Export Trade Act of 1918 (15 U.S.C. ss. 61–65), which permits United States companies to implement export cartels 'provided such association, agreement, or act is not in restraint of trade within the United States, and is not in restraint of the export trade of any domestic competition of such association' (15 U.S.C. s. 62). The same Act, in s. 4, explicitly grants to the Federal Trade Commission jurisdiction over export practices outside the United States which constitute 'unfair methods of competition'. The 1982 Foreign Trade Antitrust Improvements Act (15 U.S.C. s. 6a) has provided additional emphasis to such claims. The hostility that these moves have led to abroad has inspired some countries to enact blocking statutes that are designed to frustrate the extraterritorial enforcement of US antitrust law (see Griffin, J. P., 'Foreign Governmental Reactions to U.S. Assertions of Extraterritorial Jurisdiction' [1998] *ECLR* 64).

Public enforcement of competition law will take place, typically, where a company based in a territory carries out acts which fall to be condemned under that territory's law. Such a situation will usually raise no issues that need addressing at the international level. Two other possible scenarios are more likely to lead to problems, however. The first arises where a company is based in several states, and is carrying out activities that are illegal in some states but not in others. If the company is attacked in those states where it is infringing, but its headquarters lie elsewhere, how will the state in which it is primarily based respond? The second situation arises where a company or companies based entirely in one state engage in behaviour that is condemned in another. This was the situation in the GE/Honeywell merger, where an act that was entirely legal in the USA was condemned in the EC (see below). Not all states recognize the validity of such actions, which are generally based on the 'effects' doctrine, and the United Kingdom in particular has been hostile to moves to base jurisdiction on 'effects'. The United States readily claims such jurisdiction, and the EC achieves very similar ends by slightly different terminology.

4.2.1 The effects doctrine; 'implementation'; and the economic entity doctrine

The effects doctrine is a controversial part of international law, the position of which is not yet universally recognized. Under the doctrine a state may assume jurisdiction where an act that is committed in another state, by citizens or companies of other states, has effects in the former. This was accepted by the Permanent Court of International Justice in the *Lotus* case (*The SS Lotus (France* v *Turkey)* (1927) PCIJ ser. A, no. 10), although there continues to be strong debate amongst commentators about the exact scope of that judgment. If a group of Japanese and Korean businesses agreed to cooperate in raising prices for televisions in the EC, but were not based in the EC and sold into the EC only through agents who were themselves unconnected with the concerted action, the application of the effects doctrine might allow the EC Commission to take action against the companies, and the ECJ to uphold any fines imposed.

The United States has long applied the effects doctrine in the enforcement of antitrust law, the primary authority deriving from the case of *United States* v *Aluminum Co. of America* (*'ALCOA'*) 148 E2d 416 (2d Cir. 1945). Both private claims, including those seeking treble damages, and public cases brought by the Department of Justice may be based on actions implemented in other countries that have a significant impact in the United States. This situation is explained clearly in the Antitrust Enforcement Guidelines for International Operations, issued by the US Department of Justice in April 1995:

SITUATION: A, B, C, and D are foreign companies that produce a product in various foreign countries. None has any US production, nor any US subsidiaries. They organize a cartel for the purpose of raising the price for the product in question. Collectively, the cartel members make substantial sales into the United States, both in absolute terms and relative to total US consumption.

DISCUSSION: These facts present the straightforward case of cartel participants selling products directly into the United States. In this situation, the transaction is unambiguously an import into the US market, and the sale is not complete until the goods reach the United States. Thus, US subject matter jurisdiction is clear under the general principles of antitrust law expressed most recently in *Hartford Fire* [see below for a discussion of some aspects of this case]. The facts presented here demonstrate actual and intended participation in US commerce.

There are restrictions on the operation of these principles. The 'act of state doctrine', the doctrine of 'foreign governmental compulsion', and the principle of comity all serve to limit the extraterritorial application of the law. The first of these is a general principle of public international law that provides that national courts cannot review the actions of sovereign states where that act takes place within the state. Thus a state body would not be found to be in breach of the Sherman Act were it to engage in activity that, if undertaken by a private party, would constitute a breach. Where a private party is *required* as a matter of national law to engage in activity that breaches United States antitrust law that law will also not be enforced (see, e.g., *American Banana Co.* v *United Fruit Co.* 213 U.S. 347 (1909)). The act of state doctrine has no place within intra-European Community relationships, where the Member States may themselves be liable if they encourage, or tacitly support, breaches of the law. This position flows from art. 10 EC (see Chapter 2). The application of the principle of comity is discussed below.

In the Community legal order the most important case relating to the extra-territorial application of arts 81 and 82 is *Re Wood Pulp Cartel: A Ahlström Oy* v *Commission* (joined cases C 89, 104, 114, 116, 117, and 125–129/85 [1988] 4 CMLR 901; note that the ECJ dealt with this case twice—once on the issue of territorial jurisdiction and later on the issue of the substantive law of art. 81(1)). In this complex case (which is discussed in Chapter 9 in relation to the application of art. 81) the Commission had found that 41 producers of wood pulp, used in paper manufacture, and two trade associations had breached art. 81(1) (*Wood Pulp* 85/202 (1985) OJ L85/1). Thirty-six of these undertakings were based in the United States, Canada, Finland, or Sweden, the latter two not being part of the Community at the time the Commission decision was taken. *Inter alia* the Commission held that the members of a trade association based in the United States had concerted on price announcements, had monitored any deviations from those prices, and had concerted on transaction prices. The Commission accepted an argument from these companies to the effect that they were unaware that their conduct breached the Treaty, since that conduct was expressly covered by the Webb–Pomerene Act (see above). The argument of the companies to the effect that the Act provided a total defence was rejected by the Commission and by Advocate General Marco Darmon, on the grounds that it did not actively *compel* the companies to organize their activity in this way, but merely exempted them from the application of US antitrust law. Similar charges were levelled against a Finnish trade association and Canadian producers.

The Commission argued in its decision that

Article [81] of the EEC Treaty applies to restrictive practices which may affect trade between Member States even if the undertakings and associations which are parties to the restrictive practices are established or have their headquarters outside the Community, and even if the restrictive practices in question also affect markets outside the EEC. (para. 79)

In its submission to the Court the Commission argued that the Community's jurisdiction 'is not in breach of any prohibitive rule of international law . . . in so far as its
jurisdiction is based on the effects within the Community of conduct which
occurred elsewhere' ([1988] 4 CMLR 901, at 915). Recognizing that 'the "effects
doctrine" is still contested under international law' the Commission argued that
'the objections come primarily from the United Kingdom and not from the OECD or
other countries' (pp. 915–16). Intervening in the case the United Kingdom asked the
ECJ to resolve the issue by the application of territorial jurisdiction, that is, to find
that the agreement had to the necessary extent been operated within the EC, rather
than by any application of the effects doctrine. The Advocate General's view was
that the Community should be able to assert extraterritorial jurisdiction where the
'effects of the conduct alleged . . . were substantial, direct and foreseeable' (p. 938).

The judgment is sufficiently important to be quoted from at some length. The
key paragraphs are as follows (pp. 941–2):

> [16]   It should be observed that an infringement of Article [81], such as the conclusion of an
> agreement which has had the effect of restricting competition within the Common
> Market, consists of conduct made up of two elements, the formation of the agreement,
> decision or concerted practice and the implementation thereof. If the applicability of
> prohibitions laid down under competition law were made to depend on the place
> where the agreement, decision or concerted practice was formed, the result would
> obviously be to give undertakings an easy means of evading those prohibitions. The
> decisive factor is therefore the place where it is implemented.
>
> [17]   The producers in this case implemented their pricing agreement within the Common
> Market. It is immaterial in that respect whether or not they had recourse to sub-
> sidiaries, agents, sub-agents, or branches within the Community in order to make
> their contacts with purchasers within the Community.
>
> [18]   Accordingly the Community's jurisdiction to apply its competition rules to such con-
> duct is covered by the territoriality principle as universally recognised in public inter-
> national law . . .
>
> [22]   As regards the argument relating to disregard of international comity, it suffices to
> observe that it amounts to calling in question the Community's jurisdiction to apply
> its competition rules to conduct such as that found to exist in this case and that, as
> such, that argument has already been rejected.

In choosing to refer to the 'implementation' of the agreement instead of to the
'effect' of the agreement, the court may have been doing little more than applying
an 'effects' doctrine in language that would be acceptable to the United Kingdom,
and the application of the United States-style 'effects' doctrine and *Wood Pulp*'s
'implementation' may in practice produce equivalent results. However, this has left
some uncertainty. What, for example, would be the position where there existed
an anti-competitive agreement between Japanese producers with no direct selling
arms in the EC? Would the agreement be said to be 'implemented' where EC customers placed orders for the products directly in Japan, under contracts governed
by Japanese law? If there is a genuine distinction between 'implementation' and
'effect' it might be that in this hypothetical case there would be no jurisdiction
under Community law, and that such jurisdiction might be assumed only where

the Japanese companies were actively soliciting sales from the EC instead of passively responding to orders. A different situation could be one in which there is a market share agreement for a new product that has never been sold in the EC and that is not produced in the EC. It could be argued that this agreement would be implemented in situations either where a company will not sell the product into the EC when commercial sense would indicate that it should do so, or where it sells at an inflated price reflecting the action of the cartel. In such a case art. 81 might apply even though all participants are based entirely outside the EC.

The question of territorial jurisdiction was returned to in the case and decision relation to the *Gencor/Lonhro* merger (97/26 (1997) OJ L11/30), on appeal *Gencor Ltd v Commission* case T–102/96 [1999] 4 CMLR 971. In this case, which is discussed in Chapter 19 in relation to merger control, the Commission blocked a merger between the South African interests of the two companies. The CFI was called upon to consider both the territorial scope of the EC Merger Regulation (ECMR) (at paras 78–88), and the compatibility of the decision with public international law (at paras 89–111). In determining the territorial scope of the ECMR, the CFI confirmed the position as being that jurisdiction does not exclude concentrations which, while relating to 'activities outside the Community, have the effect of creating or strengthening a dominant position as a result of which competition in the Common Market is significantly impeded' (para. 82).

When the undertakings attempted to rely on *Wood Pulp* in order to restrict the territorial application of the Regulation the CFI held that

The applicant cannot, by reference to the judgment in *Wood pulp*, rely on the criterion as to the implementation of an agreement to support its interpretation of the territorial scope of the Regulation. Far from supporting the applicant's view, that criterion for assessing the link between an agreement and Community territory in fact precludes it. According to *Wood pulp*, the criterion as to the implementation of an agreement is satisfied by mere sale within the Community, irrespective of the location of the sources of supply and the production plant. It is not disputed that Gencor and Lonhro carried out sales in the Community before the concentration and would have continued to do so thereafter. (para. 87)

The approach of the CFI was to introduce into the extraterritorial operation of the ECMR a two-stage process. The first stage, to be answered by reference to *Wood Pulp*, is that of whether there is territorial jurisdiction. The second stage is to determine whether, having exercised jurisdiction, the substantive tests set out in the ECMR should be applied so as to block a merger. In this respect the relevant parts of the judgment are, in part, as follows:

Application of the Regulation is justified under public international law when it is foreseeable that a proposed concentration will have an immediate and substantial *effect* in the Community. (para. 90)

It is therefore necessary to verify the three criteria of immediate, substantial and foreseeable *effect* are satisfied in this case. (para. 92)

Following a further discussion of these relevant factors the Court concludes this section of the judgment by holding that 'the arguments by which the applicant denies that the concentration would have a substantial *effect* in the Community must therefore be rejected' (para. 99, emphasis added).

In 1969 the United Kingdom vigorously protested at the application of EC competition law to a UK-based company, and appears in the Competition Act 1998 to have limited the application of domestic competition law to situations in which the practice condemned 'is, or is intended to be, *implemented* in the United Kingdom' (s. 2(3), emphasis added, which relates to the Chapter I Prohibition; note that there is no need for a similar provision in relation to the Chapter II Prohibition, which applies only where the dominant position is held *in* the UK, although the dominance may also extend *beyond* the UK). The position initially adopted was summed up in the 'statement of principles according to which, in the view of the United Kingdom Government, jurisdiction may be exercised over foreign corporations in antitrust matters', which was addressed to the EEC Commission, following its decision in relation to *Dyestuffs* (JO (1969) 24 July). Under this decision the EEC Commission had found that a number of undertakings in the dyestuffs industry had operated a cartel contrary to art. 81. Fines were imposed on, *inter alia*, ICI, which had its headquarters in the United Kingdom. Article 4 of the decision provided that the decision would be notified to ICI, and to Swiss undertakings that were similarly implicated, 'at the seat of one of their subsidiaries established in the Common Market'. Before the ECJ the issue was dealt with very simply, with the Court merely relying on the fact that, via its subsidiary, ICI *was* based in the EC (*ICI* v *Commission* case 48/69 [1972] CMLR 557). This has been termed the 'economic entity doctrine', which had been explicitly rejected by the UK courts in *Re Schweppes Ltd's Agreement* [1965] 1 All ER 195. Pointing to the conflicts arising between some of the Western European states and the United States in relation to the United States' assertion of jurisdiction over matters that fell outside its territory, the UK contested the 'fundamental point concerning the reach and extent of the jurisdiction exercisable by the Commission *vis-à-vis* undertakings which are neither incorporated in the territory of a Member State of the [EEC] nor carrying on business nor resident therein'. The stance taken at that time by the UK was that 'jurisdiction should be assumed only if the foreign company "carries on business" or "resides" within the territorial jurisdiction', and that 'on general principles substantive jurisdiction in antitrust matters should only be taken on the basis of either (a) the territorial principle, or (b) the nationality principle'. The *Dyestuffs* decision turned, in this respect, on the lack of distinction drawn under Community law between the various arms of an undertaking. For the UK the parent company, in this case ICI, should not have been considered to be carrying on business in the EEC by virtue of the fact that it had subsidiary companies there. Had the fine imposed by the EEC Commission been levied *only* on the subsidiaries that decision would probably not have been contested. However, this position has now changed. Intervening in the *Wood Pulp* case the United Kingdom took a more relaxed stance. The jurisdiction asserted over anti-competitive practices that have an impact in the United Kingdom under the Competition Act 1998 is intended to be an explicit and inflexible implementation of the *Wood Pulp* case law.

In the passage of the Act Lord Simon explained that by 'copying out the test in *Wood Pulp* on the face of the Bill, we are also ensuring that in the event that EC jurisprudence develops and creates a pure effects-based doctrine, the application of the UK prohibitions will not follow suit' (Hansard (HL) 13 November 1997, col. 261). Following the modernization of EC competition law it is conceivable that, should the ECJ embrace the effects doctrine, the OFT may in the future be obliged to apply it in the context of enforcing either art. 81 EC or art. 82 EC.

Several forms of response have been made in relation to the problems raised by conflicts or potential conflicts in the application of competition law. Most loosely, the comity principle can be applied. More formally, bilateral and multilateral agreements can be concluded. Another possible solution would be the creation of a global competition order, similar to that of the trade order of the WTO. Were such a regime to be created it is likely that it would be under the auspices of the WTO, and preliminary discussions have already been held.

4.2.2 Comity and 'positive comity'

Standard international law texts are likely to draw a clear distinction between international law and international comity: the law is binding and comity is not. Thus comity has been defined as 'rules of goodwill and civility, founded on the moral right of each state to receive courtesy from others' (Shearer, I. A., *Starke's International Law*, London, Butterworths (1994), p. 18). This then is a principle of reciprocal courtesy, that may be of limited application in practice. In antitrust law comity has taken on a slightly different meaning and under the EC/US Agreement may have already generated enough law for it to be a recognition of a binding practice, akin to a legal principle.

The courts of the United States have, since the mid-1970s, turned to the doctrine of comity as a restraining factor in cases in which US antitrust law is applied to situations and parties outside the country's borders. For example, in *Laker Airways* v *Sabena, Belgian World Airlines* 731 F.2d 909, (1984) the court held that 'when possible, the decisions of foreign tribunals should be given effect in domestic courts, since recognition fosters international cooperation and encourages reciprocity, thereby promoting predictability and stability'. The approach of the courts has been to balance the interests arising out of the application of US antitrust law against the harm to comity that such an application may lead to. Four cases are of particular importance: *Timberlane Lumber Co.* v *Bank of America (Timberlane I)* 549 F.2d 597 (9th Cir. 1976); *Mannington Mills, Inc.* v *Congoleum Corp.* 595 F.2d 1287 (3d Cir. 1979); *Hartford Fire Ins. Co.* v *California* 113 S. Ct. 2891 (1993); and *United States* v *Nippon Paper Indus. Co.* 109 F.3d (1st Cir. 1997).

In *Timberlane*, which related to an alleged anti-competitive practice in Honduras, Judge Choy recognized that 'there is no doubt that American antitrust laws extend over some conduct in other nations' (p. 608), but expressed the concern that in many cases there was a danger that relatively weak interests of the United States could be asserted where it would be preferable to maintain good international relationships. He proposed a three-fold, cumulative test, by which to determine whether extraterritorial jurisdiction should be upheld (p. 615): (1) does the alleged restraint of competition affect, or was it intended to affect, the foreign trade of the USA; (2) would it fall within the Sherman Act; and (3) considering the principle of comity, should jurisdiction be asserted? These criteria were considered and refined in *Mannington Mills I* (pp. 1297–8) which concerned the allegedly anti-competitive enforcement and registration of patent rights by a United States company in 26 other countries to the detriment of Mannington Mills. The combined effect of these two cases was that the USA would assert jurisdiction where the alleged practice had direct and substantial effects, and that the courts would consider the 'balance of interests' to determine whether that jurisdiction should be upheld.

In *Hartford* the Supreme Court appears to have weakened the potency of the application of comity to antitrust cases. This case dealt with a situation in which 19 states and various private plaintiffs had complained that the defendants, which included both domestic and British companies, had conspired to restrict insurance terms in the United States. The British defendants, relying on *Timberlane*, argued that the effect of comity meant that any extraterritorial application of the Sherman Act should be struck down. At first instance this argument was successful. When the case eventually reached the Supreme Court it was held that the conduct fell within the Sherman Act, which could be applied extraterritorially where 'foreign conduct . . . was meant to produce and did in fact produce some substantial effect in the United States'. The *Hartford* judgment has been criticized both inside and outside the United States (see, e.g., Robertson, A., and Demetriou, M., ' "But that was in another country": The Extraterritorial Application of U.S. Antitrust Laws in the U.S. Supreme Court' (1994) 43 *International and Comparative Law Quarterly* 417). In *Nippon Paper* the Court of Appeals took a more hard-line approach. The claim was based on allegations that a Japanese cartel fixed the price of thermal fax paper in the United States. All the participants in the practice were Japanese; the meetings were held in Japan; and the sales to distributors were made in Japan. The Court held that the case should not, at first instance, have been dismissed, arguing that there was 'no tenable reason why principles of comity should shield [the Japanese companies] from prosecution'. The Court was swayed by the increasing amount of international commerce, and by that fact that the practice complained of would, if the allegations were sustained, be illegal in Japan as well as in the United States.

The level of court involvement in the antitrust process in the United States serves as a restraint on the application of the principle of comity. Even were the Department of Justice or the Federal Trade Commission to respect the interests and wishes of other states in the application of antitrust law, the courts are not obliged to follow their example should a case be brought by private litigants or by the individual states under their own antitrust law. It should be noted here too, that a US senate sub-committee has proposed an amendment to the antitrust laws to allow actions to be taken against anti-competitive arrangements outside the USA, even where there is no proof that US consumers have been harmed. Such a proposal is, however, unlikely to become law.

The European Commission has shown that it is ready to embrace the principle of comity where it has the discretion to do so (see, e.g., *Boeing/McDonnell Douglas* 97/816 (1997) OJ L336/16, below).

The application of the ECMR (see Chapter 19) raises particular problems with respect to the comity principle. The EC Commission does not appear to have discretion as to whether or not at least to consider any merger, wheresoever it is concluded, that falls within the threshold criteria set out in the Regulation. In some instances even such an examination is likely to be a matter of concern to other states.

There have been three important decisions which have related to mergers that would be carried out by companies whose production was entirely outside the EC. In *Gencor/Lonhro* 97/26 (1997) OJ L11/30, on appeal *Gencor Ltd v Commission* case T–102/96 [1999] 4 CMLR 971, although both companies had substantial operations in the EC, and Lonhro was a UK company, the market in question was primarily that of platinum mined in South Africa. In this case the two undertakings jointly satisfied the thresholds set out in the merger regulation (see Chapter 19) and had sales into the EEA of over €2bn at the time the concentrative joint venture was under consideration. Although the decision itself does not deal expressly with issues of jurisdiction other than to note that the thresholds were reached, it is clear that there was consideration of the South African position (see, e.g., paras 168–71). In its comment on the case in the *26th Annual Report on Competition Policy 1996*, the Commission found it 'worth underlining that, from the outset of the procedure, the South African authorities have been kept informed by the Commission of developments in this case and have attended the hearings organised in Brussels' (p. 184).

The *Boeing* case was particularly susceptible to charges of political interference in the regulatory process, although this was denied on both sides of the Atlantic. The merger between Boeing and McDonnell Douglas reduced the number of manufacturers of large commercial aircraft from three to two. As a result of this Airbus Industrie, based in Europe and part-owned by four European governments, was left facing a single dominant competitor. The Federal Trade Commission (FTC) publicly acknowledged that this level of structural restriction in the market was a problem, but then cleared the merger, holding in the process that there was no effective competition between the merging firms to be snuffed out by the merger. Notwithstanding reports in the United States press that emphasized the role of the new corporation as 'an American national champion' (e.g., *New York Times*, 17 December 1996), the FTC expressly denied that this was a consideration in its assessment of the merger. The EC Commission cleared the merger only after being given various assurances by Boeing relating to future commercial conduct. United States commentators, and Boeing's attorneys in particular, have argued that the concessions had little to do with the merger itself, but that the Commission was exploiting the situation to secure advantages for Airbus. Prior to the eleventh-hour settlement there had been speculation that if the merger proceeded contrary to Community law the severest of fines would be imposed and that Boeing planes landing in Europe might be seized. This was never a likely prospect, but the case is a perfect illustration of the problems that may arise in respect of such transactions and, notwithstanding the level of cooperation between the EC and the United States, 'diverging approaches of the competition authorities in Brussels and Washington made it impossible to reach commonly accepted solutions' (Schaub, A., 'International cooperation in antitrust matters: making the point in the wake of the Boeing/MDD proceedings', (1998) 1 *Competition Policy Newsletter*, p. 4). For further discussion and comment on this case see (1997) *Antitrust*, Fall issue, which features commentary and interviews with some of the leading players in the case. An excellent discussion of the case can also be found in Zanettin, B., *Cooperation between Antitrust Agencies at the International Level*, Oxford, Hart Publishing (2002) at pp. 93–8.

Even more controversially, in July 2001 the EC Commission blocked the proposed merger between General Electric Inc (GE) and Honeywell Inc. In doing so, the Commission took a stance which was in direct opposition to that adopted by the US authorities, which had cleared the merger. It was noted in the Commission press release (IP/01/939, 3 July 2001) that

The European Commission and the US Department of Justice have worked in close co-operation during this investigation. It is unfortunate that, in the end, we reached different conclusions, but each authority has to perform its own assessment and the risk of dissenting views, although regrettable, can never be totally excluded. This does not mean that one authority is doing a technical analysis and the other pursuing a political goal, as some might pretend, but simply that we might interpret facts differently and forecast the effects of an operation in different ways. The GE/Honeywell is a rare case where the transatlantic competition authorities have disagreed.

The Commission was particularly disappointed in this case that offers of divestment and conduct remedies put forward to the merging parties were not accepted. Three articles in the Fall 2001 issue of *Antitrust* deal with this case with interesting perspectives.

It should be recognized that although the approach of the EC Commission in the Boeing and GE cases attracted considerable criticism within the United States, the latter's authorities have similarly examined mergers in situations where production has been outside the United States. This was the case, for example, with the Guinness/Grand Metropolitan merger leading to the creation of Diageo in 1998.

Where comity requires a country to respect another's interests in the application of its national law, 'positive comity' has greater force and might suggest, *inter alia*, that a country should enforce its own competition law in order to assist another country where it might not otherwise do so were it to consider purely national interests. This principle is prominent in the EC/USA cooperation agreements, discussed below, and has led to situations in which the EC is, on behalf of the USA, investigating anti-competitive conduct which is being pursued in the Community but which is of concern to the US authorities. One such complaint, for example, has been made about the European-wide airline reservation system, 'Amadeus', which the United States authorities believe has an adverse impact on United States' commercial interests (see below).

4.2.3 **Bilateral agreements**

The EC, the UK, and the USA have all concluded bilateral agreements relating to competition enforcement with a range of parties, and in some cases with each other. As well as its agreement with the EC the USA has also concluded agreements with, amongst others, Germany, which remain in force notwithstanding the links with the EC, Canada, and Australia.

In 1991 the Commission and the US authorities had reached a formal agreement on cooperation in the application of competition laws, but, following a challenge to the legal basis of the agreement by the French government, this was struck down by the ECJ on the basis of fundamental breaches in procedure (*France* v *Commission* case C–327/91 [1994] 5 CMLR 517). The Agreement, the purpose of which 'is to promote cooperation and coordination and lessen the possibility or impact of differences between the Parties in the application of their competition laws' (art. 1(1)) has now been readopted in its correct form on the basis of arts 83, 300(3), and 308 EC (95/145/EC, ECSC, (1995) OJ L95/45).

It is a primary requirement of the Agreement that the signatories will share information about the enforcement of antitrust activities. Article II(1) thus provides that 'each Party shall notify the other whenever its competition authorities become aware that their enforcement activities may affect important interests of the other'. This notification is to be far enough in advance of the taking of formal decisions 'to enable the other Party's views to be taken into account' (art. II(4)). Officials from the relevant authorities are to meet 'at least twice each year, unless otherwise agreed' to exchange information on a range of factors, and each is to provide the other with any information that comes to its attention that relates to anti-competitive activities of which the other should be aware (art. III). Article VIII provides that no Party is required to divulge information which it would otherwise be required to treat as confidential. Further, each Party is obliged, as far as possible, to treat as confidential any information given to it by the other Party.

To the extent compatible within each of the legal orders, the Parties will cooperate with each other in enforcement activity (art. IV) and in individual cases may coordinate their activities. Where they do so they shall act 'expeditiously and, insofar as possible, consistently with the enforcement objectives of the other Party' (art. IV(2)). This cooperation was tested for the first time in the approach taken to Microsoft in 1994. Microsoft, pursued simultaneously in both the United States by the Department of Justice and the EC by the Commission, appeared itself to be grateful for the cooperation between the authorities, which allowed the position to be resolved with the minimum of disruption to the company and with the benefit to Microsoft of a single solution satisfying both jurisdictions. So advantageous to the company was the procedure that it consented to the exchange between the authorities of information that would otherwise have remained confidential. The Commission was enthusiastic about the outcome of the case which, it claimed, 'serves as an important model for the future, as it shows how the two authorities can combine their efforts to deal effectively with giant multinational companies' (Press Release IP/94/653, 16 July 1994).

Article V of the Agreement is addressed to situations in which anti-competitive activities in the territory of one Party adversely affect the interests of the other. This introduces the 'positive comity' noted above. Article V(2) and (3) is in the following terms:

2. If a Party believes that anti-competitive activities carried out on the territory of the other Party are adversely affecting its important interests, the first Party may notify the other Party and may request that the other Party's competition authorities initiate appropriate enforcement activities. The notification shall be as specific as possible about the nature of the anti-competitive activities and their effects on the interests of the notifying Party, and shall include an offer of such further information and other cooperation as the notifying Party is able to provide.

3. Upon receipt of a notification under paragraph 2, and after such discussion between the Parties as may be appropriate and useful in the circumstances, the competition authorities of the notified Party will consider whether or not to initiate enforcement activities, or to expand ongoing enforcement activities, with respect to the anti-competitive activities identified in the notification.

The notified Party is not under an obligation to act (art. V(4)), but the principles of comity and goodwill suggest that it is likely at least to consider carefully any such notification. A general principle of comity is set out in art. VI, which deals with the 'avoidance of conflicts over enforcement activities'. This principle is sometimes referred to as 'negative comity'. Under this article 'each Party shall consider important interests of the other Party in decisions as to whether or not to initiate an investigation or proceeding, the scope of an investigation or proceeding, the nature of the remedies or penalties sought, and in other ways, as appropriate'. It would appear that this principle, which is clarified further in the article, is of a stronger and more generous nature than that recognized by the US Supreme Court in *Hartford Fire Ins. Co. v California* (above). This article was applied by both the EC and the United States in the Boeing case. Here the EC 'sought an appropriate way to take account of important national interests of the United States' and the Chairman of the FTC indicated that the body would 'take into account the expressed interests of the [EC] when reaching its decision' (97/816, para. 11). The two parties concluded a further Agreement, on positive comity alone, which was signed on 4 June 1998, the EU–USA Positive Comity Agreement 1998, 98/386 (1998) OJ L173/28. This agreement, from which mergers are excluded, creates a presumption that in some cases a Party will either suspend or defer its usual enforcement measures.

The core provision is art. III, which is in the following terms:

The competition authorities of a Requesting Party may request the competition authorities of a Requested Party to investigate and, if warranted, to remedy anti-competitive activities in accordance with the Requested Party's competition laws. Such a request may be made regardless of whether the activities also violate the Requesting Party's competition laws, and regardless of whether the competition authorities of the Requesting Party have commenced or contemplate taking enforcement activities under their own competition laws.

Even before the entry into force of this agreement, the Commission had acted under the positive comity provisions of the 1991 agreement. For example, in March 1999 it decided to open a formal procedure against Air France under art. 82 in relation to the information it made available to the Amadeus computerized reservation system, which was better than that given to a reservation system owned by American Airlines (IP(99)171, [1999] 4 CMLR 581).

The *Competition Laws Cooperation Agreement 1999 (EC/ECSC/Canada)* 1999/445 (1999) OJ L175 entered into force on 29 April 1999. It makes provision for consultation, coordination, and cooperation in the enforcement of competition law. It is, in essence, similar in approach to the agreement concluded with the United States, and takes the same approach towards comity (see art. VI).

The EC has also concluded bilateral agreements with Canada (*Competition Laws Co-operation Agreement 1999 (EC/ECSC/Canada)* 1999/45 (1999) OJ L175/1), which makes provision for consultation, coordination, and cooperation in the enforcement of competition law, and with Japan (*Decision Concluding the Agreement between the European Community and Japan concerning co-operation on anti-competitive activities* 2003/520 (2003) OJ L183).

For its part, in October 2003, the UK entered into agreements with Canada, and with Australia and New Zealand. In both cases the agreements, which are in very similar terms, relate to the 'coordination of enforcement activities'. They do not extend to the criminal enforcement of the cartel offence (see Chapter 12).

4.2.4 Multilateral cooperation and globalization

4.2.4.1 *The European economic area*

There are several instances of multilateral cooperation in respect of competition policy. The most notable is that between the EU and the other members of the EEA. The importance of the EEA is declining as its members assume full membership of the European Community. The EEA, concluded between the EC and the EFTA states, with the exception of Switzerland, entered into force on 1 January 1994 ((1994) OJ L1/3). Liechtenstein acceded on 1 May 1995. As Austria, Finland, and Sweden have since joined the Community the non-EC contracting states are therefore Iceland, Norway, and Liechtenstein. Broadly the relevant law of the EEA mirrors that of the EC, arts 53 and 54 EEA reflecting arts 81 and 82 EC. Article 57 EEA essentially incorporates the ECMR into the EEA.

4.2.4.2 *The North American free trade area*

In North America, Chapter 15 of the North American Free Trade Agreement (NAFTA, 32 ILM 605 (1993)) concluded between the USA, Canada, and Mexico, commits the parties to cooperation on antitrust matters. Amongst other provisions, each of the Parties is required, by virtue of the Agreement, to 'adopt or maintain measures to proscribe anti-competitive business conduct and take appropriate action with respect thereto' (art. 1501(1)). Primarily the provisions relate to the conduct and maintenance of state 'designated' monopolies, and they do not set new standards for the regulation of private anti-competitive conduct.

4.2.4.3 *The OECD*

The OECD has published a Recommendation which calls for countries to consult with each other in appropriate situations with the aim of promoting enforcement cooperation and minimizing differences that may arise (*Revised Recommendation of the OECD Council Concerning Cooperation Between Member Countries on Restrictive Business Practices Affecting International Trade,* OECD Doc. No. C(95)130 (Final), 28 July 1995). The preamble of this Recommendation suggests that 'if Member countries find it appropriate to enter into bilateral arrangements for cooperation in the enforcement of national competition laws, they should take into account' the Recommendation, and it would appear that the EC/USA Cooperation Agreement has been so influenced. Although the OECD has expressed an interest in competition law matters which is commensurate with its membership of industrialized nations, it has not taken formal steps towards harmonization, although a working group on international antitrust cooperation is trying to reach an agreement on a 'consensus recommendation' confirming members' hostility to hard-core cartels. This group is also examining ways of resolving jurisdictional problems in relation to mergers having an international dimension. Early in 1998 a Recommendation on the prosecution of hard-core cartels was approved by the General Council.

4.2.4.4 *The WTO*

The WTO is primarily concerned with the free flow of trade, and with the elimination of trade barriers wherever possible. Its membership is nearly universal. A Draft International Antitrust Code was submitted to the members of the GATT in July 1993, although no substantial progress was made in respect of this. More important was the failure of earlier efforts leading to the Havana Charter, which the United States refused to ratify. However, because of the increasingly close relationship between trade and competition policy the WTO established a working party following the 1996 Singapore conference, under the chairmanship of the French Vice President of the *Conseil de la Concurrence* (competition council), which was due to report on whether negotiations are advisable in this area in 1998. This followed a proposal from the EC Commission, which became an EU initiative, suggesting that it might be possible to reach international agreement in some key areas, such as the response to cartels (see Commission Press Release (1995) IP/95/752, 12 July). The prospects for success are uncertain. Neither the EC nor the USA envisages a globally binding agreement. Announcing the formation of an International Competition Policy Advisory Committee, Joel Klein of the Department of Justice, Antitrust Division set out the US position in words that do not suggest that the WTO group will succeed in creating a harmonized regime:

this working group can play an important educational role in demonstrating the important contributions of antitrust to efficient national markets and open international trade, and in fostering international cooperation. We are less persuaded that the time is ripe for the negotiation of global antitrust rules.   (24 November 1997)

Matters appeared to change somewhat following the change in Presidency with the election of George Bush in 2000. The future of the possibilities for international competition cooperation in the context of the WTO was discussed at the Doha Ministerial Conference, and parties signing up to the Doha declaration accepted that there was a valid case for the WTO to negotiate and conclude a multilateral Agreement on Trade and Competition. A key reason for this was a 'fundamental shift in the US position in July 2001' (see speech by Alexander Schaub, 4 April 2002). The areas that will be focused on are the 'core principles of competition policy, such as transparency, non-discrimination and procedural fairness, commitment to outlaw hardcore cartels, [and] modalities for voluntary co-operation between antitrust authorities' (ibid.).

4.2.4.5 ICPAC, the Global Competition Forum, and the International Competition Network

On 28 February 2000 the International Competition Policy Advisory Committee (ICPAC), founded in 1997 by the US antitrust authorities, submitted its final report (this is available at **www.usdoj.gov/atr/icpac**—but is over 300 pages long). Although the report was commissioned by the US authorities and prepared by US experts, it was well received internationally. The report made recommendations in relation to multijurisdictional merger review, cooperation in cartel enforcement, and the intersection of trade and competition policy.

Specifically the report argued that the steps to be taken in the future should first centre around the creation of further bilateral agreements, but that a multilateral approach is also needed. The ICPAC group suggested that the WTO was not the natural home for competition policy initiatives, and recommended instead the establishment of a new Global Competition Initiative (GCF) for addressing the international concerns relating to competition enforcement. This proposal met with approval within the EC, and in March 2001 Dr Alexander Schaub, then Director General for Competition, made a speech in favour of the establishment of a 'Global Competition Forum', which had been discussed by international experts at a meeting in February 2001. According to Dr Schaub, this GCF:

should not be a new institution—it is not meant as an alternative to the involvement of the OECD or the WTO in competition policy. It should first and foremost be a competition authority forum, involving a minimum of permanent infrastructure, with support primarily provided by participating authorities and facilitators. However, it should draw together all interested parties—both public (e.g. other international organisations) and private (e.g. business, professional, consumer and academic bodies); these should be appropriately associated with the forum, as participants and/or facilitators.

In November 2001 the US Department of Justice (DOJ) and FTC, and the EC Commission, became the founding members of the 'International Competition Network' (ICN). This is a 'virtual' network, and has no permanent resources or institutions. Its role is to enhance cooperation between its members, which number over 50 and which include the leading developed nations (including the EC) as well as countries ranging from Armenia to Zambia. The web address of the ICN is **www.internationalcompetitionnetwork.org**.

4.3 **Private parties and the enforcement of judgments**

4.3.1 **Conflicts of laws**

There are three issues that face any private party in a dispute which involves jurisdictional matters beyond the bounds of that party's state:

(a) Where should the action be brought?
(b) Under which law should the action be brought?
(c) How will any judgment be enforced?

In practice these issues can be highly complex. It would be possible to envisage a situation in which the courts of one state would hear the action and apply the law of another state, with the judgment being enforced in the courts of yet another state. These are complex matters that lie beyond the scope of this book, and the interested reader should refer to one of the specialist texts dealing with private international law or conflicts of laws.

4.3.2 **Private actions**

There have been a number of cases in which private parties have sought remedies, or damages, in their own courts against companies based in another jurisdiction, or where claimants have sued outside their jurisdiction in the jurisdiction of the defendant. Some of these cases have been considered already in this chapter at 4.2.1, but some further developments will be noted here.

A number of claims have arisen out of the international prosecution of the vitamins cartel, which resulted in a plea bargain in the USA (see US DOJ press release, 6 April 2000), and in an infringement decision in the EC (Commission Decision 2003/2 *Vitamins* (2003) OJ L6/1). In the USA a South African company, Empagran SA, sought to recover damages from Hoffman-La Roche, one of the cartel participants. Hoffman-La Roche itself is a company based in Switzerland. The transactions between the claimant and defendant had no connection with the USA, the only relationship being that Hoffman-La Roche had pleaded to a violation of s. 1 of the Sherman Act. At first instance the District of Columbia District Court rejected the case, and Empagran appealed to the Court of Appeals for the D.C. Circuit, where the court held by a 2–1 majority that the case could proceed (*Empagran S.A.* v *Hoffman-La Roche Ltd* 315 F.3d 338 (District of Columbia Circuit,

2003))). As of Spring 2004 this case was before the US Supreme Court as *F. Hoffmann-La Roche Ltd and others* v *Empagran SA* (Docket No. 03–724). Amongst others the UK, together with Ireland and the Netherlands, submitted an *amici curiae* brief in support of the appellant. All three governments expressed their opposition to 'assertions of extraterritorial jurisdiction in private antitrust cases where foreign claimants seek to recover from foreign defendants solely for foreign injuries not incurred in the country in which the private suit is filed'. The governments argued that such litigation 'contravenes basic principles of international law and . . . would interfere with a sovereign nation's right to regulate conduct within its territory'. Concerns were also expressed that such private litigation could have the effect of undermining national leniency programmes designed to expose cartels. The same issue is also being considered by the US Supreme Court in the case of *Christie's International plc and Sotheby's Holdings, Inc and others* v *Charlotte Kruman and others*.

In the UK a similar action was brought in the case of *Provimi Ltd* v *Aventis Animal Nutrition SA and others and other actions* [2003] EWHC 961 (Comm), [2003] All ER (D) 59 (May). In this complicated case seven defendant companies were sued by three claimants in the UK courts on the basis of a breach of art. 81 EC. Some of the claimants and some of the defendants had no connection with the UK, and the claimants were relying in part upon Council Regulation 44/2001 (*on Jurisdiction and the Enforcement of Judgments in Civil and Commercial Matters* (2001) OJ L12/1) and the Lugano Convention (*Lugano Convention on Jurisdiction and Judgments in Civil and Commercial Matters 1988*, Lugano, 16 September 1988, Decision 88/592/EEC (1988) OJ L319). The cases were further complicated by the presence of jurisdictional clauses inserted into some of the contracts under which the sales were made. The court rejected the defendants' arguments to the effect that it had no jurisdiction to hear the case, and the matter proceeded to be dealt with on the substance of the claim (see further, Furse, M., '*Provimi* v *Aventis*: Damages and Jurisdiction', [2003] Comp Law 119).

4.3.3 The World Trade Organization

The WTO agreement of 1994 is intended to be directed to the restrictive acts of governments. It appears, however, to have a limited potential for private antitrust litigants. In 1995 Eastman-Kodak filed a petition with the US authorities, based on s. 301 of the 1974 Trade Act (19 USC 2411), alleging that Fuji was hindering the distribution of Kodak film in Japan by operating an exclusionary distribution system that was blocked to Kodak, and that the Japanese Government was participating in limiting access to the Japanese markets. Kodak had alternative routes: it could, for example, have attempted to persuade the Japan Fair Trade Commission to take action based on violations of arts 3, 8(1), and 19 of the Anti-Monopoly Law. The prospects for success would appear to be remote, however, and the Japanese authorities had already looked at the photographic film industry in 1974 without taking any significant remedial action. Kodak would also have had a private right of action through the Japanese courts, although art. 25 of the Anti-Monopoly Law provides that such relief becomes available only following certain formal action by the Fair Trade Commission, and again the prospect of success would be uncertain. The company could also have attempted to persuade the US DOJ to take action on the basis of an extended and aggressive effects-based approach to the application of US antitrust law. Again, such a step, although contemplated within the International Guidelines, would have been contentious and novel. In May 1995, therefore, Kodak filed a petition with the United States Trade Representative (USTR) inviting it to investigate the matter.

The USTR agreed to pursue the issue in July, and was prepared to do so not only on the basis of trade restrictions strictly interpreted, but also on the basis of the specific allegations of anti-competitive conduct made by Kodak. In the summer of 1996 the USTR found that acts which restricted the sale of photographic materials by US exporters to Japan could be attributed to the Japanese Government. Section 301 of the 1974 Trade Act gives the USTR the discretion to take action when it finds that the actions of a foreign government are 'unreasonable or discriminatory'. The choice of approach is a wide one: at one extreme the United States government can take unilateral counter-measures. Such a step is, however, contentious and carries with it the risk of retaliation by the country against whose interests the steps are being taken. The United States authorities thus decided to turn to the binding dispute resolution procedure established in the WTO at the Uruguay Round. This procedure gives members of the WTO access to a dispute mechanism in the event of a conflict based on the trade laws of the GATT. A panel of three to five members is appointed to hear any dispute. The final complaint did not rely on the basis of the specific allegations made by Kodak, but was brought on the basis that 'Japan's laws, regulations and requirements affecting the distribution' of film treated importers 'less favourably', in breach of trade obligations. Only governments have access to this procedure; the hearings are closed to the public; private parties and counsel are, by custom, excluded; and governments are the only subjects of the proceedings. By seeking a ruling to the effect that the Japanese Government was impeding imports in its tacit support of anti-competitive industrial practices maintained in Japan the dispute moved to a new level, in which Kodak and Fuji ceased to act directly as litigants. The EC Commission also joined the panel as a third party due to its economic interest in the matter (see Press Release IP/98/122). Early in 1998 the WTO disputes settlement body rejected the United States' case on the merits, although it accepted that a similar route would remain open in the future (Panel Report, *Japan—Measures Affecting Consumer Photographic Film and Paper*, WT/DS44/R, 31 March 1998; note that this has not been, as it could have, appealed). The panel also concluded that, in the appropriate circumstances, an action taken by a private party that has the effect of hindering trade may also be deemed to be governmental (para. 10.56). Such a procedure has clear advantages to the respective parties: although they are likely to be pressing their respective claims behind the scenes, they are not being required to invest heavily in the proceedings. The main drawback is that this procedure can be invoked only when it can be established that a government's action, or inaction, is involved as part of the original antitrust claim, and where the complainant can persuade its own government to bring the matter before the WTO. Although this is a somewhat tortuous route that will be beyond the reach of most companies and will require great patience, the position remains that lawyers

involved in international competition matters should keep in mind the possibility that the relevant trade agency might be convinced to bring a competition-related matter to the WTO for a resolution that might otherwise be unavailable in the antitrust system. (First, H., 'The Intersection of Trade and Antitrust Remedies' (1997) *Antitrust*, Fall, p. 21)

4.4 **Conclusion**

It is too early to envisage the creation of a global competition regime, with an international competition authority. The pattern at present is one of developing countries being encouraged to adopt competition laws, such as Zimbabwe's Competition Act 1996, and for expertise gained by states with developed competition regimes to be shared with the rest of the world. The ICN, and the WTO, appear to be the fora most engaged in this process. One result of this process is that at the present time around 100 countries are believed to have in place some form of competition law.

5

Investigation

5.1 Introduction

This chapter deals with the way in which infringements of arts 81 and 82 EC and the Chapter I and II Prohibitions are investigated and attacked in the EC and in the UK. The penalties that may be imposed following the finding of infringements are dealt with in the following chapter, and third party rights, including the role of the civil courts, are discussed in Chapter 7. Investigative powers and procedural provisions in relation to the merger control regimes are considered in Chapters 19 and 20, and market investigation references in the UK are dealt with in Chapter 17. The criminal procedures that may be applied to prosecute the cartel offence in the UK fall within Chapter 12.

Although the procedures that operate in relation to this core body of competition law cannot be characterized as belonging to the body of 'criminal' law the consequences for an undertaking found in breach of the law can be severe. In the case of the *Microsoft* decision for example (Commission Decision of 24 March 2004) Microsoft was fined €497,196,304 and was also required to take steps to alter its conduct on the market, including changing one of its products. There may well, therefore, be disputes as to whether the powers possessed by the authorities have been exercised correctly. It has been accepted that for the purposes of the human rights guarantees enshrined in the European Convention of Human Rights 1950 (ECHR) the law should be treated *as if* it were criminal. The powers set out in the Competition Act 1998, as amended by the Enterprise Act 2002 and by the Competition Act 1998 and Other Enactments (Amendment) Regulations 2004, SI 2004/1261, are similar to those of Regulation 1/2003, and the same protections will apply.

Following the modernization of EC competition law the role of national authorities in its application is greatly enhanced. While the EC Commission possesses autonomous powers to act the national competition authorities are also required to apply arts 81 and 82, and to do so under their relevant national procedures. In the UK these powers are set out in the Competition Act 1998, such that in most circumstances, it will make little difference whether the OFT is investigating a breach of the Chapter I Prohibition, or a breach of art. 81. Because national procedures are used by the members of the European Competition Network (ECN) there will, inevitably, be differences in the procedures used, and some of these will be substantial. While a study of these differences and the effects they may have on the effective enforcement of competition law would be fascinating, there is not scope here to do so, and the treatment here relates exclusively to the Commission's autonomous powers, and the powers available to the UK authorities.

5.2 **The European Community law**

The body responsible for ensuring the observance of EC competition law is, as we have seen in Chapter 2, the EC Commission. Where its acts produce legal effects it may in turn be overseen by the CFI, under the review powers conferred by way of art. 230 EC, with the possibility of further appeal to the ECJ. Articles 81 and 82 do not, in their own words, establish the necessary mechanism for enforcement of the proscriptions contained therein; the Commission's powers are set out in Regulation 1/2003, which replaced Regulation 17 of 1962 in May 2004. This regulation sets out the procedures to be adopted by the Commission when pursuing possible breaches of arts 81 and 82 EC, and the penalties that may be imposed where undertakings are found to have breached the law. The Commission may, in this respect, be characterized as investigator, prosecutor, and decision maker. For the remainder of this section the structure of the regulation will be followed.

5.2.1 **Regulation 1/2003**

Regulation 1/2003 on the implementation of the rules of competition laid down in arts 81 and 82 of the Treaty (2003) OJ L1/1, which became applicable on 1 May 2004, replaced the older regime set out in Regulation 17 of 1962 ((1962) OJ 13, 204). This latter regulation was replaced as part of the EC's modernization programme. In particular it was argued that the older regulation was ineffective in balancing the two key objectives in the EC of simplified administration and effective supervision (see Regulation 1/2003, recital (2)). While the older law is not discussed here specifically, principles established under it remain valid under the new regime, as do a number of cases, particularly those relating to the rights of the defence. These are dealt with throughout this chapter as necessary. However, some understanding of the main changes made by Regulation 1/2003 is important to an understanding of the policy underpinning the regulation.

Regulation 1/2003 made changes in three core areas: first, it fundamentally altered the way in which art. 81 (see Chapter 9) is applied. This was effected by granting direct applicability to art. 81(3), the consequences of which move are addressed fully in Chapter 9, and are also considered in Chapter 7. The regulation also, and in a related move, profoundly adjusted the relationship between the EC Commission and the Member States in the enforcement of EC competition law. This change is explained in part in Chapter 3 dealing with the relationship between

EC and national competition laws. Finally the regulation made changes to the specific powers of investigation and enforcement available to the Commission in the prosecution of alleged infringements. These latter changes are dealt with in detail in this chapter.

5.2.1.1 *The subjects of investigation*

Although it has been stressed earlier in this work that the subjects of competition law are 'undertakings', and that the term is an important one for competition lawyers to understand (see 2.2), there are increasing instances where this is not strictly the case. In the UK for example the cartel offence is targeted not at undertakings, but at individuals (the reasons for this are discussed in Chapter 12). In the EC one of the changes effected by Regulation 1/2003 was, in limited circumstances, to extend the power of the Commission to allow it to 'interview any persons who may be in possession of useful information' (para. 25—this finds formal expression in art. 19 of the regulation), and in certain cases to enter private homes if business records are kept there (para. 26, and art. 21 of the regulation). This reflects the fact that the Commission, and other authorities, have uncovered evidence in the course of previous cartel investigations that employees of undertakings are taking deliberate steps, including using their private addresses, telephone lines, etc., to avoid the detection of cartels in which they are engaged on behalf of their employer undertakings. However, individuals—unless they are simultaneously undertakings—may not be found to be in breach of the substantive provisions of arts 81 and 82. The scope of the Commission's power is purely procedural, and is designed to make easier the uncovering of infringements by undertakings.

5.2.2 **Broad powers conferred by Regulation 1/2003**

The regulation gives the Commission and the national authorities powers to make certain decisions necessary for the application of arts 81 and 82, and to take the steps necessary to lead to these decisions. The Commission has broader powers than do the national authorities, and under the terms of the regulation still sits at the apex of EC competition law.

Article 2 of the Regulation sets out the relevant burden of proof when an attempt is made to establish an infringement, or when an undertaking is seeking to rely on the legal exception provided for in art. 81(3). This is as follows:

In any national or Community proceedings for the application of arts 81 and 82 of the Treaty, the burden of proving an infringement of art. 81(1) or of art. 82 of the Treaty shall rest on the party or the authority alleging the infringement. The undertaking or association of undertakings claiming the benefit of art. 81(3) of the Treaty shall bear the burden of proving that the conditions of that paragraph are fulfilled.

This is not a controversial position, and reflects the stance taken by DG Comp and the ECJ over the previous years. In respect of the application of art. 81(3) EC it is appropriate that the party seeking to rely on it has to establish its validity. Article 81(3) applies only to situations in which art. 81(1) also applies—this is to say, to situations in which prima facie an illegal agreement is operating. Article 1(1) of the regulation provides that agreements falling within art. 81(1) EC are 'prohibited, no prior decision to that effect being required'. The onus is then on the party seeking to operate in this manner to justify the derogation from the general rule.

5.2.2.1 *Articles 4–10 of the regulation*

EC competition law may be applied at the first instance by three sets of institutions: DG Comp; national authorities; and the national courts. National authorities are empowered expressly by art. 5 to take the following decisions:

- requiring that an infringement be brought to an end;
- ordering interim measures;
- accepting commitments;
- imposing fines, periodic penalty payments, or any other penalty provided for in their national law.

It is particularly significant that the last element of this rubric makes reference to the penalties 'provided for in their national law', as this opens up the possibility in theory of some divergence, although in practice harmonization has already largely occurred in this area. The UK amended its provisions in relation to penalties to bring them into line with the Commission's powers set out in Regulation 1/2003 to coincide with modernization. Article 6 simply provides that 'National courts shall have the power to apply arts 81 and 82 of the Treaty'. The powers of national courts are considered further in Chapter 7.

5.2.2.1.1 *Termination of infringements*

The key power available to the Commission in respect of individual cases is set out in art. 7. This provides that where it finds an infringement the Commission 'may by decision require the undertakings and associations of undertakings concerned to bring such infringements to an end'. The coercive powers of the Commission in this respect are very strong indeed. Thus,

it may impose on them any behavioural or structural remedies which are proportionate to the infringement committed and necessary to bring the infringement effectively to an end

The Commission has in the past imposed a wide range of behavioural remedies. These include, for example, requiring an undertaking to resume supplies to a customer (*BBI/Boosey & Hawkes: interim measures* 87/500 (1987) OJ L286/36); requiring Microsoft to offer an amended version of one of its operating systems (*Microsoft* decision of 24 March 2004); forcing an ice cream manufacturer to alter its distribution system by removing exclusivity from freezer cabinets (*Van den Bergh Foods Ltd* 98/531 (1998) OJ L246/1). Many other examples are given in chapters dealing with the substantive provisions later in this book.

The reference to structural remedies is a new one, which was not found in Regulation 17. Indeed it had been believed that the Commission did not have the power under the old regulation to impose structural remedies, and it had never attempted to do so. These powers, however, are to be used proportionately, and not in circumstances in which less drastic remedies will resolve the problem. This position is reflected in recital (12) of Regulation 1/2003, which notes that

changes to the structure of an undertaking as it existed before the infringement was committed would only be proportionate where there is a substantial risk of a lasting or repeated infringement that derives from the very structure of the undertaking.

Member States' authorities do *not* have the power to impose structural remedies in relation to breaches of arts 81 and 82 EC. Given that the provision of the power is made express for the Commission, but is not mentioned in relation to the powers of the national authorities it is to be presumed that no such power is given, although they may impose structural remedies in relation to breaches of national law if the appropriate powers are available. Indeed, there would be jurisdictional issues arising from the attempt of one authority to impose a structural solution in relation to an undertaking located in the territory of another authority.

The Commission may also make decisions to the effect that there has been a breach of arts 81 or 82, but that no such breach is continuing. While the efficacy of this might be questioned, art. 7(1) provides that such decisions may be taken only where there is a 'legitimate interest in doing so'. Limitation periods set out in the regulation impose some further restriction on the ability of the Commission to act in such a fashion. It is most likely to do so where such a decision would act as a precedent to discourage others from participating in similar illegal conduct in the future.

5.2.2.1.2 *Interim measures*

Regulation 17 did not make explicit the power of the EC Commission to order interim measures, and it took the ECJ to confirm, in the case of *Camera Care*, that the Commission had the power to impose interim measures

when the practice of certain undertakings in competition matters has the effect of injuring the interests of some Member States, causing damage to other undertakings, or of unacceptably jeopardising the Community's competition policy. (*Camera Care Ltd* v *Commission* case 792/79R [1980] 1 CMLR 334, at para. 14)

Under Regulation 17 of 1962 the Commission ordered interim measures in only a small number of cases. In Regulation 1/2003 this power is set out on the face of the regulation, art. 8 of which provides that 'in cases of urgency due to the risk of serious and irreparable damage to competition' the Commission may order interim measures.

5.2.2.1.3 *Commitment decisions*

In addition to taking formal decisions under art. 7, the Commission may, under art. 9, accept commitments from undertakings 'to meet the concerns expressed to them by the Commission in its preliminary assessment'. The Commission may take a decision to formalize these commitments and to make them binding. This may prove to be a useful power. In the United States the practice of entering into consent decrees whereby the public authorities forsake the risks of litigation for the certainty of a binding negotiated settlement is common and has advantages for both the authorities and the undertaking in question. If nothing else this provision removes the linguistic confusion caused by the fact that the Commission in the past has accepted 'undertakings' from undertakings relating to future conduct (see, for example, *IBM* (Bull EC 10–1984) and *Digital* (IP/97/868)). These did not have binding force. The new 'commitment decisions' do not amount to either a finding, or an admission, of an infringement. They are stated in the preamble to the regulation to be 'without prejudice to the powers of competition authorities and courts of the member states to make such a finding and decide upon the case' (para. 13). The same paragraph also makes it clear that such resolutions will not be appropriate in the more serious cases where the Commission was considering the imposition of a penalty. The power to accept commitments, and make decisions in this respect, is also made available to the national authorities under art. 5.

In the United States the fact that a consent decree is being contemplated is made public, and judicial approval is required under the terms of the Tunney Act 1974 (this process was thrown into the spotlight on Valentine's Day 1995, when Judge Sporkin controversially rejected a consent decree entered into between the US Department of Justice and Microsoft Corp on the grounds that it was not in the public interest (*United States* v *Microsoft Corpn.* 56 F.3d 1448 (DC Cir. 1995)). Such decrees will be scrutinized by the lawyers acting for injured parties, and may often give rise to civil litigation, although as with the case in the EC such a decree does not form evidence on which the court may conclude that an infringement has been committed (see Furse, M., 'The Decision to Commit: Some Pointers from the US' [2004] ECLR 5). It remains at the time of writing a matter of speculation as to whether EC commitment decisions will be made with any greater frequency than has been the case in relation to the very rare acceptance of undertakings in the past, and as to what the impact of such a process might be on civil litigation.

Once a commitment decision is made the Commission may reopen the procedure in only one of three situations. The first arises where there has been a material change in the circumstances since the decision was made (art. 9(2)(a)). The second and third may occur either where the undertaking acts contrary to its commitment (art. 9(2)(b)), or where the decision was based on incomplete, incorrect, or misleading information provided by one of the parties (art. 9(2)(c)). For a good discussion of this new power see Temple Lang, J., 'Commitment Decisions Under Regulation 1/2003: Legal Aspects of a New Kind of Competition Decision' [2003] ECLR 347.

5.2.2.1.4 *Inapplicability*
In addition to decisions finding a breach of arts 81 or 82 EC, or to those imposing interim measures, or accepting a commitment, the Commission may also, where 'the Community public interest . . . so requires' find that the provisions of arts 81 or 82 of the Treaty are inapplicable to the activities of an undertaking or association of undertakings. This power is in effect the same as the power to grant negative clearance that was available under Regulation 17. In practice it is likely to be used

only exceptionally, in cases where for some reason there is genuine doubt as to the legality of particular conduct, and where a precedent is required. As noted in the preamble such decisions are most likely to be issued in respect of 'new types of agreements or practices that have not been settled in the existing case law and administrative practice' (para. 14).

5.2.2.2 Articles 11–16 of the regulation: cooperation between DG Comp and the Member States; the European Competition Network

Although the modernization process has simplified the enforcement of competition law in one key respect by allowing art. 81 EC to be applied in its entirety by any authority dealing with it, in another respect it has created a more complex relationship between DG Comp and the national competition authorities and between the national competition authorities themselves. Chapter IV of the regulation, which deals with 'Cooperation', is intended to address these issues, although there are areas which remain unclear, and it will only be with the passage of time, and the application of the new regime in practice that some matters will become clear. The broadest of statements in respect of this chapter of the regulation is found in art. 11(1) which provides simply that 'The Commission and the competition authorities of the Member States shall apply the Community competition rules in close cooperation'. To this end information shall be shared between the Commission and the NCAs (art. 11(2)) and the NCAs are obliged to inform the Commission whenever they intend to act in relation to the application of arts 81 or 82 of the Treaty.

The NCAs are obliged to notify the Commission thirty days before adopting any of the following decisions: requiring that an infringement be brought to an end; accepting commitments; or withdrawing the benefit of a block exemption regulation (see Chapter 10). The Commission shall be provided with a summary of the case, and, at its request, any other relevant documents. This information may then be made available to the competition authorities of the other Member States (art. 11(4)). If the Commission itself decides to open proceedings against the undertakings in question the relevant authorities of the Member States shall be relieved of their competence to apply arts 81 or 82 to that situation. However, where a NCA is already examining the practice in question the Commission shall not act without first consulting it (art. 11(6)).

Matters relating to the exchange of information are highly sensitive, and undertakings are greatly concerned at the increased flow of information among the members of the ECN. Article 12, which should be read alongside art. 28 ('professional secrecy'), governs the way in which information may be exchanged amongst members of the network. The information that may be exchanged expressly includes 'confidential information' (art. 12(1)), although all information exchanged may 'only be used in evidence for the purpose of applying arts 81 or 82 of the Treaty and in respect of the subject matter for which it was collected by the transmitting authority' (art. 7(2)). This means that information supplied to the OFT by other NCAs or DG Comp may not, for example, be used in relation to the prosecution of the cartel offence under domestic law. Article 12(3) imposes further limits on the way in which exchanged information can be used to support the imposition of sanctions on *natural persons*, which would again extend to the cartel offence. Article 28 requires both that information collected by the Commission in the application of its powers (see below) 'shall be used only for the purpose for which it was acquired', and that all such information, or information collected and exchanged by the members of the ECN, shall not be disclosed where it is 'of the kind covered by the obligation of professional secrecy' (art. 28(2)).

Article 13 of the regulation sets out the conditions under which an investigating authority shall terminate or suspend proceedings. Although the article does not preclude two or more authorities from acting against an agreement or practice, it does provide that wherever one authority is doing so this 'shall be sufficient grounds for the others to suspend the proceedings before them or to reject the complaint' (art. 13(1)). A concern that has been widely discussed relating to the operation of the ECN is that it may lead to a number of actions being taken against the same practice. Article 13 is designed in part to alleviate this.

The role of the Advisory Committee, discussed in Chapter 2 at 2.3.4.2, is set out in art. 14.

Cooperation between the Commission and the national courts, and the requirements of articles 15 and 16, have been considered in Chapter 3.

5.2.2.3 Informal guidance on novel questions

Regulation 1/2003 does not contain within it procedures under which matters may be notified to the Commission for consideration or guidance. However, DG Comp has recognized the possibility that new matters may still arise, in relation to which there is a lack of assistance in the existing case law, and recital (38) of the regulation acknowledges this. In such circumstances the parties may ask DG Comp for guidance. Such requests will be dealt with only where the relevant goods or services are economically important, and/or the practice is widespread, and/or there are substantial investments linked to the operation concerned. Further, the Commission will act only on the basis that it does not itself need to seek further information. Neither will the Commission consider hypothetical situations (see generally *Commission Notice on informal guidance relating to novel questions concerning articles 81 and 82 of the EC Treaty that arise in individual cases (guidance letters)* (2004) OJ C101/78).

5.2.2.4 Articles 17–22: fact finding

The specific powers of investigation provided for by Regulation 1/2003 are set out in Chapter V of the regulation, arts 17–22. These are backed up by powers in arts 23 and 24 to impose financial penalties on those who fail to cooperate with investigations.

5.2.2.4.1 Investigations into sectors of the economy, or types of agreements

Article 17 gives the Commission a general power to conduct wide-ranging investigations either into particular types of agreements, or across sectors of the economy.

These powers reflect a similar provision found in art. 12 of Regulation 17 that appeared to have fallen into abeyance. The only two occasions on which this power appeared to have been used related to inquiries carried out into the market for beer and the market for margarine. The article gives the Commission the power to publish a report, but in the absence of specific breaches of arts 81 or 82 by specific undertakings the Commission has no general power to deal with market failure in the way that is available to the UK authorities under the market investigation reference provisions of the Enterprise Act 2002 (see Chapter 17). It is doubtful whether this power will ever be used.

5.2.2.4.2 *Requests for information*

Article 18 of the Regulation gives the Commission the power to obtain information from undertakings and associations of undertakings. This power may be exercised either by request, or by decision. There are few limitations in the wording of this article, although there is a requirement that the information sought by the Commission be 'necessary'. It has been held by the CFI that 'necessary information' is anything which has a relationship with possible infringements of arts 81 and 82 (see *SEP* v *Commission* case T–39/90 [1992] 5 CMLR 33). At the same time as making any request or decision the Commission is required to forward a copy of this to the competent authority of the relevant Member State (art. 18(5)).

The procedure established by this article is not a two-stage one (unlike the position under Regulation 17). The Commission has the choice of issuing either a request or a decision when it is gathering information. Where the Commission sends a simple request to an undertaking it is required to state the legal basis of the request and its purpose, to specify the information required, to fix a time limit for its production, and to indicate the penalties that are available under art. 23 for supplying incorrect or misleading information (art. 18(2)). Similar obligations are imposed by virtue of art. 18(3) which relates to decisions requiring that information be supplied. However, in this case there is the added obligation on the Commission to indicate the penalties that are available under art. 24 for non-compliance, and the right of review of that decision before the ECJ under art. 230 EC.

The obligations of art. 18 may be imposed only on undertakings, and it is their owners, or their representatives, which shall supply the information. Duly authorized lawyers may act for their clients in this regard, but in the event that incomplete, incorrect, or misleading information is supplied it is the undertaking itself which remains responsible for the breach.

5.2.2.4.3 *The taking of statements*

A new power is given to the Commission in this regulation to take statements from any natural or legal person 'who consents to be interviewed' (art. 19(1)). However, the Commission does not have the power to compel a natural person to submit themselves to an interview, although a power to ask questions in the course of an investigation is set out in art. 20 (see 5.2.2.4.4). It is likely that this power will be used most often in non-contentious cases, as for example would be the case where

Investigation **85**

the Commission was gathering information from a customer or competitor of an undertaking whose activity was subject to scrutiny. The Commission must inform the relevant authority of the Member State in whose territory the interview is taking place if this is at the premises of an undertaking, although there is no obligation to do so in other circumstances. At the request of the relevant authority, its officials may assist and accompany those of the EC Commission.

5.2.2.4.4 *Inspections*
The most intrusive power of the EC Commission is its right to conduct investigations at the premises of an undertaking. Thus art. 20(1) provides that the Commission 'may conduct all necessary inspections of undertakings and associations of undertakings'. Article 21 further provides that where 'serious' breaches of arts 81 or 82 are being investigated, the Commission may conduct inspections at private premises. In both cases they may require the cooperation of the relevant national authorities, including the courts and the police, to effect such inspections. There is no requirement on the Commission to first avail itself of the powers given in art. 18 before making use of art. 20. Indeed the first time that an undertaking may become aware of an art. 20 inspection is when the relevant officials arrive at its premises with their notification, and demand access to the premises (so-called 'dawn raids'— terminology which is not used by the EC Commission, but which has entered the language of competition law).

Article 20(2) provides that the Commission officials, and other accompanying persons (likely to be representatives of the relevant NCA), have the power

(a) to enter any premises, land and means of transport of undertakings and associations of undertakings;

(b) to examine the books and other records related to the business, irrespective of the medium on which they are stored;

(c) to take or obtain in any form copies of or extracts from such books and records;

(d) to seal any business premises and books or records for the period and to the extent necessary for the inspection;

(f) to ask any representative or member of staff of the undertaking or association of undertakings for explanations on facts or documents relating to the subject-matter and purpose of the inspection and to record the answers.

There are requirements in the article for close liaison between the Commission and the relevant authorities of the Member State on whose territory the inspection is taking place. In particular the authorities of the Member States are required to afford the Commission 'necessary assistance, requesting where appropriate the assistance of the police or of an equivalent enforcement authority so as to enable them to conduct their inspection' (art. 20(6)). Article 20(6)–(7) deals with the situation in which national judicial approval is required for any such inspection. The judicial authority may ask for detailed information, but is not permitted to 'call into question the necessity for the inspection nor demand that it be provided with the information in the Commission's file'. This follows, for example, the judgment of the ECJ in the case of *Roquette Freres SA* v *Directeur General de la Concurrence de la*

Consommation et de la Repression des Fraudes case C–94/00 [2003] 4 CMLR 1. Here the ECJ responded to a reference for a preliminary ruling from a French court concerned as to the limits on its powers to review requests for judicial approval for an investigation. The ECJ held, in part that

In accordance with the general principle of Community law affording protection against arbitrary or disproportionate intervention by public authorities in the sphere of the private activities of any person . . . a national court having jurisdiction under domestic law to authorise entry upon and seizures at the premises of undertakings suspected of having infringed the competition rules is required to verify that the coercive measures sought . . . by the Commission . . . are not arbitrary or disproportionate to the subject-matter of the investigation ordered. Without prejudice to any rules of domestic law governing the implementation of coercive measures, Community law precludes review by the national court of the justification of those measures beyond what is required by the foregoing general principle. (para. R1)

Once the Commission's officials have started the investigation the undertaking is under a duty to cooperate fully. It is not sufficient for an undertaking merely to give the officials unfettered access to all files and records, and employees must actively help the Commission find the material that it seeks (see, e.g., *Fabbrica Pisana* 80/334 (1980) OJ L75/30, in which the undertaking had made all its files available but had not assisted the Commission's officials in finding the relevant documents). An undertaking is not entitled to have a lawyer present while the investigation is in progress, although the Commission has indicated in its 12th Report on Competition Policy that it may be prepared to wait for one to arrive as long as this does not unduly delay matters.

A contentious area has been that of legal professional privilege. This was first dealt with in *AM&S Europe* v *Commission* case 155/79 [1982] 2 CMLR 264, in which the undertaking had applied to the ECJ to strike down the Commission action after it had seized material held by the undertaking's in-house lawyers. The Advocate General conducted a thorough review of the law relating to legal privilege in the Member States and the Court held that only in recognizing the privilege attaching to documents emanating from independent lawyers relating to the client's right of defence did the laws of the Member States converge to the extent necessary for a common protection to be recognized. Thus the Court affirmed that Regulation 17 was to be interpreted so as to protect such communications only. Internal lawyers are most unlikely to be covered by the protection, although the Court indicated in *Hilti AG* v *Commission* case T–30/89A [1990] 4 CMLR 602 that, in certain highly restricted circumstances, the protection might apply (see also *VW* 98/273 (1998) OJ L124/61, paras 198–9). It may be argued that this general approach is consistent with the treatment of the undertaking as an economic whole: the in-house lawyer is part of the undertaking and it cannot be logical that any one part of the undertaking should be more privileged than another.

There is debate as to the extent to which the Commission is able to exploit its power to ask for oral explanations (art. 20(2)(e)). While the regulation does not restrict the article so as to apply it only to specific officers of the undertaking, or to specific subject matter, it would appear that the Commission is not able to ask any employee of the undertaking any question. In *National Panasonic (UK) Ltd* v *Commission* case 136/79 [1980] 3 CMLR 169, Advocate General Warner suggested that the power related to 'specific questions arising from the books and business records which [the Commission officials] examine' in the course of the investigation. If this is a comprehensive statement of the Commission's power, which has been doubted, it would rule out 'fishing trips' by the Commission officials. The Commission has stated elsewhere that it is for the undertaking to nominate the appropriate persons to answer questions, as the Commission is not in the position to judge the competence or knowledge of individual employees (*Fabbrica Pisana* 80/334 (1980) OJ L75/30).

There have been many occasions on which undertakings have challenged the way in which the Commission has conducted its investigation. *National Panasonic* is one of the most significant cases. Commission officials arrived at the sales offices of Panasonic in Slough at about 10 a.m. on 27 June 1979. The officials notified the undertaking's directors of a decision taken on 22 June authorizing an on-the-spot investigation. The directors asked if the investigation could be delayed while the undertaking's solicitor travelled to the scene from Norwich and the officials stated that their authorization entitled them to act immediately. The inspection, which lasted until 5.30 p.m., began at 10.45 a.m. and the undertaking's solicitor did not arrive until 1.45 p.m. Panasonic subsequently appealed against the decision and, *inter alia*, asked the ECJ to order that the Commission return or destroy all documents seized by it. Panasonic argued that this was the first time that the Commission had proceeded to a formal investigation by way of decision without first affording the undertaking the opportunity to submit of its own volition to an informal investigation. In fact since 1973 there had been 24 other cases in which the Commission had so acted, and the Commission contended that there was too great a risk that, if both stages of the procedure were followed, documents would be destroyed or removed. The Commission claimed that, even if only the one-stage procedure were followed, there were sufficient safeguards for the undertaking concerned. In doing so it pointed to eight factors:

(a) the need for written authorization;

(b) the need for a formal decision taken by the Commission;

(c) the fact that only 'necessary' investigations could be carried out;

(d) the requirement that the decision be adequately reasoned;

(e) the requirement that the Commission consult the competent authority of the Member State concerned;

(f) the fact that the decision must state within it the right to challenge under art. 230 EC;

(g) the fact that a successful challenge would deprive the Commission of the right to use any materials obtained; and

(h) the availability of a remedy under art. 288 EC were the Commission officials to exceed their authority.

The Court rejected the general arguments made by Panasonic, and in doing so affirmed that the procedures applied did not infringe the rights invoked, unsuccessfully, by the applicant.

The Commission officials may not use force in carrying out their investigation (*Hoechst AG* v *Commission* cases 46/87 and 227/88 [1991] 4 CMLR 410, para. 31), although they may be able to fall back on the assistance of national authorities where this is necessary to compel an undertaking to comply with an investigation.

The power to inspect 'other premises' given in art. 21 of Regulation 1/2003 is more controversial than the power to inspect undertakings' premises. The evidence however is clear that documents which may shed light on the operation of cartels in particular are being stored in private premises so as to put them out of the reach of the Commission. In order to inspect 'other premises', which include 'the homes of directors, managers and other members of staff of the undertaking' (art. 21(1)) the Commission *must* seek the prior authorization of the judicial authority of the Member State concerned. Officials have the powers set out in art. 20(2)(a)–(c).

5.2.2.5 *Penalties*

Penalties levied in the case of substantive infringements of arts 81 and 82 EC are discussed in the following chapter. Penalties may also be imposed in the event of an undertaking subject to investigation committing procedural breaches. Provision is made for these in art. 23(1) of Regulation 1/2003. Where undertakings supply false or misleading information, or fail to comply with a decision requiring them to submit information, or to an inspection, or give misleading answers, they may be fined up to 1 per cent of their total turnover in the preceding business year. In addition, periodic penalty payments may be imposed of up to 5 per cent of the average daily turnover in the preceding business year per day to compel undertakings to terminate an infringement or to supply information demanded, or to submit to an inspection (art. 24). Articles 25 and 26 set out limitation periods in relation to the imposition of penalties.

5.2.2.6 *Hearings and access to file*

Once the Commission has conducted its inquiries it must, before making any decision, give the undertaking(s) concerned the chance to be heard (art. 27, Regulation 1/2003). It may also hear applications from other natural or legal persons who can 'show a sufficient interest' (para. 3).

The general procedure for these hearings is set out in Commission Regulation 773/2004, (2004), OJ L123/18. This regulation, which entered into force on 1 May 2004, makes provision for the hearing of those to whom objections are addressed (arts 11–12), applicants and complainants, and other third parties (art. 13).

Hearings are conducted by persons appointed by the Commission, 'the Hearing Officer' (art. 14, whose terms of reference are set out in Commission Decision 2001/462 (2001) OJ L162/21).

The role of the Hearing Officer has changed substantially since the post was introduced in 1982. Changes were made in 1994, and then again in 2001. This reflects in part the difficult role the Commission has had to play both as the guarantor of the rights of undertakings involved in competition proceedings, and as the agency charged with pursuing those in breach of the law. The essence of the role of the Hearing Officer is set out in Commission Press Release IP/01/736 (23 May 2001), which states in part that

This new Mandate of the Hearing Officer will substantially improve the overall accountability of the Commission's decision-making process in merger and antitrust proceedings, ensuring that all fundamental rights of parties and economic operators involved in its procedures are respected.

The key function which ensures that this aim is met is set out in Commission Decision 2001/462, art. 1, which provides that the 'Commission shall appoint one or more hearing officers ... who shall ensure that the effective exercise of the right to be heard is respected in competition proceedings before the Commission'.

The most significant change from the earlier practice introduced in the 2001 Decision is that the Hearing Officer is no longer part of the mainstream of the Competition Division of the Commission, a practice which had been previously criticized. The Hearing Officer is now attached directly to the office of 'the member of the Commission with special responsibility for competition' (art. 2(2)). During the hearings which take place the Hearing Officer 'shall ensure that the hearing is properly conducted and contributes to the objectivity of the hearing itself and of any decision taken subsequently' (art. 5).

At art. 14 of Regulation 773/2004 further details relating to the hearings are set out. Parties invited to attend either may do so in person, or may be represented by a lawyer. The oral hearings are not public, and persons may be heard separately so as to protect business secrets.

A difficult and contentious issue is the extent to which undertaking should have access to documents held by the Commission relevant to the case, some of which may well have been obtained from the undertaking's commercial rivals. Article 27(2) of Regulation 1/2003 deals with the question of access to file in the following terms:

[Parties] shall have access to the Commission's file, subject to the legitimate interest of undertakings in the protection of their business secrets. The right of access to the file shall not extend to confidential information and internal documents of the Commission or the competition authorities of the Member States. In particular, the right of access shall not extend to correspondence between the Commission and the competition authorities of the Member States, or between the latter.

The Commission recognized in its *23rd Annual Report* that 'the disclosure to the parties of any relevant information is an essential part of the procedure' (citing *Hoffmann-La Roche & Co. AG* v *Commission* case 85/76 [1979] 3 CMLR 211, (1993) *Annual Report*, point 199). In *Hoffmann* the ECJ held that any undertaking must be able to have its views heard and, in particular, must be able to comment 'on the documents used by the Commission to support its claim that there has been an infringement' (at para. 11). The matter is complicated, as was recognized in *Hoff-mann-La Roche*, by the obligation of secrecy imposed on the Commission by way of art. 28 of Regulation 1/2003.

Decision 2001/462 in effect enshrines what became known as the '*AKZO* procedure' (*AKZO Chemie BV* v *Commission* case 53/85 [1987] 1 CMLR 231). Under this procedure the Commission will notify the undertaking from which the document has been taken that it intends to allow a third party to inspect the document. The first undertaking will then have the opportunity to contest the decision before the court prior to the release of the document. In the *Soda Ash* series of cases (cases T 30–32/91 and T 36–37/91 [1996] 5 CMLR 57 ff.) the CFI annulled decisions of the Commission in part because they had violated the rights of the appellants in denying them access to various files held by the Commission. In particular the Court held that 'it is not for the Commission alone to decide which documents are useful to the defence and the advisors of the company must have the opportunity to examine documents which may be relevant'.

The Court in *Soda Ash* suggested that the Commission should either allow the undertaking's lawyers unfettered access to the documents held by it prior to the hearing, or make available a list of *all* documents in its possession. This judgment will make life difficult for the Commission, and has been criticized as imposing impractical demands in operation (see, e.g., Ehlermann, C. D. and Drijber, B. J., 'Legal Protection of Enterprises: Administrative Procedure, in particular Access to Files and Confidentiality' [1996] *ECLR* 375). The response of the Commission has been to issue a notice in 1997 'on the internal rules of procedure for processing requests for access to the file' in competition cases (1997) OJ C25/3.

It is clear from the terms of the notice that it is difficult to reconcile the opposing obligations of safeguarding the rights of the defence and protecting confidential information (see below). The notice recognizes the obligation on the Commission to provide access to all the documents making up its file, with the exception of those identified by the CFI in *Hercules Chemicals NV* v *Commission* case T–7/89 [1992] 4 CMLR 84 as being reserved, that is, business secrets, internal Commission documents which do not form part of the investigation and are not placed in the main investigation file, and any other confidential information. The Commission therefore has expressly made clear that it will not, in future, itself select which documents an undertaking may have access to and which it may not (see also *Cimenteries CBR SA* v *Commission* cases T 25–26/95, etc. [2000] 5 CMLR 204).

The failure to disclose information, such as trade-press extracts, which is in the public domain, was found not to invalidate a Decision in *Limburgse Vinyl Maatschappij NV* v *Commission* cases T 305–307/94, etc. [1999] 5 CMLR 303, at para. 496. On appeal to the ECJ this judgment was only partially annulled, although the case is illustrative of the many issues that may be raised in relation to human rights arguments (*Limburgse Vinyl Maatschappij NV (LVM)* v *Commission* joined cases C–238/99P etc. [2003] 4 CMLR 10).

5.2.2.7 *Secrecy*

Any information obtained by the Commission in the course of its investigations must be treated carefully by the Commission and can 'be used only for the purpose for which it was acquired' (art. 28). The concern of undertakings is that the power given to the Commission to examine business records is sufficiently wide as to extend to all information held by the company, with the exception of independent legal advice. The Commission has held that 'business secrecy cannot be invoked against Commission officials . . . since . . . the same Regulation provides that they shall not disclose information' (*Fides* 79/253 (1979) OJ L57/33). Thus undertakings may be required to surrender to the Commission highly sensitive information relating both to industrial processes and to marketing. The Commission has repeatedly relied on its obligation under art. 28 to deny the undertaking concerned the opportunity to withhold information. The point was made forcefully in *FNIC* (*Fédération nationale de l'industrie de la chaussure de France* 82/756 (1982) OJ L319/ 12) where the company refused to hand to the Commission certain 'confidential documents' which, the company argued, went 'far beyond the investigators' terms of reference'. The Commission reiterated its long-held view that undertakings 'may invoke the confidentiality of such documents only within the framework of [art. 20]'.

The requirement of art. 28 is that the Commission and competent authorities shall not disclose any information gained under the regulation and 'of the kind covered by the obligation of professional secrecy'. This article is itself based on art. 214 EC, which provides a more general guarantee that Community institutions and officials shall not disclose 'information of the kind covered by the obligation of professional secrecy, in particular information about undertakings, their business relations or their cost components'. The ECJ has held that this requirement is crucial as regards the rights of the undertakings in the process (*Dow Benelux NV* v *Commission* case 85/87 [1991] 4 CMLR 410), and in *AKZO* (case 53/85 [1987] 1 CMLR 231) the ECJ held that '[b]usiness secrets are thus afforded a *very special* protection' (para. 28, emphasis added). However, as the Commission notes in its notice on access to the file (see above), this remains a problem if for no other reason than that there has been no case in which the criteria for determining that any particular piece of information is a business secret have been fully discussed. In the event that any information is shared between the Commission and the NCA, the obligation in Regulation 1/2003 is binding on all bodies (art. 28(2)).

Article 30(2) of Regulation 1/2003 provides a further guarantee in that when the Commission publishes any formal decision that it takes in relation to a particular proceeding 'the publication . . . shall have regard to the legitimate interest of undertakings in the protection of their business secrets'.

The tension between the requirement of secrecy and confidentiality and the right of undertakings to have access to pertinent information in order to ensure that their rights are observed is a very clear one. The very strict position taken by the Court in *AKZO* was largely determined by the fact that the undertaking seeking access to the confidential information was the complainant, and a competitor of AKZO.

5.2.2.8 Rights of the parties and fundamental protections

At face value the powers accorded to the Commission under Regulation 1/2003 are substantial, and the only significant recognition of the rights of the defence appears in art. 27. At art. 27(2) it is stated that 'the rights of defence of the parties concerned shall be fully respected in the proceedings'. The regulation itself is largely silent on what these rights are, and in order to clarify this area it is necessary to turn to the case law of the ECJ and CFI.

The extent to which legal persons, as distinct from natural persons, should be accorded fundamental rights is a matter of intense debate: the question is one of whether it is 'appropriate to extend a privilege, which began as a protection for individuals, to an artificial entity such as a corporation' (*Environment Protection Authority* v *Caltex Refining Co. Pty Ltd* (1993) 118 ALR 392, at 553 *per* McHugh J). More pithily Lord Denning has said that a company has 'no body to be kicked or soul to be damned' (*BSC.* v *Granada TV* [1981] AC 1096).

In the EC there is a further complication in that there is no clear standard of 'fundamental rights' set out in the founding treaties. Instead the ECJ has developed, at first slowly and then with greater force, a jurisprudence of general principles of law, drawing in part on international instruments in which the Member States have participated. The ECJ confirmed in *Firma J Nold KG* v *Commission* case 4/73 [1974] 2 CMLR 338, that the European Convention on Human Rights 1950 (ECHR) is of particular importance in this regard, and all Member States of the European Community are bound equally by its provisions, although the two regimes are legally and politically distinct. This judicial activity received belated support by the Member States in the Treaty on European Union (TEU), art. 6(2) of which provides, in part, that 'the Union shall respect fundamental rights, as guaranteed by the European Convention'. This declaration notwithstanding, the EC cannot become a state party to the Convention, lacking the legal capacity to do so (Opinion of ECJ 2/94 [1996] ECR 1–1759). The application of fundamental rights jurisprudence in relation to the competition procedures has caused problems for the Court, which remains bound by the words of the legislation.

In *National Panasonic (UK) Ltd* v *Commission* case 136/79 [1980] 3 CMLR 169, the applicant's contention that its fundamental rights had been infringed was rejected, but the ECJ left open the possibility that fundamental rights could be relied upon where the Commission's actions could be shown to be disproportionate. In *AM & S Europe* v *Commission* case 155/79 [1982] 2 CMLR 264, at 322, the Court concluded that EC law 'must take into account the principles and concepts common to the laws of (the Member States)' and a similar position was reached in *Hoechst AG* v *Commission* cases 46/87 and 227/88 [1991] 4 CMLR 410, in which the Court held that 'regard must be had in particular to the rights of the defence' (at 465); and in *Soda Ash* cases T 30–32/91 and T 36–37/91 [1996] 5 CMLR 57 ff., the CFI referred to the need to achieve the general requirement of 'equality of arms'. The most substantial arguments relating to fundamental rights made to date are those in *Orkem SA* v *Commission* case 374/87 [1991] 4 CMLR 502. Here the Commission had made a decision demanding information in respect of which an earlier request had been largely ignored. The undertaking's argument was that the documents requested were potentially self-incriminating. Advocate General Darmon recognized that 'exploitation to the full of any latitude allowed by the legal rules and efforts to ensure [that the] broadest interpretation of that latitude is acknowledged to constitute a positive right are the very essence of defence' (art. 513). The Advocate General focused on the distinction between the *investigative* stage of the Commission's proceedings, the purpose of which is to allow the Commission to check the existence of 'a given factual and legal situation', and the *statement of objections* wherein 'there is a much greater protection' afforded to the undertaking. As regards the alleged right of the undertaking not to incriminate itself, the Advocate General argued that, on an inspection of the text of the regulation, it was clear that the Council which enacted the regulation 'did not intend to give undertakings to which a request for information was addressed the right not to incriminate themselves'. More strongly, he stated that the machinery of the regulation appeared to him 'to be intellectually incompatible with the right to silence'. In giving judgment the Court allowed greater protection to the individual than the Advocate General had suggested. The Court drew a somewhat uneasy distinction between documentary evidence and oral explanations. The Court held that the Commission could compel an undertaking to provide documents in its possession, but that it 'may not compel an undertaking to provide it with answers which might involve an admission on its part of the existence of an infringement which it is incumbent upon the Commission to prove'. Only purely factual answers may be required (*Mannesmannrohren-Werke AG* v *Commission* Case T-112/98 [2001] 5 CMLR 1).

The case of *Orkem* was further discussed in *Otto* v *Postbank* case C–60/92 [1993] ECR I-5683, which came before the ECJ as an art. 234 reference from the Dutch courts. The defendant in domestic proceedings had argued that national law was incompatible with Community law because it was obliged to produce incriminatory evidence. One of the arguments made by the defendant before the ECJ was that this evidence could, and probably would, come to the attention of the Commission which might use it as part of its own enforcement procedure. The Court held that the Commission would not be able to use any such evidence in order to establish an infringement of the relevant parts of the Treaty, but that in the case in question it would not interfere as the matter was strictly one between private parties and did not involve the possibility of a penalty imposed by a public authority.

In the *Modernisation White Paper* the Commission suggested an amendment to Regulation 17, 'to make it quite clear that in the course of an investigation the authorised Commission officials are empowered to ask the undertakings representatives or staff any questions that are justified by and related to the purpose of the investigation, and to demand a full and precise answer' (para. 113).

The relevant provision, which is now set out at art. 20(2)(e) of Regulation 1/2003, does somewhat clarify the position (see 5.2.2.4.4). It will be noted that the wording focuses on questions relating to explanations of facts or documents.

The relationship in particular between the law of the Human Rights Convention and the treatment of these rights under Community law remains a complex and not altogether satisfactory one. In *Funke* v *France* (1993) 16 EHRR 297, the European Court of Human Rights emphasized that the Convention's provisions apply to commercial matters as well as to personal rights, and that special provisions of law could not justify the restriction of such rights. This is in conflict with the view of the Advocate General in *Orkem* and suggests that the ECJ may need to reconsider this area if it intends to stay in line with Convention law. In *Stichting Certificatie Kraanverhuurbedrijf (SCK) and Federatie van Nederlandse Kraanver-huurbedrijven (FNK)* v *Commission* joined cases T–213/95 and T–18/96 [1998] 4 CMLR 259, the CFI in response to an argument based largely on the application of art. 6 of the ECHR, avoided any substantive discussion relating to the application of Convention law directly to competition proceedings. It did this by noting instead that 'it is a general principle *of Community law* that the Commission must act within a reasonable time in adopting decisions following administrative proceedings relating to competition policy' (emphasis added). Because the Court held that the matter fell directly within Community law, which would ensure adequate safeguards, any discussion of the Convention became unnecessary.

The CFI itself was found by the ECJ, in another case, to have acted too slowly in delivering judgment. In *Baustahlgewebe GmbH* v *Commission* case T–145/89 [1995] ECR II-987, on appeal C–185/95P [1999] 4 CMLR 1203, the appellant relied on art. 6(1) of the Convention in seeking an annulment of the CFI judgment, and of the earlier Commission Decision in *Welded Steel Mesh* 89/515 (1989) OJ L260/1. The appeal against the decision was lodged in October 1989, and it was five years and six months before judgment was delivered, and 22 months passed between the close of the hearing and the delivering of the judgment. The ECJ held, notwithstanding the fact that 'the procedure called for a detailed examination of relatively voluminous documents and points of fact and law of some complexity' (para. 36), that 'the proceedings before the [CFI] did not satisfy the requirements concerning completion within a reasonable time' (para. 47). The ECJ found, however, that this breach was insufficient to annul the proceedings in their entirety, and in the alternative the applicant was awarded a sum of €50,000 (the appellant, having lost on some of the heads of its appeal, was also obliged to pay all its own costs, as well as three-quarters of those of the Commission).

5.2.3 The European Competition Network

The ways in which cooperation between members of the European Competition Network (ECN) functions is dealt with at some length in the *Commission Notice on cooperation within the of Competition Authorities* (2004) OJ C101/43. For a discussion of the ECN from the UK perspective see also the OFT guideline *Modernisation* (OFT 442). As explained in the Commission Notice the Network

is a forum for discussion and cooperation in the application and enforcement of EC competition policy. It provides a framework for the cooperation of European competition authorities in cases where arts 81 and 82 of the Treaty are applied and is the basis for the creation and maintenance of a common competition culture in Europe.   (para. 1)

One of the key issues for the ECN to manage is case allocation. Part 2 of the notice deals with the division of work, and it is recognized that cases may be dealt with by: a single NCA (possibly with the assistance of other NCAs or the Commission); several NCAs acting in parallel; or the Commission. In most instances it will be the authority that receives the complaint, or initiates the procedure that will be in charge, and the authority will use its own procedures during the investigation. In some cases it will be necessary to reallocate the case 'for an effective protection of competition and of the Community interest' (para. 7). Indeed, there is an obligation on network members to 'endeavour to reallocate cases to a single well-placed competition authority as often as possible' (para. 7). Three factors are set out as being important in determining which authority is the best placed:

(1) the agreement or practice has substantial direct actual or foreseeable effects on competition within its territory, is implemented within or originates from its territory;

(2) the authority is able to effectively bring to an end the entire infringement i.e. it can adopt a cease and desist order the effect of which will be sufficient to bring an end to the infringement and it can, where appropriate, sanction the infringement adequately;

(3) it can gather, possibly with the assistance of other authorities, the evidence required to prove the infringement.   (para. 8)

Article 11 of Regulation 1/2003 creates a mechanism for members of the ECN to inform each other about investigations at an early stage by way of the Commission (art. 11(3)), which also has an obligation to inform the Member States (art. 11(2)) about its own investigations. Where the same practice comes before a number of members of the ECN they may suspend proceedings or reject complaints on the grounds that another member of the ECN is dealing with the matter (art. 13), although there is no obligation on the NCA to do so. Article 11(4) and (5) is intended to provide for a mechanism to ensure consistent application of the law.

5.3 **The United Kingdom**

5.3.1 **The Competition Act 1998**

5.3.1.1 *Investigation*

The powers given to the Office of Fair Trading (OFT) to investigate, remedy and punish breaches of the Competition Act 1998 are set out in Chapter III of that Act. These are also the powers that are to be used when the OFT is investigating breaches of arts 81 and 82 EC. The most important guidelines in this respect published by the OFT are: *Powers of investigation* (OFT 404); *Enforcement: Incorporating the Office of Fair Trading's guidance as to the circumstances in which it might be appropriate to accept commitments* (OFT 407); and *OFT's guidance as to the appropriate amount of a penalty* (OFT 423). There has been only a small amount of case law relating to this area as of May 2004.

The powers of investigation the Act confers are bestowed exclusively on the OFT. In the *IIB* case the CAT noted that the Act has endowed 'the [OFT], in the public interest, with wide ranging and draconian powers, exercised on behalf of the State, which may substantially affect the civil rights and obligations of those concerned' (*Institute of Independent Insurance Brokers* v *The Director General of Fair Trading* [2002] CompAR 141, para. 57).

The OFT has the power to conduct any investigation where it has 'reasonable grounds for suspecting' that either of the two prohibitions or arts 81 and 82 EC are being infringed (s. 25). Upon the presentation of a written notice to that effect the OFT may require 'any person to produce to it a specified document, or to provide it with specified information which it considers relates to any matter relevant to the investigation' (s. 26(1)). This is the provision that, according to the guideline *Powers of Investigation*, will be most frequently used. In line with the powers conferred on the EC Commission under art. 20 of Regulation 1/2003, the OFT is able to take copies of the document or of extracts from it, and to require 'any person who is a present or past officer of [the person], or is or was at any time employed by him, to provide an explanation of the document' (s. 27(6)(a)(i)–(ii)). This latter ability to require an explanation of the documents from 'any person' who has been an employee or officer of the undertaking is a substantial one, and may conflict with obligations arising under the ECHR (see above, in relation to EC law). It is inevitable that there will be disputes over the meaning of 'explanation', with undertakings insisting that they are not required to incriminate themselves when giving an 'explanation' of any particular document. Concern was expressed in the House of Lords that this provision would allow for the possibility of 'an investigating officer shimmying up to the cleaning lady and extracting from her the skeleton key' (Hansard (HL) 17 November 1997, col. 388), and the Confederation of British Industry (CBI) pressed very strongly for changes to these provisions. The Government's view, however, was that 'the statutory investigatory powers must be able to cater for the very worst case of unscrupulous concealment of evidence of a cartel or other anti-competitive behaviour', although generally 'full use of the powers provided in the [Act] should . . . be unnecessary' (col. 391). There was specific recognition that it might often be the case that secretaries and younger assistants could have a great deal of knowledge about practices referred to in documents or under investigation, whereas a more senior manager might lack the 'hands-on' involvement in a practice. The question of the extent to which there is a right to silence is to be resolved by reference to EC case law (see above).

Investigations of undertakings' premises may be conducted either with or without notice being given to the undertaking. Section 27 of the Act gives the OFT, or an 'investigating officer', power to 'enter any premises'. Although it is not expressly stated in the Act, homes may be entered only if they are also business premises, but it is envisaged that there will be situations where this is the case (see generally Hansard (HL) 25 November 1997, cols 957–61). This point was reasonably dealt with by Nigel Griffiths for the Government, in committee, when he pointed out that 'domestic premises may be entered only if they are used in connection with the affairs of an undertaking . . . the Director General's actions are subject to judicial review if he exceeds his powers' (Committee G, 16 June 1998, col. 421).

In relation to many of the investigations which will be carried out under this section the investigating officer is required to give two working days' notice before the power of entry is enforced (s. 27(2)). Section 27(3), however, provides that in situations where there is a 'reasonable suspicion' that the premises are being occupied by a party to an agreement or conduct under investigation, the two-day notice period may be waived. The period may also be waived when 'the investigating officer has taken all such steps as are reasonably practicable to give notice but has not been able to do so' (s. 27(3)(b)). The powers that relate to such an investigation are similar to those found in Regulation 1/2003. Thus the investigating officer may take any necessary equipment with them, which might include, for example, portable photocopiers, and computer disks (s. 27(5)(a)). Any person on the premises may be required 'to produce any document which [the officer] considers relates to any matter relevant to the investigation' and 'to provide an explanation of it' (s. 27(5)(b)). Any person on the premises may further be required to 'state to the best of his knowledge and belief, where any such document is to be found' (s. 27(5)(c)).

As well as permitting the officer to take copies of, or extracts from, any document (s. 27(5)(d)), a special provision relates to material held in computer systems. Where this is 'accessible from the premises' and is relevant to the investigation, this must be produced in a form 'in which it can be taken away' and in which it is 'visible and legible', which presumably means that a print-out must be provided (s. 27(5)(e)). The reference to material which is 'accessible from the premises' is an interesting one, and it appears to extend to material held on computer systems outside of the premises under investigation, but which can be accessed over a network from the site. This would mean that where the internal information system of the company under investigation was so set up, international records from a multinational company could all be accessed through a single site investigation in the UK, thus avoiding the complexities of establishing jurisdiction and enforcing warrants elsewhere. This conclusion follows if the company is using the information itself as part of its management system. Information held in hard copy at the premises and relied upon on that basis would not be protected and the undertaking should not be able to deny the investigating officers access to the information simply on the basis of which part of their computer system the material is stored on.

While investigations conducted under s. 27 of the Act require that two days' written notice be given, the OFT may use powers under s. 28 of the Act to conduct an investigation without warning following the issuing of a warrant to that effect by a judge. A warrant may be sought either where documents required to be produced under s. 26 or s. 27 have not been produced, or where there is a reasonable ground for believing that if the notice required by s. 27 was given the documents would be destroyed, removed, or concealed (s. 28(b)). A warrant may also be requested where an investigating officer acting under the powers in s. 27 has been unable to gain access to the site. Once the warrant has been issued the powers are the same as for s. 27, with the notable exception that the officer may enter the premises 'using such force as is reasonably necessary for the purpose' (s. 28(2)(a)). Although the introduction of the right to enter by force was criticized by the Opposition the Government clung to it, with Lord Simon being 'thoroughly of the view that the right to entry using reasonable force is a necessary part of ensuring that the process of investigation goes forward. It is a key element of our strategy' (Hansard (HL) 17 November 1997, col. 406). These powers are to be exercised only at 'the very limits of investigation' in 'exceptional cases in which we know that the rogues have thus far repelled all boarders', ibid., col. 409). Later the Government confirmed that force would not be used against persons, but that, if the circumstances were to arise, force could be used inside premises to gain entry to specific parts of the premises: 'every subsequent door, if closed, could be broken down to enter the premises' (Hansard (HL) 19 February 1998, col. 339).

Section 28 powers were used for the first time, although the use of force does not appear to have been necessary, in the course of the OFT investigation leading to the decision *Market Sharing by Arriva plc and FirstGroup plc* CA 98/9/2002, 30 January 2002. Here the OFT

applied to the High Court and the Court of Session for warrants to enter premises of the two undertakings in England and Scotland, and exercise powers under s. 28 of the Act. Warrants were issued on 4 and 6 October 2000. Unannounced visits to the premises took place on 10 and 11 October 2000 and copies of documents were taken.   (para. 7)

For an example of the approach taken by a court in response to an application for a warrant by the OFT see *Application for a warrant under the Competition Act 1998* [2003] EWHC 1042 (Comm), [2003] UKCLR 765. Here the OFT applied for a warrant without notice, following a suspicion held by the OFT that the unnamed defendants had been engaged in price fixing. Morrison J. was 'satisfied that what is summarised in ... skeleton argument, justifies me in concluding that there are presently reasonable grounds for suspecting that the defendants have been engaged in unlawful conduct' (at para. 3) The practical dynamics underlying such investigations are clearly explained by the judge at para. 5:

On the basis of ... the first affidavit of Edward Francis Lennon, a principal investigation officer in the Cartel Investigations Branch of the Competition Enforcement Division of the OFT, I am satisfied that there are reasonable grounds for suspecting that there are, on the premises named in the warrants, documents which the OFT are entitled to see in the course of their investigation. As to the second requirement, the evidence shows that a 'warning shot across the defendants' bows' has already been fired by the Director General of Fair Trading. The target companies, if they have been doing what the OFT suspect, are likely to have taken steps to make detection difficult and to be continuing so to act. The stakes are high, since the penalties if guilt is established are likely to be high. The entities being investigated include one of a substantial size, and whose reputation, apart from its financial position, may be damaged if incriminating material is found. There is, therefore, a strong inducement or motive for hiding the truth. The material which the OFT are most interested to see is relatively easy to conceal, given advance notice. For these reasons, I am satisfied that there are reasonable grounds for suspecting that the written material would be concealed or destroyed. It is in the public interest that if there has been wrongdoing it is uncovered and revealed.

The *Powers of Investigation* guideline follows the approach of the EC Commission in relation to the legal advice to which an undertaking may have access during the course of an investigation (paras 4.10–4.11). Thus it is made clear that an undertaking may contact its legal advisers, and that 'the authorised officer will grant a request to wait a short time for legal advisers to arrive at the premises before the inspection continues if he considers that it is reasonable to do so in the circumstances'. This provision is also set out in The Competition Act 1998 (Office of Fair Trading's) Order, (2004), para. 3. There is no definition of what constitutes 'a reasonable time' and the Order simply provides that this means 'such period of time as the officer considers is reasonable in the circumstances'.

Section 28A of the Act relates specifically to the power to enter domestic premises, providing that in such cases entry is possible only when acting under a warrant. Once a warrant has been issued the powers are substantially the same as for s. 28. Domestic premises in this context means any premises used as a dwelling, which are also used in connection with the affairs of an undertaking, or where documents relating to the affairs of an undertaking are stored (s. 28A(9)).

Any person who does not comply with a requirement imposed under ss. 26, 27, 28, or 28A is guilty of an offence, and may be liable to a fine. Where the offence has been the obstruction of an officer acting under a warrant issued under ss. 28 or 28A the person may, on conviction, be fined, or imprisoned for a maximum of two years (s. 42). Fines and/or imprisonment may similarly be imposed where any person destroys or disposes of a document that they have been required to produce under ss. 26, 27, 28, or 28A (s. 43), or where any person gives information to the Director which is materially false or misleading when that person knows it to be so, or is reckless as to its status (s. 44).

It is perhaps in recognition of the problems caused by the *AM&S* judgment (*AM&S Europe* v *Commission* case 155/79 (1982) 2 CMLR 264) that specific provisions in s. 30 of the Act relate to privileged communications. 'Privileged communication' is defined in s. 30 as being a communication 'between a professional legal advisor and his client' or 'made in connection with, or in contemplation of, legal proceedings and for the purposes of those proceedings'. No person shall be required to produce any material under any provision in the Act that falls within this definition. This is one area in which the Act explicitly is out of step with Community law, and where UK practice will not be affected by future developments in EC case law. As was clearly stated in the debates:

it is the government's intention that the [OFT] should *not* be able to require, under his investigative powers, the production of legal advice and other material enjoying legal professional privilege, whether the lawyer concerned is an external lawyer or an 'in-house' lawyer. (Hansard (HL) 17 November 1997, col. 416)

This is consistent with the approach adopted by the House of Lords in *Alfred Compton Amusement Machines Ltd* v *Customs and Excise Comrs (No. 2)* [1974] AC 405, where the Court held that no distinction could be made between the two groups.

The position in the UK now is a somewhat unfortunate one. Where the OFT is investigating a breach of the Chapter I and II Prohibitions, or is itself investigating a breach of arts 81 or 82 it is the position of s. 30 which applies. However, where the OFT is assisting the EC Commission conducting an investigation on UK soil under the powers conferred by Regulation 1/2003 it is the less restrictive approach taken by the EC which will prevail (see *Powers of investigation* part 6).

It will be clear that these powers are very substantial, and at least match those held by the Commission. In fact, given that the ECJ has made moves towards increasing the protections afforded to undertakings with reference to 'general principles of law' and the European Convention on Human Rights, the powers given to the Director may be greater than those arising under Regulation 1/2003. Some mention should be made here of the fact that the Human Rights Act 1998 was progressing through Parliament at the same time as the Competition Act 1998, and that the former requires courts and tribunals, where possible, to interpret domestic legislation so as to conform to the international obligations set out in the Human Rights Convention. It is likely that, as has been the case in the EC, cases will be brought challenging the application of the investigation powers, particularly where investigations are followed by the imposition of substantial penalties. Section 60 of the Competition Act 1998 does not apply to the investigative process, as there are relevant differences between the provisions of the Act and those of Regulation 1/2003 (see, e.g., Pertetz, G., 'Detection and Deterrence of Secret Cartels Under the UK Competition Bill' [1998] ECLR 145). However, the effect of s. 60 is to import into UK law the so-called high-level principles of EC law, such as fairness, due legal process, etc., and in these respects jurisprudence in the UK should take into account the development of these principles in the EC.

It is recognized in the *Powers of Investigation* guideline, for example, that the approach to be taken to self-incrimination is the same as under Community jurisprudence. Thus 'the OFT may compel an undertaking to provide specified documents or specified information but cannot compel the provision of answers which might involve an admission on its part of the existence of an infringement' (para. 6.6).

5.3.1.2 Interim measures

Under s. 35 the Director has the power to impose interim measures on those suspected of infringing either of the prohibitions where a reasonable suspicion to that effect exists. These powers may be exercised, and indeed are likely to be exercised, notwithstanding that an investigation is in progress. Such interim measures may be taken in order to prevent serious and irreparable harm to any person, or general damage to the public interest.

The procedures relating to interim measures are dealt with in the *Enforcement Guideline* at part 3.

5.3.1.3 Commitment decisions

In line with the new powers available to the EC Commission to accept commitments from undertakings and to formalize these, the OFT also has the power to accept commitments. This power is set out at ss. 31A to 31E of the Competition Act 1998, and is dealt with in the *Enforcement Guideline* at part 4.

5.3.1.4 Infringement decisions

The OFT has taken a number of infringement decisions in relation to the Chapter I and II Prohibitions, which are dealt with at the relevant parts of this text. Sections 32–34 of the Competition Act 1998 set out the power of the OFT to require the termination of infringements. Wherever the OFT makes an infringement decision any appeal is to be to the Competition Appeals Tribunal. This procedure applies in relation also to decisions made by the OFT in respect of arts 81 and 82 EC.

5.3.1.5 The right to be heard before a decision is taken

Wherever the OFT intends, following any investigation permitted under s. 25, to make a decision to the effect that either the Chapter I or Chapter II Prohibitions or arts 81 or 82 EC have been infringed, it must give written notice of that to the appropriate person, and give that person an opportunity to make representations (s. 31).

5.3.2 Judicial review

In principle the acts of the domestic competition authorities are subject, in accordance with the Supreme Court Act 1981 and Order 53 of the Rules of the Supreme Court, to judicial review. This is an area of law in which there has been rapid growth in recent years, and for a detailed analysis a specialist text should be referred to (and for an interesting discussion of some of the aspects of this area, see Black, J., *et al., Commercial Regulation and Judicial Review*, Oxford, Hart Publishing (1998)). Generally the greater the discretion available to any authority to act the less likely is a judicial review application to be successful. This is certainly the case where the competition authorities are concerned, both the OFT and the CC having very wide discretion in the exercise of their powers, and there is little prospect of *Wednesbury* unreasonableness (*Associated Provincial Picture Houses Ltd* v *Wednesbury Corpn* [1948] 1 KB 223) applying to a formal decision made by either body. This is particularly so when the final views of these bodies are conditioned by detailed analyses of economic principles which the courts are unlikely to review (see Sir Gordon Borrie QC, 'The Regulation of Public and Private Power' [1989] *PL* 552). The majority of the very few reported judicial review cases in this area arise out of challenges to decisions taken in relation to merger control. However, it has been established that the law of judicial review relates to the operation of the bodies responsible for competition law at the investigative stage. In *Secretary of State for Trade and Industry* v *Hoffmann-La Roche & Co. AG* [1975] AC 295, at 368, Lord Diplock held that

it is the duty of the Commissioners to observe the rules of natural justice in the course of their investigation—which means no more than that they must act fairly by giving to the person whose activities are being investigated a reasonable opportunity to put forward facts and arguments in justification of its conduct.

And in *R* v *MMC, ex parte Matthew Brown Plc* [1987] 1 WLR 1235, Macpherson J held that 'provided each party has its mind brought to bear on the relevant issues it is not in my judgment for the court to lay down rules as to how each group should act in a particular enquiry'. As has been noted above, the CC's reports tend to be very detailed and densely argued. While one might take issue with the conclusions drawn, there is only a remote possibility that an action could be founded on the basis that the CC did not bring its mind to bear on the relevant issues. A partially successful judicial review was mounted on behalf of Thomson Holidays against the Foreign Package Holidays (Tour Operators and Travel Agents) Order 1998, SI 1998/1945, which followed the MMC report into the supply of foreign package holidays (Cm. 3813, 1998) (*R* v *Secretary of State for Trade and Industry, ex parte Thomson Holidays* [2000] UKCLR 189). In part the Order was struck down because it would prohibit restrictions that were not found by the MMC to operate against the public interest. A further partial success arose in *Interbrew SA and Interbrew UK Holdings Ltd* v *The Competition Commission and the Secretary of State for Trade and Industry* [2001] UKCLR 954 in which it was found that a remedy required following a merger report was unreasonable in the light of the lack of opportunity the undertaking concerned had had to comment on the proposed remedy in the course of the inquiry. However, the CC's substantive findings regarding the public interest were left largely intact (see CC press release 20/01, 23 May 2001, [2001] UKCLR 734).

The fact that so many of the decisions may be taken by the OFT or the CC in the exercise of their specific powers under the relevant Acts is likely to reduce the grounds on which judicial review may be sought. See, for example, 20.2.6.

6

Penalties

6.1 Introduction

The issue of how best to compel corporate or individual compliance within a system designed to modify corporate conduct is a difficult one. Whereas individual unlawful acts may be presumed to be committed for the immediate gain of the perpetrator, the decision-making process within complex organizations, such as the modern company, is less focused and harder to direct externally. There is a substantial body of literature which considers the decision-making process within companies and the methods by which this may be affected. A large amount of this is American, and differences in corporate and legal cultures mean that such material may not necessarily relate to the situation in Europe, although in introducing the cartel offence into UK law the Government was clearly swayed by America's experience (see Chapter 12). An interesting survey of compliance and deterrence in relation to UK and EC competition law was carried out by Frazer in 1994 and is reported on at (1995) 58 *MLR* 847. Frazer found that respondents in UK-registered companies with a turnover of at least £200 million were 'motivated more by questions of legitimacy than by the desire to avoid penalties' (p. 855).

In industrial economics a general presumption is that companies have as their main goal profit maximization. If this was strictly true the issue for competition law would be relatively straightforward: the task of the law would be to create a structure of penalties where the *likely cost* of unlawful anti-competitive conduct more than outweighed the *likely benefit* to the company of engaging in that conduct. In fact it is not apparent that all companies have profit maximization as their goal all of the time. Even were they to do so, there may be a difference between the goals of the organization as a whole and those of its individual officers. Competition within a company might have the effect of encouraging managers to take risks that are disproportionate to the potential rewards where those risks are not borne directly by that manager: if an unlawful informal agreement between managers in two companies works well, the revenue flow to that manager's division may be greatly improved; if the agreement is discovered the punishment will be spread across the company as a whole. There have been occasions where individual officers have demonstrated a blatant disregard for the strictures of competition law. For example, in *Pioneer* 80/256 (1980) OJ L60/21 a letter written by one, of the officers involved in the maintenance of a restrictive practice read: 'I am well aware of EEC rules regarding parallel exports but quite frankly at times I am more concerned with justice than with the law itself'. Similarly, during the course of negotiating an arrangement between a leading toy manufacturer and two high-street retailers an e-mail setting out the arrangement was sent to, amongst others, one of the manufacturer's sales directors. His reply made it clear that the firm knew that such arrangements sat uncomfortably with the requirements of competition law:

Ian . . . This is a great initiative that you and Neil have instigated!!!!!!!!! However, a word to the wise, never put anything in writing, its highly illegal and it could bite you right in the arse!!!! suggest you phone Lesley and tell her to trash?   (*Agreements between Hasbro UK Ltd, Argos Ltd and Litlewoods Ltd fixing the price of Hasbro toys and games* CA98/2/2003 [2003] UKCLR 553, at para. 53)

One of the issues for competition law is that of whether penalties should be imposed on only the company as a whole, or on individual managers too, where they can be shown to be responsible for the infringement. At the Community level the fines permitted under Regulation 1/2003 may be levied only against the undertaking which is the subject of Community law. Under domestic law fines may be imposed against the company in breach of the Chapter I and Chapter II Prohibitions of the Competition Act 1998, and individual officers may be fined or imprisoned where they have obstructed an investigation or provided misleading information (see Chapter 5). Criminal penalties are available in relation to the cartel offence, and this is dealt with separately in Chapter 12.

6.2 The types of penalty

The weapons in the enforcers' arsenal are conduct remedies, structural remedies, and fines and imprisonment. The power to order the modification of corporate conduct (e.g., to determine the price at which a product may be sold), which may go so far as the complete break-up of a company, may be the most powerful weapon. There are two significant objections to such modifying orders. The first is that they may often require a continued supervision to ensure compliance, which is burdensome on the relevant enforcer; the second is that they do not always sit well within a framework of free-market economics which competition law is often intended to support. Lastly, third-party remedies—injunctions and damages—also have a role to play. These are considered in the following chapter.

Incarceration is a well-publicized feature of the American system, and since the entry into force of the Enterprise Act 2002 has been an option in the UK in relation to hard-core cartel conduct. In fact imprisonment for antitrust offences is not widely used in America, although some writers have suggested that such a method of enforcement should be potent. It has been pointed out in one study that company officers are, as a group, 'exquisitely sensitive to status deprivation' (Geiss, G., 'Deterring Corporate Crime' in Ermann, M. D., and Lundmann, R. J. (eds), *Corporate and Governmental Deviance*, Oxford, OUP (1978), p. 278). In the late 1950s the 'electrical conspiracy cases' resulted in imprisonment for some company officers, and enforcement officials believed that these convictions had a salutary effect on conduct over the immediately following years; but over time these effects diminished. There have been a number of high-profile cases in recent years, including convictions secured against executives of Hoffmann-La Roche, and the owner of Sothebys, Mr Taubman.

The argument in favour of the efficacy of fines is a persuasive one: companies take part in anti-competitive conduct in order to boost profits; remove those profits and the incentive for illegal conduct vanishes. Elzinga, K., and Breit, W., in *The Antitrust Penalties*, New Haven, Yale UP (1976) argue in favour of the imposition of massive fines, which are more efficient than the other options. Incarceration is an expensive choice for society—longer periods of incarceration are increasingly expensive—but to impose a higher fine is generally no more costly for society than the imposition of a lesser one. Within the Community and the separate European jurisdictions there is now a consensus in favour of the imposition of fines based on turnover. Whether this is the appropriate measure is less certain. While turnover figures have the advantage of being available through the requirements to maintain accounts, and are not readily open to manipulation, they are not always an accurate indicator of an ability to pay. A company fined 5 per cent of turnover in a high-turnover, low-profit-margin business will be harder hit than a company fined 5 per cent of turnover in a low-turnover, high-profit-margin business. However, the solution advanced by Viscount Trenchard, 'to devise a maximum penalty which would have an equal effect in its application to all companies' (Hansard (HL) 30 October 1997, col. 1176), is clearly flawed. A single-figure maximum does *not* have an equal effect on all companies. If the maximum fine were, say, £10m, this would have less deterrent effect, and less impact, on a company with a turnover of £1 bn than it would on a company with a turnover of £50 m. Further, a set figure allows companies to conduct cost–benefit analyses as to whether to break the law or not. Such strategic behaviour can be redressed only by a variable level of penalty, such that the wrongdoer cannot, before the event, calculate its risk with certainty, or, as is the case in the EC, by the expectation that *at the minimum* the fine will recover all profit reaped by the illegal activity. The UK adopted in the 1998 Act the same measure as the EC, which is to say that fines may be levied at up to 10 per cent of turnover (see below). Even this measure was described in the debate on the Bill as being 'grossly excessive' (Lord Fraser of Carmyllie, Hansard (HL) 30 October 1997, col. 1152).

6.3 **The European Community**

6.3.1 **Fines**

Article 23 of Regulation 1/2003 gives the Commission the power to impose on undertakings fines where breaches of procedural law have occurred, or where substantive breaches of arts 81 and 82 have occurred. Article 23(1) sets the tariff in respect of procedural breaches, such as a refusal to supply information following a Decision ordering it, or the supply of incorrect or incomplete information. In this case the penalties can be up to a maximum of 1 per cent of turnover in the preceding business year. This is a significant change from the position set out in Regulation 17, where there was a limit of €5,000. However, the more important provision is that in art. 23(2) in which it is provided that

The Commission may by decision impose fines on undertakings and associations of undertakings where, either intentionally or negligently:

(a)   they infringe art. 81 or art. 82 of the Treaty; or

(b)   they contravene a decision ordering interim measures under art. 8; or

(c)   they fail to comply with a commitment made binding by a decision pursuant to art. 9.

For each undertaking and association of undertakings participating in the infringement, the fine shall not exceed 10 per cent of its total turnover in the preceding business year.

Article 23(5) provides that decisions taken under arts 1 and 2 'shall not be of a criminal law nature'. Lastly, by virtue of art. 24 the Commission may impose periodic penalty payments up to 5 per cent of the daily turnover of the undertaking in order to compel it to: (a) terminate an infringement; (b) comply with an interim measures decision; (c) comply with a binding commitment; (d) supply complete and correct information ordered by way of a decision; and (e) submit to an inspection ordered by a decision.

The range within which the fines for substantive infringements may fall is a wide one, and it was only at the end of 1997 that the Commission considered the setting of clear guidelines ((1998) OJ C9/3). That the Commission has a wide discretion both as to whether a fine should be imposed at all, and as to the level of any such fine, flows from the wording of art. 23 itself. Article 23(3) provides in addition that 'in fixing the amount of the fine, regard shall be had both to the gravity and the duration of the infringement'. This discretion is fettered by the general principles of law developed in the context of art. 230 EC. However, when challenges against the level of fines have been upheld this has generally been on the grounds that the factual findings of the Commission have been incorrect, not that it has acted beyond its powers in imposing the fine at all. In *Miller International Schallplatten GmbH* v *Commission* case 19/77 [1978] 2 CMLR 334, Advocate General Warner argued that

a fine of 10 per cent of turnover may be taken to be appropriate to an intentional infringement of the gravest kind and of considerable duration. At the other end of the scale, a fine of less than 1 per cent is appropriate for a merely negligent infringement, of the most trivial kind and continuing only for a short time, in a case where, nonetheless, the circumstances warrant the imposition of some fine.   (p. 346)

Under the guidelines,

a base sum defined with reference to the duration and of the gravity of the infraction will be calculated without reference to turnover. It will then be raised when aggravating circumstances exist or reduced to take into account . . . attenuating circumstances. Corrections could be made to the resulting amount to take account of the individual circumstances of the case.   (ibid.)

The guidelines thus appear to dismiss altogether the calculation of fines by reference to turnover, and the only recognition of this as a determining factor appears where the Commission notes that 'it goes without saying that the final amount calculated according to this method may not in any case exceed 10 per cent of the world-wide turnover of the undertakings'. In assessing the level at which any fine should be imposed the article itself makes reference only to the 'gravity' and the 'duration' of the infringement, and the guidelines make clear that the basic amount will be defined in reference to these.

The determination of the level at which the undertaking would be fined prior to the guidelines had involved the consideration of a number of factors, most of which are reflected in the guidelines. Within the structure as set out in the guidelines the gravity of the infringement will be determined with reference to three criteria: the nature of the infringement; its impact on the market; and the size of the relevant geographical market. The application of these criteria will result in a restriction being placed in one of three categories:

Minor infringements: These might be trade restrictions, usually of a vertical nature [see Chapter 8], but with a limited market impact and affecting only a substantial but relatively limited part of the Community market. Likely fines: €1,000 to 1 million.

Serious infringements: These will more often than not be horizontal or vertical restrictions [see Chapter 8] of the same type as above, but more rigorously applied, with a wider market impact, and with effects in extensive areas of the common market. They might also be abuses of a dominant position . . . Likely fines: €1 million to 20 million.

Very serious infringements: These will generally be horizontal restrictions such as price cartels and market-sharing quotas, or other practices which jeopardise the proper functioning of the single market . . . and clear cut abuses of a dominant position by undertakings holding a virtual monopoly . . . Likely fines: above €20 million.

These figures will be subject to variation, both to allow the requisite individual treatment of the position of each undertaking and to allow the 'duration' to be factored in. The impact of the duration on the level of fine set out above is as follows: short term (generally less than one year)—no impact; medium term (one to five years)—an increase of up to 50 per cent on the amount determined for gravity; long term (five years plus)—an increase of up to 10 per cent per year. Even having published the guidelines the Commission is not under an obligation to spell out precisely how it arrives at the final figure for a penalty imposed on it in an adverse decision. In *Mo Och Domsjo AB* v *Commission* case C–283/98P [2001] 4 CMLR 322 the ECJ held that it was sufficient for the Commission to indicate in its decision 'the factors which enabled it to determine the gravity of the infringement and its duration' (para. 44).

The fact that fines are to be increased in direct proportion to the longevity of the infringement is designed to put further pressure on cartels, an issue which is dealt with in part by the Commission's reducing the penalties on cartel members who 'blow the whistle' (see below).

The fining guidelines also set out aggravating and attenuating circumstances that will affect the basic amount. The non-exhaustive list of aggravating circumstances is as follows:

- repeated infringement of the same type by the undertaking;
- non-cooperation or obstruction during the course of the Commission investigation;
- a leading role in the infringement;
- any retaliatory measures taken against other undertakings designed to reinforce the anti-competitive actions;
- consideration of any profits made by virtue of the unlawful conduct when it is possible to calculate this (see the discussion of this aspect of the calculation of penalties in section 6.4.1.1).

The list of attenuating circumstances is as follows:

- a passive, or 'follow my leader' role taken in a cartel;
- less than full compliance with any restrictive agreement;
- prompt termination of the infringement following the intervention of the Commission;
- reasonable doubt on the part of the undertaking as to the fact that the conduct was in breach of Community law;
- infringement negligently or unintentionally committed;
- cooperation with the Commission in the course of the proceedings.

Undertakings have persistently called for a clarification of the Commission's fining policy, and some pressure has also come from cases in the human rights field, such as *Société Stenuit* v *France* (1992) 14 EHRR 509. In *Musique Diffusion Française SA* v *Commission* cases 100–103/80 [1983] 3 CMLR 221, the Commission argued (at 263) that:

since there are so many unquantifiable criteria to be taken into consideration, no mathematical formula of general application is possible. Different approaches may be used in different cases. Even where it is possible to connect the size of the fine to a quantifiable criterion, such as turnover, the decision as to what must be the relationship between the fine and the criteria thus measured is a question of appraisal rather than simple calculation.

The guidelines strike what may be an acceptable compromise between calculation and judgement. The criteria were largely drawn from existing practices, reflecting the approach both of the Commission and of the Court of Justice. It has always been the case that the Commission has been particularly concerned by breaches of art. 81 which are likely to lead to the division of the common market, and any practice threatening economic integration will be strongly condemned. Thus, for example, in *IPTC Belgium* 83/773 (1983) OJ L376/7, the Commission made the point that

It is well known that business practices seeking to prevent parallel imports and to erect artificial trade barriers within the Community, and thus to undermine the unity of the common market, are regularly investigated and condemned by the Community authorities. (para. 15)

The Commission has been particularly harsh on recidivism. In *Flat glass* 84/388 (1984) OJ L212/13, the Commission emphasized the fact that two of the parties were guilty of previous infringements. The fact that they had negotiated an agreement with the Commission and then observed the letter, but not the spirit, of the undertaking, led to the imposition of a higher fine than would otherwise have been the case. The fines imposed in *LdPE* 89/191 (1989) OJ L74/21 were also influenced by the fact that several of the parties had previously been the subject of Commission action in *Dyestuffs* (*ICI* v *Commission* case 48/69 [1972] CMLR 557) In *Tetra Pak II* 92/163 (1992) OJ L72/1, the Commission imposed a then record fine of €75 million on the undertaking, and in doing so stressed that it would attempt to recover illicit profits where these could be identified. This point was reiterated in the *21st Report on Competition Policy*:

The financial benefit which companies . . . have derived from their infringements will become an increasingly important consideration. Wherever the Commission can ascertain the level of this ill-gotten gain, even if it cannot do so precisely, the calculation of the fine may have this as its starting point. (point 139)

While the profit level will not, under the guidelines, be the starting point for the assessment of the fine, the fact that the Commission will attempt at the absolute minimum to recover any profit made remains a guiding principle.

The Commission has reduced the fines imposed in the past where participants in cartels have played a reduced role in relation to the hard-core members. This was the case in *LdPE* (above) where Shell and BP were fined reduced amounts, reflecting the restricted level of their involvement in the cartel meetings. Undertakings may have their fines reduced if they are merely responding to another's illegal activity (*Welded steel mesh* 89/515 (1989) OJ L260/1). Cooperation during the course of the investigation was rewarded in *IPTC Belgium* (above). The 'reasonable doubt' attenuation provision of the guidelines reflects the fact that undertakings have been subjected to lesser penalties in the past where the Commission has not previously penalized the behaviour which is the subject of the fine. For example, in *BDTA* 88/477 (1988) OJ L233/15 the Commission dealt with the actions of a trade association which organized trade exhibitions. It reduced the fine because this was the first exhibition policy case in which one had been imposed. In *Wood pulp* 85/202 (1985) OJ L85/1 the Commission reduced or removed altogether the fines for undertakings that were based in the United States and were operating within American antitrust law (see further Chapter 4).

It is clear that over time the average amount of the fines imposed by the Commission has greatly increased. From 1970 to 1974 the average level was €411,604; from 1990 to 1994 the average level was €4,135,220. This reflects partly the fact that the Commission is taking a greater proportion of its proceedings against larger undertakings and cartels, where both the impact of the infringement and the ability to pay are greater. It also reflects the fact that the Commission has quite deliberately increased the tariff from time to time to strengthen the enforcement of competition policy. This was the case, for example, in *Pioneer* 80/256 (1980) OJ L60/21, where the fines imposed amounted to between 2.4 and 4 per cent of turnover, whereas previously fines had amounted to 2 per cent of turnover at the most. The Commission argued that this was necessary in view of the increasing maturity of the Community regime, and that in deciding to increase levels generally they had not exceeded their discretion. On appeal (*Musique Diffusion Française SA* v *Commission* cases 100–103/80 [1983] 3 CMLR 221) the Court agreed with the Commission, holding that 'the proper application of the Community competition rules requires that the Commission may at any time adjust the level of fines to the needs of that policy' (para. 109). In January 1998 the Commission broke the record that it had established in *Tetra Pak* by imposing a fine of €102 million on Volkswagen following a finding that the company had, in breach of art. 81(1), prevented Italian dealers in its cars from reselling these to customers from other parts of the Community (*VW* 98/273 (1998) OJ L124/61, on appeal *Volkswagen AG* v *Commission* case T–62/98 [2000] 5 CMLR 853—as a result of which the fine was reduced (to €90 million). The decision is a further demonstration of the extremely strong stance that the Commission will take against any practice which results in the re-creation of the trade barriers it has sought so hard to dismantle. In September 1998 record fines totalling €273 million were imposed on parties to the Trans-Atlantic Conference Agreement following a finding that they had abused a position of joint dominance under art. 82 (IP/98/811, 16 September 1998). In 2003, in its decision in relation to the vitamins cartel, Hoffman-La Roche alone was ordered to pay €426m (*Vitamins* 2003/2/EC, (2003) OJ L6/1) and in 2004 Microsoft was fined €497,196,304 (*Microsoft*, 21 April 2004).

On the other hand, where infringements are genuinely committed negligently, fines may be only token. For example, in *1998 Football World Cup* 2000/12 (2000) OJ L5/55 the Commission drew the conclusion that the French ticketing authorities adopted arrangements similar to those taken in earlier competitions, and that the area was so specific that clear guidance could not be drawn from earlier decisions. As a result, having found the relevant undertaking to have abused its dominant position, the Commission imposed a fine that was only €1,000.

6.3.1.1 *Leniency for 'whistle-blowers'*

The Commission is attempting to use its fining policy to put particular pressure on cartels, which it has admitted are hard to detect (see Chapter 5). This pressure stems in part from the Commission Notice on Immunity from fines and reduction of fines in cartel cases (2002) OJ C45/03. The notice is aimed at 'secret cartels between two or more competitors aimed at fixing prices, production or sales quotas, sharing markets including bid-rigging or restricting imports or exports' (para. 1). The problem for undertakings engaged in cartels is that the fines increase for every year of participation if the cartel is detected, and some members may be looking for a way out. However, the increased fines mean that members might be reluctant to disclose the existence of the cartel to the authorities. The Commission has taken the view that the 'interests of consumers and citizens in ensuring that secret cartels are detected and punished outweigh the interest in fining those undertakings that enable the Commission to detect and prohibit such practices' (para. 4). Accordingly the Commission notice is aimed at encouraging undertakings involved in cartels to come forward with the evidence the Commission needs to take action.

Total immunity from any fine that would ordinarily be imposed by the Commission is guaranteed where either:

8(a) the undertaking is the first to submit evidence which in the Commission's view may enable it to adopt a decision to carry out an investigation in the sense of [art. 20 of Regulation 1/2003] in connection with an alleged cartel affecting the Community; or

(b) the undertaking is the first to submit evidence which in the Commission's view may enable it to find an infringement of article 81 EC in connection with an alleged cartel affecting the Community.

In respect of para. 8(a) the immunity will apply as long as the Commission did not already have sufficient evidence to launch an investigation, and under para. 8(b) the requirement is that the Commission did not have the evidence, and no other undertaking had been granted immunity from fines under para. 8(a). However, there are also three further conditions to the grant of immunity, set out in para. 11. First the undertaking must cooperate fully throughout the investigation. Secondly, the undertaking must end its own involvement in the cartel at the same time as it provides the necessary information to the Commission, and thirdly the undertaking must not have taken any steps to coerce any other undertaking to join the cartel.

Even in situations where an undertaking does not qualify for a total immunity from a fine penalties may be reduced. This will particularly be the case where the undertaking in question provides information which has a 'significant added value with respect to the evidence already in the Commission's possession' (para. 21). The first undertaking to meet this point will earn a reduction of some 30–50 per cent, the second a reduction of 20–30 per cent, and any subsequent undertaking a reduction of up to 20 per cent.

This version of the notice addresses criticisms made in respect of an earlier version of which it was argued that undertakings were not given sufficiently clear guidance to enable them to assess their risk properly. While the notice is less conditional than the earlier version, there will still be some situations in which undertakings are unable to determine whether it is better to approach the Commission to seek leniency, or to hold their collective breath in the hope that no action will follow.

Some concern has been raised in relation to the operation of the leniency programme within the context of modernization and the European Competition Network. This matter is dealt with in the *Commission Notice on cooperation within the Network of Competition Authorities* (2004) OJ C101/43 in which it addresses the problem of a lack of harmonization in this area in the following terms:

In the absence of a European Union-wide system of fully harmonised leniency programmes, an application for leniency to a given authority is not to be considered as an application for leniency to any other authority. It is therefore in the interest of the applicant to apply for leniency to all competition authorities which have competence to apply article 81 of the Treaty in the territory which is affected by the infringement and which may be considered well placed to act against the infringement in question. In view of the importance of timing in most existing leniency programmes, applicants will also need to consider whether it would be appropriate to file leniency applications with the relevant authorities simultaneously. It is for the applicant to take the steps which it considers appropriate to protect its position with respect to possible proceedings by these authorities.   (para. 38)

It is to be regretted that there is no single leniency procedure by which an applicant may make an approach to the EC Commission and be assured leniency in all the Member States, and it is possible that this divergence may, to an extent, undermine the application of the leniency programme.

6.3.2 **Other orders**

Articles 7–9 of Regulation 1/2003, discussed in Chapter 5, deal with the decisions that the Commission may make in respect of conduct which infringes arts 81 and 82. While it is not strictly correct to characterize these as 'penalties', to the undertaking subject to any such decision it may well feel as if a punishment is being imposed. The central power here is that held by the Commission to 'require the undertakings and associations of undertakings concerned to bring such infringement to an end'. In order to achieve this termination of an infringement the Commission 'may impose on them any behavioural or structural remedies which are proportionate to the infringement committed and necessary to bring the infringement effectively to an end' (art. 7(1)). The wording of this provision allows the Commission to make any order that it considers to be appropriate, although all such orders may be challenged by way of art. 230 before the CFI.

The power to order structural remedies (typically divestiture, or the break-up of a company), is a new one, and it is anticipated that this will be employed only in exceptional circumstances, where a behavioural remedy will not be readily available. It is not the case that all infringement decisions will be accompanied by behavioural orders. In many cases the Commission merely requires that the infringement be terminated, but does not prescribe behaviour, rather leaving it to the undertaking to determine what is required so as to bring its conduct within the bounds of legal acceptability. A typical behavioural remedy might be to resume supplies to a customer where these have been illegally stopped (as was the case in *BBI/Boosey & Hawkes: Interim measure* 87/500 (1987) OJ L286/36)), or to withdraw a threatened predatory price cut (see *ECS/AKZO: Interim measure* 83/462 (1983) OJ L252/13)).

6.4 The United Kingdom

6.4.1 The Competition Act 1998

6.4.1.1 *Fines*

The Competition Act 1988 incorporates a penalty system that is similar to that of Community law. By virtue of s. 36 of the Act, the OFT may impose a penalty where either the Chapter I or the Chapter II Prohibitions are infringed. Section 36(8) provides that 'no penalty fixed by the [OFT] under this section may exceed 10 per cent of the turnover of the undertaking (determined in accordance with such provisions as may be specified in an order made by the Secretary of State)'. Turnover is to be calculated in accordance with the Competition Act 1998 (Determination of Turnover for Penalties) Order 2000, SI 2000/309 as amended by the Competition Act 1998 (Determination of Turnover for Penalties) (Amendment) Order 2004, SI 2004/1259. 'Section 36(8)' turnover is not restricted to the turnover in the relevant product and geographic market.

The turnover threshold may be amended by order of the Secretary of State, but it is unlikely that this figure would ever be revised upwards. Companies may appeal against any fines levied, which become recoverable by the OFT as if they were a civil debt (s. 37). Turnover is to be UK turnover, not worldwide or EC turnover. Appeals may be made against decisions of the OFT, to the Competition Appeals Tribunal (CAT) and then to the Court of Appeal (s. 49(1)(b)). Unlike the Court of First Instance, the CAT reviews the decision taken by the OFT from scratch, in relation both to penalties and to any required conduct changes and is required to consider the case 'on the merits' (Sch. 8, para. 3(1)), and if it is necessary and appropriate to 'make any other decision which the OFT could have made' (Sch. 8, para. 3(2)(e)). In regard to penalties the CAT may raise, lower, or revoke altogether any penalty (Sch. 8, para. 3(2)(b)). Also, the CAT is not bound by any guidance issued by the OFT in relation to penalties, and as the CAT recognized in *Napp Pharmaceuticals Holdings Ltd* v *The Director General of Fair Trading* [2002] CompAR 13, 'the CA98 contains no provision which requires the Tribunal to even have regard to that

Guidance' (para. 497). The general approach whereby the CAT would start from first principles, although in doing so it would clearly have in mind any penalty imposed by the OFT is, the CAT commented in *Napp*, consistent with the requirements of the European Convention on Human Rights, art. 6. In the case it was accepted by all parties that the penalties are 'criminal' within the meaning of the Convention, even though they are characterized in English law as a 'civil debt'. An appeal may be made from the CAT to the Court of Appeal in relation to the level of any penalty imposed (s. 49(1)(b)).

Given the emphasis in the 1998 Act on conformity with Community law, it is likely that fines will be assessed in a way similar to that employed by the EC Commission. It was confirmed by the CAT in *Napp* that in determining the broad policy relating to fines Community law should be followed (see para. 455). However, in relation to the calculation of the exact fine within the broad parameters set out in the Act, dealt with in the relevant guideline (see below), the CAT took the view that differences between the approach taken by the OFT and that taken by the EC Commission's guideline were 'relevant' for the purposes of s. 60 of the Act. This is to say that the CAT did not feel obliged to take into account the EC guidelines in making its own decisions. In situations where the condemned conduct has also been subject to the imposition of a penalty under Community law by the Commission, the OFT is to have regard to that penalty in assessing the level of the fine under domestic law.

'Small agreements', as defined by secondary legislation (and see s. 39), and 'conduct of minor significance' otherwise falling within the Chapter II Prohibition (s. 40) have limited immunity from the imposition of fines. However, this immunity may, in certain circumstances, be withdrawn by the OFT. The relevant thresholds are set out in the Competition Act 1998 (Small Agreements and Conduct of Minor Significance) Regulations 2000, SI 2000/262. These provide that small agreements (s. 39(1)) are those where the combined applicable turnover in the year preceding the infringement did not exceed £20 million (para. 3). The threshold in respect of s. 40(1) is £50 million (para. 4).

The approach that will be taken to the setting of penalties is set out in the OFT's *Guidance as to the Appropriate Amount of a Penalty*, which the OFT had a statutory duty under s. 38(1) of the Act to produce. The tone of the guidance is set at the outset, where the OFT explains the policy objectives underlying the approach. These are 'to impose penalties on infringing undertakings which reflect the seriousness of the infringement and to ensure that the threat of penalties will deter undertakings from engaging in anti-competitive practices'. Accordingly, the OFT intends 'to impose financial penalties which are severe' (para. 1.5).

The broad approach is similar to that adopted by the EC Commission. A five-step approach is taken:

1. calculation of the starting point by applying a percentage determined by the nature of the infringement to the 'relevant turnover' of the undertaking;
2. adjustment for duration;

3. adjustment for other factors;
4. adjustment for further aggravating or mitigating factors;
5. adjustment if the maximum penalty of 10 per cent of the turnover would be exceeded, and to avoid double jeopardy.

These factors are discussed further in the guidelines.

The first penalty imposed by the OFT under the Act was a fine of £3.21m levied against Napp Pharmaceuticals (*Napp Pharmaceutical Holdings Ltd* CA98/2/2001 [2001] UKCLR 597, on appeal *Napp Pharmaceuticals Holdings Ltd* v *The Director General of Fair Trading* [2002] CompAR 13). The undertaking had been condemned for discriminatory predatory pricing to one customer base, and for excessive pricing to another. One of the points which concerned the CAT related to an attempt by the OFT to recover any profits made as a result of Napp's illegal conduct. Such an adjustment is dealt with as part of the third step in the calculation of the penalty, the amount of profit made being 'another factor'. The first concern of the CAT related to the difficulty of calculating what the gain actually was. In the case in question the parties were unable to agree within a million pounds. Even were a figure produced the CAT felt that this would most likely underestimate the gain, as it would not be able to take into account the long-term benefit to the undertaking of an enhanced reputation for toughness and competitiveness. The CAT expressed the view that 'this method of calculation, so it seems to us, is more suited to the process for assessing the damages in civil litigation, rather than the fixing of a deterrent penalty' (para. 508).

The operating of a compliance programme is expressly recognized as a mitigating factor (penalty guidance, part 3), but in order for this to apply the parties must show that the programme is active, visibly supported by senior management, backed up by appropriate procedures and appropriate training, and properly audited and reported.

6.4.1.2 *Leniency for 'whistle-blowers'*

The OFT approach to 'whistle-blowers' was more influenced by the similar US programme than by the one operated by the EC Commission. It is now, however, following revisions to the EC scheme (discussed above) similar to that scheme. It was invoked for the first time in the decision *Market Sharing by Arriva plc and First-Group plc* (CA98/9/2002, 30 January 2002), in which both companies benefited from the operation of the scheme as they provided the OFT with evidence of cartel activity. Arriva's fine was reduced by 36 per cent, and FirstGroup avoided penalty altogether. FirstGroup did not approach the OFT until after the investigation had begun, but was the first of the two parties to do so. A letter offering a 100 per cent reduction was issued on 2 November 2000, and was conditional on FirstGroup providing evidence of the cartel, cooperating with the OFT throughout the investigation, and complying with all the conditions set out in the *Guidance on Penalties* (paras 70–71). Under the UK guidelines the OFT 'will offer *total immunity* from financial penalties . . . to a member of a cartel who is the first to come forward and who satisfies the requirements set out in para 9.3.2 [or] 9.3.4' (para. 9.1). Paragraph 9.3.2 relates to those who come forward *before* an investigation has commenced. The conditions are that the undertaking in question must:

(a) give full disclosure of relevant information;

(b) cooperate fully throughout the investigation;

(c) not have compelled any other undertaking to join the cartel, have instigated the cartel, or played a leading role; and

(d) cease any involvement in the cartel from the time it comes forward.

Paragraph 9.3.4 relates to those who come forward once an investigation has commenced. In this case immunity may be available where the undertaking is the first to come forward before the Director has given written notice of his intention to make a decision to the effect that the Chapter I Prohibition has been breached, and the conditions set out above are also met. The Director will, so far as is possible, attempt to maintain confidentiality as to the identity of any undertaking coming forward under this part of the procedure (para. 9.7). However, given the dynamics involved in the investigation of a cartel, and the fact that there will already be in place links between the undertakings concerned, it is difficult to see how this will work in practice. Copies of draft letters setting out the terms and conditions on which the leniency programme operates are available on the OFT website.

6.4.2 **The Enterprise Act 2002**

6.4.2.1 *The cartel offence*

The cartel offence, set out in Part 6 of the Enterprise Act 2002, is the only substantive area of competition law operating in the UK to be criminal in nature. Any person in breach of s. 188 may, on conviction, face a term of imprisonment of up to five years. The offence is dealt with in more detail in Chapter 12.

6.4.2.2 *Directors' disqualification*

Although the cartel offence has received the lion's share of attention, the threat of director' disqualification following breaches of competition law is likely to have at least as much impact on ensuring compliance with the law. The Government signalled its intention to make provision in this area in the White Paper, *A World Class Competition Regime* (Cm. 5233, July 2001), suggesting that it would be 'in the public interest that directors who have engaged in serious breaches of competition law should be exposed to the possibility of disqualification on that ground alone' (para. 8.24).

Section 204 of the Enterprise Act amends the Company Directors Disqualification Act 1986 (CDDA) inserting new ss. 9A–9E. In May 2003 the OFT published *Competition disqualification orders: Guidance*. Section 9A of the CDDA provides that the appropriate court must make a competition disqualification order (CDO) against a person following an application by the OFT (or other concurrent regulator), where the conditions are met. The first condition is that an undertaking of which that person is a director commits a breach of competition law—this applies in relation to the Chapter I and II Prohibitions, and to arts 81 and 82 EC. The second condition is that 'the court considers that his conduct as a director makes him unfit to be concerned in the management of a company'. In making this assessment the court is required to consider the matters set out in s. 9A(6). These are that the person's conduct contributed to the breach, that their conduct did not contribute to the breach but that the person had reasonable grounds to suspect the breach and took no steps to prevent it, or that they did not know of the breach but should have known of it. The court may also consider the involvement of the director in any other breaches of competition law. Where a breach has occurred 'it is immaterial whether the person knew that the conduct of the undertaking constituted the breach' (s. 9A(7)). The OFT may also, instead of proceeding with the formal steps, accept a competition disqualification undertaking (CDU) from a person, which, once made, operates in a very similar way to a formal CDO.

In the event that a director is disqualified under these provisions the maximum period of disqualification is 15 years (s. 9A(9)). During the term of the disqualification it is a criminal offence for the person to: be a director of a company; act as a receiver of a company's property; in any way, whether directly or indirectly, be concerned to take part in the promotion, formation, or management of a company; or to act as an insolvency practitioner (s. 1(1)).

In its guidance the OFT indicates that it will follow a five-step process in considering whether to apply for a CDO. Thus it will:

1. consider whether an undertaking which is a company of which the person is a director has committed a breach of competition law;
2. consider whether a financial penalty has been imposed for the breach;
3. consider whether the company in question benefited from leniency;
4. consider the extent of the director's responsibility for the breach;
5. have regard to any aggravating and mitigating factors.

When considering the role of the director in question the primary factor will be 'the extent of the director's responsibility for or involvement in the breach, whether by action or omission' (para. 4.15). The OFT is 'likely' to apply for a CDO against a director who has been directly involved in a breach, and is 'quite likely' to apply for a CDO where a director failed to take corrective action against the breach. It also does not exclude the possibility that it may apply for a CDO where it considers that the director 'taking into account that director's role and responsibilities, to have failed to keep himself or herself sufficiently informed of the company's activities which constituted the breach of competition law' (para. 4.16). This is to say, ignorance may not be an excuse. In the event that a company has benefited from the leniency the OFT will *not* apply for a CDO against a director of that company.

In the event that any director is convicted of a cartel offence the convicting court has the power to make a disqualification against that person, and in these cases the OFT will not make use of its powers under the CDDA.

6.4.2.3 *Market investigation references and merger investigations*

The orders that may be made, and remedies that may be imposed in relation to market investigation references and merger investigations are dealt with in Chapters 17 and 20 respectively.

7

Complaints and third-party rights

7.1 Introduction

Although this chapter is addressed to the rights of third parties rather than to the position of those in breach of the law, or of society as a whole, it should be recognized that there is a relationship between third-party rights and the enforcement of competition law (see the previous chapter). In particular, the effect on the infringing party of paying damages is little different than if a fine were being levied. The effect upon the legal system, however, is more noticeable, and the burden of enforcement will pass from the relevant public authorities to wronged individuals, who may often have greater motivation to bring actions. This is a very obvious and prominent feature of the American antitrust system, where individual enforcement is a vital part of the regime, and is encouraged by the availability of triple damages under s. 4 of the Clayton Act, which provides that

[a]ny person who shall be injured in his business or property by reason of anything forbidden in the antitrust laws may sue therefor ... and shall recover threefold the damages by him sustained, and the cost of suit, including a reasonable attorney's fee. (15 USC s. 15)

The nature of the regimes in the European Community and the United Kingdom is that public regulation is to the fore, and any individual rights are ancillary to this. There is also a very clear difference between the legal culture of the United States, where parties bring actions much more readily, and of Europe, where there is a greater reluctance to involve the courts in commercial matters. This factor has clearly been a matter of some exasperation to the EC Commission, which would like to see far more actions brought directly by injured parties in the Member States. During debates on the passage of the Competition Act 1998 suggestions were made by members on the Conservative benches that the penalties for breaches of the new UK law should be reduced as enforcement would flow from third parties. However, the Government recognized that

ordinary consumers and small companies, who will commonly be the victims of anti-competitive agreements and abuses by small and medium sized enterprises, are less likely and less able to pursue their rights through courts than would a big business. (Hansard (HL) 17 November 1997, col. 436)

And Lord Borrie, former DGFT, made the point that

small businesses have been extremely reluctant to take action themselves because of the expense. With some reason they have thought that the [OFT], set up especially to enforce the law, should take action at public expense. That is the real deterrent. (ibid.)

It is in part because of these factors that the Government introduced strong publicly imposed penalties in the new law.

For an excellent general discussion of this area see Jones, C. A., *Private Enforcement of Antitrust Law in the EU, UK, and USA*, Oxford, OUP (1999).

As part of the modernisation process the EC Commission has published guidelines designed to assist both private actions before the courts (*Guidelines on co-operation between the Commission and the National Courts* (2004) OJ C101/54) and complainants bringing matters to the attention of the relevant national competition authority (*Commission notice on the handling of complaints by the Commission under arts 81 and 82 EC* (2004) OJ C101/65). In the latter guideline the Commission makes clear that it 'wishes to encourage citizens and undertakings to address themselves to the public enforcers to inform them about suspected infringements of the competition rules' (para. 3). Under the enforcement regime established under Regulation 1/2003 a complainant has a choice as to whether to bring a matter to the attention of the Commission, or to a relevant national competition authority, or before a national court in the form of a private action. Paragraph 8 of the notice explains clearly the basic position facing those with a grievance:

While national courts are called upon to safeguard the rights of individuals and are thus bound to rule on cases brought before them, public enforcers cannot investigate all complaints, but must set priorities in their treatment of cases. The Court of Justice has held that the Commission, entrusted by art. 85(1) of the EC Treaty with the task of ensuring application of the principles laid down in arts 81 and 82 of the Treaty, is responsible for defining and implementing the orientation of Community competition policy and that, in order to perform that task effectively, it is entitled to give differing degrees of priority to the complaints brought before it. [See further the case of *Automec srl* v *Commission* below at 7.2.1]

Regulation 773/2004 (OJ L123/18) *relating to the conduct of proceedings by the Commission pursuant to Articles 81 and 82 of the EC Treaty* makes further provision in relation to complainants. Here the Commission indicates that 'complaints are an essential source of information for detecting infringements of competition rules' (recital (5)). Article 5 of the Regulation sets out the rules relating to the admissibility of complaints, which shall contain the information specified in Form C, attached to the Regulation. Form C requires the complainant to give full details about the undertaking whose activity is being complained about, along with

in detail the facts from which, in your opinion, it appears that there exists an infringement of [arts 81 or 82 EC]. Indicate in particular the nature of the products (goods or services) affected by the alleged infringements and explain, where necessary, the commercial relationships concerning these products. Provide all available details on the agreements or practices of the undertakings or associations of undertakings to which this complaint relates. Indicate, to the extent possible, the relative market positions of the undertakings concerned by the complaint. (Form C, para (3))

The Commission itself has indicated that it intends to focus its enforcement efforts on cases in which it is best placed to act, concentrating its efforts on the most serious of cases, or on those cases in which the Commission needs to define Community competition policy in order to ensure the coherent application of arts 81 or 82.

7.2 European Community law

7.2.1 Involvement in proceedings

Historically the Commission has received many complaints from third parties about anti-competitive activity, but is significantly overburdened and not able to take effective action in all appropriate cases. In 2002, for example, 321 new cases were registered, of which 101 were based on complaints made by third parties; 363 cases were closed; and 805 cases were left outstanding. These figures were not encouraging for third parties seeking redress through an administrative route, although the Commission focused its activity on the most serious breaches.

Regulation 1/2003, art. 7(2) provides that '[t]hose entitled to lodge a complaint for the purposes of paragraph 1 are natural or legal persons who can show a legitimate interest and member states'. There is little law on what constitutes a 'legitimate interest', and the practice of the Commission has been generally to assume that if a party was making a complaint it *did* have a legitimate interest. In essence the view of the Commission is that where undertakings operating in the market are affected by the alleged anti-competitive conduct, or where conduct is likely to have a direct and foreseeable effect on that undertaking, a legitimate interest will arise. This follows the approach taken by the CFI in cases such as *Bureau Européen des Medias et de l'Industrie Misicale (BENIM)* v *Commission* case T–114/92 [1996] 4 CMLR 305.

In *Automec srl* v *Commission* case T–24/90 [1992] 5 CMLR 431, the applicant relied on art. 232 EC in an attempt to compel the Commission to act in response to a complaint. Article 232 is in the following terms:

Should the European Parliament, the Council or the Commission, in infringement of this Treaty, fail to act, the Member States and the other institutions of the Community may bring an action before the Court of Justice to have the infringement established.

The action shall be admissible only if the institution concerned has first been called upon to act. If, within two months of being so called upon, the institution concerned has not defined its position, the action may be brought within a further period of two months.

Any natural or legal person may, under the conditions laid down in the preceding paragraphs, complain to the Court of Justice that an institution of the Community has failed to address to that person any act other than a recommendation or an opinion.

The Court held that the Commission was entitled to prioritize its workload, that the emphasis in enforcement policy would inevitably shift from time to time in response to the wide range of factors that the Commission was expected to consider, and that the Commission was not obliged necessarily to follow every case presented to it, but was entitled to select which cases it could address its attention to. This case has been often cited by the Commission in its attempts to persuade courts and authorities in the Member States to assume more of the burden of enforcement, and has also been relied on by the OFT in the UK.

Where the Commission has taken action in response to a complaint, the person who made that complaint will have the necessary *locus standi* to bring an action challenging the act on the basis of art. 230 (see, e.g., *Timex Corp* v *EC Council and Commission* case 264/82 [1985] 3 CMLR 431). The relevant part of this article is as follows:

Any natural or legal person may, under the same conditions, institute proceedings against . . . a decision which, although in the form of a regulation or a decision addressed to another person, is of direct and individual concern to the former.

The link between these two articles was emphasized in *Guerin Automobiles* v *Commission* case C–282/95P [1997] 5 CMLR 447. The Court of Justice held in *Guerin* that the Commission was obliged to take a decision in a reasonable period of time where it had received a complaint. However, the decision taken may be merely a formal statement that the Commission does not intend to pursue the matter. If the decision is not taken following a complaint, the complainant may rely on art. 232 to enforce the obligation, and may use art. 230 to challenge the decision when it is eventually made. While the case appears slightly to strengthen the position of a complainant beyond that established in *Automec*, in that it emphasizes that the Commission must act definitively, the number of procedural hurdles to be overcome, and the time and cost that this can entail, are likely to be beyond the reach of many applicants. Nevertheless, in *UPS Europe SA* v *Commission* case T–127/98 [2000] 4 CMLR 94, the plaintiff was successful in its art. 232 action.

A successful challenge to a rejection of a complaint was also mounted in *Micro Leader Business* v *Commission* case T–198/98 [2000] 4 CMLR 886. Here the applicant had complained to the Commission about various practices engaged in by Microsoft that restricted the ability of Micro Leader Business to obtain Microsoft products in Canada for resale in the EC. The Court held that the evidence put forward by the complainant was sufficient at least to indicate that there might be an abusive practice, and that the Commission should have examined this part of the complaint more carefully. The Commission's rejection of the complaint was therefore annulled, and the Commission was obliged to consider the complaint again, as well as to pay the costs of the complainant's court action. Similarly, in *Union Française de l'Express (UFEX)* v *Commission* case T–77/95 [2001] 4 CMLR 35 the CFI held that the Commission had failed adequately to assess the seriousness and duration of the complained-of infringements and had not therefore been in a position to determine whether the Community interest would best be served by pursuing the complaint.

It is uncertain what criteria have to be met for a third party falling in art. 230 EC to show 'a sufficient interest'.

In Regulation 773/2004 (OJ L101/18) *relating to the conduct of proceedings by the Commission pursuant to Articles 81 and 82 of the EC Treaty* complainants are given a role to play in proceedings once the Commission has issued a statement of objection to the undertaking whose conduct has been complained of. Article 6 provides that

(1) Where the Commission issues a statement of objections relating to a matter in respect of which it has received a complaint, it shall provide the complainant with a copy of the non-confidential version of the statement of objections and set a time-limit within which the complainant may make its views known in writing.

(2) The Commission may, where appropriate, afford complainants the opportunity of expressing their views at the oral hearing of the parties to which a statement of objections has been issued, if the complainants so request in their written comments.

A complainant does not have the *absolute* right to be heard during the oral proceedings (*Kish Glass & Co Ltd* v *Commission* case T–65/96 [2000] 5 CMLR 229, paras 32–3). For further consideration of the Commission's approach to complaints see the *Notice on the handling of complaints*.

7.2.2 **Direct effect and** *Garden Cottage Foods*

Given that there is no direct access to the ECJ other than through the 'judicial review' provisions of the Treaty (arts 230, 232, and 288), the individual plaintiff seeking to rely on EC law must do so through the courts of Member States under the principle of direct effect. When the Treaty of Rome originally entered into force in 1958 it was not clear that it was intended to give rise to such actions on the part of individuals. However, in the landmark case of *NV Algemene Transport-en Expeditie Onderneming Van Gend en Loos* v *Nederlandse Belastingadministratie* case 26/62 [1963] 1 CMLR 105, it was established that where articles of the Treaty are clear, precise, and unconditional they are capable of creating rights vested in individuals which can be enforced against Member States ('vertical direct effect').

In *Defrenne* v *Sabena (No. 2)* case 43/75 [1976] 2 CMLR 98, the principle was extended to allow such rights to be enforced against other persons not being part of the state ('horizontal direct effect'). The principle applies equally to regulations, which are, by the wording of art. 249 'binding in [their] entirety and directly applicable in all Member States'. Both art. 81 and art. 82 meet the criteria for direct effect set out in *Van Gend*. The effect of this then is that an undertaking engaging in conduct that falls within the prohibitions may therefore face actions before national courts by those harmed by that action (see, e.g., *Belgische Radio en Télévisie (BRT)* v *Société Belge des Auteurs, Compositeurs et Editeurs (SABAM)* case 127/73 [1974] 2 CMLR 238). The case of *Francovich* v *Italian Republic* cases C 6 and

9/90 [1993] 2 CMLR 66, in which it was established that a Member State becomes liable for its breaches of Community law to those who can show harm as a result of the breach where an identifiable right has been infringed, and should then compensate accordingly, placed further emphasis on the place of remedies in the Community legal order. It should be noted that art. 81(3) has only had direct effect since 1 May 2004 by virtue of the entry into force of Regulation 1/2003. This reflects a fundamental shift in enforcement of the article. Prior to this date art. 81(1) had direct effect as did art. 81(2), but the Commission had exclusive competence to apply art. 81(3). The effect of this was that neither national courts nor national competition authorities could rule on the application of the article in its entirety. Where a complainant or a defendant relied on art. 81(1), e.g., to avoid a contractual obligation, the national court would be able to rule only on this part of the article, and would either have to ask the party relying on the contract to refer it to the Commission for a decision, which could take a considerable period of time, or in the alternative seek to avoid any discussion of the competition law aspects of the case. One of the thrusts of the modernization programme has been to facilitate the application of EC competition law by the national courts by removing this practical obstacle to the effective administration of justice.

The most important early case in the United Kingdom dealing with these issues in relation to competition law is that of *Garden Cottage Foods Ltd* v *Milk Marketing Board* [1983] 2 All ER 770, HL. The plaintiff was a distributor of butter sold in bulk that obtained its supplies from the defendant, and then made a profit by distributing the butter to purchasers elsewhere in the Community. The plaintiff, over the relevant period, made 90 per cent of its purchases from the defendant, and made 95 per cent of its sales to a single Dutch company. In March 1982, the defendant, which was a statutory body and undeniably in possession of a dominant position in the market in England and Wales, announced a new sales policy. The effect of this was that it would in the future sell bulk butter to only four companies, which did not include the plaintiff. The result of this decision was that the plaintiff would in the future be required to pay more for any butter that it obtained. The substance of the case revolved around the issue of whether an injunction would be granted to restrain the defendant from altering its selling practices. At the Court of Appeal an injunction had been granted ([1982] 3 All ER 292, CA) and this decision was reversed by the House of Lords. What was important in this case was not the approach of the Court to the granting of an injunction in competition cases, although that is a matter of note, but the *obiter dictum* of Lord Diplock relating to the duty imposed by art. 82. His Lordship, first referring to the judgment of the ECJ in *BRT* v *SABAM*, suggested that

The rights which the article confers on citizens in the United Kingdom accordingly fall within section 2(1) of the [European Communities Act 1972]. They are without further enactment to be given legal effect in the United Kingdom and enforced accordingly.

A breach of the duty imposed by article [82] not to abuse a dominant position in the Common Market or in a substantial part of it can thus be categorised in English law as a breach of statutory duty that is imposed not only for the purpose of promoting the general economic prosperity of the Common Market but also for the benefit of private individuals in whom loss or damage is caused by a breach of that duty.

If this categorisation be correct, and I can see none other that would be capable of giving rise to a civil cause of action in English private law on the part of a private individual who sustained loss or damage by reason of a breach of a directly applicable provision of the EEC Treaty, the nature of the cause of action cannot, in my view, be affected by the fact that the legislative provision by which the duty is imposed takes the negative form of a prohibition of particular kinds of conduct rather than the positive form of an obligation to do particular acts.   (pp. 775–6)

This is now generally accepted as the correct position, although there has been inevitable debate about the characterization of the right of action as being one for breach of statutory duty. In practice this pigeon-holing of the action, which is a consequence of the dualist approach taken by the United Kingdom to international law, is of little significance, and the route taken to obtain a Community-derived remedy is less important than the fact that the remedy is available.

There have been only a very few cases in the EC in which damages have been awarded to a complainant alleging harm as a result of a breach of EC competition law, and as of May 2004 none had been reported in the UK. The most substantial of these cases was determined before the Swedish Court of Appeal in *Scandinavian Airlines System* v *Swedish Board of Civil Aviation* (unreported), also known as the Arlanda Terminal 2 case. In this case SAS was obliged to pay for an expansion of the main Stockholm airport's new terminal 2, although after using the terminal SAS found that it was not appropriate for its needs and it pulled out. Following a general change to the operation of the airport system in Sweden SAS had been charged a landing tariff at the terminal, in addition to its contribution to the building costs. The essence of SAS's case was that the dual charges, which it uniquely faced, amounted to price discrimination and was in breach of art. 82(c). On appeal the claim was upheld and SAS was awarded very substantial damages, in the sum of nearly €100m. For a thorough review of this case see Pettersson, T., and Alwall, J., 'Discriminatory pricing: comments on a Swedish case' [2003] ECLR 295, and Bernitz, U., 'The Arlanda Terminal 2 Case: substantial damages for breach of article 82' [2003–2004] *Comp Law* 195.

A substantial case was launched in the UK in 2003 following an infringement decision made by the EC Commission in relation to an illegal cartel operating in the vitamins market (*Vitamins* 2003/2 (2003) OJ L6/1). The claimant alleged that it had suffered loss as a result of the operation of the cartel, and sought damages on that basis. An early attempt to have the case rejected was unsuccessful (*Provimi Ltd* v *Aventis Animal Nutrition SA and others* [2003] All ER (D) 59 (May)). See further Furse, M., '*Provimi* v *Aventis*: Damages and jurisdiction' [2003] *Comp Law* 119.

There are difficulties in pursuing cases in national courts. One of these is that the courts in the UK have shown themselves to be generally reluctant to deal with the economic issues that competition law raises (see Chapter 21 for the approach taken by the courts under common law) and have little expertise in this area. Another is that the courts are understandably reluctant to contribute to a multiplicity of actions. In *MTV Europe* v *BMG Records (UK) Ltd* ((1995) 17 July, CA (unreported)) the plaintiff was seeking damages for an alleged breach of arts 81 and 82 and was at the same time pressing a complaint before the EC Commission. The defendant succeeded in persuading the Court of Appeal to confirm the decision of the judge at first instance delaying proceedings at least until the Commission had considered the matter.

The advantages of bringing private actions directly before the national courts are set out by the Commission in its *Guidelines on co-operation between the Commission and the National Courts*. At para. 10 the Commission notes that national courts must work in a way which is compatible with Community law and that case law of the ECJ has accumulated according to which

(a) where there is an infringement of Community law, national law must provide for sanctions which are effective, proportionate and dissuasive;

(b) where the infringement of Community law causes harm to an individual, the latter should under certain conditions be able to ask the national court for damages;

(c) the rules on procedures and sanctions which national courts apply to enforce Community law
   • must not make such enforcement excessively difficult or practically impossible (the principle of effectiveness) and they
   • must not be less favourable than the rules applicable to the enforcement of equivalent national law (the principle of equivalence).

National courts faced with a dispute relating to the application of either art. 81 or art. 82, or both, may turn to the Commission for assistance in accordance with Regulation 1/2003, art. 15. Article 15(1) provides that in relevant proceedings national courts may 'ask the Commission to transmit to them information in its possession or its opinion on questions concerning the application of Community competition rules'. Further, national competition authorities may, on their own initiative, submit to courts dealing with such disputes written observations, and with the permission of the court may make oral representations (art. 15(3)). The Commission may also, 'where the coherent application of art. 81 or art. 82 of the Treaty so requires' submit written observations to the courts of Member States.

National courts ruling on directly effective Community law may also have recourse to the art. 234 EC procedure. This provides a formal link between any court or tribunal in a Member State and the ECJ:

The Court of Justice shall have jurisdiction to give preliminary rulings concerning:

(a) the interpretation of this Treaty;

(b) the validity and interpretation of acts of the institutions of the Community.

Where such a question is raised before any court or tribunal of a Member State, that court or tribunal may, if it considers that a decision on the question is necessary to enable it to give judgment, request the Court of Justice to give a ruling thereon.

Where any such question is raised in a case pending before a court or tribunal of a Member State against whose decisions there is no judicial remedy under national law, that court or tribunal shall bring the matter before the Court of Justice.

The article, the purpose of which is to restrict the scope for divergence in the application of EC law by national courts and to facilitate the availability of Community law rights, does not serve as an appeal process—questions must be asked in the abstract and the answers provided by the ECJ are unlikely to be such as to determine the outcome of the case on the facts. The jurisdiction of the CFI does not extend to art. 234 references (art. 225(1)), all references being made directly to the ECJ. Domestic courts have shown themselves to be willing to make references in competition cases. Article 10 EC would be applicable were they reluctant to do so; the courts, being emanations of the state to which the duties of art. 10 are addressed, are equally bound to cooperate in the application of Community law.

A problem that is particularly noticeable in domestic law is that established case law makes it difficult to obtain injunctions in relation to competition law matters. The criteria for the granting of injunctions set out in *American Cyanimid Co.* v *Ethicon Ltd* [1975] AC 396, HL, mean, *inter alia*, that injunctions will not be granted where damages are an adequate remedy. This was clearly a problem for the plaintiff in *Garden Cottage Foods*.

Throughout proceedings in national courts the general principle is that it is national procedures which apply, and remedies and sanctions are generally matters for national law. Although there have been calls for the Commission to introduce a directive on remedies, thus ensuring some consistency across the EC, and a reduction in 'forum shopping', this has been resisted. However, national courts are, in some circumstances, under an obligation to adapt national procedures to fulfil EC obligations. In particular, national rules which prevent a complainant obtaining a remedy in appropriate circumstances might have to be set aside as a result of the requirement to effectively apply Community law.

7.3 United Kingdom law

7.3.1 The Competition Act 1998

Third-party rights under the Competition Act 1998 are intended to mirror those available under arts 81 and 82 EC. The Enterprise Act 2002 further reinforced these rights, and introduced some new procedures designed to facilitate the bringing of private claims.

7.3.1.1 Third-party involvement in public enforcement

There are some provisions in the Act that allow for specific consideration of third-party interests. Chief of these is s. 35, which provides that the OFT may impose interim measures if 'it is necessary for him to act under this section as a matter of urgency for the purpose:—(a) of preventing serious, irreparable damage to a particular person'. Generally the involvement of third parties in the Act's procedures will be limited to that of making representations to the OFT complaining about anti-competitive conduct, and the circumstances in which third parties may be involved in the proceedings are restricted.

Section 47, which was amended by the Enterprise Act 2002, s. 17, provides the main procedure under which third parties may appeal against decisions of the OFT. As originally written the section provided that appeals were to the OFT itself, whereas they are now made directly to the CAT. This followed criticisms made of the original appeal process by the then CCAT in the case of *IIB* (*The Institute of Independent Insurance Brokers* v *The Director General of Fair Trading* [2001] CompAR 62, at para. 270). The operative requirement is that a person may appeal under this provision 'only if the Tribunal considers that he has a sufficient interest in the decision with respect to which the appeal is made' (s. 47(2)). There is no definition provided of what constitutes 'a sufficient interest', and this remains to be worked out through case law. However, it does appear to be the case that *locus standi* here is likely to be wider than is the case in respect of the operation of art. 230 EC.

The decisions that may be challenged by third parties are those falling within s. 47, and include those, as to whether the Chapter I or II Prohibitions or arts 81 and 82 EC have been infringed, and decisions to make, or not make, directions.

Those who can appeal to the CAT are those whom the CAT finds to have 'a sufficient interest in the decision with respect to which the appeal is made' (s. 47(2)).

There have been a number of cases in which the OFT has objected to appeals against its decisions on the grounds that it had not, in fact, made a decision capable of being appealed. The matter first arose for consideration in the case of *Bettercare*. Here correspondence had passed between Bettercare and the OFT relating to a complaint made by the undertaking. The OFT closed the file and refused to reopen the matter when requested to do so by Bettercare. On appeal the OFT argued that it had not made a decision within the meaning of the Competition Act 1998. The CAT found, however, that in the absence of any definition of 'decision' in the Act itself it had to look at the 'question of substance, not form' (*Bettercare Group Ltd* v *The Director General of Fair Trading* [2002] CompAR 226). The CAT found that the OFT had, in reaching the view that the entity complained of was not an undertaking, made a decision to the effect that the Chapter II Prohibition had not been infringed. Similarly in *Freeserve.com plc* v *Director General of Telecommunications* [2003] CompAR 1 the CAT found that that correspondence between Oftel and the complainant constituted a decision capable of being appealed. The relevant law was summed up in the case of *Claymore Dairies Ltd and Express Dairies Plc* v *Director General of Fair Trading* [2004] CompAR 1 at para. 122. The CAT here drew a distinction between a situation in which the OFT had merely exercised administrative discretion, and one in which it had made a decision as to the existence or otherwise of an infringement. The test, the CAT said, is that of whether the OFT has genuinely abstained from expressing a view, one way or the other, even by implication, on the question whether there has been an infringement. A related issue arose in the case of *Pernod-Ricard SA and Campbell Distillers Ltd* v *OFT* [2004] CompAR 181.

In this case the OFT had initiated an action against the Bacardi Group following the receipt of a complaint relating to its selling practices. Following the making of certain assurances by Bacardi the action was terminated. The complainant argued a decision had been taken, although the matter was not resolved by the CAT.

In the case of *Aquavitae (UK) Limited* v *The Director General of Water Services* [2004] CompAR 117 the CAT exceptionally found that a closure of a file by Ofwat did not constitute a decision capable of being appealed. In that case the applicant had expressly stated to Ofwat at the time the action was initiated that it was not making a complaint under the Competition Act 1998.

7.3.1.2 *Claims for damages before the CAT*

Claims for damages brought by those injured by anti-competitive conduct falling within the Act may be brought generally before the courts (see 7.3.1.3), or by an alternative procedure under s. 47A of the Competition Act 1998, which was inserted into the Act by s. 18 of the Enterprise Act 2002. This section applies to 'any claim for damages' or 'any other claim for a sum of money' brought by any person 'who has suffered loss or damage as a result of the infringement of a relevant prohibition' (s. 47(A)(1)). Claims under this head may be made directly before the CAT with the claimant relying upon the fact that a breach of either arts 81 or 82 EC, or the Chapter I or II Prohibitions of the Competition Act, has been established by a relevant authority, and either that an appeal has been unsuccessful, or that there has been no appeal within the time limit set for this. In such a case the sole task of the CAT will be to establish that harm has occurred, is caused by the breach identified in the infringement decision, and the amount of the harm. Although it is not made clear in any of the relevant guidelines it is likely that general principles of EC law mean that decisions made by other national authorities in other Member States in relation to arts 81 and 82 EC may also be invoked and relied upon in the appropriate circumstances before the CAT.

In the White Paper, *A World Class Competition Regime* (Cm. 5233, July 2001), which presaged the Enterprise Act 2002, the Government set out a proposal to facilitate claims where a number of consumers had been harmed by the effect of anti-competitive action:

The Government wishes to take specific steps to facilitate damages actions on behalf of consumers. Often such cases will involve a large number of harmed parties—each of whom may only have suffered relatively small loss. In such cases, it is much more sensible that claims are brought on behalf of those that suffer by representative consumer bodies.

Section 47B of the Competition Act 1998 makes provision for representative claims to be brought before the CAT on behalf of a number of consumers by designated bodies. This option is only available in respect of goods or services received 'otherwise than in the course of a business' (s. 47B(7)) and hence is limited to consumers rather than intermediate businesses harmed by upstream conduct. The consumers must be specified in the claim, although it is possible for claims initiated by the consumers already to be consolidated into a representative claim. In the event that damages are awarded these will be to 'the individual concerned' (s. 47B(6)), although the CAT may, 'with the consent of the specified body and the individual, order that the sum awarded must be paid to the specified body'. As of May 2004 no such claims had been launched.

7.3.1.3 *Private actions in the courts*

As originally written the Competition Act 1998 did not make specific references to third-party actions in the civil courts, although during the debate on the passage of the Act Lord Simon confirmed that 'it is true that third parties have rights to seek damages in the courts as a result of actions there' (Hansard (HL) 17 November 1997, col. 456). Section 58 of the Act, however, makes oblique reference to third-party actions, in providing that factual findings of the OFT are, in most situations, binding in proceedings brought otherwise than by the OFT. Section 60 of the Act, which requires domestic law to be interpreted and applied consistently with EC law, includes a specific reference to 'civil liability of an undertaking for harm caused by its infringement of Community law'.

The Enterprise Act 2002 inserted a new s. 58A into the Competition Act 1998, making clearer the link between public enforcement and private rights. This now makes express the fact that there may be proceedings before the courts in which damages may be claimed. In any such proceedings any court is bound by decisions of the OFT or the CAT to the effect that relevant provisions of the Competition Act 1998 have been infringed. There is no reference in this section to claims other than those brought for damages or other monetary relief, and on the face of it therefore appears not to apply to claims for other forms of relief, such as injunctions, or specific performance. However, as s. 58 applies to all claims, it may be that s. 58A will likewise do so, or that in the alternative it does little more than make clear the effect of s. 58.

As of May 2004 a number of private actions had been reported under the Act, and none of these was an unqualified success for the complainant. The first reported case was brought on the basis of an alleged breach of the Chapter II Prohibition (*Claritas (UK) Ltd* v *The Post Office and Postal Preference Service Ltd* [2001] UKCLR 2). This was unsuccessful when the Court found that the alleged abuse had not taken place on a 'relevant market for the purposes of s. 18' and dismissed the application. However, the OFT later found that there was a relevant market, and stressed that 'in order to establish an infringement of the Chapter II Prohibition it is not necessary to show an abuse on the market which an undertaking dominates' (*Consignia plc and Postal Preference Service Limited* CA98/4/2001 [2001] UKCLR 846—following *Tetra Pak International SA* v *EC Commission* case C–333/94P [1997] 4 CMLR 662).

In *Synstar Computer Services (UK) Ltd* v *ICL (Sorbus) Ltd and International Computers Ltd* [2001] UKCLR 585 there was an allegation that a software maintenance contract system maintained by the defendant was in breach of both the Chapter I

Prohibition and the Chapter II Prohibition. The complainant had also made a complaint to the OFT, and the Court stayed the proceedings pending the outcome of the OFT investigation which it was considered likely would be appealed to the CAT. All parties in the case recognized that the CAT was better equipped to deal with the sensitive issues, and in particular market definition, which this case was likely to revolve around. The OFT subsequently made a finding that there had been no breach of the Act, and no appeal was made to the CAT (*ICL/Synstar* CA98/6/2001 [2001] UKCLR 902).

More substantial arguments were developed in *Hendry and others* v *The World Professional Billiards and Snooker Association Ltd* [2002] UKCLR 5. Here the claimants were snooker players and a company incorporated for the purpose of exploiting the Internet in relation to snooker. They argued that World Professional Billiards and Snooker Association (WPBSA) rules were in breach of both the Act's prohibitions. The Court found that Rule A5 of the WPBSA rules was in breach and was void. Rule A5 provided in part that 'members shall not enter or play in any snooker tournament, event or match without the prior written consent of the Board'. The Court found that this may not have been intended to restrict competition, but that its effect was to do so, by limiting the sources of income to which players could have access. Damages sought by the claimants were not awarded, however, as the bulk of the claim was dismissed.

In a number of cases injunctions have been sought, although there have been no reported cases in which final injunctions have been granted. The first reported case in which an interim injunction was granted was *Network Multimedia Television LTd (t/a Silicon.Com)* v *Jobserve Ltd* [2001] UKCLR 814. In this case the claimant successfully argued that the defendant had acted in breach of the Chapter II Prohibition when it refused to accept job advertisements from clients who had also advertised with the claimant. It was held 'without hesitation, that there is a serious issue to be tried in relation to the alleged abuse' (at para. 88). An appeal was dismissed (*Jobserve Ltd* v *Network Multimedia Television* [2001] UKCLR 184) on the grounds that there was a complex and serious matter to be tried. Not all claims have been as successful as this. In *Getmapping plc* v *Ordnance Survey* [2002] UKCLR 410, an application for interlocutory relief was rejected by Laddie J on the grounds that the claimant had no credible case. Here the claimant had sought to argue that Ordnance Survey had abused its dominant position when setting specifications for certain mapping services, which resulted in the exclusion of the claimant. In *Suretrack Rail Services Ltd* v *Infraco JNP Ltd* [2002] EWHC 1316 Laddie J held that

applications for interlocutory relief, whether mandatory or prohibitory, should not be seen as means by which a court can be persuaded to grant relief on the basis of a claim to rights which it is fairly confident would not be upheld at the trial. The more confident it is that the claimant will fail at the trial, the less likely it is that an interlocutory injunction will be appropriate. (para. 14)

7.3.2 **Super-complaints**

Sections 11 and 205 of the Enterprise Act make provision for 'super-complaints'. Section 11 applies in situations where 'a designated consumer body makes a complaint to the OFT that any feature, or combination of features, of a market in the United Kingdom for goods or services is or appears to be significantly harming the interests of consumers'. The OFT has published guidance to assist super-complainants (*Super-complaints: Guidance for designated consumer bodies*, July 2003). It is for the Secretary of State to designate a body as a super-complainant, and the DTI has issued guidance for those who aspire to this status. Super-complaints do not lead to a specific outcome, but rather give the OFT, or other appropriate concurrent regulator, the chance to evaluate a situation and determine what action, if any, is appropriate. This process is explained in para. 2.4 of the OFT guidance:

The super-complaint process is intended to be a fast-track system for designated consumer bodies to bring to the attention of the OFT and the Regulators, market features that appear to be significantly harming the interests of consumers. When deciding whether or not to make a super-complaint, careful thought should be given as to whether the super-complaint process is the most effective route. It may be that specific competition or consumer legislation would provide a more immediate and/or effective means of satisfying and addressing the issue. For example when the feature of a market that is, or appears to be, significantly harming the interests of consumers relates to single firm conduct.

Super-complaints are required to be dealt with within a strict timetable, and the OFT or regulator will keep the super-complainant informed of the proceedings. As of May 2004 the OFT had considered four super-complaints, relating to: private dentistry, as a result of which a consumer information campaign was launched by the OFT; doorstep selling, which the OFT then examined as a market study; mail consolidation, which was then examined by the concurrent regulator Postcomm; and care homes, following an 'informal super-complaint' made by the Consumers' Association. In the latter case the OFT launched a market study into the area.

7.3.3 **The Enterprise Act 2002**

Certain third-party rights are also available in relation to concluded market investigation references which have resulted in the imposition of orders, or the acceptance of undertakings, or in relation to the merger control process in the UK. These are considered further in the relevant chapters below.

8

An introduction to the economics of
agreements, collusion, and parallel conduct

8.1 Introduction

Multi-firm conduct is often a more difficult phenomenon to analyse and to identify than is single firm or monopoly conduct. It is dealt with in this book ahead of unilateral conduct because that is the order in which the EC Treaty deals with them. At the most general level the point is simply made: if a single firm can damage the market and produce unwelcome welfare effects, then so too can a group of firms which act together *as if* they were a single firm. This is known as the 'cartel', or 'cartelization'. The difficulty inherent in the economic analysis of multilateral conduct has meant that the legal response in the EC and UK is to attack such situations either where observed market conduct is indicative of anti-competitive behaviour, or where physical evidence, such as documents and communications, shows that firms have attempted, even if unsuccessfully, to coordinate conduct. Legislation in this area usually makes reference to 'agreements, decisions, or concerted practices' between firms. In practice the distinction is often not made, and in this chapter the word 'agreement' is taken to apply to all three situations. The economic analysis here would apply equally to the cartel offence of the Enterprise Act 2002, although the way the offence is structured removes the need to engage in sensitive economic analysis.

8.2 Horizontal restraints

The issue of horizontal agreements, which is to say agreements between firms at the same level of production or distribution, will in most cases be of concern to authorities, as the inevitable tendency of such agreements is to approximate the circumstances of monopolistic competition, and such agreements will be often proscribed. Thus in America one of the long-standing rules of antitrust is that price fixing is to be condemned per se, and is not brought within the 'rule of reason' (*United States* v *Trans-Missouri Freight Association* 166 US 290 (1897)). Even where the ostensible purpose of such agreements is apparently benign, such as to agree standards or to harmonize technology, the underlying purpose may in fact be anti-competitive. The attainment of monopoly pricing by a cartel is likely to be accompanied by more deleterious effects than in the case of a true monopoly; a group of smaller firms is unlikely to have attained the efficiencies of production that flow from a monopolist's economies of scale. Cartels and collusion are discussed in Bishop, S., and Walker, M., *The Economics of EC Competition Law*, London, Sweet & Maxwell (2nd edn, 2002) (hereinafter *The Economics of EC Competition Law*), paras 5.07–5.31.

8.2.1 The problem of oligopoly

In atomistic markets where there are a great number of competitors, agreements between firms operating at the same level of production are unlikely to be of concern to competition authorities (although note that in *Vereniging van Samenwerkende Prijsregelende Organisaties in de Bouwnijverheid (SPO)* v *Commission* case T–29/92 [1995] ECR–II 289 an investigation into the Dutch building industry involved thousands of undertakings). Much effort would be required to put an agreement in place, and in the absence of a mechanism to punish firms that broke the agreement—which would be illegal under almost all regimes—cheating would be inevitable. The more concentrated the market is, the more likely it is that the firms will be able successfully to agree to dampen or restrict competition. An oligopolistic market is one in which only a few firms compete, or in which a few firms hold the bulk of the market power, albeit with numbers of smaller competitors at the periphery (banking, petrol, etc.). It is in these markets, where business managers may be unable to resist 'a bit of corporate nookie' (Lord Lucas, Hansard (HL) 30 October 1997, col. 1161), that competition concerns arise most readily. A problem for any authority or complainant becomes that of distinguishing between conduct which is based on agreements, whether formal or informal, and conduct which is the result of each firm responding rationally to the actions of the others. For example, if petrol prices generally rise by the same margin within a short time, is that because the companies have agreed to raise their prices together, or because once one company does so it makes sense for the others to follow suit? The MMC has consistently held that the petrol market in the UK is competitive, in spite of public concerns to the contrary (see, e.g., Cm. 972, *The Supply of Petrol* (1990)).

It was early suggested by the economist Cournot, in 1838, that, even assuming *independent decisions* made by oligopolists, prices in such markets would be higher than in perfectly competitive markets, and such markets can achieve what is now referred to as a 'Nash–Cournot equilibrium'. Distinguishing between the anticipated higher price of oligopolistic industry and 'artificially' maintained higher prices is one of the central problems facing competition authorities.

8.2.2 **Cartels**

A cartel may be defined as 'an explicit arrangement designed to eliminate competition' (Kaserman, D. L., and Mayo, J. H., *Government and Business: The economics of antitrust and regulation*, Fort Worth, The Dryden Press (1995), p. 152). Cartels are attractive to participants: if the cartel succeeds, total profits to the participants will be higher than would be the sum of individual profits in what would otherwise be a competitive market. A perfect cartel would be one in which the group as a whole set production where marginal cost for the group equalled marginal revenue, which is to say that the cartel would collectively behave exactly like a single-firm monopoly. In practice such perfection will be unobtainable.

For the EC Commission the danger of cartels is that they

generate situation rents for the most powerful companies since they need not make an effort either to improve the quality of their products or to improve productivity. At the same time, however, cartels artificially keep the least efficient companies in the market, weaken the productive apparatus and thus inflict considerable damage on the economy in general and eventually also on EU jobs.   (IP (98) 1068, 3 December 1998 [1999] 4 CMLR 13)

The example of a cartel that is most often used in economics texts is that of the Organization of Petroleum Exporting Countries (OPEC), which continues to have a strong influence on the world market in oil. Even here, in a situation in which the participants, being sovereign nations, are not subject to the rigours of national antitrust laws, the cartel is unable to raise prices to the level that would have been obtained under a monopoly situation. The challenge for antitrust enforcement with respect to cartels is to exacerbate the inherent weaknesses in order either to make membership so unattractive as to force the abandonment of the cartel, or to minimize the effects of the anti-competitive arrangements.

There are two major problems that economists have identified as facing any cartel: these may be characterized as the problems of 'agreement' and 'adherence'. In the mid-1950s emphasis was placed on the difficulties cartel members would have in agreeing on matters of fundamental policy, such as the correct response to make to a new entrant, or the trade-off between short- and long-term profits. One researcher identified a cartel where prices had not changed for 10 years, in spite of rising costs, because the two largest members which were able to block any changes preferred to maintain low prices to keep new entrants out of the market (Fog, B., 'How are Cartel Prices Determined?' (1956) 5 *Journal of Industrial Economics* 16). There are several factors that make it difficult for cartels to reach agreement. For example, product differentiation will require cartel members to agree on what may be a very complex price schedule, rather than a single price. This is a problem for OPEC, as oil is not a homogeneous product but is produced at different grades with different sulphur contents. Differences in the costs facing firms in the industry will also make agreement harder: larger firms in the cartel, which are more likely to benefit from economies of scale, may want lower prices than the smaller firms, and it may become difficult to put into place arrangements acceptable to all to limit production.

Once the agreement problem is overcome, the second, more significant, problem relates to adherence. The problem facing cartels is as follows:

If a cartel is successful in restricting its joint output and raising price, it creates an incentive for individual member firms to cheat, expand their outputs, and undermine the cartel. A *single* firm will always profit by cheating on the cartel. But *all* firms have this same incentive, and if all firms expand their output, the cartel breaks down. On this reasoning, cartels are inherently unstable. (Martin, S., *Industrial Economics: Economic Analysis and Public Policy*, London, Macmillan (2nd edn, 1994), p. 162)

The position may be explained by reference to game theory, on which most cartel/ oligopoly models are now based. Game theory, which was developed by John von Neumann and Oskar Morgenstern (*Theory of Games and Economic Behaviour*, Princeton, Princeton UP (1944)), is, at its most elaborate, incredibly complex, but a simple demonstration will show how the problem may be addressed. A branch of game theory deals with the 'Prisoner's Dilemma' which can be related to the behaviour of two competing oligopolists. Consider the following situation: Joan and Graham rob an off-licence; they are arrested by Colin, who is convinced of their guilt but does not have the evidence to obtain a conviction unless he can obtain a confession. Colin does have the evidence to obtain convictions on a lesser charge of dangerous driving, and if convicted of this offence both the prisoners will go to prison for one year. If either one of the prisoners confesses and is prepared to testify against the other, that prisoner will receive no gaol term at all and the other will go to prison for 10 years. If both prisoners confess each will go to prison for five years. The prisoners are held separately in the police station and do not have the opportunity to coordinate their conduct. The resulting strategic position therefore looks like this:

		Joan's strategies	
		Don't confess	Confess
Graham's strategies	Don't confess	–1, –1	–10, 0
	Confess	0, –10	–5, –5

(For example, if Graham does not confess, and Joan does, Graham faces 10 years in prison, and Joan none.)

In this position the combined welfare of the parties dictates that neither should confess, and both will go to prison for one year. The incentive for each of the parties to break the fraternal criminal bond and grass on the other is strong, but of course if both do this then each faces a longer prison sentence than if each had remained silent. Only if the two prisoners can exchange information during the process, and are prepared to forgo some short-term benefit in order to improve their collective position, can it be assured that the outcome will be optimal to the two. If two companies are substituted for Joan and Graham, and profit figures for the prison sentences, the game becomes applicable to a two-firm cartel situation.

Finding physical, documentary evidence of the existence of cartels is a difficult matter. Baroness O'Caithan drew attention in the Lords to a case resolved by the Restrictive Practices Court (RPC) under the old UK regime:

The paint-makers' price fixing cartel, which was ended by an undertaking to the [RPC] in early June [1997] had been going on for years. It was quite obvious that the companies involved knew exactly what they were doing and knew it was illegal. Why else would they have used assumed names to book hotel conference facilities? (Hansard (HL) October 30 1997, col. 1167)

Given the difficulties of establishing the existence of cartels, a tactic employed by most authorities is to implement measures designed to destabilize cartels, which find their expression in leniency programmes.

Analysis of the instability of cartels is based largely on pioneering work done by George J. Stigler ('A Theory of Oligopoly' (1964) 72 *Journal of Political Economy* 44). Stigler focused on the fact that much of the conduct in a cartel will be furtive, and that a poor flow of information will mean that strategic activity is carried out largely on the basis of conjecture and guesswork. A price-cutting firm is unlikely to announce the fact, and published prices may reflect no change at all. Instead any price cuts are likely to be agreed discreetly with customers. In a cartel situation firms will in any case be facing a reduced demand as price rises with the implementation of the cartel, and it will be difficult for firms to determine if demand reductions are the result of this inevitable process or the cheating of other members. Firms will also be used to a variation in sales, and only if the reduction is below their expectations may they suspect cheating. Stigler's results show that the greater the number of firms in the cartel, the greater is the likelihood of cheating being able to go undetected. On the other hand, if firms are able to pool their information the probability of detection of any cheating rises dramatically. It is then clear that one of the tasks of competition policy is to make such information exchange risky, and in most regimes the availability of hard physical evidence of cartelization is likely to bring swift condemnation.

The prediction that there is an inverse relationship between numbers in cartels and the likely success of cartels is a logical one. In a cartel with 15 members there is a total of 105 paired relationships between members. This rises to 190 relationships in a cartel of 20 members, and 1,225 in a cartel with 50 members (formally the number of paired relationships is given by $N(N-1)/2$). Only if a central control mechanism, normally through a trade association or perhaps via the appointment of a specific cartel management team (as was the case in *Pre-Insulated Pipe Cartel* 1999/60 (1999) OJ L24/1), can be established are larger cartels ever likely to be successful. The activities of trade associations tend to be closely scrutinized by competition authorities. A survey of antitrust actions against cartels taken in the United States found that where only a few firms were involved, and the market conditions were relatively uncomplicated, there were few instances of formally structured collusion. In 606 cases studied the average number of participants was just under 17, and as the number of participants in each case increased, so too did the complexity of the arrangements that were put in place to facilitate the success of the cartel (Fraas, A. G. and Greer, D. F., 'Market Structure and Price Collusion: An Empirical Analysis' (1977) 26 *Journal of Industrial Economics* 21).

8.2.3 Price leadership

It can be difficult to distinguish between cartels in which prices are maintained across a range of producers or suppliers, and other situations in which price leadership is present. Markham distinguished three categories of price leadership, none of which is likely to be condemned by competition authorities without further evidence of actual collusion (Markham, J. W., 'The Nature and Significance of Price Leadership' (1951) 41 *American Economic Review* 891).

Dominant firm leadership occurs where in any market one firm is sufficiently large in relation to other producers to be the only one capable of significantly affecting the market. In such a case the dominant firm is likely to set prices as if it were a monopolist, and the smaller firms will have little to gain from diverging much from this price. Competition law will accept such situations, and does not require firms to price at what would be irrational levels in order to maintain a fiction of vigorous price competition.

Barometric price leadership is more complex, and is a characteristic of markets in which the price leader changes frequently, and in which the response to any change in price tends to be less swift than in the situation where there is a single dominant firm. Whether a price will be followed will depend not on the identity of the company setting the price, but on whether the change, even if set by a small company, reflects a generally perceived need in the market for a price adjustment. This was considered to be the case by the EC Commission in *Zinc producer group* 84/405 (1984) OJ L220/27.

The third situation, which poses the greatest problem for competition law, arises in markets where the product is homogenous, and where there are few producers facing similar costs. Here any one firm would accurately reflect the situation facing each firm, and it is likely that any one firm choosing to adopt a price leadership role would be followed. Conditions similar to these may be found in the United Kingdom in the banking and petrol industries, although the position in the petrol market is changing following the entrance into the market of supermarket chains.

In *Industrial Market Structure and Economic Performance*, Frederic Scherer and David Ross set out some interesting case studies of price leadership (Boston, Houghton Mifflin (3rd edn, 1990), pp. 250–60).

8.3 Vertical restraints

In the case of most goods, and some services, there is a chain of production before the product reaches the consumer. Typically this will extend from the gathering of the raw material, and its first processing, to the retailer with whom the customer deals. Thus, for example, in the case of the motor industry the vertical chain begins with steel and plastics manufacturers, through the various stages of production of components and the cars themselves, to distributors and individual retailers. A vertical agreement is one between firms at different stages of the chain of production, and it will be immediately apparent that this is an essential and pervasive feature of commercial life. In the absence of vertical agreements the raw material would not arrive at the manufacturer's plant, and the finished car would not end up on a garage forecourt. A vertical agreement is to some extent a substitute for vertical integration. It was a matter of some surprise, therefore, when the EEC Commission, as it then was, attacked an agreement between a manufacturer and a distributor as being anti-competitive in a very early competition decision (*Re Grundig* 64/556/EEC [1964] 1 CMLR 489; on appeal *Establissements Consten SARL and Grundig-Verkaufs-GmbH* v *Commission* cases 56 and 58/64 [1966] CMLR 418; see further discussion of this case in the following chapter). Concerns as to the effects of vertical restraints have also underpinned several inquiries in the UK, including, for example, that into *Foreign Package Holidays*, completed in 1997. The question whether vertical restraints are anti-competitive remains a matter of debate, with the Chicago school in the 1980s arguing broadly that any and all vertical restraints should be legal, although the authors of the Commission Green Paper (below) note that a consensus is emerging, with economists being reluctant to generalize in what is a difficult area. In 1996 the OFT published its 12th Research Paper 'Vertical Restraints in Competition Policy' (Dobson, P. W., and Waterson, M.; and see also Bond, C., 'Vertical Restraints' (1997) *Fair Trading*, Summer, p. 7), and in early 1997 the EC Commission published its *Green Paper on Vertical Restraints in EC Competition Policy* (COM(96) 721 final).

Broadly, the argument made in favour of examining vertical restraints is that while they may encourage inter-brand competition, for example competition between Nissan and Toyota cars, they may restrict intra-brand competition, for example competition between two sellers of Nissan cars.

If vertical restraints or agreements are to be considered a problem, the analysis must take into account situations in which firms at the lower level of the chain, nearer consumers, exercise power over firms higher up the chain. Thus the OFT report recognizes that retailers hold increasing power in setting the contract terms on which they will deal with suppliers, and suggests that competition concerns may be raised where either party in the chain is in possession of market power. The threefold consideration put forward in the report is as follows:

(a) Is there horizontal market power at either the level of manufacturer or the level of retailer?

(b) Is the consumer likely to be significantly affected by the restriction?

(c) Is the result of the restriction to generate efficiency gains?

If the answer to (a) is in the affirmative then consideration of (b) and (c) may allow a determination of whether the restriction is against the public interest. Even if the answer to (b) and (c) would be in the affirmative, the authors conclude that in the absence of horizontal market power there is unlikely to be any benefit from conducting further examination of the practice for anti-competitive effects.

It is a common assumption that vertical restraints are necessarily imposed to benefit the party higher up the chain of production, but this is not always the case. One of the strongest forms of vertical restraint is resale price maintenance (RPM), under which resellers are restricted in their ability to set prices. Usually the manufacturer or supplier specifies a minimum price below which the reseller may not sell the product. It is not easy to create scenarios in which this operates to the benefit of the supplier, and the immediate beneficiary tends to be the retailer. These sorts of restraints therefore may be requested by retailers, and are a particularly effective way to ensure that cheating is minimized in price-fixing cartels. It is perhaps in response to this possibility that, until the Competition Act 1998, the taking of any steps to enforce RPM was the only activity condemned per se in the UK regime. Chicagoan economists have argued that this supposition cannot be correct as there will be too much competition at the retail level to allow the retailers to impose conditions on those supplying to them. This conclusion is probably wrong, and it has been pointed out by Porter that retailers tend to operate in oligopolistic markets because they are dependent in turn on the ability of local customers to travel to them (Porter, M. E., *Interbrand Choice, Strategy, and Bilateral Market Power*, Cambridge Mass, Harvard UP (1976)).

Vertical restraints are discussed in *The Economics of EC Competition Law*, paras 5.32–5.56.

9

Article 81 EC

1. The following shall be prohibited as incompatible with the common market: all agreements between undertakings, decisions by associations of undertakings and concerted practices which may affect trade between Member States and which have as their object or effect the prevention, restriction or distortion of competition within the common market, and in particular those which:

   (a) directly or indirectly fix purchase or selling prices or any other trading conditions;

   (b) limit or control production, markets, technical development, or investment;

   (c) share markets or sources of supply;

   (d) apply dissimilar conditions to equivalent transactions with other trading parties, thereby placing them at a competitive disadvantage;

   (e) make the conclusion of contracts subject to acceptance by the other parties of supplementary obligations which, by their nature or according to commercial usage, have no connection with the subject of such contracts.

2. Any agreements or decisions prohibited pursuant to this Article shall be automatically void.

3. The provisions of paragraph 1 may, however, be declared inapplicable in the case of:

   — any agreement or category of agreements between undertakings;

   — any decision or category of decisions by associations of undertakings;

   — any concerted practice or category of concerted practices;

   which contributes to improving the production or distribution of goods or to promoting technical or economic progress, while allowing consumers a fair share of the resulting benefit, and which does not:

   (a) impose on the undertakings concerned restrictions which are not indispensable to the attainment of these objectives;

   (b) afford such undertakings the possibility of eliminating competition in respect of a substantial part of the products in question.

9.1 Introduction

Article 81 is intended to apply to any agreed coordinated conduct, howsoever structured, between two or more undertakings, and is more concerned with the economic impact of a practice than with its legal form. In *La Technique Minière* v

Maschinenbau Ulm GmbH case 56/65 [1966] 1 CMLR 357, the ECJ held that the condemnation of any restrictive practice will depend 'not so much on its legal nature as on its relations, on the one hand, with "trade between the Member States" and, on the other, with "the play of competition"' (p. 374). Recognizing that the ingenuity of undertakings to devise new ways of structuring or describing arrangements between them knows no bounds, the choice of words is deliberately as wide as possible, and the phrase 'all agreements between undertakings, decisions by associations of undertakings and concerted practices' should be interpreted as extending to almost all multilateral coordinated conduct (see below). Although the article applies to any formally drafted contract, it applies equally to situations where undertakings act in concert with each other by informal means. It is this aspect in particular that makes the application of the article fraught with problems. As we have seen in Chapter 8, in oligopolistic markets it has proven very difficult to distinguish between conduct which is collusive and conduct which is the natural result of the market structure. In this chapter the word 'agreement' is used to apply to all three of these heads unless the discussion is specifically about 'decisions' or 'concerted practices'.

Further problems arise because the prohibition of art. 81(1), which is sufficiently precise as to be directly effective, applies to a great number of contracts entered into by undertakings, and on the face of it would proscribe more beneficial than harmful economic conduct. Many steps have therefore been taken to limit the application of art. 81(1) only to those situations where the conduct identified is harmful, or likely to be harmful: under art. 81(3) agreements may be exempted (or 'excepted') on an individual case-by-case basis (see below) or en bloc (see Chapter 10) where the relevant criteria are fulfilled, and the ECJ has established that the article does not apply unless the harm caused by the agreement is substantial. The situation thus approximates to, but is not the same as, that in the United States where the 'rule of reason' has been developed to limit the scope of the application of s. 1 of the Sherman Act (see 9.7 below).

In this chapter the general principles covering art. 81 will be considered; the specific block exemption regulations will be examined in the next chapter. It is easiest to approach the article by analysing each of its parts, and then by considering its operation as a whole. For the meaning of 'undertaking', see Chapter 2.

9.2 Article 81(1): the prohibition

It is immediately apparent that the effect of art. 81 is to make conduct falling within its ambit illegal, and the article may be relied upon by injured competitors. Undertakings in breach are liable to be fined by the Commission, and many of the largest fines handed out have been to those engaged in illicit cartels (see Chapter 6, and 9.3.2.1). As noted in the introduction to this chapter, the article is drafted so as to apply to any form of multilateral anti-competitive conduct, and 'has been interpreted so broadly and formalistically that any restriction on the freedom to act has been deemed to fall under the prohibition, irrespective of its impact on competition' (Amato, G., in *Robert Schuman Centre Annual on European Competition Law 1996*, p. 126). The Commission does not always distinguish between the various forms that a breach of the article may take, and indeed in some cases has expressly refused to do so. In *Cartonboard* 94/601 (1994) OJ L74/21, for example, the Commission said that it did not consider it 'necessary, particularly in the case of a complex infringement of long duration, for the Commission to characterise it as exclusively an agreement or concerted practice. Indeed, it may not even be feasible or realistic to make any such distinction' (para. 128) (decision upheld on appeal in *Cascades SA* v *Commission* case T–308/94 [2002] 4 CMLR 33 and *Stora Kopparbergs Bergslags AB* v *Commission* case T–354/94 [2002] 4 CMLR 34, although some penalties were reduced). However, the approach taken to evidence of the breach, particularly by the courts, and perhaps to the penalty, may depend on the form that the proscribed conduct takes.

9.2.1 Agreement between undertakings

That any contract between two undertakings may be held to fall within art. 81 is clear, and many distribution, franchise, and service agreements have been examined, modified, and at times condemned. However, 'agreement' does not require that a formal contract be in place, or indeed that any more than one party behaves in a certain manner. The primary requirement of this part of art. 81(1) is that at least two parties must be involved. The article cannot in any circumstance be applied to entirely unilateral conduct. See, for example, *Bayer AG* v *Commission* case T–41/96 [2001] 4 CMLR 4, discussed at 9.3.1.3, and see 9.2.6.

In *Polypropylene* 86/398 (1986) OJ L230/1, for example, the Commission found that the producers of polypropylene had been party 'to a whole complex of schemes, arrangements and measures decided in the framework of a system of regular meetings and continuous contact' (para. 80). Although the parties contended that no agreement was in place, the Commission held that it was not necessary for it to establish the presence of an agreement 'intended as legally binding upon the parties'. In the Commission's view an agreement exists wherever there is the necessary consensus between the parties 'determining the lines of their mutual action or abstention from action in the market', and it was certainly not necessary for the agreement to be made in writing. This point was emphasized in *National Panasonic* 82/853 (1982) OJ L354/28, where National Panasonic UK somehow managed to operate a dealership system throughout the UK without the benefit of written agreements. The company did not dispute that an agreement existed, and in fact had provided the Commission with evidence of the terms and conditions that it expected dealers to comply with if they were to be admitted into the network.

It has been stressed already that art. 81 cannot apply to unilateral conduct, which may be addressed only if art. 82 is applicable, but there are situations in which it appears as if only one party may be acting. In *Johnson & Johnson* 80/1283 (1980) OJ L377/16, the Commission investigated a situation in which the undertaking and its subsidiaries, including Ortho UK, acted to prevent the export from the UK to Germany of pregnancy-testing kits. In January 1977 Ortho had changed the contracts of sale that applied between it and its dealers so as ostensibly to permit the export of the testing kits within the EC. However, on investigation the Commission found that the company had acted unilaterally in making threats to dealers to withhold supplies, or to delay supplies, if the dealers in fact made exports even within the Community. While it is possible that this conduct could have been attacked under art. 82, the Commission chose to proceed under art. 81 and found that although the action was apparently unilateral the dealers all knew what the position was and that in effect the contracts of sale 'were still, therefore, subject to prohibitions of exports, which prohibitions formed an integral part of agreements within the meaning of art. [81(1)]' (para. 28).

9.2.2 Decisions by associations of undertakings

It is standard practice in many industries for those in the industry to belong to an association that acts on behalf of its member companies. Such actions might include industry-wide promotional campaigns, public education, market research, standards setting, and perhaps even charitable functions on behalf of workers in the industry. These associations may also act as a front for collusive activity: a unilateral statement from the association as to, for example, the desirability of price stability might be followed by action by all its members, each of them denying that they have in any way colluded with the others.

A classic example of such a situation arose in *Roofing felt* 86/399 (1986) OJ L232/15, where the action taken related primarily to the Cooperative Association of Belgian Asphalters (Belasco) which represented seven members in the industry. The members had collaborated in drawing up an agreement, initially valid for five years but thereafter renewable, which provided for, *inter alia*: bans on bribes to induce customers to choose a particular supplier; joint advertising; and the studying of ways of standardizing and rationalizing the production and distribution of roofing felt. While all of these are laudable aims, and by themselves would have been unlikely to attract the attention of the EC Commission, further objectives set out in the agreement included: the adoption of a price list and minimum prices for all roofing felt supplied in Belgium; the allocation of quotas between members; and penalties for breaches of decisions made under the agreement, which taken together would fall within the prohibition set out in art. 81(1). Although the Commission was able to establish the presence of agreements between the individual members of Belasco, and some outside parties, it pointed too to the role played by Belasco, which it found 'was involved in a number of ways in the operation of the agreement'. In particular, it was Belasco which had managed the quota system, unilaterally employing an accountant for the purpose and administering the compliance mechanism.

Where an association of undertakings is found to exist the steps that it takes do not have to be binding on its members to fall within art. 81(1). If this were to be a requirement avoidance would be all too easy. In *Fire insurance* 85/75 (1985) OJ L35/20 (on appeal *Verband der Sachversicherer eV* v *EC Commission* case 45/85 [1988] 4 CMLR 264) for example, an association of undertakings was found to exist, but argued in its defence that the 'recommendation' it had made was expressly described as 'non-binding'. However, the Commission was not persuaded to this view and made its position clear:

In spite of the fact, therefore, that the title of the recommendation describes it as being 'non-binding', the recommendation was in the nature of a 'decision' by an association of undertakings within the meaning of Article [81]. It is sufficient for this purpose that the recommendation was brought to the notice of members as a statement of the association's policy. (para. 23 of the Decision)

Here the association's objective was to represent, promote, and protect the business interests of insurers providing industrial fire insurance in Germany. Following a long period during which insurance premiums in the sector had fallen, although there had been no apparent reduction in the risks being insured or their costs, a recommendation, described as 'non-binding', laid down a collective flat rate and an across-the-board rise in premiums. By its decision taken in 1984 the Commission rejected an application for negative clearance and the association appealed. The Court, taking into account the nature of the recommendation, noted that shortly after it was made the members of the association altered their contracts of reinsurance so as to comply with the recommendation. The statutes of the association gave it the power to coordinate the activities of its members, particularly in relation to competition, and decisions or recommendations taken by a special committee set up under it were deemed to be 'definitive'. In view of these facts the Court held that the recommendation 'regardless of what its precise legal status may be, constituted the faithful reflection of the applicant's resolve to coordinate the conduct of its members . . . it must therefore be concluded that it amounts to a decision of an association of undertakings' (para. 32).

This case was followed by the EC Commission in *Fenex* 96/438 (1996) OJ L181/28, in which action was taken against an association of undertakings in the freight market in The Netherlands. The association had, for nearly 100 years, issued 'recommendations' to its members relating to various scales of charges. In its defence the association argued that the recommendations were non-binding and were therefore not 'decisions' within the meaning of art. 81. The Commission noted that: the system had been in existence for a long time; the recommendation was drawn up and updated annually by a specialist body within the association; the recommendation would then be adopted by the board of directors of the association; and it would be published accompanied by a circular drafted in strong terms, such as, for example, 'in view of the result arrived at members are *urgently recommended* to pass on the above mentioned tariff increase [5 per cent] in full' (at para. 38, emphasis added). In the light of these facts the Commission held that 'the recommendation must be interpreted as being the faithful reflection of the association's resolve to coordinate the conduct of its members on the relevant market' (para. 41).

Consistently the Court has expressed concern that the rules governing trade associations should not be more than is necessary to achieve the *legitimate* objectives of that association. The fact that this was not the case was important in *Gottrup-Klim Grovvareforeninger* v *Dansk Landbrugs Grovvarelskab* case C–250/92 [1996] 4 CMLR 191. Here an association existed that had as its task facilitating cooperative purchasing of supplies, and the Court held that 'in order to escape the prohibition laid down in Article [81(1)] of the Treaty, the restrictions imposed on members by the statutes [of the association] must be limited to what is necessary [to ensure the legitimate aims of the association]'. There will even be situations in which the rules of a trade association may be such as to make the creation of the association, or membership of it, a breach of art. 81(1) without the need for the Commission to consider the actual operation of the association in practice. This appears to have been the case in *National Sulphuric Acid Association* 80/917 (1980) OJ L260/24, where the Commission indicated that the terms of the association in question were automatically such as to breach art. 81(1) (paras 29–36).

9.2.3 Concerted practices

Concerted practice is the most nebulous of the three categories and covers a wide range of conduct, ranging from a situation in which an agreement appears to exist but is difficult to establish evidentially, to the very difficult situations in which the conduct that is observable in the market diverges from that which would be expected so as to suggest that firms are in some degree colluding. In an American antitrust case it was pointed out that 'the picture of conspiracy as a meeting by twilight of a trio of sinister persons with pointed hats close together belongs to a darker age' (*William Goldman Theatres Inc.* v *Loew's Inc* 150 F2d 738, 743n. 15 (3rd Cir 1945)) and the modern-day enforcers of competition policy are confronted with companies using a full range of practices by which to coordinate their behaviour, whether by way of conventions held in luxury hotels, unrecorded telephone calls and e-mails, or apparently innocent market announcements in the press.

The first significant case in which the ECJ dealt with concerted practices was *ICI* v *Commission*, '*Dyestuffs*', case 48/69 [1972] CMLR 557, in which it upheld a Commission decision where the undertakings were condemned on the basis of evidence of collusion in the setting of prices. The definition of concerted practice applied in that case was approved and expanded on in the next important case, *Suiker Unie* (*Coöperatieve Vereniging 'Suiker Unie' UA* v *Commission* cases 40–48/73, 50/73, 54–56/73, 111/73, 113–114/73 [1976] 1 CMLR 295), when the Court held that

The concept of a 'concerted practice' refers to a form of coordination between undertakings which, without having been taken to the stage where an agreement properly so-called has been concluded, knowingly substitutes for the risks of competition cooperation in practice between them which leads to conditions of competition which do not correspond to the normal conditions of the market, having regard to the nature of the products, the importance and number of the undertakings as well as the size and nature of the said market. Such cooperation in practice amounts to a concerted practice *inter alia* when it enables the persons concerned to consolidate established positions to the detriment of effective freedom of movement of the products in the Common Market and of the freedom of consumers to choose their suppliers.   (paras 26–7 of the judgment)

The difficulties of establishing the existence of such a situation are compounded in particular where the market is an oligopolistic one, in which case a degree of similarity of conduct is to be expected: if it is appropriate for one producer to raise its prices it is quite probably appropriate for all to do so. In such a situation it is not the fact that prices have risen at the same time, by possibly the same level, that will induce condemnation under art. 81(1). The task of the Commission is to show that this has been achieved by other than the operation of normal market forces—it is the method, and not the result, that is being condemned. This is made clear by the Court in the *Dyestuffs* case:

while it is permissible for each manufacturer to change his prices freely and to take into account for this purpose the behaviour, present and foreseeable, of his competitors, it is, on the other hand, contrary to the competition rules of the Treaty for a manufacturer to co-operate with his competitors, in whatever manner, to determine a coordinated course of action relating to an increase in prices.   (para. 118)

It is exceptionally difficult to distinguish between situations in which an under-taking acts *intelligently* in response to another's conduct (which is quite lawful), and acts *with knowledge* of another's conduct (which may be in breach of art. 81(1)). In *Cimenteries CBR SA v Commission* joined cases T 25–26/95, etc. [2000] 5 CMLR 204 (in summary only) the CFI explained that

The concept of concerted practice implies the existence of reciprocal contacts. That condition is met where one competitor discloses its future intentions or conduct on the market to another when the latter requests it or, at the very least, accepts it. Thus, failure by an applicant to object to or express reservations where a competitor reveals its position regarding the relevant market will deny the former the defence of being a purely passive recipient of information unilaterally passed on without any request on the part of the applicant.   (para. 1849)

A similar stance was taken in *Tate & Lyle plc, British Sugar plc and Napier Brown plc v Commission* joined cases T–202/98, etc. [2001] 5 CMLR 22 where the Court held that an undertaking would be implicated in the existence of a concerted practice where it attended a meeting whose purpose was limited 'to the mere receipt of information concerning the future conduct of their market competitors' (para. 58). This would apply even where that information could be obtained through legitimate channels by the undertakings.

In *Zinc producer group* 84/405 (1984) OJ L220/27, the Commission investigated coordination in the market for zinc under an agreement that extended from 1964 to 1977. When the agreement ended in 1977 the market structure meant that there was no one firm that could break ranks and set its own prices independently of the rest of the market. In such a situation, known as 'barometric price leadership' (see Chapter 8), undertakings do not have true economic independence but, in law, are not acting in a concerted fashion where all companies set the same prices. The Commission was careful to isolate this position from that which existed between 1964 and 1977, and did not condemn the undertakings in relation to subsequent conduct, notwithstanding the similarity in behaviour (paras 75–6).

There are, in essence, two ways in which the Commission may attempt to establish the existence of collusive conduct. The first, and most satisfactory, is to collect the physical evidence that supports such a conclusion. Records of meetings, copies of letters, statements by company personnel, and evidence presented by customers may all provide the necessary evidence. Although such evidence may often lead to the conclusion that an agreement is in place it may fall short of the required formality but still be indicative of collusion. An alternative, and more difficult, route is for the Commission to base a case on the analysis of the market in question, arguing that there is a divergence between the conduct that would be predicted under competitive conditions and the conduct observed, and that the only explanation for such a divergence is that the relevant undertakings are colluding. This was the way in which the Commission proceeded in its decision in relation to *Wood pulp* 85/202 (1985) OJ L85/1 (on appeal *Re Wood Pulp Cartel: A Ahlström Oy* v *Commission* cases C 89, 104, 114, 116, 117, and 125–129/85 [1993] 4 CMLR 407; note that at [1988] 4 CMLR 901 the issue of territorial jurisdiction was dealt with—see Chapter 4.

In *Wood pulp* the Commission took action against 43 undertakings producing bleached sulphate pulp, used in the manufacture of fine quality paper, based in both the Community and other producing states, including Canada and the United States. Worldwide about 800 companies produced bleached wood pulp, with over 50 firms selling into the Community. There were a large number of customers based in the Community, and one firm alone supplied about 290 different paper manufacturers. Producers announced prices in advance for the following quarter-year. Such announcements were highly visible and were reported in the specialist trade press, and were likely to be followed quickly by similar announcements from competitors. Over a number of years prices in the Community rose steadily, irrespective of the fact that over some of this period the stocks of pulp held by producers were increasing, and that production costs varied. Prices were also constant irrespective of the source of the product, when it might have been expected that imports from Canada and the United States would be more expensive than those from Scandinavia. The core of the Commission's argument was that

The fact that the addressees of this Decision have coordinated their market conduct contrary to Article [81(1)] of the EEC Treaty is proved by:

— their parallel conduct in the years 1975 to 1981 which, in the light of the conditions obtaining on the market in question and following a proper economic analysis, cannot be explained as independently chosen parallel conduct in a narrow oligopolistic situation . . .

Given the particular competitive conditions obtaining on the pulp market, such uniform market behaviour can be explained only by a concerted practice on the part of the addresses of this Decision.   (paras 82–3)

The factors that the Commission considered to be determinative of the issue included the following:

- the presence on the market of 50 producers and several hundred customers;
- the fact that some of these producers were large enough to pursue an independent competitive policy;
- the wide range of products offered the potential for the introduction of price competition;
- the deliberate creation of a transparent market by the system of early announcements of prices;
- the fact that prices rose evenly and uniformly, with none of the divergences that would be expected were the firms moving independently towards a new equilibrium price;
- the uniform approach to prices could not be explained by the presence of a single market leader, as no company held this position;
- the absence of any explanation of the rapid spread of price information across products, companies, and countries;
- coincidence was ruled out; and
- prices bore little relationship to fluctuations in costs.

Following the imposition of fines, and the negotiation of an undertaking with which the Commission would be satisfied, several of the companies appealed to the ECJ. The Court's rejection of the Commission's main arguments was robust. The question whether the mere system of price announcements denounced by the Commission could itself constitute an infringement of art. 81(1) was rejected by the Court. The stance taken by the Court was that each individual price announcement was made by a producer to a consumer or consumers, and not to other producers. This being so, no one announcement would 'lessen each undertaking's uncertainty as to the future attitude of its competitors' (para. 64 of the judgment). There was, the Court suggested, no guarantee that any one price announcement would be followed by that undertaking's competitors. In fact the announcement could result in a competitor taking the opportunity to announce a lower, more competitive price. The fact that 'the Commission [had] no documents which directly establish the existence of concertation between the producers concerned' meant that the Court took a rigorous approach to the conclusion reached by the Commission. The key paragraphs in the judgment are as follows:

In determining the probative value of those different factors, it must be noted that *parallel conduct cannot be regarded as furnishing proof of concertation unless concertation constitutes the only plausible explanation for such conduct.* It is necessary to bear in mind that, although Article [81]

EEC prohibits any form of collusion which distorts competition, it does not deprive economic operators of the right to adapt themselves intelligently to the existing and anticipated conduct of their competitors . . .

Accordingly it is necessary in this case to ascertain whether the parallel conduct alleged by the Commission cannot, taking account of the nature of the products, the size and the number of the undertakings and the volume of the market in question, be explained otherwise than by concertation.   (paras 71–2, emphasis added)

Unusually in this case the Court commissioned its own expert report into the characteristics of the market in question. The experts' conclusions differed from those of the Commission; in particular the experts pointed out that the system of price announcements had been requested by customers, rather than being imposed by producers. This, the experts said, was the result of the cyclical nature of the market, and the fact that producers of paper wanted to know as soon as possible what the biggest constituent cost of their end product was going to be. The fact that the response to price announcements was almost simultaneous was explained by the applicants as being the result not of concertation, but of the highly transparent nature of a market in which both producers and customers were sophisticated and well informed. This analysis too was supported by the Court's experts. In a second report requested by the Court the experts concluded that the parallelism in prices could also be explained by the natural structure of the market. Following these analyses the response of the ECJ was to accept that 'in this case, concertation is not the only plausible explanation for the parallel conduct' (para. 126).

In annulling this decision the Court has made it difficult for the Commission to proceed against collusive practices. Although it is likely that in the majority of cases the Commission will be able to find physical evidence of collusion, there are likely to be some situations where the Commission is unable to do so. In such cases it is still going to have to fall back on economic analysis. The level of economic debate and evidence brought in the *Wood pulp* case takes it beyond the expertise of lawyers and into the realms of pure industrial economists. Given the differences of approaches to this subject it is likely that in many cases alleged wrongdoers will be able to commission a reputable economist to produce an argument that runs counter to that brought forward by the Commission. Only if the Commission is able to anticipate each and every possible argument will it be able to build a case that will, if *Wood pulp* is followed, satisfy the ECJ.

The more recent action in the *Ferry operators—currency surcharge* decision (97/84 (1997) OJ L26/23) hints at the range of approaches that the Commission may now take. Here various operators of ferry services between the UK and continental Europe imposed surcharges on customers who had paid in sterling following the 17 per cent fall in the value of the pound in September 1992. The additional charges, which were designed to protect the operators from the full impact of the devaluation of the currency, were levied at the same amount, and their imposition took effect at the same time and was announced in identical terms. The Commission both indicated that this was not a plausible result in light of the fact that the operators faced very different cost structures dependent upon their size and management systems, and also relied on evidence and admissions of collusion collected in the course of an investigation.

Concerted practices may be distinguished from naked cartels (or 'hard-core' cartels), where there is an explicit agreement between undertakings. In practice, however, the link is blurred as evidence of the agreement may be difficult to obtain. Cartels are discussed below at 9.3.2.1.

9.2.4 Peripheral involvement in restrictive conduct

The fact that an undertaking has only a peripheral role in any breach of art. 81, and is not a driving force in the illegal conduct, is not a defence to any action brought under the article. However, if fines are imposed on the offending undertakings these may be less for those undertakings that have played a less significant role in the activity. Thus, for example, in the *Polypropylene* decision (86/398 (1986) OJ L230/1) the Commission drew a distinction between the four largest producers which between them 'formed the nucleus of the arrangements and constituted an unofficial directorate' and other members that had played a less prominent role. However, the fact that Shell 'did not attend the plenary sessions', or that Hercules 'did not communicate its own detailed sales figures to other producers' was in neither case considered to be a mitigating factor in assessing the existence of a breach by those undertakings.

The strictness of this approach was even more evident in *LdPE* 89/191 (1989) OJ L74/21, which again related to a cartel operating in the plastics market. The decision related to 17 undertakings, but three, BP, Shell, and Monsanto, required 'special examination'. None of these undertakings took a central role in the cartel, and the Commission acknowledged that, at worst, their participation could be considered 'only a partial one'. As the Commission recognized, 'mere knowledge of the existence of a cartel does not constitute involvement in the infringement'. Neither would it constitute an infringement to have knowledge of a cartel's existence and to base one's own conduct on the basis of that knowledge. This was the argument made by BP and Shell, which both argued that documents obtained by the Commission that showed they were aware of impending price rises and planned their own rises in the light of that knowledge were simply the result of their making use of 'legitimate market intelligence' or other published sources (para. 32). The three companies were all allocated quotas by the cartel, but argued that this was unconnected with them and simply the result of the cartel opti-mistically setting quotas for all the producers in the industry. It is clear from the terms of the decision that the Commission found these arguments persuasive, but the Commission had established that the undertakings had attended at least some of the meetings of the cartel. 'In the absence of any evidence of attendance at meetings or other contacts the Commission might well have given these three undertakings the benefit of the doubt' (para. 33), but even the minimal contact that could be shown was considered to be sufficient to establish the applicability of art. 81(1) to those undertakings. The fines that the undertakings were required to pay, however, were far less than those meted out to the other participants: BP, for example, was fined €750,000, compared to Bayer AG's fine of €2.5 million.

9.2.5 'Object or effect'

It should be apparent from the wording of the article that an agreement may be condemned if it has *either* the object *or* the effect of preventing, restricting, or distorting competition. It would be an unusual position were undertakings to be allowed to conspire, ineffectually, to breach the law and be condemned only were they successful. In *La Technique Minière* v *Maschinenbau Ulm GmbH* case 56/65 [1966] 1 CMLR 357, the Court examined a distribution agreement between a German producer of industrial earth-levellers and a French distributor. Following a disagreement between the parties La Technique Minière had asked the Cour d'Appel in Paris to declare the contract void on the grounds that it breached art. 81(1). Maschinenbau Ulm argued that the agreement did not partition the market and did not therefore fall within the prohibition. As this case arose under art. 234 EC the Court was not being asked to resolve the issue, but in its answers to the Cour d'Appel the Court indicated that

these [criteria] are not cumulative but alternative conditions, indicated by the conjunction 'or', suggest[ing] first the need to consider the very object of the agreement, in the light of the economic context in which it is to be applied. . . . Where, however, an analysis of the said clauses does not reveal a sufficient degree of harmfulness with regard to competition, examination should then be made of the effects of the agreement.   (p. 375)

That the Commission is willing to bring actions against cartels even where they are not entirely successful is demonstrated by, *inter alia*, *Polypropylene* 86/398 (1986) OJ L230/1. During the course of investigations into the market for bulk thermoplastic polypropylene throughout the Community, the Commission uncovered substantial documentary evidence of 'an institutionalised system of meetings between representatives of the producers at both senior and technical managerial levels' (para. 1). At these meetings, 'the producers developed a system of annual volume control to share out the available market between themselves according to agreed percentage or tonnage targets, and regularly set target prices' (para. 1). The appendices attached to the decision, listing meeting dates and venues, show the extent to which the Commission may be able to obtain irrefutable evidence of attempts to coordinate activity. Such conduct is a classic example of cartelization, where producers seek collectively to limit supplies, raise prices, and monitor observance of the agreement to alleviate the risk of its collapsing through strategic cheating on the part of the cartel members. As the Commission put it:

By planning common action on price initiatives with target prices for each grade and national currency effective from an agreed date, the producers aimed to eliminate the risks which would be involved in any unilateral attempt to increase prices. The various quota systems and other mechanisms designed to accommodate the divergent interests of the established producers and newcomers all had as their ultimate objective the creation of artificial conditions of 'stability' favourable to price rises.   (para. 89)

In fact the agreement was not as successful as the participants had hoped. The price level achieved in the market generally lagged some way behind the targets set at the meetings, and the price initiatives often ran out of steam, occasionally resulting in a sharp drop in prices. Over the period in question the industry was characterized by substantial over-capacity, and in such circumstances the temptation on the part of the cartel members to cheat would have been hard to resist. Faced with the evidence garnered by the Commission some of the producers in fact appeared to rely on their own cheating as a defence, pointing to sometimes substantial discrepancies between the delivery targets they had been set and the actual deliveries they had made. In one particular year, 1980, the targets for tonnage deliveries had to be revised continually. Some of the alleged participants pointed also to the fact that market shares had changed substantially over the relevant period, a fact that they said was evidence of 'unrestricted' competition. The Commission rebutted most of these arguments. It argued that while there had been price instability this was usually arrested by a revision of the targets and agreements, and that further falls which would have benefited consumers were thus prevented. That market shares had changed had been envisaged under the targets which had taken into account the ambitions of some of the newer entrants into the market. However, as the Commission also made clear, art. 81(1) would have been applicable notwithstanding failures in the cartelization of the market:

> The fact that in practice the cartelisation of the market was incomplete and did not entirely exclude the operation of competitive forces does not preclude application of article [81]. Given the large number of producers, their divergent commercial interests and the absence of any enforceable measures of constraint in the event of non-compliance by a producer with agreed arrangements, no cartel could control totally the activities of their participants. (para. 92)

The 15 identified participants in the cartel were fined a total of €5,785,000.

A similar position was reached in *Ferry operators—currency surcharge* 97/84 (1997) OJ L26/23 (discussed above) where the fact that the operators found it extremely difficult actually to impose the charge that they had agreed to levy did not serve to exonerate them from the fact that they had, in breach of art. 81, colluded to impose the charge.

Even in the case of a concerted practice the ECJ has indicated that it would be possible for a breach of art. 81(1) to flow from the mere contact preliminary to a concerted practice (see for example *Huls v Commission* case C–199/92P [1999] 5 CMLR 1016 at para. 163). While this does not seem an intuitive position it must be remembered that even in the case of a concerted practice some form of coordination, other than mere intelligent reflection, is called for.

9.2.6 **Unilateral conduct**

For the prohibition of art. 81(1) to be invoked there must be multilateral conduct. Unilateral conduct will be condemned under EC competition law only where it falls within art. 82. However, there are situations in which it may appear at first sight that art. 81 has been applied to unilateral conduct. Such a situation arose in *AEG-Telefunken* v *Commission* case 107/82 [1984] 3 CMLR 325, in which the undertaking contested a Commission decision (82/267 (1982) OJ L117/15) on the grounds that there had been no other undertakings involved in the condemned conduct. AEG had maintained a selective distribution system and refused to supply certain distributors which met the criteria laid down by AEG but which had a reputation for price cutting—AEG itself described its strategy as a 'high price policy'. It appeared from the wording of the decision that AEG was indeed the only offending party, and the decision was addressed only to it. However, when the undertaking appealed, the conclusion reached by the ECJ was that the refusals to supply, which had been endemic, were an integral part of the operation of the distribution system, and involved all the members of that system, who stood to benefit from the refusals. In effect, the ECJ found that the nexus of interest between AEG and its distributors was such that it was implicit in the agreements between AEG and each of the distributors that AEG would refuse to supply price-cutters. There have been other cases since where the Commission has pursued a similar line, notably *Sandoz* 87/409 (1987) OJ L222/28 and *Vichy* 91/153 (1991) OJ L75/57 (see also Lidgard, H. H., 'Unilateral Refusal to Supply: an Agreement in Disguise?' [1997] *ECLR* 352). In two more recent cases the Commission failed to persuade the CFI that it had correctly found multilateral conduct in situations in which a producer either reduced quantities available for parallel trade, or issued a circular asking retailers to adhere to certain prices (*Bayer AG* v *Commission* case T–41/96 [2001] 4 CMLR 4 and *Volkswagen AG* v *Commission* case T–208/01 [2004] 4 CMLR 14).

9.3 The prevention, restriction, or distortion of competition: the application of article 81(1)

An agreement between two or more undertakings will not be caught within art. 81(1) where it does not prevent, restrict, or distort competition.

There is a substantial and vibrant debate about the way in which the Commission has applied this part of art. 81(1). It is clear that not all clauses within agreements prevent, restrict, or distort competition, and that there are situations in which agreements, even at the horizontal level, are incapable of having such an effect, or the only distortion of competition may be a beneficial one (see in particular the *Guidelines on the Applicability of Article 81 to Horizontal Cooperation Agreements*, 2000, at para. 3). The debate is similar to that surrounding the application of the rule of reason in American antitrust law which is referred to at the end of this chapter.

In one of the leading cases in this respect, *Gottrup-Klim* v *Dansk Landbrugs Grovvareselskab* case C–250/92 [1994] ECR I-5641, the ECJ held that the extent to which clauses in contracts were compatible with EC competition law could not be assessed 'in the abstract', but depended on both their content, and the 'economic conditions prevailing on the markets concerned'. In this case the ECJ ruled that it was not necessarily anti-competitive for a cooperative association to include a rule which prohibited members from also joining other cooperatives. The Court found that membership of competing cooperatives could impinge upon the proper operation of the cooperative, and its contractual arrangements. Accordingly, the term in question could potentially 'have beneficial effects on competition' (paras 31 to 34).

In its *Guidelines on Vertical Restraints*, the Commission sets out the factors that are important in determining whether a vertical agreement falls within art. 81(1) (see para. 121, and the subsequent discussion in paras 123–33). These are:

(a) market position of the supplier;

(b) market position of competitors;

(c) market position of the buyer;

(d) entry barriers;

(e) maturity of the market;

(f) level of trade;

(g) nature of the product; or

(h) other factors.

In *European Night Services* v *Commission* joined cases T–374/94, etc. [1998] ECR II-3141 the matter was expressed this way:

in assessing an agreement under [art. 81] account should be taken of the actual conditions in which it functions, in particular the economic context in which the undertakings operate, the products or services covered by the agreement and the actual structure of the market concerned unless it is an agreement containing obvious restrictions of competition such as price-fixing, market-sharing or the control of outlets. In the latter case, such restrictions may be weighed against their claimed pro-competitive effects only in the context of [art. 81(3)] of the Treaty, with a view to granting an exemption . . . It must be stressed that the examination of conditions of competition is based not only on existing competition between undertakings already present on the relevant market but also on potential competition, in order to ascertain whether, in the light of the structure of the market and the economic and legal context within which it functions, there are real concrete possibilities for the undertakings concerned to compete among themselves or for a new competitor to penetrate the relevant market and compete with the undertakings already established in it.   (paras 136–7, references omitted)

Much earlier than this the Court in *Remia* v *Commission* case 42/84 [1985] ECR 2545 had held that a clause in an agreement relating to the transfer of a business, under which the seller agreed not to compete with the new owner of the business, would not fall within art. 81. The EC Commission had found that such a clause did fall within the prohibition, and had offered only a limited concession in its application of art. 81(3) (*Nutricia/Zuid—Hollandse Conservenfabriek* 83/670 (1983) OJ L376/22). The Court held on appeal that against the background in which the agreement operated 'non-competition clauses . . . have the merit of ensuring that the transfer has the effect intended. By virtue of that very fact they contribute to the promotion of competition' (para. 19). *Remia* was cited with approval by the Commission in *Glaxo Wellcome* 2001/791 (2001) OJ L302/1, relating to a system designed to restrict the flow of parallel imports of cheap pharmaceutical products from Spain into the more expensive EC Member States. In response to an application for negative clearance, the Commission held *inter alia* that

The Court of Justice (and Court of First Instance) have always qualified agreements containing export bans, dual-pricing systems or other limitations of parallel trade as restricting competition 'by object'. That is to say, prohibited by art. 81(1) without there being any need for an assessment of their actual effects. In principle they are not eligible for exemption pursuant to art. 81(3).

This reference to certain restrictions as being restrictive of competition 'by object' (see also *Volkswagen AG* v *Commission* case T–62/98 [2000] 5 CMLR 853, paras 89 and 178) brings the approach under art. 81(1) close to the US approach to the 'rule of reason' although the EC Commission has stated that such a rule has no place to play in the art. 81 system (see section 9.7).

The principles developed in these cases may also be seen at play in *Visa International* 2001/782 (2001) OJ L293/94 in which the Commission made a decision of negative clearance in respect of the agreement between some 20,000 financial institutions responsible for the operation of the Visa network system. The Commission held that the rules relating to the operation of the agreement were not restrictive of competition. In particular a rule under which a member of the Visa network could not acquire the right to join without issuing cards exploiting the network was not restrictive of competition as it ensured a large card base, thereby making the system as a whole more attractive to merchants (paras 18 and 65). In a later Decision—*Visa International (Multilateral Exchange Fee)* 2002/914 (2002) OJ L318/17—the Commission granted an individual exemption under art. 81(3) in relation to the intra-regional interchange fee scheme of Visa for consumer cards as applied to cross-border point-of-sale Visa card transactions between Member States.

Perhaps the clearest discussion of the state of the law relating to this difficult issue is that given by Advocate General Lenz, in *Union Royale Belge des Societes de Football Association ASBL* v *Jean-Marc Bosman* case C–415/93 [1995] ECR I-4921 at paras 262-9).

Where undertakings operating in different markets, and which are not current competitors, enter into an agreement relating to a third market this *may* fall outside the remit of art. 81(1). This was the case, for example, in *Elopak/Metal Box—Odin* 90/410 (1990) OJ L209/15, where Elopak and Metal Box collaborated in a joint venture to produce a new form of packaging carton for foodstuffs. The Commission held that the joint venture agreement fell outside the terms of art. 81 as the parties were not competitors, and the joint venture company, Odin, would effectively operate as an independent entity. This decision, along with *Konsortium ECR 900* 90/446 (1990) OJ L228/31, is an example of the Commission applying some of the principles of a 1983 policy statement on a 'realistic' approach to competition.

A similar approach was taken in the late 1990s case of *Cegetel* (1999) OJ L218/14 in which the Commission found that a joint venture relating to the provision of a fixed-voice telephony service in France, the founding companies of which were large operators in France, Germany, and the USA, did not fall within art. 81(1). The Commission held that as the parent companies were each unable to enter this market by themselves the existence of the joint venture did not restrict either actual or potential competition.

Generally, however, the Commission will take a broad view of the potential danger of restrictive conduct, and is more likely to find that such situations are encompassed within art. 81(1) but may benefit from an exemption (see, e.g., *KSB/Goulds/Lowara/ITT* 91/38 (1991) OJ L19/25).

9.3.1 Vertical agreements

Article 81(1)(a)–(e) set out some of the classes of restriction to which the article is intended to apply. This list is not intended to be exhaustive, however. The article applies to both inter-brand and intra-brand competition. Inter-brand competition is that *between different brands*, for example, competition between Ford and Nissan motor cars. Intra-brand competition is that *between goods of the same brand*, for example, competition between different retailers of Nissan motor cars. Typically this means that EC competition law is applicable to vertical restraints (see generally Chapter 8), which are often considered to have a pro-competitive effect, the aim being to improve methods of distribution and to make it easier to bring products to the market. This conclusion, which seems to flow obviously from the wording of the prohibition, is one of the most contentious reached in the application of EC competition law and came as a surprise to many when the position was first established. It was driven largely by the fact that one of the underlying imperatives of EC competition law is to facilitate the integration of the national markets. Where vertical restraints obstruct such an integration, by, for example, allocating particular national or regional markets and territories to particular distributors, they are likely to be condemned. The key decision was that in *Etablissements Consten SARL and Grundig-Verkaufs-GmbH* v *Commission* cases 56, 58/64 [1996] 1 CMLR 418, which remains the most important case to be considered under art. 81, and one that demonstrates the application of most aspects of that article. It is therefore discussed here in some detail.

9.3.1.1 *Consten and Grundig*

Grundig-Verkaufs-GmbH was a German manufacturer of consumer electronic goods (radios, tape recorders, television sets, and dictating machines). In April 1957 it entered into an exclusive distribution contract with the French firm Etablissements Consten. Under the terms of this contract Consten was to be Grundig's sole representative in France, the Saar, and Corsica. Consten was required, *inter alia*, to purchase a certain minimum percentage of Grundig's exports into France, to adequately promote Grundig's products, and to provide an adequate after-sales service and maintain supplies of spare parts. Along with these obligations Consten undertook not to sell competing products, and not to make any deliveries, direct or indirect, of its supplies to territories outside its contract area. Similar terms were to be found in the contracts Grundig maintained with its distributors in other European territories, and with the main German wholesalers. Grundig itself was enjoined from supplying, other than through Consten, the relevant goods into Consten's allocated territory. In order to reinforce Consten's exclusive rights it was assigned in France the trade mark GINT (Grundig International), which was carried on all Grundig products. The effect of this was that Consten would be able to bring an action, based on the infringement of its intellectual property rights, against any importer of Grundig's goods into France. Under the terms of the assignment if Consten ceased being Grundig's sole distributor in the relevant territory it was to return the GINT trademark to Grundig. The firm UNEF obtained Grundig products from German distributors in spite of the fact that they were not meant to supply such customers, and sold them into France at prices below those charged by Consten. Consten brought two actions against UNEF in the French courts, one based on the French law of unfair competition, the other for infringement of the GINT trade mark. In 1962 the case was adjourned following an application made by UNEF to the Commission which sought a declaration to the effect that the agreement between Consten and Grundig was in breach of art. 81(1). Grundig notified its agreements with both Consten and its other exclusive distributors to the Commission on 29 January 1963, and sought a decision to the effect that art. 81(1) did not apply to such an agreement, or that if it did the agreement should be exempt by virtue of the application of art. 81(3). By a decision of 23 September 1964 (*Re Grundig's Agreement* 64/566/EEC; the official text is not published in English, but see [1964] CMLR 489) the Commission held that the contracts in question, and the assignment of the trade mark, constituted an infringement of the provisions of art. 81. Both Consten and Grundig brought actions to have the decision annulled. When the cases came before the ECJ the Italian and German governments were admitted as intervening parties, both of them in support of the two firms.

After rehearsing the facts Advocate General Karl Roemer noted that the case had 'taken on unusual proportions because of the economic and legal importance of the problems dealt with and the number of parties involved'. Various technical points made by the applicants were dismissed by the Advocate General, who then dealt in more detail with the more significant arguments about the applicability of art. 81(1) to vertical restraints. Consten had argued that it was incumbent on the Commission to provide a theoretical justification for the position it had taken. Advocate General Roemer roundly dismissed this suggestion, pointing instead to the limited body of case law already decided by the ECJ in the area of restrictive agreements. Following on from the first such case considered by the Court (*Bosch v De Geus* case 13/61 [1962] 1 CMLR 1), he noted that the Court had held that it was not possible in that case to come to a general conclusion about the application of art. 81(1) to a particular class of agreements, and that the task instead was to decide in each particular case whether the article was applicable. It was of no doubt, the

Advocate General said, that 'contracts involving exclusive supply and purchase undertakings can have the effect of limiting competition, especially when they are accompanied by an absolute territorial protection'. Grundig had suggested that the absolute territorial protection afforded under the contract was irrelevant, for even without it the distributor would be the only 'offeror' of the product in question. Clearly this 'argument could not be supported, for it was precisely the presence of other 'offerors', in particular UNEF, that had led to Consten bringing action before the French courts to enforce its territorial claims.

There were, however, points that concerned the Advocate General. In particular he was concerned that the approach of the Commission was apparently to consider only the 'object' of the agreement and not its concrete 'effect'. 'Article [81(1)]' the Advocate General said, 'requires really the comparison of two market situations: that which arises after the conclusion of an agreement and that which would arise in the absence of the agreement'. Such a concrete examination, if undertaken, might lead to the conclusion that an agreement in a particular case 'only has effects which are likely to *promote* competition'. In particular this might be the case, it was suggested, where it would not be possible for a manufacturer to gain a purchase on the market unless it were to do so by way of appointing an exclusive distributor. Thus, the Advocate General opined, 'such an examination might have led to a finding that in the Grundig–Consten case the *suppression* of the sole sales agency would have involved a noticeable reduction in the offer of Grundig products on the French market'. A second argument was made by the German government which the Advocate General felt 'deserves complete approval'. This was that a consideration of the competition between various distributors of Grundig products missed the point, and that any consideration of the market should have as its starting point an analysis of the competition between *similar competing* products. This is the distinction between intra-brand and inter-brand competition that is still a matter of debate. The Advocate General was of the opinion that the Commission was simply 'wrong in taking *exclusive* account of that internal competition . . . and in neglecting completely in its consideration competition with similar products'. Competition, it was suggested, should be judged in this case at the level of the wholesaler, where the dealers were technically competent to distinguish between the different brands of equipment, and to pass on the relevant details to the retailers. In fact, the market share held by Grundig in France in tape recorders and dictating machines was only about 17 per cent. There must therefore have been vigorous competition from other brands of similar, although not identical, products. In the market for televisions and radios it appeared that the competition, particularly from foreign imports, was intense, and there was evidence that the prices charged for Grundig products had been reduced in response to this on several occasions. Taking these factors into account the Advocate General felt that 'the conclusions reached by the Commission in examining the criterion of "interference with competition" should be considered as insufficiently based and consequently should be disregarded'.

The Commission, in considering the requirement that the practice 'may affect trade' (see below), had found it sufficient to demonstrate that 'following an agreement restricting competition the trade between Member States develops in *other* ways than it would have done without the agreement'. It was the Commission's contention that this requirement was merely a 'criterion of competence', but the Advocate General was 'convinced that the very text of 'article [81(1)] prevents justification of that opinion'. His view was that in some of the Treaty's official languages the requirement was that there be an *unfavourable* influence on trade and that it was insufficient merely to demonstrate an influence. In the Advocate General's view it was the suppression of such exclusive arrangements that could have a harmful effect on trade and obstruct the integration of the market, as such steps could in fact reduce the flow of goods between the Member States. These various criticism, he felt, were sufficient to annul the decision. Further arguments merely reinforced this view. Prominent amongst these was the fact that the Commission had found simply that the agreement was in breach of the article. The Advocate General, however, felt that this position led to 'intolerable' legal uncertainty, and that, particularly at such an early stage in the development of the law relating to restrictive agreements, undertakings should be told precisely what *clauses* of the agreement were in breach. This would both lend greater clarity and precision to the Commission's decisions, and also give the undertakings concerned the chance to amend their agreements to bring them into line with Community law without requiring them to lose all the legal benefits flowing from those agreements.

The Advocate General considered also the refusal of the Commission to grant an exemption to the contested agreement under art. 81(3). The Commission had accepted that it might be possible to contend that the agreements contributed to improving production and distribution, but not that consumers received any share in the resulting benefit. This, the Commission had held, would be impossible as long as the agreement conferred absolute territorial protection on Consten. Noting that the German Law against Restraint on Competition, one of the strictest regimes in the Community, took a lenient approach to exclusive distribution agreements, the Advocate General felt that the Commission should do likewise in the application of art. 81(3), because 'as a general rule competition between *similar* products of different producers constitutes a sufficient regulator of the market'. In its application to the Court the Commission had argued that because art. 81(1) provided the *rule*, and art. 81(3) only the *exception*, it fell to the undertakings in particular cases to justify the application of the exemption. This would allow the Commission to adopt a role that was, in the view of the Advocate General, unacceptably passive. Thus it was argued that the role of the Commission was to 'raise questions on its own initiative and make conscientious enquiries together with the undertakings concerned'. Whether the individual criteria for the grant of an exemption had been fulfilled was also a matter of some debate. Although accepting that the agreement could lead to the requisite improvement in production and distribution, the Commission had suggested that the requirement that Consten undertake promotion of the products on behalf of Grundig was a restraint that was unnecessary. The Commission had not, the Advocate General felt, adequately argued this point, and had failed to show that the bearing of this cost by Consten had not resulted in any benefit to the market. For an exemption to be granted consumers are expected to reap some of the benefits of the restrictive agreement along with the undertakings themselves. The Commission had argued that that was not the case here. As the Advocate General noted, this requirement is 'a particularly delicate and difficult criterion to grasp', and found the submission of the German government particularly helpful on this point. This had suggested that it should be sufficient to show that there was lively competition between manufacturers of different products, as 'that guarantees at the same time that the consumers have a fair share in the profit, because [they] should only pay the price which develops on the market under the influence of effective competition'. Pointing to the likelihood that such exclusive dealing arrangements would promote competition the Advocate General suggested that consumers might then be sharing the rewards and, as important to his conclusion, that the Commission had failed to consider this aspect. In conclusion Herr Roemer, supporting the arguments of the applicants and the two interested Member States, argued that the contested decision should be annulled *in toto* and referred back to the Commission for reconsideration.

As is usual in Community case law the judgment is somewhat shorter than the Advocate General's submission (13 pages and 46 pages respectively). On the question of whether art. 81(1) could be applied to vertical restraints, which was a matter that the Italian government had strongly contested, the Court held that

Neither the wording of article [81] nor that of article [82] gives ground for holding that the two articles are limited in effect according to the positions of the contracting parties in the economic process. Article [81] refers in a general way to all agreements which distort competition within the Common Market and does not establish any distinction between those agreements as to whether or not they were made between operators competing at the same stage or between non-competing operators placed at different stages. In principle no distinction should be made where the Treaty does not make any distinction.

The Court was equally dismissive of the arguments made by the Advocate General, the German government, and the parties to the effect that the conferment of absolute territorial protection in a case where there existed competition at the level of the producers need not necessarily be condemned. The Court pointed to the basic objectives of the Treaty: 'The Treaty, whose preamble and text aim at suppressing the barriers between Member States and which in several provisions gives evidence of a stern attitude with regard to their reappearance, could not allow undertakings to restore such barriers'.

The Court further agreed with the Commission that the primary purpose of the requirement that trade between Member States be affected was to allow for jurisdictional competence to be determined. The Commission was not therefore required to show that trade would have been greater had the agreement not been in place. The Court, in holding that 'the fact that an agreement favours an increase, even a large one, in the volume of trade' brings the agreement within art. 81, could not have made the position clearer, nor more roundly rejected the argument of the Advocate General.

On the questions of the benefits of inter-brand over intra-brand competition, particularly advanced by the German government, the ECJ found that it was quite acceptable for the Commission's analysis to proceed solely with reference to the competition in the market for Grundig's products, and held that

Although competition between producers is generally more noticeable than that between distributors of the same make, it does not thereby follow that an agreement tending to restrict the latter kind of competition should escape the prohibition of article [81(1)] merely because it might increase the former.

Lastly, the Court was satisfied that the Commission had properly considered the points relating to the award of an art. 81(3) exemption. The Commission's decision was annulled by the Court only in so far as it related to the entire agreement concluded between the parties, the Court holding that those parts of the agreement which did not breach the art. 81(1) prohibition could not be condemned by the Commission.

While *Consten and Grundig* saw the Commission and Court taking a relatively inflexible approach to the nature of competition in so far as it applied to exclusive distribution agreements, a more flexible approach may be seen in *Metro-SB-Grossmärkte GmbH & Co. Kg* v *Commission* case 26/76 [1978] 2 CMLR 1. In this case a selective distribution system operated by SABA, a German manufacturer of radios, television sets, and tape recorders, was approved by the Commission (*SABA 76/159* (1976) OJ L28/19). This followed a complaint by a cash-and-carry wholesaler which, by reducing the level of service that it offered to consumers, was able to charge lower prices than would usually be charged by SABA's distributors. Metro had argued to the Commission that it was denied access to the distribution system established by SABA, and that this distribution system was in breach of art. 81(1) and therefore unlawfully maintained. Referring to the flexibility afforded by the concept of 'workable competition', the ECJ held that the nature of the competition could vary depending on the products and services in question, and the structure of the market. The Commission had found selective distribution systems to be unobjectionable as long as the resellers were chosen on the basis of objective criteria which had a genuine relationship to the product in question and as long as such criteria were not applied in a discriminatory manner. The argument was raised by Metro that such systems could lead to higher prices for consumers, and that the application of art. 81(1) required that price competition be maintained effectively. The Court's response was that

It is true that in such systems of distribution price competition is not generally emphasised either as an exclusive or indeed as a principal factor. . . . However, although price competition is so important that it can never be eliminated, it does not constitute the only effective form of competition or that to which absolute priority must in all circumstances be accorded. The powers conferred upon the Commission under article [81(3)] show that the requirements for the maintenance of workable competition may be reconciled with the safeguarding of objectives of a different nature and that to this end certain restrictions on competition are permissible. . . . For specialist wholesalers and retailers the desire to maintain a certain price level, which corresponds to the desire to preserve, in the interests of consumers, the possibility of the continued existence of this channel of distribution in conjunction with new methods of distribution based on a different type of competition policy, forms one of the objectives which may be pursued without necessarily falling under the prohibition contained in article [81(1)]. (para. 21)

Thus, although recognizing the primacy of price competition, which in the Court's words 'is so important that it can never be eliminated', the Court and the Commission both recognized that there could be situations in which some restriction on price competition would be acceptable if that restriction fostered other types of competition. Here the nature of the product was such that a number of large and medium-scale producers offered products that consumers would regard as being generally interchangeable. In such a circumstance any restrictions on prices maintained by one producer would be constrained by the existence on the market of acceptable substitutes, and could be justified if the effect of the constraint was to make available to the consumer a level of supply, service, and after-sales commitment that would not be available in the absence of the restraint.

9.3.1.2 *Agency agreements*

The Commission's *Guidelines on Vertical Restraints* at paras 12–20 deals with agency agreements. These, according to the *Guidelines,*

cover the situation in which a legal or physical person (the agent) is vested with the power to negotiate and/or conclude contracts on behalf of another person (the principal), either in the agent's own name or in the name of the principal, for the:

— purchase of goods or services by the principal, or

— sale of goods or services supplied by the principal.

Genuine agency agreements do not fall within art. 81(1). Non-genuine agency agreements are likely, subject to the market share provisos, to fall within block exemption 2790/99, discussed in Chapter 10. The determination of whether an agency agreement is genuine or not goes to the question of the allocation of risk. If the agent does not bear the risks for the contracts negotiated, or bears only a minimal risk, then it is a 'genuine' agency agreement. In these cases the agent is, in effect, not exercising any independent economic activity, and is subsumed within the principal undertaking.

9.3.1.3 *Vertical restraints—the current position*

There has been substantial debate about the approach to take to vertical restraints in EC competition law since the decision in *Consten*. In 1997 some of these debates were rehearsed in the Commission *Green Paper on Vertical Restraints in Competition Policy* (COM96) 721 final, 22 January 1997). The introductory paragraphs set out the core of the problem:

(1) The single market represents an opportunity for EU firms to enter new markets that may have been previously closed to them because of government barriers. This penetration of new markets takes time and investment and is risky. The process is often facilitated by agreements between producers who want to break into a new market and local distributors. Efficient

distribution with appropriate pre- and after-sales support is part of the competitive process that brings benefits to consumers.

(2) However, arrangements between producers and distributors can also be used to continue the partitioning of the market and exclude new entrants who would intensify competition and lead to downward pressure on prices. Agreements between producers and distributors (vertical restraints) can therefore be used pro-competitively to promote market integration and efficient distribution or anti-competitively to block integration and competition. The price differences between Member States that are still found provide the incentive for companies to enter new markets as well as to erect barriers against new competition.

(3) Because of their strong links to market integration that can be either positive or negative, vertical restraints have been of particular importance to the Union's competition policy. Whilst this policy has been successful in over 30 years of application a review is now necessary.

The Commission invited comments as to its next steps towards legislative reform, indicating at the same time that it would not countenance any system within which absolute territorial protection would be tolerated. In 1998, in response to the consultation process, the Commission published a white paper (COM(1998) 546 final) in which it made clear that its aim was to develop a 'more economics based approach' in which 'vertical agreements should be analysed in their market context'. This policy found shape in the block exemption regulation 2790/99 on the application of art. 81(3) of the Treaty to categories of vertical agreements and concerted practices (1999) OJ L336/21, discussed in the following chapter.

There is a plethora of cases dealing with territorial restrictions in distribution agreements, and work carried out on behalf of the government during the passage of the Competition Act 1998 demonstrated that single-market considerations played the leading role in many of the cases dealing with vertical restraints. More recent decisions include *Novalliance/Systemform* 97/123 (1997) OJ L47/11, in which the infringing company quickly amended the terms of its distribution agreements following their notification to the Commission; *ADALAT* 96/478 (1996) OJ L201/1, dealing with export bans imposed in relation to a range of medicinal products by Bayer AG; and *BASF Lacke + Farben AG and Accinauto SA* 95/477 (1995) OJ L272/17, dealing with the market for car paints, upheld on appeal, *BASF Coating AG* v *Commission* case T–175/95 [2000] 4 CMLR 33.

The *ADALAT* decision was appealed to the CFI, and overturned (*Bayer AG* v *Commission* case T–41/96 [2001] 4 CMLR 4), a judgment later confirmed by the ECJ in *Bundesverband der Arzneimittel-Importeure EC and Commission* v *Bayer AG* cases C–2/01 P and C–3/01 P [2004] 4 CMLR 13. The central question here was whether the export restrictions were the result of unilateral or agreed action. The Commission had argued that by limiting the amount of drugs available for parallel export— in effect by limiting supplies to any Member State to the requirements of that state—Bayer had entered into a series of implied agreements with distributors who accepted the conduct as part of the terms of entry into the distribution network. The CFI found that no such agreement existed, holding that the action was unilateral and therefore not subject to the terms of art. 81(1). The ECJ agreed with the

CFI that it was right to consider that the fact that wholesalers wished to continue to order products for export suggested a lack of concordance of wishes between the parties. A similar approach was taken by the CFI in the case of *Volkswagen AG v Commission* case T–208/01 [2004] 4 CMLR 14. This followed the second infringement decision the Commission had made in respect of VW's conduct in a relatively short space of time (*VW (II)* 2001/711 (2001) OJ L262/14) finding that the company was in breach of art. 81(1) by virtue of a circular sent to dealers asking them not to sell the VW Passat below certain prices. As with *ADALAT* the CFI found that the Commission was incorrect to impute an agreement where none existed.

The €102m fine imposed on Volkswagen in January 1998 (*VW* 98/273 (1998) OJ L124/61)—on appeal (*Volkswagen AG v Commission* case T–62/98 [2000] 5 CMLR 853) the fine was reduced by the Court to €90m—is in itself proof of the Commission's abhorrence of distribution agreements which are operated so as to prevent parallel imports. In that case Italian distributors of the manufacturer's cars were effectively prevented from reselling them to Austrian and German consumers.

On a further appeal to the ECJ the judgment of the CFI was confirmed (*Volkswagen AG v Commission* case C–338/00P [2004] 4 CMLR 7). A similar approach to that adopted in *VW* was taken by the Commission in *Mercedes-Benz* 2002/758 (2002) OJ L257/1 in which restraints were imposed on distributors preventing parallel trade between Member States. Correspondence obtained by the Commission included a letter in which Mercedes-Benz states that it was convinced that 'by adhering strictly to this policy, we can effectively combat internal competition . . . we therefore count on your unconditional support' (para. 78). DaimlerChysler AG, which had become the parent company was fined €71.825 million.

In *JCB* 2002/190 (2002) OJ L69/1 the Commission took strong action against conditions in JCB's distribution agreements for its construction and earth-moving equipment and spare parts. This followed a complaint by a French company which sought to import this equipment into France from the UK, where prices were appreciably lower. As early as 1975, following an approach made by JCB, the Commission had informed the company that export bans in their agreements were illegal and should be deleted. Evidence showed that JCB continued to prevent such parallel imports. For example, in a fax sent from a UK distributor to a French distributor relating to a machine purchased in the UK, but found in France, the UK distributor wrote: 'we cannot be held responsible for this customer's actions, but as a result from this sale we will not be trading with this customer again' (para. 82). The Commission emphasised again the censure placed upon territorially restrictive agreements under art. 81 in no uncertain terms when it argued that such restrictions 'jeopardise the proper functioning of the single market, frustrate one of the principal aims of the Community and have been held for decades as infringements of [art. 81]' (para. 248). JCB was fined €39,614,000. An infringement decision was also made in respect of the distribution of video games in respect of which parallel imports were prevented (*Nintendo* 2003/675 (2003) OJ L255/33).

In May 2000, to coincide with the entry into force of Regulation 2790/99 on 1 June 2000, the Commission published its *Guidelines on Vertical Restraints*. At paras 119–36 these set out general rules for the assessment of vertical restraints. The starting point is the recognition of the fact that 'for most vertical restraints competition concerns can only arise if there is insufficient inter-brand competition', and that in unconcentrated markets, defined as those where the Herfindahl–Hirshman Index (HHI) is less than 1,000 (the use of the HHI formula is discussed below in relation to horizontal agreements), it will be assumed that non-hard-core vertical restraints will not have appreciable effects. On the other hand, vertical restraints which have the effect of reducing inter-brand competition will be analysed with greater concern. Some analysis of specific categories of vertical restraint is provided in paras 137–229 of the *Guidelines*. The practices dealt with there are: single branding, exclusive distribution, exclusive customer allocation, selective distribution, franchising, exclusive supply, tying, and recommended and maximum resale prices. In each case, the *Guidelines* should be read through carefully.

9.3.2 **Horizontal agreements**

The treatment in this section is broken into two parts: anti-competitive agreements; and potentially benign agreements (which may also be referred to as 'cooperation agreements'). For the present purposes the first category refers to those agreements, typically in the forms of cartels, that are unlikely to have redeeming features. The second refers to categories of agreements which may, on the face of it, be entered into for pro-competitive reasons, but where it may be possible for harm to flow depending on the exact way, and the circumstances, in which the agreement operates.

9.3.2.1 *Anti-competitive agreements*

A number of anti-competitive horizontal agreements have been considered already in this chapter. In particular the position in relation to concerted practices has been dealt with above at 9.2.3, and although it may be doubted that a 'concerted practice' equates to an 'agreement', the fact is that the *effect* of a concerted practice is the same as the effect of an agreement. In most of the cartel decisions referred to in this section the EC Commission has recognized that certain conduct might be the result either of a cartel or of a concerted practice. However, the cases presented here are more clearly 'cartel' cases, and have often been tackled as a result of a whistle-blower providing information about specific agreements to the Commission.

In recent years, partly as a result of a particular drive by DG Comp, there has been a relatively large number of actions brought against cartels. At the end of 1998 the Commission created a new unit expressly to fight cartels (IP (98) 1068, 3 December 1998, [1999] 4 CMLR 13). One of the best examples of cartel decisions is *Pre-Insulated Pipe Cartel* 1999/60 (1999) OJ L24/1, an infringement that began with a national cartel in Denmark in 1990, and by 1994 had been extended to cover the entire Community. The list of restrictions of competition set out in para. 147 of the decision is an impressive one, and, even allowing for some reductions in the level of fines imposed in accordance with its notice on the non-imposition of fines in cartel cases (see Chapter 6), the total fines amounted to €92,920,000. The decision was upheld by the CFI on appeal (*LR AF 1998 A/s v Commission* case. T–23/99 [2002] 5 CMLR 10. A very good description of the operation of this cartel, and the steps taken to counteract it, written by the head of the Cartels unit of DG Comp, may be found in *Competition Policy Newsletter* (1999) February, p. 27.

One of the most high-profile cartel cases of recent years attracted the attention of competition authorities around the world when the existence of the cartel was exposed to the FBI. In the EC the investigation, during which competition authorities cooperated, culminated in the EC Commission decision *Amino Acids Cartel—Archer Daniels Midland Co and others* 2001/418 (2001) OJ L152/24. Here a number of leading companies in the production of amino acids, led by the US company Archer Daniels Midland, put in place elaborate cartel arrangements to market-share and fix prices. The story of the uncovering of the cartel is told in Eichenwald, K., *The Informant*, New York, Broadway Books (2000), which is highly recommended. In *Archer Daniels Midland v Commission* case T–224/00 [2003] 5 CMLR 12 the CFI upheld the Commission decision, although it reduced the amount of the penalty imposed.

The uncovering of this cartel led to investigations in a number of related industries, involving many of the same undertakings. For example, in *Citric Acid* 2002/742 (2002) OJ L239/18 the Commission took action against a cartel which pursued four main objectives: the allocation of sales quotas to each member; the fixing of target and 'floor' prices; the elimination of price discounts; and the exchange of specific customer information. Between 1991 and 1995 the members of this cartel held around 20 multilateral meetings, and also held special meetings, known within the cartel as 'Sherpa' meetings, in order to deal with grievances between the cartel members. Substantial penalties were imposed, and the Commission did not feel constrained by the fact that some of the cartel members had already paid criminal fines in the USA and Canada in respect of the same conduct.

In 2001 the Commission took 10 cartel decisions, and imposed fines totalling €1,836 million. In the *Vitamins* case alone (2003/2 (2003) OJ L6/1) a fine of €855.23 million was imposed on the various parties (see Commission Press Release IP (02) 1744, 27 November 2002 in relation to the plasterboard cartel). At nearly 800 paragraphs the *Vitamins* decision is exceptionally long, and the facts are complex. The cartel was notified to the Commission by one of the participants, Rhone-Poulenc, seeking to benefit from the leniency programme. This application was facilitated by the fact that the company 'played only a passive role in the vitamin D3 infringement. It did not attend any of the cartel meetings and was not allocated an individual market share' (para. 725). Eleven different cartels were identified in the decision by the Commission, relating to different vitamins, folic acid, beta-carotene, and carotinoids. Although in each case different facts were brought to light, the cartels generally flowed from a period of intense price competition during which prices fell dramatically. In the summer of 1989 at least two top-level meetings were held in Zurich between executives of Hoffmann-La Roche AG and

BASF AG. The discussions that took place at the second meeting were described in some detail by BASF:

On the first day senior executives responsible for vitamin marketing in each company, together with some product managers, identified the size of the market for vitamins A and E then agreed the allocation between the four producers of the world and regional markets on the basis of their respective achieved sales in 1988.

In summary, the underlying objective was to stabilise the world market share of each producer. Market shares were frozen at 1988 levels: as the market expanded, each company could increase its sales only in accordance with its agreed quota and in line with market growth and not at the expense of a competitor.

On the second day, the chairmen of the fine chemicals division or the equivalent and the heads of vitamins marketing of each company joined the meeting to approve the agreed quotas and to establish 'confidence' between the participants that the arrangements would be respected. The maxim 'price before volume' was accepted as the underlying principle of the cartel. Specific pricing levels were also discussed. (paras. 163–5).

The cartel expanded, both in terms of products and markets covered, and the participants. It was eventually attacked in a number of jurisdictions, including the USA where prosecutions were brought on the basis of s. 1 of the Sherman Act. The fines eventually imposed by the EC Commission set a new benchmark, with Hoffmann-La Roche alone being required to pay a total of €462.3 million.

A price-fixing cartel was also tackled in *Graphite Electrodes* 2002/271 (2002) OJ L100/1. ('Graphite electrodes are ceramic-moulded columns of graphite used primarily in the production of steel in electric arc furnaces' (para. 4).) Eight undertakings were found to have been party to an agreement (or concerted practice) covering the entire EC under which they: fixed the prices of the product; put into place a mechanism to facilitate the price fixing; allocated markets; restricted output; agreed to retain certain technologies only to the participants (so as to limit the growth in potential competition); and set up procedures by which adherence to the agreement could be monitored and enforced. Individuals participating in the cartel management were instructed to take particular care to conceal their contacts with competitors. The Commission decision followed dawn raids carried out in France and Germany which produced evidence that fitted in with material also found by US and Japanese authorities on their own territories. Some of the cartel members then chose to cooperate with the Commission in the hope of benefiting from reduced penalties. Total fines of €218.8 million were imposed.

A smaller cartel was dealt with in *Luxembourg Brewers* 2002/759 (2002) OJ L253/21 in which the five main brewers in Luxembourg reached an agreement between them to ensure the mutual observance and protection of the tied agreements entered into with outlets in Luxembourg. The agreement came to light after it was notified to the Commission by Interbrew SA which had taken control of a Luxembourg brewer, and instructed its two subsidiaries in the market to stop implementing the agreement. Interbrew benefited from total leniency under the Commission's leniency policy. Similarly in *Industrial and Medical Gases* 2003/355 (2003) OJ L84/1 the Commission took action against a price-fixing agreement between Dutch producers of certain gases.

Other recent cartel cases include: *Plasterboard* (Commission Press Release IP (02) 1744, and (2003) OJ C161/E/72—Commission response to a parliamentary question); *Seamless steel tubes* 2003/382 (2003) OJ L140/1; *Zinc phosphate* 2003/437 (2003) OJ L153/1; *French beef* 2003/600 (2003) OJ L209/12; and *Food flavour enhancers* 2004/206 (2004) OJ L75/1.

9.3.2.2 *Potentially benign horizontal agreements*

The range of material about which undertakings at a horizontal level may agree is vast, and includes not only prices and market sharing, but also practices which are wholly pro-competitive, or whose pro-competitive effects may outweigh the anti-competitive effects. We have already seen at 9.3 that in the case of *European Night Services* v *Commission* joined cases T–374/94, etc. [1998] ECR II-3141 the Court drew a distinction between different types of horizontal agreements. The first task, the Court said, was to assess carefully the competitive conditions in which such agreements operated. It might be the case that a horizontal agreement would not even fall within art. 81(1) if it had no deleterious effect on competition. However, where certain restrictions are present, set out in the case as being price fixing, market sharing, or the control of outlets (para. 136), it must be presumed automatically that art. 81(1) applies. It would then become necessary to analyse carefully the competitive conditions in order to see if the requirements for the application of art. 81(3) were met.

Guidelines on the Applicability of Article 81 EC to Horizontal Cooperation Agreements were published in January 2001. These *Guidelines* replace a number of earlier guidelines and notices, including, importantly, the 1968 *Notice on Agreements, Decisions and Concerted Practices in the Field of Cooperation between Enterprises* ((1968) OJ C75/3).

The difficulty in dealing with benign horizontal cooperation is that there is always a risk that parties will coordinate in an anti-competitive fashion, and that such coordination can have serious consequences both for economic welfare, and for the integration of the single market. Thus it is recognized in the introduction to the *Guidelines* that

1. In most instances, horizontal cooperation amounts to cooperation between competitors
. . .

3. Companies need to respond to increasing competitive pressure and a changing market place driven by globalisation, the speed of technological progress and the generally more dynamic nature of markets. Cooperation can be a means to share risk, save costs, pool know-how and launch innovation faster. In particular for small- and medium-sized enterprises cooperation is an important means to adapt to the changing market place.

However:

2. Horizontal cooperation may lead to competition problems. This is for example, the case if the parties to a cooperation agree to fix prices or output, to share markets, or if the co-operation enables the parties to maintain, gain or increase market power and thereby causes negative market effects with respect to prices, output, innovation or the variety and quality of products.

The *Guidelines*, which go some way to clarifying the position in relation to horizontal cooperation and should be read carefully, focus on cooperation between competitors, which includes both 'actual' and 'potential' competitors. They have a further limitation in that they are concerned only with cooperation which may generate efficiency gains, by which the EC Commission means 'agreements on R&D, production, purchasing, commercialisation, standardisation, and environmental agreements' (para. 10). Research and development agreements, and production agreements, which include specialization agreements, are considered in the following chapter, because they are subject to block exemptions.

The *Guidelines* deal first with the situations in which such agreements may fall within art. 81(1). Some agreements are unlikely to fall within art. 81(1), particularly where there will be no coordination of competitive conduct. This will be the case where the parties are not competitors, or where (as was the case in *Elopak/Metal Box—Odin* 90/410 (1990) OJ L209/15, discussed above at 9.3) the parties could not independently carry out the activity covered by the cooperation. In these cases, notwithstanding that there is an element of cooperation, it will be in an entirely new activity. This new activity would not exist without that level of cooperation, and therefore pre-existing competition is not being undermined.

Agreements will almost always fall within art. 81(1), and will almost always be prohibited, where they 'have the object to restrict competition by means of price fixing, output limitation or sharing of markets or customers' (para. 25). Agreements that do not fall within these categories have to be analysed more fully to determine whether they fall under art. 81(1).

The central consideration will be 'the position of the parties in the markets affected by the cooperation' (para. 27), because it is the undertakings' market power which is likely to be determinative of whether harmful effects flow from the agreement. The base line of the Commission is that such agreements cannot be tolerated where they have the effect of 'eliminating' competition (see art. 81(3)).

One of the indices used by the Commission is the Herfindahl–Hirshman Index, or HHI, which is a tool employed by the US authorities in merger control. It provides a useful first indicator of market concentration. Formally the HHI is the sum of the squared market shares of the companies on the relevant market, or $\Sigma s1^2 \ldots sn^2$ (where sn is the market share of firm n). Thus, in a market with four firms, each of which has a 25 per cent market share, the HHI would be $25^2 + 25^2 + 25^2 + 25^2 = 2,500$. In a total monopoly market the HHI would be 10,000 (100^2), and in a market of 100 firms, each with only 1 per cent market share, it would be 100. Where the HHI is less than 1,000, the concentration will be characterized as low, between 1,000 and 1,800 it will be moderate, and over 1,800 high. As the *Guidelines* make clear, a post-cooperation HHI may in some cases 'be decisive for the assessment of the possible market effects of a cooperation'. It refers to the following example:

A market consisting of four firms with shares of 30%, 25%, 25% and 20%, has a HHI of 2,550 (900 + 625 + 625 + 400) pre-cooperation. If the first two market leaders would cooperate, the HHI would change to 4,050 (3,025 + 625 + 400) post-cooperation.   (footnote 22, para. 29)

As well as conducting such analysis it must be demonstrated that the requirements of art. 81(3) are met (which are discussed below). For a detailed consideration of the approach to be taken in relation to each of the categories of agreement referred to in the *Guidelines* reference should be made to the relevant section in the *Guidelines*.

9.3.2.3 *Information agreements*

The *Guidelines* do not deal with information-sharing agreements. There has not been a great deal of case law in relation to these. In its 1968 *Notice on Cooperation Agreements* the Commission indicated that certain information agreements would not be caught by art. 81. These agreements were:

(1) Agreements having as their sole object:
   — an exchange of opinion or experience,
   — joint market research,
   — the joint carrying out of comparative studies of enterprises or industries,
   — the joint preparation of statistics and calculation models.

Agreements whose sole purpose is the joint procurement of information which the various enterprises need to determine their future market behaviour freely and independently, or the use by each of the enterprises of a joint advisory body, do not have as their object or result the restriction of competition. But if the scope of action of the enterprises is limited or if the market behaviour is coordinated either expressly or through concerted practices, there may be a restraint of competition. This is in particular the case where concrete recommendations are made or where conclusions are given in such a form that they induce at least some of the participating enterprises to behave in an identical manner on the market.

Although this notice has been replaced by the horizontal guidelines, it remains the most substantial source of comment relating to information agreements. It implies that agreements relating to the exchange of information between actual or potential competitors are therefore capable of being in breach of art. 81. A distinction should in this respect be made between three classes of information agreements:

(a) information exchanges concerning price;
(b) information exchanges which do not relate to price, but do contain information that may underpin other anti-competitive activity, such as, for example, information that allows firms in an industry to pinpoint exactly who is making what sales to whom; and
(c) information which is neither about price nor about other anti-competitive activity.

In the case of the first two categories the Commission is likely to take the approach that the agreement invites condemnation, having the object, if not in fact the effect, of being anti-competitive. In the third category the Commission will examine the situation more carefully, the presumption being that there is no anti-competitive object, but that there may nevertheless be an anti-competitive effect in practice. The Commission will be highly swayed by the extent to which the information is individualized. In its *7th Annual Report on Competition Policy* it explained its position at some length. In short the position is that the 'provision of collated statistical material is not in itself objectionable' but that 'the organised exchange of individual data from individual firms . . . will normally be regarded by the Commission as practices . . . which are therefore prohibited' as having the object or effect of preventing, restricting, or distorting competition. The leading cases in this respect are *UK Tractors Information Agreement* 92/157 [1992] OJ L68/19 and *Fatty Acids* 87/1 (1987) OJ L3/17.

In the latter case an agreement was entered into by the four major producers in the EC of various chemicals. Under the agreement the parties, having first established their respective average market shares over the previous three years, set out to exchange information regarding their total sales in Europe for each quarter, with the intention of allowing each party to monitor the behaviour of each other, and to adjust its own conduct accordingly. As the Commission noted the information exchanged was 'of a kind normally regarded as business secrets' (para. 1). At para. 45 of the decision the Commission held that an agreement

based on an exchange of confidential information on the one hand about traditional market positions and on the other hand providing a means of monitoring their future performance, has inherent restrictive effects upon competition. . . through the exchange of information they artificially increased transparency between them by obtaining knowledge of each other's activities which they would not have had in the absence of the agreement. The Commission considers that this will inevitably have led them to temper their competitive behaviour towards each other.

9.3.2.4 *Standards-setting agreements*

Agreements relating to standards setting are dealt with in Part 6 of the *Guidelines*. Standardization agreements are defined as those which 'have as their primary objective the definition of technical or quality requirements with which current or future products, production processes or methods may comply' (para. 159). In high-tech industries, such as computing, where equipment needs to be able to interface with other equipment, standards setting is increasingly important. Standards may be set by either public or private bodies. In the case of public bodies it is unlikely that competition law will involve itself, and the only requirement in the EC is that any such standards do not distort competition, and are not used to raise barriers to trade.

In relation to private standards setting the general principles set out in the *Guidelines* follow previous decisions taken by the Commission. Where standards are 'open' they are unlikely to fall within art. 81(1). An open standard is one which is open to all, and is not discriminatory or exclusionary. For example, in *TUV/Cenelec* (*28th Annual Report on Competition Policy* 1998, p. 159) the Commission negotiated a settlement whereby a standard developed by Cenelec was 'opened' up to all qualified certifiers, a procedure which the Commission hoped would 'serve as a model for application procedures in related fields'. Standards may, however, be used to restrict competition by setting criteria which are unattainable by some parties. The question then becomes one of whether art. 81(3) may be applied. If that is to be the case the standard must serve a valid end, and meet the general criteria for exemption discussed below.

The leading decision dealing with the application of art. 81(3) to a standards-setting agreement is that of *X/Open Group* 87/69 (1987) OJ L35/36. In this case a number of significant undertakings in the computing industry, such as Bull, Ericsson, and ICL notified the Commission of an agreement to standardize various matters relating to the use of the computer operating system UNIX. The objective was to increase the number of applications that could be written to work with UNIX. The group intended to limit its membership, with a requirement that applicants be 'major manufacturers in the European information technology industry, with their own established expertise concerning UNIX'. The revenue of any applicant to the group would be expected to be about US$500m from information technology activity. The Commission found that the agreement would fall within art. 81(1), but that it would be exempt under art. 81(3). A crucial factor was that the standards created by the group would be well publicized and relevant technical information would be made widely available. The Commission further found that

the advantages involved in the creation of an open industry standard (in particular the intended creation of a wider availability of software and greater flexibility offered to users to change between hardware and software from different sources) easily outweigh the distortions of competition entailed in the rules governing membership which are indispensable to the attainment of the objectives of the Group Agreement.   (para. 42)

9.3.2.5 *Professional rules*

Rules regulating professions, for example, lawyers, doctors, architects, may fall within art. 81(1), although whether this is the case will depend on an analysis of the rule in question. The fact that a professional rule contains an element of restriction will not necessarily bring it within the prohibition. Thus in *Wouters, Savelbergh and Price Waterhouse Belastingadviseurs BV* v *Algemene Raad Van de Nederlandse Orde Van Advocaten* case C–309/99 [2002] 4 CMLR 27 the ECJ dealt with the question, *inter alia*, of whether it was a breach of art. 81(1) for the Dutch Bar Council to impose a rule preventing its members from entering into certain multidisciplinary partnerships. The first two named claimants were therefore prevented from entering into a partnership with accountants. The Court found that it was reasonable for the Dutch Bar 'to consider that members of the Bar might no longer be in a position to advise and represent their clients independently' (para. 105) if they belonged to such a partnership. The restrictions inherent in the professional rules in this case did not, the Court held, 'go beyond what is necessary in order to ensure the proper practice of the legal profession' (para. 109), and in conclusion the Court held that the rules did not infringe art. 81(1).

9.3.3 **Mergers and joint ventures**

The application of art. 81 to mergers and joint ventures is considered in Chapter 19.

9.4 **Article 81(2): void agreements**

Where art. 81(1) has been found to apply to any agreement an important consequence is that the agreement, or relevant parts of it, is void. Because of the nature
of the prohibition there need not be any formal decision to the effect that art. 81(1)
applies for this to be the case. This position is made clear in *Beguelin Import Co.* v *GL
Import Export SA* (case 22/71 [1972] CMLR 81) where the Court held that 'since the
nullity imposed by Article [81(2)] is absolute in character, an agreement which is
void because of that provision has no effect between the contracting parties and
cannot be pleaded against third parties' (para. 29). Thus any national court dealing
with the issue may find that a contract or parts of that contract are void where one
of the parties to an action can demonstrate that art. 81(1) applies to the situation.

The effect of art. 81(2) runs either from the date at which art. 81(1) became
effective, or the date of the conclusion of the agreement, whichever is the later.

Article 81(2) does not necessarily apply to an agreement in its entirety. Where the
offending clauses can be separated from the agreement without stripping the
essence of the agreement, this will be permitted but is primarily a matter of
national, not Community, law. Whether this is possible is to be determined in the
light of all the relevant circumstances objectively and not necessarily by reference
to the views of the parties themselves. Thus in *La Technique Minière* v *Maschinenbau
Ulm GmbH* case 56/65 [1966] 1 CMLR 357, the Court held (at 376) that

The automatic nullity in question applies only to those elements of the agreement which are
subject to the prohibition or to the agreement as a whole if those elements do not appear
severable from the agreement itself. Consequently, all other contractual provisions which are
not affected by the prohibition, since they do not involve the application of the Treaty, fall
outside the Community law.

The Court has also held that where the matter falls to be decided before a national
court the test of severability is to be that which would normally be applied in
equivalent national law (*Société de Vente de Ciments et Bétons de L'Est SA* v *Kerpen and
Kerpen GmbH* case 319/82 [1985] 1 CMLR 511). There is therefore the potential for a
different result to be arrived at depending on the country in which an action
is brought, although it is unlikely that this will be a matter of great difficulty in
practice.

As has been discussed in Chapter 7, competition law is not used as a sword
as often as it could be. One of the most common ways for EC competition law
to be introduced before the national courts is for a party contesting a contractual
obligation to raise what has become known as the 'Euro-defence' (or 'competition
defence'). In such a case the defendant pleads that there is no obligation because
the clause or contract in question is in breach of art. 81(1) (see, e.g., *Chemidus
Wavin Ltd* v *Société pour la Transformation et l'Exploitation des Resines Industrielles SA*
[1978] 3 CMLR 514). English courts have tended to be wary of these 'defences',
recognizing the potential of such a defence to serve as an effective obfuscating

tactic: if an art. 234 reference is made in such a case the matter may take up to 18 months to be resolved. Nevertheless if the argument is made it will have to be addressed properly at trial. Such 'defences' may also be raised on the basis of art. 82 although this is less likely. Again the courts may be sceptical of the claims made (see, e.g., *Hoover plc* v *George Hulme (Stockport) Ltd* [1982] FSR 565).

It is for national courts to rule on the validity of contracts falling within art. 81 in actions relying on the direct effect of EC law. There has been uncertainty as to the approach that would be adopted by courts in the UK. The issue has been discussed particularly in cases arising out of challenges to leases between pub tenants and breweries. The key question was whether either party could, to any extent, rely on a contract falling within art. 81(1), as such a contract was presumed to be 'illegal'.

The issue was referred to the ECJ by way of an art. 234 reference from the Court of Appeal in the cases of *Crehan* v *Courage Ltd and others* [1999] UKCLR 110 and 407. Late in 2001 the ECJ gave its response (*Courage Ltd* v *Crehan* case C–453/99 [2002] UKCLR 171) and held in particular that, while it was for the national court to determine the appropriate procedures by which the rights given under art. 81 should be invoked, national courts should take into account 'the economic and legal context in which the parties find themselves and . . . the respective bargaining power and conduct of the two parties to the contract' (para. 32). The Court stressed that in cases where a small agreement was concluded within a network of similar agreements 'the party contracting with the person controlling the network cannot bear significant responsibility for the breach of art. 81, particularly where in practice the terms of the contract were imposed on him by the party controlling the network' (para. 34).

When the case returned for further consideration to the national court, Park J. held that the contractual ties in question did not have the effect of preventing, restricting, or distorting competition, so did not find it necessary to rule on the question of damages, although he made it clear that had the contracts fallen within art. 81(1) damages would have been available (*Crehan* v *Inntrepreneur Pub Company and Brewman Group Ltd* [2003] EWHC 1510 (Ch), [2003] UKCLR 834).

9.5 Trade between Member States

The importance of the phrase 'trade between Member States', and its application has been considered at 3.4.1 above. It is the agreement which must affect trade.

It is worth noting that in the 2001 notice on agreements of minor importance (2001) OJ C368/13 the Commission recognizes that 'agreements between small and medium-sized undertakings . . . are rarely capable of appreciably affecting trade between member states' (para. 3). For these purposes small and medium-sized undertakings are defined as those with fewer than 250 employees and having an annual turnover not greater than €40m, or an annual balance sheet total not greater than €27m. And in *The Dutch Acceptance Giro System* 1999/687 (1999)

OJ L271/28 the Commission found that an agreement between undertakings in The Netherlands relating to inter-bank commission payments, with only a negligible involvement by banks from other Member States, would not affect trade between Member States.

9.6 Limits on the application of article 81(1) and (2)

From the above it becomes apparent that the prohibition of art. 81(1) is broad and indiscriminate. It applies to multilateral anti-competitive conduct irrespective of the form that the conduct takes; it applies to a wide range of practices; and the jurisdictional test of an effect on Community trade is not a demanding one. At the same time as the prohibition has been widely drawn the limits on the application of the prohibition have become more clearly defined. Most obviously the article is ameliorated in the application of art. 81(3). The ECJ has also developed *de minimis* criteria which are not themselves set out in the article.

9.6.1 Article 81(3)—exemptions and exceptions

Article 81(3) of the Treaty

sets out an exception rule, which provides a defence to undertakings against a finding of an infringement of Article 81(1) of the Treaty. Agreements, decisions of associations of undertakings and concerted practices caught by Article 81(1) which satisfy the conditions of Article 81(3) are valid and enforceable, no prior decision to that effect being required. (*Guidelines on the application of article 81(3) of the Treaty*, (2004) OJ C101/81 para 1)

Article 81(3), has, as does art. 81(1) and art. 81(2), direct effect. While this may seem unexceptional this position has existed only since 1 May 2004, and is a result of the modernization process encapsulated in, but not confined to, Regulation 1/2003. It is provided in that Regulation that:

Agreements, decisions and concerted practices caught by art. 81(1) of the Treaty which satisfy the requirements of art. 81(3) of the Treaty shall not be prohibited, no prior decision to that effect being required. (art. 1(2))

This is not the appropriate place to expand at length on the history of the application of art. 81(3), but some understanding of that development is essential to an understanding of the fundamental nature of the change that has been made. Prior to 1 May 2004 art. 81(3) did not have direct effect, and the EC Commission had *exclusive* power to rule on its application. There were, in essence, two ways in which art. 81(3) could be invoked: either by making an individual application to the Commission; or by structuring an agreement so as to fall within a block exemption regulation (see the following chapter). The Commission was, as a result of hundreds of notifications each year, overstretched and resorted to administratively convenient, but legally uncertain, measures to resolve cases. In particular it developed the use of the 'comfort letter' under which it bound itself, but not others, as to the result. Crucially, whenever the application of art. 81(1) was pleaded before a national court, the party seeking to rely on the contract or agreement could not plead the application of art. 81(3), and their only recourse was to persuade the national court to stay the proceedings while an application for individual exemption was made to the Commission. This led to some considerable dissatisfaction with the process. For example, in the case of *Crehan* (discussed above), the judge accepted that 'I can understand that Mr Crehan and his professional advisers feel disenchanted by the way in which Inntrepreneur caused their counterclaim to be held up for years while Inntrepreneur pursued a European route to get rid of it' (*Crehan* v *Inntrepreneur Pub Company and Brewman Group Ltd* [2003] EWHC 1510 (Ch), [2003] UKCLR 834, at para. 146). The decision was therefore taken that

The present system should therefore be replaced by a directly applicable exception system in which the competition authorities and courts of the Member States have the power to apply not only art. 81(1) and art. 82 of the Treaty, which have direct applicability by virtue of the case law of the Court of Justice of the European Communities, but also art. 81(3) of the Treaty. (Regulation 1/2003, recital (4))

Where any party seeks to rely on what is now more properly referred to as the 'legal exception' (although it is likely that the term 'exemption' is so entrenched it will be used for some time) it is for that party to establish its application. Thus, art. 2 of Regulation 1/2003 provides that

The undertaking or association of undertakings claiming the benefit of art. 81(3) of the Treaty shall bear the burden of proving that the conditions of that paragraph are fulfilled.

In essence, the appropriate procedure for the application of art. 81(3) now is for the parties seeking to rely on the legal exception—if it is accepted that the agreement might fall within the scope of art. 81(1)—to make their own evaluation of the exception's application, and to be prepared to defend this before a national court or national competition authority. A key document to be considered in any such case is the Commission *Guidelines on the application of art. 81(3) of the Treaty* (2004) OJC 101/97.

In some circumstances undertakings may make applications to the relevant member of the network of competition authorities to seek clarification that their assessment of the application of art. 81(3) is correct, and the Commission has retained the power to rule in novel cases. Article 10 of Regulation 1/2003 therefore provides that the Commission may, 'where the Community public interest relating to the application of arts 81 and 82 of the Treaty, so requires', make a finding that the conditions of art. 81(3) are satisfied. The Commission has published a *Notice on informal guidance relating to novel questions concerning arts. 81 and 82 of the EC Treaty that arise in individual cases (guidance letters)* (2004) OJ C101/78 in which it recognizes that the way in which art. 81(3) functions may create legal uncertainty, and permits undertakings to approach it where cases 'give rise to genuine uncertainty because they present novel or unresolved questions' (para. 5). At the time of writing the OFT was consulting on its approach to applications for guidance.

The Commission anticipates that the guidance that is available in its vertical and horizontal guidelines, along with the *Notice on the application of art. 81(3)* and previous case law, will provide undertakings with most of the information that they need to make their own assessment of the situation, and will assist the courts and members of the network of competition authorities to rule as appropriate.

In key areas, and in particular in relation to vertical agreements and certain categories of cooperation agreements, block exemption regulations are also in place that will automatically exempt from the application of art. 81(1) a large number of agreements. These are discussed in the following chapter.

9.6.2 **Article 81(3)—substance**

The wording of art. 81(3) provides that the legal exception will be available where the agreement or concerted practice in question

contributes to improving the production or distribution of goods or to promoting technical or economic progress, while allowing consumers a fair share of the resulting benefit, and which does not:

(a) impose on the undertakings concerned restrictions which are not indispensable to the attainment of these objectives;

(b) afford such undertakings the possibility of eliminating competition in respect of a substantial part of the products in question.

It was confirmed in *Atlantic Container Line AB* v *Commission* case T–395/94 [2002] 4 CMLR 28, following earlier case law, that the four conditions set out in art. 81(3) are cumulative, such that 'non-fulfilment of only one of those conditions' would make it impossible for an undertaking to benefit from the application of the provision. According to the notice 'the four conditions of art. 81(3) are also exhaustive. When they are met the exception is applicable and may not be refused' (para. 38).

The notice deals with the substantive application of the criteria in some detail, and should be relied on to provide useful guidance in this respect. The first condition for the application of art. 81(3) is that there is an efficiency gain as a result of the restriction. Any such gain must be clearly substantiated, so that it is possible to evaluate: (a) the nature of the claimed efficiencies; (b) the link between the agreement and these efficiencies; and (c) the likelihood and magnitude of each of the efficiencies claimed of the agreement. Efficiencies either may be of cost, or may take the form of new or improved products. Under the third condition of the article it must also be demonstrated that the restrictions in the agreement are necessary to the attainment of these efficiencies.

Consumers must benefit from the gain, but the general expectation is that in markets which are competitive—and the article does not permit the elimination of competition—these will be passed on as part of the inevitable process of competition. For example, in the *Metro* case the Court first considered the fact that the agreement assured 'a more regular distribution' of the goods in question to the benefit of both producer and retailer (para. 43). Then the Court held that

In the circumstances of the present case regular supplies represent a sufficient advantage to consumers for them to be considered to constitute a fair share of the benefit resulting from the improvement brought about by the restriction on competition permitted by the Commission . . . the grant of exemption may . . . in the present case be considered as sufficiently justified by the advantage which consumers obtain from an improvement in supplies.   (para. 48)

This is not always the case, however. In condemning the operation of an association of building contractors in The Netherlands market the Commission, supported by the CFI, found that although the contractors undeniably benefited from the operation of the rules determined by the association this benefit was not passed on to the customer. As the Court put it, 'the claimed limitation of transaction costs operates almost exclusively to the benefit of the contractors'. Even accepting that some of the benefits the contractors claimed did exist, because, for example, the customer would have to consider fewer bids, 'that benefit is limited by comparison with the disadvantages which he must bear and the benefits obtained from that system by contractors' (*Vereniging van Samenwerkende Prijsregelende Organisaties in de Bouwnijverheid (SPO)* v *Commission* case T–29/92 [1995] ECR-II 289, para. 295).

The meaning of 'consumer' is not necessarily limited to the end-user of a product purchasing it through a retail outlet. The industrial user of a product, or a manufacturer purchasing a component to be used in its production process, may also be a consumer for the purposes of art. 81(3). For example, in *Kabel-metal-Luchaire* 75/494 (1975) OJ L222/34, an agreement between two industrial companies was exempted when 'electrical-equipment and motor-vehicle manufacturers and their customers, obtain[ed] a fair share of the benefits . . . for as a result of this agreement they have at their disposal in the common market goods tailored to their needs' (para. 11).

Some concern has been expressed that in giving pre-eminence to the role of price competition the Commission has not permitted the consumer to benefit from other types of competition in some cases. For example, in *VBBB/VBVB* 82/123 (1982) OJ L54/36 (on appeal *Vereniging ter Bevordering van het Vlaamse Boekwezen (VBVB) and Vereeniging ter Bevordering van de Belangen des Boekhandels (VBBB)* v *Commission* cases 43/82 and 63/82 [1985] 1 CMLR 27) the Commission considered an agreement operated by the main Dutch and Belgian book publishers and sellers under which resale price maintenance was applied. This position had its counterpart in the Net Book Agreement operated in the United Kingdom. Under the terms of the agreement booksellers would be prevented from increasing their individual market share by competing with other booksellers on price. In seeking an exemption for this agreement the parties claimed that it produced benefits that were shared by the consumers. In particular it was claimed that the agreement increased both the range of books published and the number of outlets in which they could be purchased.

Similar arguments were made before the ECJ following the Commission's finding that the agreement was in breach of art. 81(1) and that no exemption would be granted. The applicants also relied, unsuccessfully, on art. 10 of the European Convention on Human Rights which guarantees the right to freedom of expression. As was the case in *Metro*, the applicants claimed that while the effect of the agreement was to restrict price competition, here by resellers in relation to each individual book, it left unimpaired competition between the various publishers. The applicants felt that by taking the view that price competition was the essential ingredient in competition the Commission had ignored the particular characteristics of the book market. The Commission did not share the applicants' view that for the consumer the consideration put on the price of a book was secondary to that relating to the diversity of stocks. The Court, noting the Commission's argument that 'the resale price maintenance system totally eliminates price competition at retail level' (para. 43 of the judgment), rejected the applicants' arguments. Accepting that there might be situations in which art. 81(1) would not be breached by a restriction on price competition that was more than balanced by other factors, the Court nevertheless held that in this case the agreement's effects were too marked to be removed from the scope of the prohibition by the granting of an art. 81(3) exemption.

On the other hand, in *REIMS II* 1999/687 (1999) OJ L275/17 the EC Commission exempted an agreement between 16 European postal operators which fixed the fees for the costs of delivering cross-border mail (so-called terminal dues). At para. 65 the Commission noted that 'it has to be acknowledged that the REIMS II Agreement is a price-fixing agreement with unusual characteristics'. Some sort of arrangement was clearly necessary in order for the postal system to work, and in the absence of a general agreement there would need to be a system of bilateral agreements, with the costs entailed by this. Further, the agreement would clearly produce the substantial advantage of an increase in the quality of cross-border mail services (paras 69–76).

A difficulty facing the courts is that the language of the notice is very much about 'efficiency', whereas the Commission has, in the past, taken into account wider considerations. In September 1998, for example, an art. 81(3) comfort letter was issued to members of the European Council for Automotive Research and Development (EUCAR) relating to an agreement between major manufacturers to collaborate in research aimed, *inter alia*, at reducing car emissions. In doing so, the Commission noted that 'research must be at the pre-competitive stage' (Press Release IP/98/832, 25 September 1998). Environmental concerns also led to the Commission granting an art. 81(3) exemption in respect of an agreement between manufacturers and importers of washing machines to reduce sales of the least efficient machines (*CECED Agreement* 2000/475 [2000] OJ L187/47). In *Metro* the Commission took into consideration the fact that several Member States had enacted legislation that differentiated between resale and wholesale outlets with the aim of providing a limited protection to retailers from competition from wholesalers, in order to increase the range of outlets. The Court's view was that it was acceptable for the Commission to apply a similar policy when deciding whether to grant an exemption under art. 81(3) to the selective distribution system maintained by SABA (at para. 29 of the judgment). This is of concern to some commentators who would prefer that the scope of the review be limited strictly to competitive matters. However, the fact that the Court has held repeatedly that Community competition policy is to be reviewed in the light of the other objectives of the Treaty would suggest that such a wider application is appropriate—another objective of the Treaty should not be obstructed by a rigid interpretation of art. 81(3) (see also *Remia BV* v *Commission* case 42/84 [1987] 1 CMLR 1, at para. 42).

9.6.3 Article 81(3) and article 82

The fact that an undertaking has the benefit of an exception will not necessarily serve as a defence to an action brought on the basis of art. 82. The exception relates specifically to the application of art. 81(1) and not to EC competition law in general. This point was clarified by the CFI in *Tetra Pak Rausing SA* v *Commission* case T–51/89 [1991] 4 CMLR 334, where the Court rejected Tetra Pak's argument to the effect that the principle of legal certainty would be undermined if an art. 81(3) decision could not be relied on in all circumstances. A similar view was taken by the Commission in *Cewal* 93/82 (1993) OJ L34/20 (at para. 20) where it held that the fact that the parties benefited from one of the block exemptions did not prevent the application of art. 82.

9.6.4 *De minimis* rules and the notice on agreements of minor importance

On its face art. 81(1) prohibits all anti-competitive agreements where trade is affected, irrespective of the size of the parties in question or the impact that the agreement will have. Were this in fact the case the article would paralyse business activity, and steps have been taken to remove from its scope the great majority of situations where agreements are in place. The initial approach of the Commission and the Court was to remove from the application of the article those agreements where the market share of the parties concerned was only minimal. For example, in the case of *Franz Völk* v *Ets Vervaecke SPRL* case 5/69 [1969] CMLR 273, an agreement was not condemned under art. 81(1) even where it contained clauses that, in other contexts, would have been clearly in breach. The agreement was an exclusive distribution agreement providing absolute territorial protection, between a German producer of washing machines and a distributor based in Belgium. The manufacturer's market share was, at 0.6 per cent, considered to be insignificant, and the agreement related to only 600 units. In these circumstances the Court held that 'an agreement escapes the prohibition of Article [81] when it only affects the market insignificantly, account being taken of the weak position held by the parties on the market in the products in question' (para. 3). It should be noted, however, that art. 81 will still apply at market shares greatly below those necessary to establish the presence of a dominant position under art. 82.

These *de minimis* decisions have been 'codified' in a Commission *Notice on agreements of minor importance*, which has been regularly overhauled since the first notice was introduced. While such notices cannot have the force of law, and do not bind the Commission, they are considered to be of the status of at least 'soft law' by those seeking guidance from them, and are likely to reflect accurately current Commission policies. In the most recent version of the notice the Commission makes it clear that where undertakings rely on the notice in good faith and assume that an agreement is covered by the notice the Commission will not impose fines on them if it subsequently finds them to be in breach. In cases where the notice does apply 'the Commission will not institute proceedings either upon application or its own initiative' (para. 4).

The most recent version of the *de minimis* notice was published in 2001 ((2001) OJ C368/13) and is the most detailed version of the notice published to date and, according to the accompanying press release (IP/02/13, 7 January 2002), 'reflects an economic approach'. Thresholds provided for in the earlier versions of the notices have been raised. Under the 2001 notice the relevant thresholds for the application of art. 81(1) are different depending on whether agreements are made between competing or non-competing undertakings. In the case of competitors, or potential competitors, the threshold is 10 per cent of any of the relevant markets affected by the agreement(s) (para. 7(a)). Where the undertakings are not competitors or potential competitors the threshold is 15 per cent (para. 7(b)). In situations in which it is not readily easy to determine whether the relevant undertakings are competitors or not the lower threshold is to be the applicable one.

For the first time the notice sets out a threshold to apply to situations in which there exists a network of small agreements which have a cumulative effect, although in this respect the formula is a little more complex. Both the thresholds set out in para. 7 are reduced to 5 per cent in respect of individual agreements, and a cumulative foreclosure effect is considered to be unlikely to exist if less than 30 per cent of the relevant market is affected by a network of parallel agreements. This is to say that, for example, where there is a network of parallel agreements which covers 20 per cent of the market, and a new one is entered into between parties which have less than 5 per cent of the overall market, both the individual agreement and the network of similar agreements will be found not to be appreciable.

Certain 'hard-core' restrictions are considered sufficiently onerous as to invite condemnation even where they are entered into by parties whose market shares would be such as to fall within the application of the notice. In relation to competitors these are agreements which have as their object the fixing of prices when selling the products to third parties, the limitation of output or sales, and the allocation of markets or customers (these are the same exceptions as found in block exemption 2790/99—see Chapter 10). In the case of agreements between non-competitors the following restrictions are prohibited: those which restrict the ability of a buyer to determine its minimum sale price, the maintenance of absolute territorial protection, various restrictions relating to the operation of selective distribution systems, and restrictions on the ability of a supplier of components to a manufacturer that would limit the ability of the supplier to make those components available as spare parts (these are the same exceptions as found in block exemption 2658/2000—see Chapter 10).

The fact that an agreement or conduct falls above the thresholds set out in the notice does not mean that such agreements necessarily appreciably restrict competition. It is noted in para. 2 of the notice that such agreements 'may still have only a negligible effect on competition and may therefore not be prohibited by Article 81(1)'. However, such agreements would not benefit from the shortcut to safety provided by the *de minimis* notice.

9.7 Article 81 and the rule of reason

Similarities between the approach of arts 81 and 82 EC and that of the Sherman Act, ss. 1 and 2, have encouraged speculation as to the place of doctrines developed in the American context in Community law. There has been much discussion of the place of the 'rule of reason' in EC law. Section 1 of the Sherman Act is, in part, in the following terms:

Every contract, combination in the form of trust or otherwise, or conspiracy, in restraint of trade or commerce among the several States, or with foreign nations, is declared to be illegal. Every person who shall make any contract or engage in any combination or conspiracy hereby declared to be illegal shall be deemed guilty of a felony.

As was noted in Chapter 1, on its face this provision would condemn a wide range of competitive activity, much of it beneficial. American courts responded to this legislative straitjacket by developing an approach, itself based on the common law, in which the question is asked whether the restraint under attack 'is one that promotes competition or one that suppresses competition' (*National Society of Professional Engineers* v *United States* (1978) 435 US 679 at 691). The test was first introduced in *Standard Oil Co. of New Jersey* v *United States* (1911) 221 US 1, and was given some shape in 1918. Thus the

true test of legality is whether the restraint imposed is such as merely regulates and perhaps thereby promotes competition or whether it is such as may suppress or even destroy competition. To determine that question the court must ordinarily consider the facts peculiar to the business to which the restraint is applied; its condition before and after the restraint was imposed; the nature of the restraint and its effect, actual or probable. The history of the restraint, the evil believed to exist, the reason for adopting the particular remedy, the purpose or end sought to be attained, are all relevant facts.   (*per* Brandeis J in *Chicago Board of Trade* v *United States* (1918) 246 US 231 at 238)

Under the rule of reason a plaintiff must generally show first that the practice in question is likely to damage competition. If this can be demonstrated it is then for the defendant to establish that there are clear benefits that flow from the restraint, and that the restraint is necessary in order for those benefits to be achieved. *Inter alia* vertical restraints fall to be considered under the rule of reason and it is unlikely that a vertical restraint will be condemned except in situations where inter-brand competition is very weak (see, e.g., *Tunis Bros Co.* v *Ford Motor Co.* (1991) 952 F.2d 715).

In the case of *Metropole* the CFI expressly ruled that there was no rule of reason applied in relation to art. 81 (*Metropole Television (M6) and others* v *Commission* case T–112/99 18 September 2001). Here the applicants relied in part upon earlier judgments, including *European Night Services*, to establish the existence of a 'rule of reason'. The approach of the court was to say that

These judgments cannot, however, be interpreted as establishing the existence of a rule of reason in Community competition law. They are, rather, part of a broader trend in the case-law according to which it is not necessary to hold, wholly abstractly and without drawing any distinction, that any agreement restricting the freedom of one or more of the parties is necessarily caught by the prohibition laid down in [art. 81(1)] of the Treaty.   (para. 76)

However, the approach of the court is somewhat disingenuous. Earlier on in the judgment the CFI was even more emphatic holding that 'contrary to the applicants' assertions the existence of such a rule has not, as such, been confirmed by the Community courts' (para. 72). At para. 74 though, the CFI notes that it is only in the framework of art. 81(3) that 'the pro and anti-competitive competition aspects of a restriction may be weighed'. The entire argument developed here is predicated on there being a restriction to be evaluated. As we have seen above in relation to the application of art. 81(1) there are a number of cases in which there clearly are restrictions on the parties within the ordinary understanding of the term, but where the Commission and the courts have held that there is not a restriction for the purposes of art. 81(1). The language of *Metropole* appears to be applicable *only* to those circumstances in which a restriction already exists, and in that case the CFI was stating only the obvious. It is also possible to read *Metropole* as supporting the proposition that art. 81(1) encompasses only economic efficiency based analysis, and that any other considerations are to be dealt with via the application of art. 81(3).

While many have been unable to resist the temptation of comparing the operation of the rule of reason with the process whereby matters are considered under art. 81, the argument is a complex one and of doubtful value. The availability of the art. 81(3) exception has meant that major problems have not been created for undertakings when their arrangements are brought within the scope of art. 81(1). The analysis undertaken for the purposes of art. 81(3) is akin to, but not the same as, that carried out in applying the rule of reason. Generally arguments based on an application of the rule of reason in relation to art. 81 are designed to remove from the scope of the article altogether many of the agreements which now fall to be considered under art. 81(3), and would thus deprive the operation of art. 81 of much of its current flexibility.

In its *Modernisation White Paper* the Commission accepted that it was, in effect, advocating an approach similar to that taken under the rule of reason, and noted, in relation to arguments about the rule of reason, that

the Commission has already adopted this approach to a limited extent and has carried out an assessment of the pro- and anti-competitive aspects of some restrictive practices under art. [81(1)] . . . However, the structure of [art. 81] is such as to prevent greater use being made of this approach.   (para. 57)

10

Block exemption regulations under article 81 EC

10.1 Introduction

The authority for the making of block exemption regulations stems from art. 83 EC, which provides that the secondary legislation necessary to give effect to the principles set out in arts 81 and 82 'shall be laid down by the Council, acting by a qualified majority on a proposal from the Commission'. Such legislation may be designed, *inter alia,*

(b) to lay down detailed rules for the application of Article [81(3)], taking into account the need to ensure effective supervision on the one hand, and to simplify administration to the greatest possible extent on the other.

Block exemption regulations are made on the basis of the experience gained by the EC Commission in the application of art. 81(3), and are designed to clarify the application of art. 81(3) in specific categories of agreements. Two Council Regulations establish the general framework within which block exemption regulations may be made. These are Regulation 19/65 ((1965) JO 533) and Regulation 2821/71 ((1971) JO L285/46). Regulation 19/65 gave the Commission the authority to issue regulations relating to bilateral exclusive dealing arrangements, and Regulation 2821/75 an equivalent power applicable to categories of agreements relating to intellectual property. Regulation 19/65 was amended in 1999 by Regulation 1215/99 (1999) OJ L148/1, which was part of the follow-up to the *Green Paper on Vertical Restraints* discussed in the previous chapter. Recital (9) of Regulation 1215/99 made clear the thrust of the changes that were to be effected, stating that 'the Commission should be empowered to replace the existing legislation with legislation which is simpler, more flexible and better targeted, and which may cover all types of vertical agreements'.

Importantly, in relation to the balance of power between the Member States and the Commission a new para. 7(2) was added to Regulation 19/65, which gives the Member States the power to withdraw the benefit of a block exemption regulation in cases where an agreement falling within its terms has 'certain effects which are incompatible with the conditions laid down in art. 81(3) . . . in the territory of a Member State, or in part thereof, which has all the characteristics of a distinct market'. The block exemptions considered in this chapter are those that were enacted under these instruments. Further authorization has been given in specific areas such as transport and insurance.

Provision is further made in Regulation 1/2003 in art. 29 (Chapter IX of the regulation) for the withdrawal of the benefit of a block exemption regulation in individual cases. Article 29(2) is in similar terms to art. 7(2) of Regulation 19/65, but art. 29(1) provides in addition that in the case of any block exemption regulation the Commission may

acting on its own initiative or on a complaint, withdraw the benefit of such an exemption Regulation when it finds that in any particular case an agreement, decision or concerted practice to which the exemption Regulation applies has certain effects which are incompatible with art. 81(3) of the Treaty.

The following are the main block exemptions as of May 2004:

- Regulation 2790/99 on the application of art. 81(3) of the Treaty to categories of vertical agreements and concerted practices (1999) OJ L336/21;

- Regulation 2658/2000 on the application of art. 81(3) of the Treaty to categories of specialization agreements (2000) OJ L304/3;

- Regulation 2659/2000 on the application of art. 81(3) of the Treaty to categories of research and development agreements (2000) OJ L304/7;

- Regulation (EC) 1400/2002 on the application of art. 81(3) of the Treaty to categories of vertical agreements and concerted practices in the motor vehicle sector (2002) OJ L203/30;

- Regulation (EC) 772/2004 on the application of art. 81(3) of the Treaty to categories of technology transfer agreements (2004) OJ L123/11.

In addition to these regulations the Commission has also published a number of guidelines and explanatory notes which further clarify the rules set out within the regulations. Of particular importance are the *Guidelines on Vertical Restraints* (2000) OJ C291/1, *Guidelines on the applicability of Article 81 to Horizontal Agreements* (2001) OJ C3/2, *Guidelines on the application of Article 81 of the EC Treaty to technology transfer agreements* (2004) OJ C101/2, and an explanatory brochure on *Distribution and Servicing of Motor Vehicles in the European Union* (available on the DG Comp web site **http://europa.eu.int/comm/competition/antitrust/legislation**).

The current block exemption regulations are in part an attempt to reflect economic considerations and the needs of business. They are therefore less prescriptive than earlier versions, and in a number of cases set a benchmark share of the relevant market within which they are applicable. The relevant market shares range from 30 per cent in the case of vertical agreements, to 20 per cent in the case of certain technology transfer agreements, and specialization agreements.

10.2 **Vertical agreements**

10.2.1 **Regulation 2790/99**

It has already been seen in the previous chapter that the approach taken in *Etablissements Consten SARL and Grundig-Verkaufs-GmbH* v *Commission* cases 56, 58/64 [1966] CMLR 418 confirmed, to the surprise of some, that art. 81 could be applicable to vertical agreements, including those designed to facilitate the marketing and distribution of goods.

As was discussed in Chapter 8 the approach taken by the vast majority of economists to vertical agreements is that, in the absence of significant market power, they are likely to be more beneficial than harmful, and allow in particular a producer to offer an incentive to a retailer to invest in the distribution and promotion of the good or service in question.

In practice the great majority of such agreements would have benefited from an individual exemption under art. 81(3) under the pre-modernization system, and would now benefit from the legal exception. However, when notifications were required, and when the Commission had exclusive competence in this area, the burden falling on the Commission nearly led to the collapse of the system. This was particularly the case in the early days of the system, when a great many such agreements were notified to the Commission. The present block exemption regulation applicable to general vertical agreements, Regulation 2790/99, replaced two earlier block exemption regulations, which themselves replaced the first such regulation, introduced in 1967.

Regulation 2790/99 should be read alongside the Commission Notice, *Guidelines on Vertical Restraints*, published in May 2000.

Recital (3) of the Regulation identifies a range of vertical agreements which can normally be regarded as satisfying the conditions laid down in art. 81(3). This category

includes vertical agreements for the purchase or sale of goods or services where these agreements are concluded between non-competing undertakings, between certain competitors or by certain associations of retailers of goods; it also includes vertical agreements containing ancillary provisions on the assignment or use of intellectual property rights.

This includes not only standard distribution agreements, but also franchising agreements, and the *Guidelines*, at paras 42–44, deal with the assignment of know-how that is central to franchise agreements.

The recitals to the regulation iterate the arguments made in favour of such agreements in the case law and previous decisions. The recitals are an integral part of the regulation and on several occasions the ECJ interpreted provisions of Regulation 67/67 in the light of its recitals, as, for example, in *De Norre* v *NV Brouwerij Concordia* case 47/76 [1977] 1 CMLR 378. It is recognized in the recitals therefore that

(6) Vertical agreements of the category defined in this Regulation can improve economic efficiency within a chain of production or distribution by facilitating better coordination between the participating undertakings; in particular they can lead to a reduction in the transaction and distribution costs of the parties and to an optimisation of their sales and investment levels.

(7) The likelihood that such efficiency-enhancing effects will outweigh any anti-competitive effects due to restrictions contained in vertical agreements depends on the degree of market power of the undertakings concerned.

It is this focus on market power which marks the most significant difference between the operation of this regulation, and its predecessors. Where the earlier regulations set out detailed lists of acceptable, 'white' clauses, and unacceptable, 'black' clauses, the new regulation provides that, with some limited exceptions, all vertical restraints are acceptable unless they are coupled to significant market power. Recognizing that there may still be some situations in which the effect of agreements may be harmful, and in particular those in which there are parallel networks of vertical agreements which have a foreclosure effect, there is mention in recital (13), and later in the regulation, of the power of the Commission to with-draw the benefit of the exemption (see also art. 6, and Regulation 1/2003, art. 29).

Article 1 of the regulation defines basic terms relevant to its application, and the core provision is that of art. 2, which provides that:

Article 81(1) shall not apply to agreements or concerted practices entered into between two or more undertakings each of which operates, for the purposes of the agreement, at a different level of the production or distribution chain, and relating to the conditions under which the parties may purchase, sell or resell certain goods or services ('vertical restraints').

The exemption applies also to agreements between associations of undertakings and their members as long as all members are retailers of goods, and if no individual member has a turnover in excess of €50m. This does not affect the possible applica-tion of art. 81(1) to horizontal agreements between members of the association (art. 2(2)). The three main elements of this definition are set out in para. 24 of the *Guidelines*. The agreement must be between two or more undertakings, and agreements with final consumers not operating as an undertaking do not there-fore count. It does not matter if each undertaking operates at various levels of the market, as long as the specific agreement is between elements operating at a different level, and the purpose of the regulation is to 'cover purchase and distribution agreements'. Rent and lease agreements are not covered.

Article 2(3) includes provisions relating to the assignment of intellectual property rights where the assignment is a legitimate part of a vertical agreement otherwise covered by the exemption. Five conditions are set out for this to be valid, the main purpose being to 'ensure that the [Regulation] applies to vertical agreements where the use, sale or resale of goods or services can be performed more effectively because IPRs are assigned to or transferred for use by the buyer' (*Guidelines*, para. 31).

The limiting principle is set out in art. 3, para. 1, which provides that the exemption provided for in art. 2 shall apply on condition that the market share held by the supplier does not exceed 30% of the relevant market on which it sells the contract goods or services.

A similar market share of 30 per cent applies in relation to buyers where the vertical agreement relates to exclusive supply obligations (art. 3(2)). Agreements as a whole will not be covered by the exemption in situations in which, either by themselves or in combination with other factors, they have one of a number of objectives (art. 4). These include:

(a) setting fixed or minimum sale prices (maximum prices may be set in some circumstances);

(b) setting territorial restrictions except in certain defined, limited circumstances;

(c) restricting cross-supplies in a selective distribution system;

(d) restrictions accepted by a buyer of components which prevent the supplier of those components from selling them as spare parts to end-users or repairers not approved of by the buyer.

The approach to territorial restrictions follows that long established by the Commission, in that the protection of exclusively assigned territories must permit passive sales, although active sales may be prevented. The *Guidelines* provide definitions of 'active' and 'passive' sales, that for the first time deal also with the issue of marketing over the Internet. The definitions, in full, are as follows:

'Active' sales mean: (1) actively approaching individual customers inside another distributor's exclusive territory or exclusive customer group by, for instance, direct mail or visits, or (2) actively approaching a specific customer group or customers in a specific territory allocated exclusively to another distributor through advertisement in media or other promotions specifically targeted at that customer group or targeted at customers in that territory, or (3) establishing a warehouse or distribution outlet in another distributor's exclusive territory.

'Passive' sales mean responding to unsolicited requests from individual customers, including delivery of goods or services to such customers. General advertising or promotion in media or on the Internet that reaches customers in other distributors' exclusive territories or customer groups but which is a reasonable way to reach customers outside those territories or customer groups, for instance, to reach customers in non-exclusive territories or in one's own territory, are passive sales.   (para. 50)

The question of Internet sales is an important one, and it is generally recognized that the development of e-commerce threatens to change radically concepts of 'exclusivity' and assigned territories. At para. 51 of the *Guidelines* the Commission deals with the issue at some length, taking as the starting point the basic principle that

[e]very distributor must be free to use the Internet to advertise or sell products. A restriction on the use of the Internet by distributors could only be compatible with the [Regulation] to the extent that promotion on the Internet or sales over the Internet would lead to active selling into other distributors' exclusive territories or customer groups.

The Commission considers the situation where a customer contacts a distributor through the distributor's web site, and places an order, to be one of passive selling.

Further, the language used on the web site will be irrelevant. Outright bans on selling on the Internet will be permitted only where there is an objective justification. The position here is likely to have been influenced by the experience gained in America, where the issue of Internet selling has already led to some difficulties. It was reported in 1998, for example, that Tupperware had prohibited its more than 7,000 'sales consultants' from selling Tupperware through the consultants' own web sites. Tupperware had argued that the product needed live demonstrations in order to be most effectively sold.

In Regulation 1400/2002, relating to motor vehicle distribution (discussed at 10.2.2) it is also expressly provided that the right to passively sell the goods subject to the agreement in question 'should include the right to use the Internet or Internet referral sites' (recital (15)).

Article 5 provides that certain obligations within an agreement will not be covered by the block exemption, although to the extent to which these can be separated out from the agreement as a whole, the latter will still benefit. There are few of these, and the first two relate to various non-completion obligations, while the third relates to any provision under which members of a selective distribution system are prevented from selling competing brands.

The right of Member States to withdraw the benefit of the block exemption in accordance with the conditions laid down in Regulation 19/65 is confirmed in art. 7.

Article 9 relates to the issue of the calculation and assessment of market share. Although the regulation resolves many of the problems that flowed from the overly formalistic approach adopted under the earlier block exemptions, it does not provide a solution to every problem that will always be simple. To some extent it has replaced formalistic legal analysis with sophisticated economic analysis, and although for a great many small- and medium-sized undertakings this will not present any problem, there will be a class of firms for which there may be genuine doubt whether they are operating at the 30 per cent threshold. Paragraph 1 of art. 9 refers to the by now standard definition of goods or services 'sold by the supplier, which are regarded as interchangeable or substitutable by the buyer, by reason of the products' characteristics, their prices and their intended use'. The effect of this is to require the analytical framework of the Commission *Notice on Market Definition* (discussed in Chapter 14) to be applied. Market shares are to be calculated on the previous year's data where these are available, and they may, for a two-year period, exceed 30 per cent as long as they do not rise above 35 per cent. If they are initially below 30 per cent, but then rise to above 35 per cent, the period of grace shall be limited to one year.

The application of Regulation 2790/99 was considered in the Commission infringement decision *JCB* 2002/190 (2002) OJ L69/1. Here the Commission condemned, following a notification some 27 years earlier, a distribution agreement entered into between the JCB Group and various appointed distributors in respect of construction and earthmoving equipment and spare parts. In 1996 a complaint was lodged with the Commission by a French undertaking alleging that JCB had taken active steps to prevent it sourcing supplies from the UK, where they were cheaper than in France. The Commission found, *inter alia*, that Regulation 2790/99 was not applicable to the agreements in question as the market share of JCB for backhoe loaders was 40 per cent by value and 45 per cent by volume, and that even were a wider market definition adopted, bringing the market share within the 30 per cent threshold, the agreements incorporated hard-core restrictions contrary to art. 4(a)–(d) of the Regulation (see paras 198–9). On appeal (*JCB Service* v *Commission* case T–67/01, [2004] 4 CMLR 24) the CFI substantially upheld the decision in so far as it related to territorial restrictions, although it did find that the Commission had failed to establish adequately some of the other alleged breaches.

10.2.2 Motor vehicle sector agreements—Regulation 1400/2002

Regulation 1400/2002, which entered into force on 1 October 2002, replaced Regulation 1475/95 on the application of art. [81(3)] of the Treaty to certain categories of motor vehicle distribution and servicing agreements (1995) OJ L145/25 which was heavily criticized over a number of years. The very broad approach underpinning the regulation is that stricter rules than those set out in Regulation 2790/1999 are necessary in the case of vertical agreements in the motor sector, and there is too a recognition of the fact that 'motor vehicles are expensive and technically complex mobile goods which require repair and maintenance at regular and irregular intervals' (recital (21)). In its explanatory brochure the Commission cites research showing that the cost of purchasing a car and the cost of maintaining it both account for about 40 per cent each of the full cost of ownership (para 3.2).

A full analysis of Regulation 1400/2002 is beyond the scope of this text, and an introduction only is given here. Those seeking further details are referred in particular to the explanatory brochure (running to over 90 pages) available on the DG Comp web site. A critical analysis of the regulation written by members of an automotive sector group may also be found at [2003] ECLR 254 (Automotive Sector Groups of Houthoff Buruma and Liedekerke Wolters Waelbroeck Kirkpartick, 'Flawed Reform of the Competition Rules for the European Motor Vehicle Distribution Sector').

The vertical agreements covered by Regulation 1400/2002 are the following:

vertical agreements for the purchase or sale of new motor vehicles, vertical agreements for the purchase or sale of spare parts for motor vehicles and vertical agreements for the purchase or sale of repair and maintenance services for such vehicles where these agreements are concluded between non-competing undertakings, between certain competitors, or by certain associations of retailers or repairers. (recital (3))

The regulation applies to various types of vertical distribution agreements entered into in relation to the sales of vehicles, spare parts, and servicing arrangements. For the purposes of the regulation selective distribution systems are divided into two categories: qualitative selective distribution systems where the supplier uses criteria which are exclusively determined by quality, whatever the results in terms of the numbers of distributors this leads to; and quantitative selective distribution systems where criteria are used which directly limit the number of distributors (art. 1(g) and (h)). Manufacturers are no longer able to choose between a combination of selective and exclusive distribution systems, but instead have to make a choice between the two at the outset. Motor vehicles are defined as being 'a self propelled vehicle intended for use on public roads and having three or more road wheels' (art. 1(n)). Spare parts are defined as 'goods which are to be installed in or upon a motor vehicle so as to replace components of that vehicle, including goods such as lubricants which are necessary for the use of a motor vehicle' (art. 1(s)), although this excludes fuel.

Article 2 of the regulation sets out its basic scope. This is that art. 81(1) EC shall not apply, subject to the provisions of the regulation, to 'vertical agreements where they relate to the conditions under which the parties may purchase, sell or resell new motor vehicles, spare parts for motor vehicles or repair and maintenance services for motor vehicles' (art. 2(1)). However, this exemption applies only where the agreement is a vertical one, and the parties are not competitors, unless the agreement is not reciprocal and: (i) the turnover of the buyer does not exceed 100m; or (ii) the supplier both manufactures and distributes goods, while the purchaser does not manufacture competing goods; or (iii) the buyer does not compete at the level of trade at which the service is provided by the seller.

The relevant market shares are that the supplier's share of the relevant market be less than 30 per cent except that the threshold shall be 40 per cent in the case of agreements establishing quantitative selective distribution systems for the sale of new motor vehicles. Article 8 makes provision for the calculation of market shares. In practice it is likely that the market shares will normally be significantly below these levels. In its examination of the market for the supply of new motor cars in the UK the UK Competition Commission found that no one company had a market share in excess of 25%, and most fell well below this figure (*New Cars: A report on the supply of new motor cars within the UK* (Cm. 4660, 2000). In the case of qualitative selective distribution systems these thresholds do not apply (art. 3(1)). These criteria are further elaborated on in art. 3. Where the vertical agreement contains exclusive supply obligations the exemption applies as long as the market share held by the buyer does not exceed 30 per cent of the relevant market on which the purchases are made (art. 3(2)). This is a cumulative condition to that set out in art. 3(1)). One effect of this is that it should, if it operates as hoped, make it easier for retailers to sell different brands on the same location, and the Commission has stated that 'the aim of the regulation as far as multi-branding is concerned is to increase competition between brands of different suppliers' ('Frequently Asked Questions' about the regulation on the DG Comp web site).

The distributor or repairer must be permitted to transfer the rights and obligations arising under the agreement to another distributor or repairer within the system (art. 3(3)), and the supplier may not terminate the agreement without giving notice in writing including 'detailed, objective and transparent reasons for the termination' (art. 3(4)). This latter obligation is designed to prevent a supplier from terminating an agreement because the purchaser engages in practices which are not otherwise restricted under the regulation, for example by making passive sales outside the allocated territory, which would be permitted under the regulation, but which might run contrary to the wishes of the supplier.

Any agreement falling within the block exemption regulation must be concluded by the supplier of new motor vehicles for a period of at least five years, with at least six months' notice to be given of an intention not to renew the agreement (art. 3(5)(a)), or the agreement is to be concluded for an indefinite period, with at least two years' notice of termination being given by either party, although in some circumstances this period may be reduced to one year (art. 3(5)(b)). By virtue of art. 3(6) the agreement must make provision for independent arbitration in the event of certain disputes, although this right is without prejudice to the ability of either party to refer a dispute to their national court.

Article 4 sets out an extensive list of hard-core restrictions the presence of which will invalidate the exemption. As with all the block exemption regulations the central requirements here are that the agreement may not restrict the ability of the reseller to determine their sales price (art. 4(1)(a)), and may not impose absolute territorial protection (art. 4(1)(b), (d), and (e)). In relation to the sales of new motor vehicles only, there must be not restriction on the ability of the distributor to sell any new motor vehicle corresponding to a model within the contract range (art. 4(1)(f)), or on the ability of the reseller (subject to certain technical requirements) to subcontract the provision of repair and maintenance services to authorized repairers (art. 4(1)(g)). Other hard-core restrictions are set out in relation to the supplies of repair and maintenance services, and spare parts. Finally,

the exemption shall not apply where the supplier of motor vehicles refuses to give independent operators access to any technical information, diagnostic and other equipment, tools, including any relevant software, or training required for the repair and maintenance of these motor vehicles or for the implementation of environmental protection measures. (art. 4(2))

Other terms that may be found in such agreements will not benefit from the exemption, although their presence will not invalidate the agreement as a whole. These are set out in art. 5, and include non-compete obligations. One cumulative effect of these obligations is that manufacturers' warranties issued in one Member State must be honoured under the same conditions in all Member States, although manufacturers are free to choose how to implement this requirement.

Where a parallel network of similar vertical restraints covers more than 50 per cent of a relevant market the Commission may, by way of a regulation, declare that the block exemption regulation does not apply to vertical agreements containing specific restraints relating to that market (art. 7(1)), although in the unlikely event that any such regulation is made there shall be a period of one year before it becomes effective to allow the parties time to adjust their agreements in order to comply with the change in law.

The Commission is required regularly to monitor the application of the regulation, and to draw up a report on its operation by 31 May 2008 at the latest (art. 11). The regulation is due to expire on 31 May 2010.

10.2.3 Technology transfer agreements—Regulation 772/2004

Regulation 772/2004 is the third set of legislation to deal with the application of art. 81(3) EC to vertical agreements under which technology is transferred from one party to another. It entered into force on 1 May 2004, although in respect of earlier agreements falling within the terms of Regulation 240/96 (on the application of art. [81(3)] of the Treaty to certain categories of technology transfer agreements (1996) OJ L31/2) which was repealed by Regulation 772/2004 there is a transitional period extending up to 31 March 2006 (art. 10). Regulation 240/96 itself replaced and consolidated the law found in two earlier regulations, but was criticized for its rigid approach, and in 2000 the Commission published an *Evaluation Report on the Transfer of Technology Block Exemption Regulation No 240/96*. The response to suggestions for reform was generally favourable, and the new regulation reflects a greatly simplified approach. A Commission notice providing *Guidelines on the application of art. 81 of the EC Treaty to technology transfer agreements* has been published at (2004) OJ C101/2 and this sheds further light on the operation of the regulation. The regulation is due to expire on 30 April 2014.

It is a matter of common commercial practice that the originators of intellectual property or new technologies are often not those who themselves are best in a position to directly exploit them, and will instead license this task to a second party or parties. As recognized in recital (5) to the regulation,

Technology transfer agreements concern the licensing of technology. Such agreements will usually improve economic efficiency and be pro-competitive as they can reduce duplication of research and development, strengthen the incentive for the initial research and development, spur incremental innovation, facilitate diffusion and generate product market competition.

As with the other block exemption regulations the position of the parties to the agreement on the relevant market is considered to be important:

The likelihood that such efficiency enhancing and pro-competitive effects will outweigh any anti-competitive effects due to restrictions contained in technology transfer agreements depends on the degree of market power of the undertakings concerned and, therefore, on the extent to which those undertakings face competition from undertakings owning substitute technologies or undertakings producing substitute products.   (recital (6))

The Commission took the view early on that patent licensing would fall within art. 81(1) EC unless the licence merely confirmed the existence of the property right in the patent in question. The most important case in this respect is that of *LC Nungesser KG and Kurt Eisele* v *Commission* case 258/78 [1983] 1 CMLR 278 ('the *maize seed* case'). This dealt with the commercial exploitation of a modified type of maize seed, where the right owner, an agency of the French Government, INRA, granted an exclusive licence to a German resident, Eisele. An agreement was concluded in 1965 under which Eisele was granted territorial protection in relation to the seed variety in Germany. When Eisele sought to enforce his rights in the German courts to prevent parallel imports, following which a settlement was reached, a complaint was subsequently made to the EC Commission, which found that both the grant of the right and the settlement of the case were in contravention of art. 81(1). An application for an exemption under art. 81(3) was rejected. An appeal was made to the ECJ which ruled that although the grant of the exclusive licence itself did not violate art. 81(1), a 'closed licence' may contravene art. 81(1). In this context a 'closed licence' is one which not only confirms an exclusive licence in a given territory on the licensee, but further affects the position of third parties, i.e. by restricting their ability to distribute the product in that territory. The ECJ preferred a model of an 'open licence' which merely confirmed the grant of the licence, and an obligation on the licensor itself not to compete with the licensee. At the same time the ECJ linked the benefits of the open licence with the need to disseminate *new* technology, and suggested that if the technology licensed was not sufficiently new, then even an open licence might contravene art. 81(1). This approach has been followed by the EC Commission on a number of occasions since, and in particular the Commission has stressed that while restrictions might be permissible in the early years of a development of new technology, they cannot be permitted to continue indefinitely. While this case dealt with 'plant-breeder's rights' the ECJ indicated that the same approach could be applied to other types of intellectual property, including, presumably, patents and know-how.

Article 1 of the regulation provides the basic definitions necessary to understanding the later terms of the regulation. Most important of these is the definition of a technology transfer agreement. This is

a patent licensing agreement, a know-how licensing agreement, a software copyright licensing agreement or a mixed patent, know-how or software copyright licensing agreement, including any such agreement containing provisions which relate to the sale and purchase of products or which relate to the licensing of other intellectual property rights or the assignment of intellectual property rights, provided that those provisions do not constitute the primary object of the agreement and are directly related to the production of the contract products; assignments of patents, know-how, software copyright or a combination thereof where part of the risk associated with the exploitation of the technology remains with the assignor, in particular where the sum payable in consideration of the assignment is dependent on the turnover obtained by the assignee in respect of products produced with the assigned technology, the quantity of such products produced or the number of operations carried out employing the technology, shall also be deemed to be technology transfer agreements. (art. 1(b))

'Intellectual property rights' are further defined in art. 1(g) to include 'industrial property rights, know-how, copyright and neighbouring rights'. Know-how, which is not generally defined in the law of intellectual property, is defined in art. 1(i) as being 'a package of non-patented practical information' which meets three further criteria. It should be (1) secret; (2) substantial; and (3) identified. It might be asked why such a definition is actually necessary as it would be unlikely that anyone would pay for a right to the use of know-how that was neither secret, nor substantial, nor capable of being clearly identified and explained.

The basic exemption from the application of art. 81(1) provided by the regulation is set out in art. 2, and the time period of the exemption in any particular case is the period of the existence of the intellectual property right in question, which may vary depending on the type of intellectual property, and by which body or bodies the right has been recognized. In the case of know-how the time period extends for as long as the know-how remains secret. The relevant market share thresholds are set out in art. 3. These are 20 per cent in the case of competing undertakings, and 30 per cent in the case of non-competing undertakings. The calculation and application of these thresholds is further expanded on in art. 8. In particular a 'safe harbour' is provided whereby the exemption shall continue for a period of two years following an increase of the market share above the levels specified in art. 3.

Prohibited hard-core restrictions are set out in art. 4. The standard prohibition on restricting the ability of a party to determine its selling price, and limitations on output (in this case subject to certain conditions), and the allocation of customers or markets are all found here. The licensor may impose restrictions on the *type* of use to which the technology is put, i.e. the licence may be for a particular purpose only (art. 4(1)(c)(i)). What is perhaps worthy of particular note is that some territorial restrictions may be imposed which go further than are permitted under any of the other block exemption regulations, and which go further than would be suggested by the general application of art. 81(1). Thus art. 4(1)(c)(iv) *permits* 'the restriction, in a non-reciprocal agreement, of active and/or *passive sales* by the licensee and/or the licensor into the exclusive territory or to the exclusive customer group reserved for the other party' (emphasis added). Similarly, in the case of licences between undertakings which are not competing with each other passive sales may be restricted into an exclusive territory or to an exclusive customer group (art. 4(2)(b)(i)) or to the customers of another licensee during the first two years that the licensee is selling that product (art. 4(2)(b)(ii)). It is to be presumed that the licensee may *not* refuse to supply, within its own territory, a known parallel exporter, although this is much harder to monitor, and the effect of these terms of the regulation is to allow for much greater market division than is the case elsewhere in the application of EC competition law.

Article 5 sets out certain excluded restrictions, the presence of which does not serve to invalidate the agreement as a whole, but which individually will not benefit from the exemption provided for in art. 2. These include: an obligation on a licensee to compulsory license back, or to assign to the licensor or a nominated third party 'severable improvements' that it creates in relation to the new technology; and any direct or indirect obligation not to challenge the validity of the intellectual property which forms the subject matter of the agreement.

The Commission may withdraw the benefit of the block exemption in individual cases in accordance with art. 6. The list of circumstances in which this may happen is not a closed one, but includes situations where the parties, 'without any objectively valid reason' do not exploit the technology (art. 6(1)(c)), or where parallel networks of similar agreements restrict competition (art. 6(1)(a) and (b)).

10.3 The horizontal block exemptions

Not all cooperation between undertakings that are competitors, or potential competitors, is necessarily bad, and two special cases are dealt with by way of block exemption regulations. In their broad approach, both these regulations resemble Regulation 2790/99.

10.3.1 Research and development

There is a general commitment on the part of the EC to the fostering of research and development (R&D) which is emphasized in the Treaty itself. Article 163, introduced by the Single European Act, is, in part, in the following terms:

1. The Community shall have the objective of strengthening the scientific and technological bases of Community industry and encouraging it to become more competitive at international level, while promoting all the research activities deemed necessary by virtue of other chapters of this Treaty.

2. For this purpose the Community shall, throughout the Community, encourage undertakings, including small- and medium-sized undertakings, research centres and universities in their research and technological development activities of high quality; it shall support their efforts to cooperate with one another, aiming, notably, at enabling undertakings to exploit the internal market potential to the full, in particular through the opening up of national public contracts, the definition of common standards and the removal of legal and fiscal obligations to that cooperation.

Generally, R&D agreements are among the small class of horizontal agreements that are actively encouraged by the competition authorities, and the Commission has made it clear that in many cases it does not consider that R&D agreements are in any way restrictive of competition, and are not therefore caught by art. 81(1). In its *14th Annual Report on Competition Policy* (1984) the EC Commission recognized the importance of R&D to the development of the EC economy:

Competition . . . relies increasingly on innovation . . . The introduction of new processes and products on the market stimulates competition within the common market, and helps to strengthen the ability of European industry to compete internationally. . . . R&D plays an essential role. In fact R&D promotes and maintains dynamic competition, characterised by initiation and imitation and in doing so assures economic growth.

. . . in many cases the synergy arising out of a cooperation is necessary because it enables the partners to share the financial risks involved and in particular to bring together a wider range of intellectual and mental resources and experience, thus promoting the transfer of technology. In the absence of such cooperation, the innovation may not take place at all, or otherwise not as successfully or efficiently. Also the present situation in the Community demands more rapid and effective transformation of new ideas into marketable products and processes, which may be facilitated by joint efforts by several undertakings.

The Commission has always shown a favourable attitude towards R&D cooperation provided that competition is maintained by the existence of different independent poles of research.

While statements such as these demonstrate a flexible attitude to R&D agreements, evidence of which can also be found in previous Commission decisions, it is a general requirement, consistent with the wording of art. 81(3), that such agreements should not contain restrictions which go beyond those necessary to undertake the project successfully and to exploit its fruits. Particular attention will be paid to terms which limit the conduct of the participants after the conclusion of the project. Further, greater concerns will be raised in markets which are highly concentrated. These factors have informed the block exemption, in which R&D is defined as

the acquisition of know-how relating to products or processes and the carrying out of theoretical analysis, systematic study or experimentation, including experimental production, technical testing of products or processes, the establishment of the necessary facilities and the obtaining of intellectual property rights for the results.   (art. 2(4))

The regulation exempts from the application of art. 81(1) agreements under which undertakings pursue

(a) joint research and development of products or processes and joint exploitation of the results of that research and development;

(b) joint exploitation of the results of research and development of products or processes jointly carried out pursuant to a prior agreement between the same parties; or

(c) joint research and development of products or processes excluding joint exploitation of the results.   (art. 1(1))

Ancillary restrictions which are not directly about R&D but the presence of which is a necessary component of the agreement will also be covered by the operation of the block. Article 3 sets out four conditions for the granting of an exemption. These are, in brief, that

(a) all parties must have access to the results;

(b) where the agreement is only in relation to pure R&D the parties must be free to exploit it in any way they wish;

(c) where the agreement includes provisions for joint exploitation this can only be permitted where the results are protected by intellectual property, and are 'decisive for the manufacture';

(d) where the agreement makes provision for manufacture by way of specialization, the undertakings engaged in such manufacture must fulfil orders from all the parties, unless the agreement also provides for joint distribution.

Article 4 provides the market share test that is similar to that of Regulation 2790/99, and which is 'consistent with an economics based approach which assesses the impact of agreements on the relevant market' (recital (7)). Where the parties are not competing at the time of the agreement the exemption will last for the duration of the R&D. When the agreement provides for the joint exploitation of results the exemption will last for seven year from the date at which the contract products are first put on the market (art. 4(1)). At the end of this period the exemption will continue to apply for as long as the market share of the parties does not exceed 25 per cent (art. 4(3)). This balances the fact that it is likely to be the case that R&D agreements may lead to the development of a market in which the parties are the only players, and will have a 100 per cent market share, against the fact that without the joint R&D such a market might not exist at all. It is thus possible to have a seven-year exemption in respect of a very high market share where the parties do not start off as competitors. Where two or more of the parties are competing in the market for products which can be improved or replaced by the contract products, the exemption shall last for the same period as set out in art. 4(1), but only for as long as the parties do not have a combined market share of more than 25 per cent of the relevant market (art. 4(2)).

Article 5 of the regulation removes from its scope entire agreements that have one of 10 objectives. These include: (a) the elimination of independent poles of research; (b) agreements which purport to prevent challenges to the validity of intellectual property rights; (c) limiting output or sales; (d) price fixing; (e)–(j) a number of territorial restrictions, having their origins in various practices.

Provisions in art. 6 relating to the calculation of market shares are similar to those set out in regulation 2790/99.

Article 7 sets out the power of the Commission to withdraw the benefit of the block exemption from individual agreements in a range of circumstances. In addition to the market share tests of art. 6, these provisions allow the Commission to act where the agreement's existence impairs substantially the scope for third parties to carry out R&D in the relevant field because of limited research capacity available elsewhere (art. 6(a)). The remainder of these provisions are largely concerned with situations in which, for a number of possible reasons, effective competition in relation to the products in question is impaired. The regulation will apply until 31 December 2010 (art. 9).

10.3.2 Specialization agreements

In the *Guidelines on the Applicability of Article 81 to Horizontal Cooperation Agreements* (2001) OJ C3/2 published at the same time as the horizontal block exemption regulations, specialization agreements are dealt with as part of the wider set of 'production agreements'. This recognizes the fact that there are a number of forms in which production agreements can manifest themselves, and that specialization agreements, in which 'the parties agree unilaterally or reciprocally to cease production of a product and to purchase it from the other party' (*Guidelines*, para. 79), are merely one such form. The benefits of specialization agreements are referred to in recital (8) of the regulation, which recognizes that

Agreements on specialisation in production generally contribute to improving the production or distribution of goods, because the undertakings concerned can concentrate on the manufacture of certain products and thus operate more efficiently and supply the products more cheaply. Agreements on specialisation in the provision of services can also be said to generally give rise to similar improvements. It is likely that, given effective competition, consumers will receive a fair share of the resulting benefit.

The agreements covered by the block exemption are set out in art. 1, and include: (a) unilateral specialization agreements, (b) reciprocal specialization agreements; and (c) joint production agreements. Related purchasing and marketing agreements are also covered (art. 3). The market share limit set out in art. 4 is a combined market share of 20 per cent, a level lower than that set out in the R&D block exemption, reflecting the fact that the restrictions on competition in the case of specialization agreements can be more severe than that in R&D. Where the market shares are initially less than 20 per cent they may rise to a maximum of 25 per cent for two consecutive years, or may exceed 25 per cent for one year, without the benefit of the exemption being lost (art. 6(2) and (3)).

Article 5 sets out the categories of agreements which cannot benefit from the block exemption, which are those that: (a) fix prices; (b) limit output or sales; and (c) allocate markets or customers. However, to the extent that it is necessary to set prices or produce agreed amounts in the context of a production joint venture, this will be permitted as part of the integration of functions within the joint venture.

The benefit of the block exemption may be withdrawn in accordance with art. 7 where the Commission finds that it has effects which are incompatible with the conditions set out in art. 81(3). In particular this may be the case where: (a) the agreement is not yielding the expected results; or (b) there is no effective competition in respect of the products which are the subject of the agreement in the common market, or a substantial part of it. The regulation shall apply until 31 December 2010.

In situations in which the market shares set out in the Regulation are exceeded it is almost certain that the requirements of art. 81(1) will be met, and an individual analysis under art. 81(3) will be necessary. The Commission, however, is still inclined to take a favourable view of such agreements (see, e.g., *Bayer/Gist-Brocades* 76/172 (1976) OJ L30/13, and *Jaz-Peter* 78/194 (1978) OJ L61/17).

11

The Chapter I Prohibition

11.1 Introduction

Section 2 of the Competition Act 1998 puts into place a prohibition on anti-competitive agreements that is similar to that of art. 81 EC. Section 2 is set out here in full:

2.—(1) Subject to section 3, agreements between undertakings, decisions by associations of undertakings or concerted practices which—

    (a)   may affect trade within the United Kingdom, and

    (b)   have as their object or effect the prevention, restriction or distortion of competition within the United Kingdom,

are prohibited unless they are exempt in accordance with the provisions of this Part.

(2) Subsection (1) applies, in particular, to agreements, decisions or practices which—

    (a)   directly or indirectly fix purchase or selling prices or any other trading conditions;

    (b)   limit or control production, markets, technical development or investment;

    (c)   share markets or sources of supply;

    (d)   apply dissimilar conditions to equivalent transactions with other trading parties, thereby placing them at a competitive disadvantage;

    (e)   make the conclusion of contracts subject to acceptance by the other parties of supplementary obligations which, by their nature or according to commercial usage, have no connection with the subject of such contracts.

(3) Subsection (1) applies only if the agreement, decision or practice is, or is intended to be, implemented in the United Kingdom.

(4) Any agreement or decision which is prohibited by subsection (1) is void.

(5) A provision of this Part, which is expressed to apply to, or in relation to, an agreement is to be read as applying equally to, or in relation to, a decision by an association of undertakings or a concerted practice (but with any necessary modifications).

(6) Subsection (5) does not apply where the context otherwise requires.

(7) In this section 'the United Kingdom' means, in relation to an agreement which operates or is intended to operate only in a part of the United Kingdom, that part.

(8) The prohibition imposed by subsection (1) is referred to in this Act as 'the Chapter I prohibition'.

Because of the overriding nature of s. 60 (see section 3.5.1), requiring this provision to be interpreted consistently with EC law, it should be applied in much the same way as art. 81 EC. However, the extent to which single market issues have been determinant in some of the EC case law may lead to divergence and to some difficulty. The relevant guidelines in respect of the Chapter I Prohibition are *Article 81 and the Chapter I Prohibition, Vertical agreements, Assessment of conduct,* and *Trade associations, professions and self-regulating bodies.*

11.2 Exceptions and exemptions

Section 3 of the Competition Act 1998 sets out generalized exclusions which include: mergers and concentrations, which are dealt with under the relevant provisions of the Enterprise Act 2002 (see Chapter 20); and agreements which are examined under other Acts, which may include activities that are supervised directly by one or other of the industry regulators (Sch. 2). The Secretary of State has been given the power to modify these excluded classes, by either adding to the list or removing from the list those items already on it. Further, the prohibition will apply only where an agreement has an appreciable effect on trade and competition. Section 6 makes provision for block exemption regulations, and s. 10 introduces 'parallel exemptions' which apply where a practice benefits from the legal exception of art. 81, or would benefit were art. 81 applicable. The legal exception regime is the same as for the application of art. 81, with the criteria in s. 9 of the Act mirroring those of art. 81(3). Under the 'old' regime, only.

A small number of agreements were notified to the OFT for consideration for either a negative clearance or exemption. For example, following consultation leading to some adaptation of the agreement a decision of negative clearance was made in respect of the standard conditions for licensing the commercial exhibition of films (*Film Distributors' Association Ltd* CA98/10/2002, [2002] UKCLR 243). Exemptions were granted to *Link Interchange Network Limited* CA98/7/2001 [2002] UKCLR 59, and in respect of the *Memorandum of Understanding on the Supply of Fuel Oils in an Emergency* CA98/8/2001 [2002] UKCLR 74.

11.2.1 *Block exemptions*

Block exemptions may be made to cover categories of agreements which fall within the terms of s. 9. Any such exemption must be proposed and published by the OFT (ss. 6 and 8), and may be made by the Secretary of State as an Order in Parliament. As of May 2004 only one block exemption had been created—the Competition Act 1998 (Public Transport Ticketing Schemes Block Exemption) Order 2001, SI 2001/319. A guideline relating to the application of this block exemption was published in August 2002 (OFT 439).

11.2.2 *Parallel exemptions*

In s. 10 it is provided that '[a]n agreement is exempt from the Chapter I prohibition if it is exempt from the Community prohibition', i.e., from art. 81(1). In effect this merely recognizes the requirement imposed by Regulation 1/2003, art. 3(2). The provision in fact goes further than this, for it applies not only to agreements which are excepted from art. 81(1), but also to those which would be, by virtue of the operation of a block exemption, where the agreement in question is not actually subject to Community law because it has no impact on trade between the Member States (s. 10(2)). One effect of this section then is to import wholesale into the United Kingdom domestic arena, which falls outside the ambit of Community law, all Community block exemptions. The OFT is granted the power to cancel the benefit of the parallel exemption (s. 10(5)).

11.3 *De minimis* thresholds and appreciability

During the passage of the Competition Act the Government indicated that, subject to later consultation, classes of agreements would be exempt from the imposition of financial penalties, but not from any other adverse consequences of breach in accordance with s. 39 ('small agreements') where the turnover of the parties in question was between £20m and £50m (Hansard (HL) 17 November 1997, col. 434). The relevant thresholds are set out in the Competition Act 1998 (Small Agreements and Conduct of Minor Significance) Regulations 2000, SI 2000/262. These provide that small agreements (s. 39(1)) are those where the combined applicable turnover in the year preceding the infringement did not exceed £20m (para. 3). The threshold in respect of s. 40(1) is £50m (para. 4). This 'safe harbour' does not affect the application of art 81 EC by the OFT.

The appreciability test is the same for the EC—see section 9.6.4.

11.4 Horizontal and vertical agreements

Section 2(2) of the Competition Act 1998 includes the list of examples of anti-competitive agreements which mirrors that of art. 81. As with art. 81 this 'is a non-exhaustive, illustrative list and does not set a limit on the investigation and enforcement activities of the OFT. The guideline *Article 81 and the Chapter I Prohibition* does not deal in detail with various types of unlawfully coordinated conduct. However, the EC guidelines on horizontal and vertical agreements discussed in Chapter 7 will be applied in the UK.

11.4.1 Horizontal agreements—Infringement decisions

The first cartel to be penalized by the Director under the new regime demonstrated sharply the improvements that the Competition Act 1998 has made to the system of competition enforcement in the UK. While anti-competitive conduct in the bus industry had bedevilled the operation of the Competition Act 1980, in

Market Sharing by Arriva plc and FirstGroup plc CA98/9/2002, [2002] UKCLR 322, the Director was able to deal decisively with this market. In the case in question the Director concluded that the two undertakings had breached the Chapter II Prohibition by entering into a market-share agreement in respect of bus routes within Leeds. The OFT investigation followed the receipt of an anonymous complaint which alleged that Arriva Yorkshire had entered into an agreement with First Leeds to swap bus routes. The market affected was small, and the initial complaint referred only to two local routes. On-site investigations were carried out in October 2000, and both companies benefited from the operation of the leniency scheme in relation to the operation of cartels (see Chapter 6). One of the board members of Arriva Yorkshire, Mr Peter Harvey, had arranged a meeting in a private room at a Yorkshire hotel where the participants were senior staff of both Arriva and FirstGroup. These meetings were not declared by the FirstGroup participants on a form linked to training in compliance procedures with the Competition Act, which asked the participants to note all contacts with competing companies. The Director found that the object of the agreement reached between the undertakings was 'clearly to share markets geographically by mutual withdrawal from the relevant bus routes' (para. 42). Penalties were imposed, although FirstGroup's was reduced to nil following the application of the leniency scheme.

One of the more unusual horizontal cases considered by the OFT related to an agreement between cattle auctioneers in Northern Ireland which fixed commission rates. This was announced to farmers by way of a press release sent to the *Irish News and Farmers Life*. The OFT condemned the arrangement, but did not issue a penalty given the dire straits in which the industry found itself at the time the arrangement was entered into, as a result of both the BSE and foot and mouth disease epidemics (CA98/1/2003 [2003] UKCLR 433).

There have, in fact, been very few horizontal cases brought under the Competition Act, although there was a horizontal element in *Agreements between Hasbro UK Ltd, Argos Ltd and Littlewoods Ltd fixing the price of Hasbro toys and games* CA98/2/2003 [2003] UKCLR 553, which is discussed below at 11.4.2.1.

11.4.2 Vertical agreements

Early on in its preparation for the 1998 Act, the DTI indicated that it was intended to remove most vertical agreements from the scope of the Chapter I Prohibition. Research carried out on behalf of the DTI indicated that in the majority of formal decisions and cases decided in relation to vertical agreements under EC law, single-market considerations were to the fore. Such considerations would clearly be largely irrelevant in the UK, and Lord Simon, in the House of Lords, suggested that

There remains a case therefore for special treatment of vertical agreements under the Bill to avoid the burden of unnecessary notification and to ease the so-called 'straitjacket' which existing European block exemptions impose.   (Hansard (HL) 9 February 1998, col. 901)

In February 2000 the Government introduced the Competition Act 1998 (Land and Vertical Agreements Exclusion) Order 2000, SI 2000/310 to give effect to this policy. Even before the modernization programme was put into place the Government had announced its intention to withdraw the exclusion order following concerns that it dampened private litigation in cases where genuine harm was being caused, and a recognition that in fact much of the OFT's work was, nevertheless, taken up with vertical agreements. Modernization provided a further spur to this intention, and SI 2000/310 was repealed by the Competition Act 1998 (Land Agreements Exclusion and Revocation) Order 2004 SI 2004/1260, although this does not take effect until 1 May 2005 to permit a transition period. The law relating to vertical agreements in the UK is dealt with in the guideline *Vertical agreements*, and is also discussed briefly in Part 7 of *Assessment of conduct*.

11.4.2.1 *Infringement decisions*

Vertical price fixing has been attacked by the OFT on a number of occasions. In *John Bruce* a UK distributor of 'automatic slack-adjusters', used primarily in commercial vehicles, agreed minimum prices with it dealers, including Unipart. John Bruce argued that without the price maintenance the supplies would simply not be viable, and the OFT appears in part to have accepted this, noting that there were 'special circumstances' and 'pro-competitive effects arising from John Bruce's actions' (para. 97) in fixing the penalty. Still, a penalty *was* imposed, the OFT taking the view that resale price maintenance 'is a very serious infringement of the Chapter I Prohibition' (*Price fixing agreements involving John Bruce (UK) Limited, Fleet Parts Limited and Truck and Trailer Components* CA98/12/2002 [2002] UKCLR 435). Vertical price fixing was also condemned in *Lladro*, in which the manufacturer of luxury figurines operated a selective distribution system, and strongly discouraged retailers from offering promotional discounts or sales (*Agreements between Lladro Comercial SA and UK retailers fixing the price of porcelain and stoneware figurines* CA98/04/2003 [2003] UKCLR 652). Lladro was concerned that such actions might damage the perceived value of the brand. Somewhat controversially the OFT both recognized, as it was bound to do so, that legitimate steps could be taken to protect the value of the Lladro trademark, but held at the same time that

restrictions amounting to resale price maintenance (whether directly or indirectly imposed), including those which restrict a retailer's ability to advertise resale prices, cannot be object-ively justified on the grounds that they are necessary to protect the reputation or image of a trademark. In the [OFT's] view, any such reputation or image derives not from the supplier's ability to control the resale price of the products or services bearing the trademark, but from other factors, including (in particular) the actual quality of those products or services and the environment in which they are sold.   (para. 76)

While many economists would agree with this, it is nevertheless the case that many consumers do equate price to quality, particularly in respect of 'luxury' branded goods.

Two more significant cases have resulted in a great deal of litigation, in part because they have involved a number of parties and different sets of arrangements.

The first of these related to price fixing in the market for toys (*Agreements between Hasbro UK Ltd and distributors fixing the price of Hasbro toys and games* CA98/18/2002 [2003] UKCLR 150), and the second in relation to replica football kits.

Hasbro was the leading manufacturer of toys in the UK, and in February 2001 the OFT launched an investigation into suspected agreements between it and 10 distributors. This followed the receipt by the OFT of a circular originating in one of the Hasbro distributors. This was in the following terms:

All distributors, that is the Club Group and Youngsters, have had to sign new distributor contracts that forbid any discounting off Hasbro list prices. This means that no-one, Youngsters included, can offer any settlements, retrospective rebates or ordinary discount off Hasbro list prices.   (cited at para. 10 of the decision)

Information requests and on-site inspection visits were made, and Hasbro agreed to cooperate, thereby benefiting from the leniency programme. When asked, one of Hasbro's directors, David Bottomley, admitted that 'Yes, I was the instigator of it'. Hasbro was subsequently fined £4.95 million, having been given a 45 percent reduction for its cooperation with the investigation. Hasbro lodged an appeal with the CAT, but subsequently withdrew this.

Following this decision the OFT made a further one in February 2003 in relation to agreements entered into between Hasbro and Argos, and Hasbro and Littlewoods (*Agreements between Hasbro UK Ltd, Argos Ltd and Littlewoods Ltd fixing the price of Hasbro toys and games* CA98/2/2003 [2003] UKCLR 553). The OFT found in this respect that sometime in 1998–9 a pricing initiative undertaken by Hasbro led directly to an overall agreement and/or concerted practice between the three undertakings. By 1 March 2000, the date at which the Competition Act 1998 became effective in this respect, agreements were at least in place in relation to Action Man and core games. The importance to Hasbro of this arrangement was that these two catalogue stores were the price leaders for other high-street retailers. The market in toys and games is highly competitive. Were prices to be reduced, thereby restricting sellers' profit margins, retailers would be reluctant to stock a wide range of toys and games. By maintaining higher margins Hasbro was able to place more of its toys into retail outlets. One of Hasbro's executives told the OFT that

We put [a] plan together to put profit into [the] retail sector. Had discussions with Argos, but they were unwilling to take on the plan because they were concerned about other retailers undermining them. Initiative was discussed with other retailers. Other retailers were always going to follow prices of Argos and Index. So other retailer[s] felt whatever Argos and Index did was crucial to strategy.   (para. 42)

A joint email was then sent to members of the Hasbro sales team by the account managers for the Argos and Littlewoods accounts. This began:

Neil and I have spoken to our respective contacts at Argos and Index and put together a proposal regarding the maintenance of certain retails within our portfolio. This is a step in the right direction and it is fair to say that both Accounts are keen to improve margins but at the same time are taking a cautious approach in case either party reneges on a price agreement . . .

It goes without saying that Action Man and Games prices will be maintained as per earlier agreements. . . . The proof of the pudding will be when both Catalogues are published, but Neil and I are confident that they will play ball.   (para. 49)

This drew a prompt response from a Sales Director:

Ian . . . This is a great initiative that you and Neil have instigated!!!!!!!!!!! However, a word to the wise, never ever put anything in writing, its highly illegal and it could bite you right in the arse!!!! suggest you phone Lesley and tell her to trash? Talk to Dave. Mike.

The initiative worked, and was subsequently repeated in later catalogues.

The OFT found that three agreements and/or concerted practices existed: two vertical agreements, and also a horizontal agreement between the two retailers, in which Hasbro played the role of facilitator. One problem facing the OFT was that not all evidence received by it during the course of the investigation was consistent, but the approach that the OFT took was that it was proper to place more reliance on statements that were consistent with written evidence, and particularly those which were supported by contemporaneous documentary evidence (paras 15 and 97). Hasbro received a 100 percent reduction in penalty, Argos was fined £17.28 million, and Littlewoods £5.37 million. Argos and Littlewoods promptly appealed, leading the CAT to resolve a number of procedural points. When the case came before the CAT the OFT sought to rely in part upon three important witness statements that had not been put before the parties during the proceedings leading up to the making of the decision. The CAT decided to remit the matter back to the OFT (*Argos Ltd and Littlewoods Ltd v OFT* [2004] CompAR 80), which subsequently published an amended version of its decision, reaching the same conclusions on the substance of the abuse (*Agreements between Hasbro UK Ltd, Argos Ltd and Littlewoods Ltd fixing the price of Hasbro toys and games* CA98/8/2003, 21 November 2003). This was then subject to a further appeal, which had not been concluded as of 1 May 2004. The second large case was decided by the OFT in August 2003 (*Price-fixing of replica football kit* CA98/06/2003 [2003] UKCLR 6). The investigation was launched following a complaint from Sports Soccer Ltd alleging that price fixing in this market was widespread. After making extensive inquiries the OFT identified the presence of a number of agreements: between Umbro (the manufacturer) and Sports Soccer in relation to the England home replica kit, and on all new licensed kit; between Umbro, Sports Soccer, and four leading retailers in relation to England replica shirts at the time of Euro 2000; between Umbro and Manchester United and at least two retailers; between at least JJB, Sports Soccer, and Umbro in relation to Manchester United and England replica shirts for the remainder of 2000 and 2001. Penalties were imposed on a number of parties including £158,000 on the Football Association, and £1,652,000 on Manchester United. Umbro was fined £6,641,000. As of May 2004 the appeal was before the CAT.

11.4.3 Trade associations, the professions, and self-regulating bodies

A clear discussion of the relevant rules in relation to trade associations, the professions, and self-regulating bodies is set out in the relevant guideline. The original position under the Chapter I Prohibition was that professional rules could be subject to an exclusion from the Act following an application from the relevant professional body to that effect. However, the OFT was concerned about the possible anti-competitive effects of such rules, and in March 2001 a report prepared by the economic consultancy LECG into this subject was published ([OFT 328, [2001] UKCLR 352). Following this the OFT gave a response in which it noted that

Restrictions on supply in the case of professional services, just as with other goods and services, will tend to drive up costs and prices, limit access and choice and cause customers to receive poorer value for money than they would under properly competitive conditions. Such restrictions will also tend to inhibit innovation in the supply of services, again to the ultimate detriment of the public.

The general exclusion has now been withdrawn, and the professions are subject to the same principles as all other providers of goods and services.

12

The cartel offence

12.1 Introduction

After a hiatus of 330 years Part 6 of the Enterprise Act 2002 made it a criminal offence to engage in cartel activity implemented in the UK. The last legislation to impose criminal sanctions in respect of anti-competitive conduct in the UK, enacted in the reign of Edward VI, provided, *inter alia*, for an offender to 'sit in the pillory and lose one of his ears'. This Act was repealed in 1772, and the penalties provided for in the cartel offence provisions of the Enterprise Act 2002 are slightly less dramatic, the maximum penalty for a breach of s. 188 of the Enterprise Act 2002 being a term of imprisonment of five years. During the extensive debates on this part of the Act the Opposition dismissed these provisions as 'great for a headline but not much else' (Mr Waterson, Hansard, 17 June 2002, col. 112). Elsewhere, however, it has been noted that this is 'possibly one of the most intriguing developments in English criminal law of recent years' (Harding, C., and Joshua, J., 'Breaking Up the Hard Core: The Prospects for the Proposed Cartel Offence' [2002] Crim LR 933 at 933).

In introducing this offence the UK has joined three other EC Member States—Germany, France, and Ireland (Austria repealed a law imposing personal criminal sanctions in 2003)—although there is no power within the EC Treaty itself to allow criminal liability to be imposed in respect of EC competition law. The cartel offence is thus purely a matter of domestic law, although one expressly acknowledged by virtue of Regulation 1/2003, recital (8) of which provides that

this Regulation does not apply to national laws which impose criminal sanctions on natural persons except to the extent that such sanctions are the means whereby competition rules applying to undertakings are enforced.

There are, nevertheless, concerns to be raised about the way in which the operation of the offence will interact with the application of EC competition law, as the same body, the OFT, is primarily responsible for both aspects of the competition law regime within the UK. In particular care will need to be taken to separate civil and criminal investigations to ensure that the rights of the defence in criminal cases, which are stronger than in civil cases, are adequately protected.

The question of the effectiveness of civil penalties has been discussed in Chapter

6, and there is disagreement in the literature as to whether incarceration, or large financial penalties, are the more effective mechanism by which to ensure compliance with competition law. For a discussion of these issues see Elzinga, K. G., and Breit, W., *The Antitrust Penalties*, Yale, Yale UP (1976); Hylton, K. N., *Antitrust Law: Economic Theory and Common Law Evolution*, Cambridge, CUP (2003), at ch. 3 and Wils, W. P. J., *The Optimal Enforcement of EC Antitrust Law: Essays in Law and Economics*, London, Kluwer Law International (2001). In the White Paper, *A World Class Competition Regime* (Cm. 5233, July 2001), the Government argued that existing levels of civil penalties available under the Competition Act 1998, and EC competition law, were inadequate to deter all anti-competitive conduct:

if fines are to deter firms and their executives effectively, they need to be set at a level which is greater than the expected gains from participating in a cartel.

US evidence shows that cartels often raise prices by around 10%. Increasing prices will have some dampening effect on demand, so a cartelist might increase its profits by a smaller proportion. Conservatively they might do so by around 5%. *If the cartel operates for six years (as the average US cartel is thought to do)*, then the total benefit might be 30% of annual turnover.

The Competition Act 1998 allows fines to be imposed at this level . . . But not all cartels will be caught. *In the US, estimates suggest that only a sixth of cartels are detected.* (Box 7.3, emphasis. added)

In 2001 the OFT published a substantial report commissioned to examine whether a new criminal offence should be introduced into domestic law, and this remains important reading for those interested in this area (*The Proposed Criminalisation of Cartels in the UK—A report prepared for the Office of Fair Trading by Sir Anthony Hammond KCB QC and Roy Penrose OBE QPM* (November 2001) [2002] UKCLR 97 (hereinafter the Penrose Report)). This in turn followed a joint DTI/Treasury Department report which concluded that

Although the Competition Act 1998 strengthens the deterrent effect against anti-competitive behaviour, the project team is concerned that it may not go far enough. In particular, the penalties for engaging in cartels may not be enough to deter such action. (Quoted in the Penrose Report, at para. 1.3)

The project team concludes that American, and other experience, suggests that there is a strong case for introducing criminal penalties, including custodial sentences, for those who engage in cartels, alongside a new civil sanction of director's disqualification.

It is not possible in this book to provide a full analysis of all aspects of the offence, and detailed matters of criminal law, and particularly procedure, which are subject to frequent legislative change, are not dealt with here. Rather, this short chapter focuses on the substance of the offence. For a full statement of the law as at May 2004 see Furse, M., and Nash, S., *The Cartel Offence*, Oxford, Hart Publishing (2004). It is not anticipated that the first cases to be prosecuted will complete their way through the courts until at least 2006, and possibly even later, as the matters to be dealt with are likely to be complex, both in fact and in law.

The essential features of the cartel offence are that it is (1) a stand-alone offence, unconnected to the remainder of the competition law operative in the UK; and (2) directed towards individuals and not towards undertakings, which remain the exclusive subjects of the application of arts 81 and 82 EC, and the Chapter I and II Prohibitions of the Competition Act 1998. The offence extends to the whole of the UK.

12.2 **The offence**

The essential ingredients of the offence are set out at s. 188 of the Enterprise Act 2002. Section 188(1) provides:

An individual is guilty of an offence if he dishonestly agrees with one or more other persons to make or implement, or to cause to be made or implemented, arrangements of the following kind relating to at least two undertakings (A and B).

Section 188(2) sets out six categories of arrangement the implementation of which will be deemed to fall within the terms of the offence. Thus it is provided that

The arrangements must be ones which, if operating as the parties to the agreement intend, would—

(a) directly or indirectly fix a price for the supply by A in the United Kingdom (otherwise than to B) of a product or service,

(b) limit or prevent supply by A in the United Kingdom of a product or service,

(c) limit or prevent production by A in the United Kingdom of a product,

(d) divide between A and B the supply in the United Kingdom of a product or service to a customer or customers,

(e) divide between A and B customers for the supply in the United Kingdom of a product or service, or

(f) be bid-rigging arrangements.

Even before the offence entered into effect on 20 June 2003 the Serious Fraud Office (SFO) was using existing powers to investigate a cartel. On 9 November 2003 the *Sunday Times* reported that 'on the morning of April 10 last year, the senior executives of several British drug companies were awakened by the sound of police banging on their front doors' ('Strong Medicine', *Sunday Times*, 9 November 2003, Business Section, p. 5). It was reported that 'Operation Holbein', an investigation into allegations of fraud and price fixing in the supply of generic drugs to the NHS was the Serious Fraud Office's 'largest and possibly most expensive inquiry ever'. The link was inevitably made to the new offence, with the report's authors claiming that if the head of the SFO, Robert Wardle, was successful, he could 'pave the way for his office to become inquisitor general of Britain's commercial cartels'. See also *R (on the application of Kent Pharmaceuticals Limited) v Director of the Serious Fraud Office* [2003] EWHC 3002 (Admin), [2003] All ER (D) 298, where the court dealt with the extent to which seizure of various documents in the course of the investigation was lawful.

The SFO has, following a memorandum entered into with the OFT, been given the lead role in prosecuting the cartel offence, and apart from the specific provisions relating to the offence in the Enterprise Act will be substantially reliant on its powers provided by the Criminal Justice Act 1987. Section 2 of this Act gives the SFO the necessary powers to obtain search warrants, to compel persons to answer questions and to provide information and produce documents for the purposes of the criminal investigation. In Scotland the Criminal Law (Consolidation) (Scotland) Act 1995 provides that the Lord Advocate can nominate a person to exercise the same powers as the SFO, and the Head of the International and Financial Crime Unit has been so appointed. The OFT itself, via its Cartels Investigation Branch, will play a key role in investigating breaches of the offence, and will work closely with the SFO in this respect.

12.2.1 Situations in which the offence may be applied

It was always going to be the case that the offence would extend only to hard-core cartel conduct. Thus in the White Paper it was explained that

7.19 The new criminal offence will cover hard-core cartels only—widely recognised as the most serious form of competition breach. The most common form of hard-core cartel involves illegal price-fixing—where a number of firms agree what price should be charged for a particular product. In most cases, this will be above what the competitive market price would be.

7.20 However, cartels can also involve conduct which achieves the same economic result by different means. This includes agreeing not to compete for each other's customers—which leaves each firm free to set higher prices (market sharing). Or firms could agree to reduce levels of output—which also increases the price that they can charge.

7.21 In some cases, firms will agree to inflate the price charged in a tender-bidding process and enter bids which ensure that one company in the cartel will win, but on better terms than would otherwise be the case (collusive tendering). The OFT believes that public sector contracts are particularly vulnerable to these practices. As such, they could hit taxpayers hard—because Local Authorities or Government departments have to pay more for public services.

7.22 In all these cases, the effect is the same—prices rise and consumers pay more than they should. The Government intends that the new criminal offence will cover each of these different types of cartel.

This closely followed the approach recommended in the Penrose Report, which considered in part whether the offence might extend to vertical, as well as to horizontal, conduct:

We understand the view of those who are experts in the field of competition law is that the criminal offence should only be applicable to *horizontal* agreements between individuals representing 'competing' undertakings operating at the same level of the supply-chain for the purposes of the agreement in question. It should not apply to vertical agreements, many of which are considered to have pro-competitive or other beneficial effect.   (para. 1.12)

Price fixing at the horizontal level, whether it be direct or indirect, is prohibited. While the most obvious form of price fixing would be that which set a single price, or set of prices, for a customer or customers, it is also possible to envisage situations in which there might be coordination on discounts, quantity rebates, and so on. Any such arrangement that would have the same effect as a direct agreement to set selling prices may fall foul of the provision.

For the offence to be operative arrangements must be made between two parties. Because the offence is defined as making such arrangements, it is not necessary that they be implemented. However, where arrangements are entered into outside the UK it is a requirement that the arrangement is implemented in the UK. The four categories of arrangement that are condemned are: price fixing; limitation of production or supply; the sharing of markets; and bid rigging. These are generally considered to be the most serious forms of anti-competitive activity.

It is provided in addition in s. 188(3) that in the case of s. 188(2)(a), (b) and (c) (see above), both firms (A and B)—as defined above—must be engaged in the anti-competitive practice. This requirement is set out clearly in the *Explanatory notes to the Enterprise Act* published by the DTI at para. 408 in the following terms:

Subsection (3) requires, in the case of price-fixing or limitation of production or supply, that for the offence to be committed the other party must reciprocally have intended that the agreement, if implemented according to the intentions of the parties, should result in one of these activities. This means that agreements are not criminal where the agreement only requires one party to fix prices or limit production or supply as defined. This further requirement does not apply in the case of market-sharing and bid-rigging where the activities are by definition reciprocal.

Further conditions relating to the horizontal nature of the arrangements are set out in s. 189. In each of the instances set out in s. 188, it is necessary, as an additional element of the offence, that the supply of the product or service by A would be 'at a level in the supply chain at which the product or service would at the same time be supplied by B in the United Kingdom' (s. 189(1)).

12.2.1.1 *Section 188(2)(a)—price-fixing arrangements*

Section 188(2)(a) relates to horizontal price-fixing arrangements—the most generally recognized form of cartel. For this section to apply the relevant arrangements must be such as to constitute a direct, or indirect, reciprocal fixing of a price by both A and B for a product or service in the UK to a third party or parties. Although s. 188(2)(a) makes reference only to A, s. 188(3) provides that B must also be an active party to the arrangement. There is no requirement for the product or service to be identical, or indeed even substitutable but, by virtue of s. 189(1) it is necessary for the prosecution to demonstrate that 'A's supply of the product or service would be at a level in the supply chain at which the product or service would at the same time be supplied by B' in the UK. The arrangement as to price would not necessarily have to be one which led to an increase in prices by both parties. Even an arrangement which led to the parties lowering their prices—for example to provide a joint response to the threat of entry into the market affected—would be caught if it could be shown to have been entered into dishonestly. Equally, an arrangement under which B would maintain its price at a constant level while A increased its price would be caught.

12.2.1.2 *Section 188(2)(b) and (2)(c)—limitations of supply or production*

Sections 188(2)(b) and (c) relate to the limiting of production or supply. For the arrangements to fall within the offence both A *and* B must limit the production or supply of goods or services which would be supplied at the same level in the supply chain. It would appear that an agreement between A and B to refuse to supply C could be caught by this subsection as well as a more generic agreement to reduce supplies overall. There is no requirement that the goods or services being produced be supplied in the UK.

A difficulty could arise in respect of both of these elements of the offence (as well as with bid rigging) if parties were not to act simultaneously. Suppose, for example, A were to cut its production or supply of a product in 2005, and B were to do so in 2006. It might be somewhat difficult to demonstrate—particularly in the absence of supporting documentation setting out communication between the parties—that there had been an arrangement to do so. It would, it is suggested, be incumbent on the prosecuting authority to bring forward some documentary or testamentary evidence to establish in such circumstances the existence of the ingredients of the offence.

12.2.1.3 *Section 188(2)(d) and (2)(e)—market sharing arrangements*

For an arrangement to infringe either of subsections (2)(d) and (e) it must be one which would lead to a division of the market or customers, between A and B in the UK. Any such division need not necessarily be on the basis of a geographical allocation, but could be by any means whereby individual customers were denied the choice of supplier of the product or service in question.

12.2.1.4 *Section 188(2)(f)—bid rigging*

Bid-rigging arrangements are defined in s. 188(5) as being

arrangements under which, in response to a request for bids for the supply of a product or service in the United Kingdom, or for the production of a product in the United Kingdom—

(a) A but not B may make a bid, or

(b) A and B may each make a bid but, in one case or both, only a bid arrived at in accordance with the arrangements.

It is further provided in s. 188(6) that bid-rigging arrangements are excluded from the scope of this provision where the person requesting the bids was notified of the arrangements at or before the time of the making of the bid. It is interesting therefore that in the *Explanatory notes* the position is taken that '[b]id-rigging is the only one of the prohibited activities where for all practical purposes the carrying out of the activity described in this section will in itself invariably indicate a dishonest intention' (para. 409), and it has been argued by a number of parties that bid-rigging arrangements are to be regarded as per se dishonest.

12.2.2 **Dishonesty**

There was some debate as to the standard of conduct that would be required for an offence to be committed. In the Penrose Report dishonesty was the preferred option:

The advantage of this approach is (a) it signals that the offence is serious and should attract a substantial penalty and (b) it would go a long way to preclude a defence argument that the activity being prosecuted is not reprehensible or that it might have economic benefits or is an activity which might have attracted exemption domestically or under EC law. The possible disadvantage is that some might argue that an offence which depends on an approach of 'dishonesty' may be difficult for juries to understand. However, given the context in which hard core cartels take place, we believe that, in most cases, the facts will demonstrate that the parties realised what they were doing was dishonest and was contrary to the law. (para 2.5).

In the White Paper it was further emphasized that

To be effective, it is critical that the offence is defined in a way which is both clear and easy for business and the courts to understand. It must also be actively applied so that its deterrent effect is genuinely felt. The Government recognises that defining the offence is a complex task.   (para 7.33)

The test for dishonesty in England and Wales, which is a question of fact to be determined by the jury, was established in the case of *R* v *Ghosh* [1982] 2 All ER 689. The question of whether the defendant has acted dishonestly is a matter of fact for the jury to determine. In *Ghosh* Lord Lane CJ observed that it was necessary to consider whether the dishonesty in question related to a course of conduct or described a state of mind. In a judgment which has stood the test of time, the Court of Appeal settled on a double test for dishonesty which involves both objective and subjective considerations. Thus the *Ghosh* direction requires that

In determining whether the prosecution has proved that the defendant was acting dishonestly, a jury must first of all decide whether according to the ordinary standards of reasonable and honest people what was done was dishonest. If it was not dishonest by those standards, that is the end of the matter and the prosecution fails.

In determining if it was dishonest by those standards, then the jury must consider whether the defendant himself must have realised that what he was doing was by those standards dishonest. In most cases, where the actions are obviously dishonest by ordinary standards, there will be no doubt about it. It will be obvious that the defendant himself knew that he was acting dishonestly. It is dishonest for a defendant to act in a way which he knows ordinary people consider to be dishonest, even if he asserts or genuinely believes that he is morally justified in acting as he did.   [1982] 2 All ER 689 at 696

Thus, the jury is required to determine whether the act done would, according to the standards of reasonable people, be considered to be dishonest, and then to consider whether the defendant would have realized that this was the view of reasonable people. If the answer to both questions is in the affirmative, then dishonesty is established.

The position is a little more complex in Scotland, where it remains unclear if dishonesty is a feature of certain aspects of criminal law.

Although the purpose of basing the offence on the standard of 'dishonest' conduct was to define it tightly—and to mark a move to acting against the object of agreements—it was suggested in the debates on the passage of the Act that the definition was anything but tight. It has been suggested that the persons drafting this legislation failed to understand fully the role of dishonesty in the criminal law and used it to 'bridge a perceived weakness in the objective definition of the prohibited conduct'. See Harding, C., and Joshua, J., 'Breaking Up the Hard Core: the Prospects for the Proposed Cartel Offence' [2002] Crim LR 933–944 at 939. An opposition amendment to replace 'dishonestly' with 'knowingly or recklessly' was resisted by the Government on the grounds that that would have significantly *expanded* the scope of the offence. According to the Under-Secretary of State,

[the] sort of evidence that would point to dishonesty is likely to include a failure to seek legal advice, combined with attempts to disguise or hide activity. For example, holding secret meetings and the absence or destruction of records, and other such practices, would be instances of such evidence.   (*Hansard*, Standing Committee B, col. 136)

This implies also that there is a need for some positive act, and not merely a failure to act, for the offence to be established. Peretz and Lewis have recognized that the standard of 'dishonesty' is one that will be familiar to criminal lawyers, although not to the competition bar. They are probably correct when they write that in the context of the cartel offence

the question of whether individuals acted dishonestly is likely to be determined by the extent to which they were open about what they were doing. If, for example, the agreement operated by covert meetings held under a soubriquet, with all records being destroyed, it will probably not be hard to establish dishonesty, the badges of fraud being present.   (Peretz, G., and Lewis, J., 'Go directly to jail: Losing badly in "Monopoly"' (2003) NLJ 99)

12.3 The relationship of the offence with the Competition Act 1998 and EC competition law

Because the offence is a stand-alone provision, there is in theory no relationship between it and the civil provisions of the Competition Act 1998 and arts 81 and 82 EC. In practice, however, it is possible that the same conduct will be investigated and attacked under both the civil law, in an action against undertakings, and the criminal law in an action against persons. The OFT is generally precluded from using evidence obtained in the course of a civil investigation under the Competition Act 1998 in order to pursue a cartel prosecution, although it may use statements made in the course of interviews where these counteract evidence subsequently given in the criminal procedure.

One issue in which there is likely to be an overlap arises in relation to the leniency programmes operated in relation to the civil laws, and 'no-action letters' (see 12.4) operated in relation to the cartel offence. At the time the offence was introduced the OFT indicated that it had engaged in extensive discussions with the EC Commission. relating to the new offence, and had considered in particular the impact of the offence on leniency policies:

We have worked closely with the European Commission to ensure that the interface between Community and national law is carefully worked out. This has included discussions with the Commission on leniency policies. An undertaking should apply for leniency to both the OFT and the Commission where the cartel involves more member states than the UK. The first undertaking to apply in a cartel should be eligible under the EU civil leniency policy and the UK civil leniency policy for full leniency unless they were the instigator of the cartel, compelled others to take part or played the leading role. . . . In this way we have ensured the compatible working of the EU and UK regimes. The OFT will discuss with the Commission the handling of individual EC cartel cases where the UK may wish to mount a criminal prosecution. These will be considered case by case.   (Bloom, M., 'Key Challenges in Public Enforcement: A Speech to the British Institute of International and Comparative Law', 17 May 2002, OFT web site, **(www.oft.gov.uk)**))

It is clear that an offence may be committed by the instigators of a cartel operating in Europe where the arrangements are 'implemented' in the UK. However, there are limitations on the ability of the OFT to recycle the information and evidence obtained relating to any action taken by the EC Commission or by another national competition authority to sustain a prosecution in relation to the offence. It is also unlikely that the OFT will use both its civil and criminal powers in relation to a cartel operating in the UK. Were it to do so human rights considerations would require that the civil action would follow the criminal action. A more likely scenario is that cartel arrangements involving undertakings in the UK and elsewhere in the EC might be attacked under art. 81 EC and by the OFT under this Part of the Act, although the two actions would proceed independently. In this case, it is possible that persons participating in the cartel in the UK might face penalties that went beyond those imposed on other cartel members. There would appear to be nothing in principle, however, that would prevent the OFT prosecuting all members of the cartel.

MacCulloch has expressed the concern that the operation of the offence may have an impact on the way in which the OFT fulfils its functions as a member of the NCA network (MacCulloch, A., 'The Cartel Offence and the Criminalisation of UK Competition Law' [2003] JBL 616). It is possible for example that the OFT will feel it is obliged to give primacy to the enforcement of art. 81 EC, or the Chapter I Prohibition, and may not prosecute the cartel offence where it is not envisaged that there is a very strong prospect of success.

12.4 'No action letters'

As we saw in Chapter 6, leniency programmes operated by the EC Commission and the OFT are an important plank in the detection of cartels in particular, and one of the concerns expressed vociferously about the introduction of the cartel offence was that the threat of criminal penalties would in fact undermine the approach to leniency. This concern was raised in the Penrose Report:

5.9 The difficulty faced by the OFT is how to provide sufficient comfort against criminal prosecution and the imposition of custodial sentences for potential whistleblowers who inform on other cartel participants. In particular, the OFT would need a policy which would:

- provide sufficient 'certainty' to whistleblowers that they would not personally face criminal prosecution, and
- be consistent with the existing leniency policies operated under civil procedures in both the UK *and* the EC in respect of undertakings whilst maintaining the integrity of the SFO as the prosecuting authority and the criminal justice system in the UK as a whole.

Express provision is made in the Act for the leniency programme at s. 190(4):

Where, for the purpose of the investigation or prosecution of offences under section 188, the OFT gives a person written notice under this subsection [a no-action letter], no proceedings for an offence under section 188 that falls within a description specified in the notice may be brought against that person in England and Wales or Northern Ireland except in the circumstances specified in the notice.

The OFT has issued guidance, *The Cartel Offence: Guidance on the issue of no-action letters for individuals*, which sets out the terms of its approach to leniency. At the outset it should be noted that the position of no-action letters is a little different in Scotland than is the case in the remainder of the UK. The OFT cannot bind the Lord Advocate in Scotland, whose prosecutorial discretion is absolute. However, it was pointed out in committee that a similar procedure under which Customs and Excise employs a leniency programme has given rise to no substantial problems, and that concerns will be allayed by the good working relationship between the OFT, the SFO, and the Scottish authorities.

The leniency programme operated in relation to the cartel offence finds its expression in the instrument of 'no-action letters'. These are explained in the following terms in the relevant guidance:

In the context of the cartel offence, immunity from prosecution will be granted in the form of a 'no-action letter', issued by the OFT under section 190(4) of the Enterprise Act. A no-action letter will prevent a prosecution being brought against an individual in England and Wales or Northern Ireland for the cartel offence except in circumstances specified in the letter. Whilst guarantees of immunity from prosecution cannot be given in relation to Scotland, cooperation by an individual will be reported to the Lord Advocate who will take such cooperation into account.   (para. 3.2)

There are five main conditions that must be met in order for a no-action letter to be issued by the OFT. These are that the individual must: (1) admit participation in a criminal offence; (2) provide the OFT with all available information regarding the cartel; (3) cooperate completely and continuously throughout the investigation; (4) not have coerced another to participate in the cartel; and (5) cease participation in the cartel, unless instructed to continue by the OFT or other investigating authority. It is thus clear that the OFT contemplates that there may be occasions when it has an informant operating under supervision inside a cartel, passing back all relevant information to the OFT or SFO.

While satisfaction of these conditions is necessary for the issuance of a no-action letter, it is not sufficient. Where the OFT already has sufficient information to bring a successful prosecution against the applicant individual, or is in the process of gathering that information, it will not grant a no-action letter. The effect of this policy must be to encourage early applications where an investigation is under way. In addition, in order to benefit from a no-action letter the approach must come from the individual, or a lawyer representing that person to the OFT. It appears from the OFT guidance that the OFT will not itself initiate the process. Any such approach made by a lawyer may be made at the first instance on an anonymous basis. Approaches may also be made on behalf of a named individual, or a group of named individuals by an undertaking or by a lawyer representing that undertaking in the course of an investigation into breaches of either the Chapter I Prohibition of the Competition Act 1998 or art. 81 EC in accordance with the terms of the relevant leniency notices. In the latter case the relevant notice applies to undertakings, but where an undertaking qualifies for full immunity from penalties it is anticipated that named individuals within that undertaking, or ex-employees or directors of that undertaking, will be granted the benefit of a no-action letter.

In the event that any such approach is made, the Director of Cartel Investigations will give 'an indication' as to whether the OFT might be prepared to issue a no-action letter. If the OFT is prepared to issue a no-action letter, any individual who hopes to benefit from one will be interviewed, although information given in these interviews will not subsequently be used against them in criminal proceedings, unless either they 'knowingly or recklessly provided information that is false or misleading in a material particular' (para. 3.7) or the letter is subsequently revoked.

At the end of the interview process three results are possible. The first of these is that the OFT concludes that the applicant is not at risk of criminal prosecution. In this case the OFT will not issue a no-action letter, but will instead confirm its conclusion in writing. While the exact legal status of such a communication is unclear, it will at the least raise a legitimate expectation on behalf of the recipient that no criminal action will follow. There does remain the possibility, however, that the OFT may obtain further information subsequently which might influence it to reassess the position. In such a case it would be reasonable to believe that the OFT would reconsider the application, and would be minded to do so favourably.

The second possible result is that the OFT determines that without a no-action letter there would be a possibility of criminal prosecution, but that the applicant confirms that they will meet the criteria for the grant of a no-action letter, in which case the letter will be issued. Where the prosecution would be brought in Scotland the cooperation will be reported to the Lord Advocate with a request that an early decision be made as to whether the individual remains liable for prosecution. A third possibility is that the OFT determines that a prosecution is a possibility, and that the individual does not meet, or would not in the future meet, the criteria to be issued a no-action letter. In this case, as we have seen, the interview may not be used against the individual. This would imply that there is little to be lost in making an application. In practice, however, there may be some concerns that while the OFT may not use the information given at the interview, it may be encouraged to pursue lines of inquiry as a result of the interview that it might otherwise have overlooked.

No-action letters may be revoked in two circumstances. The first of these arises where the recipient of the letter ceases to satisfy the conditions for the grant of a letter discussed above. The second arises where the recipient has 'knowingly or recklessly provided information that is false or misleading in a material particular' (para. 3.11). If a no-action letter is revoked any immunity conferred by the letter will cease to exist as if it had never been granted. A particular consequence of this is that any information given at the initial interview may be used in the course of any subsequent prosecution. Before revoking a no-action letter the OFT will give the recipient notice of the decision in writing, and will give the recipient a reasonable opportunity to make representations. The OFT may, but is not required to, give the applicant the opportunity to remedy any breach of the compliance conditions within a reasonable time after an explanation as to the breach of the conditions has been given.

12.5 **Conclusion**

It remains to be seen whether breaches of the cartel offence will be vigorously pursued, although the OFT, naturally, insists that the provisions will constitute a vital plank in acting against hard-core anti-competitive conduct. For example, in a speech delivered in May 2002, Margaret Bloom dealt in part with the new offence:

Are these new powers necessary? Will they be used? The short answer is 'Yes'. We are uncovering around one cartel a month. We are now uncovering more serious ones. This activity is equivalent to theft. It has no redeeming features. Effective deterrence is very important. However, we will select carefully the cartels for criminal prosecutions, concentrating on the serious ones. We expect that there will be a relatively small number of prosecutions—but they will have a significant deterrent effect. The first prosecutions will reach the courts in a few years'.   (Bloom, M., 'Key Challenges in Public Enforcement: A Speech to the British Institute of International and Comparative Law', 17 May 2002, OFT web site (**www.oft.gov.uk**))

Many find it tempting to draw such a clear comparison between the cartel offence and theft, although this is perhaps somewhat inappropriate. Theft may be characterized as a wholly coerced transaction; the customer of, or supplier to, a cartel, enters into the transaction voluntarily, but receives false information about the transaction mechanisms. On the other hand, given that the intention under-pinning the Act was to place emphasis on dishonest conduct, the analogy is understandable, and appears to have taken root. Certainly it was frequently made in the parliamentary debates. What is clear is that those engaged in business are now faced with a strong indication of the determination of the Government that cartels be vigorously tackled.

13

An introduction to the economics
of monopoly abuse

13.1 Introduction

The arguments advanced in Chapter 1 support the need for some intervention in
the competitive structure, but do not necessarily justify action against individual
monopolists. The Harvard/Chicago debate is not a purely theoretical one, and
nowhere is this more significant than in relation to the policy prescriptions relating
to the control of monopoly conduct. If the extreme Chicago approach is correct
there would be little need to apply competition law to the conduct of privately
maintained monopolies. Article 82 EC (see Chapter 14) could, along with the
Chapter II Prohibition (see Chapter 15), be abandoned, leaving competition regulators to focus on the twin problems of distortions to the competitive structure
resulting from state conduct and the maintenance of cartels. State aids and state-
maintained, or created, barriers to entry have indeed received increasing attention
from the EC Commission, and much time has been taken up in the UK with deregulation initiatives in the utilities sectors (see the discussion of natural monopolies,
at 13.2.5). If, on the other hand, the Harvard school adherents are correct the
anti-competitive conduct of a single firm in possession of a significant degree
of market power may still raise genuine concerns that cannot be resolved by the
operation of the market place in the absence of regulatory intervention. This is
the assumption underpinning art. 82 and its domestic equivalents. The economics
of monopoly control is considered in Bishop, S., and Walker, M., *The Economics of
EC Competition Law*, London, Sweet & Maxwell (2nd edn, 2002), ch. 6.

13.2 Individual monopolies

To the economist a monopoly is, quite simply, a market in which the industry is in
the hands of one producer. Competition law, however, extends to situations which
are monopolistic—which is to say a market in which there are a number of sellers,
into which new firms may enter, but in which each firm has a degree of control over
price by virtue of selling products that are not identical to those of its competitors.
Generally, potentially anti-competitive actions undertaken by a single firm will be

subject to legal proceedings only where that firm has a significant degree of market power. It is a source of some confusion that legislation and case law make reference to 'monopoly' to describe such market power, disregarding the stricter economic definition. Market shares are usually used as a proxy by which to establish, prima facie, the appropriate market power at which intervention may be triggered. In the EC shares of around 50 per cent generally require the undertaking to demonstrate that it is *not* in a dominant position (see further at 14.2.5.1); and in the USA a share of at least 50 per cent, and likely around 70 per cent, will establish the degree of monopoly power required under the Sherman Act (see, for a survey of the relevant authorities, *Domed Stadium Hotel, Inc.* v *Holiday Inns, Inc* 732 F.2d 480 at 489–90).

The attractions to company directors of attaining monopoly have never been better expressed than in *The Godfather*:

Like any good businessman he came to understand the benefits of undercutting his rivals in price, barring them from distribution outlets by persuading store owners to stock less of their brands. Like any good businessman he aimed at holding a monopoly by forcing his rivals to abandon the field or by merging with his own company. . . . Like many businessmen of genius he learned that free competition was wasteful, monopoly efficient.   (Puzo, M., *The Godfather* (1969), ch. 14)

Expressed this way the strategy may not be far removed from that adhered to in many boardrooms, although clearly Don Vito Corleone was prepared to resort to anti-competitive practices that would be better addressed by way of the criminal law than by way of competition law. The problems to be addressed by competition law are that, first, monopolies may not always be efficient and, secondly, the pursuit of predatory or exclusionary tactics may have harmful welfare effects as well as, less abstractly, damaging individual target firms, along with their investors and managers.

The allegations faced by monopolists most frequently are that:

(a) the monopoly price is higher than the price would be in a competitive market, which is the area that is usually of most concern to consumer advocates;

(b) output is lower and therefore potential demand that could be efficiently met is going unanswered, a corollary of which is that the income that would have been spent on the monopolist's product is being spent elsewhere, distorting other prices in the economy;

(c) predatory behaviour may directly damage the interests of other legitimate competitors and indirectly harm consumers; and

(d) the monopolist, in order to protect a profitable position, may erect barriers that prevent new entrants coming into the market to correct the behaviour referred to in (a) and (b).

Ancillary concerns are that monopolists, contrary to the Godfather's view, may be *less efficient* than firms in a more competitive market and may stifle innovation. Following Leibenstein this type of inefficiency is sometimes called 'X-inefficiency', and relates primarily to an inefficient use of existing resources. X-inefficiency arises if the same inputs might result in more outputs (Leibenstein, H., 'Allocative Efficiency v. X-Efficiency', (1966) 59 *American Economic Review* 392). Competition law is not well placed to deal directly with X-efficiency concerns, which would require a strongly interventionist approach, or with the problem of reduced monopoly output. Instead the focus of the law is on facilitating the emergence of stronger competition to the monopolist by tackling predation, exclusion, and barriers to entry. *Ceteris paribus* stronger competition should reduce the other identifiable harms. Depending on the emphasis given to individual rights and consumer welfare in the relevant regime, other issues such as high pricing or refusal to deal may be addressed where they are readily identifiable.

13.2.1 Higher prices/lower output

The formal proof by which higher pricing and lower output arises in monopoly markets is a standard feature of industrial economics and is not unduly technical. The aim of all firms is assumed to be profit maximization, and although this may not be the case in all situations, it is a reasonable working assumption. The consequence of this is that, when considering what quantity of any product to market, firms will set the level where the marginal cost (MC) of production is equal to the marginal revenue (MR) the firm makes from that unit of production: if the MC is £5 and the MR is £10 a profit-maximizing firm would produce the extra unit as it would make a £5 profit on the sale; if the MC is £10 and the MR is £5 the firm would not produce it as it would make a £5 loss.

Whereas in perfect competition the firm has no control whatsoever over the price at which the item is sold, and takes the price set by the market, a monopolist *makes* the price. Adam Smith famously suggested that 'the price of monopoly is upon every occasion the highest which can be got' (Smith, A., *An Inquiry Into the Nature and Causes of the Wealth of Nations* (1776), Book One, Ch. VII). It is the essence of monopoly that the monopolist has the power to set the price of his product, which is effected by altering the amount that is supplied. As with perfect competition, marginal cost will be set equal to marginal revenue, but the outcome is very different, as Figure 13.1 shows. In the case of perfect competition price = MC, with the outcome being PC, QC. In the case of monopoly MR = MC, with the outcome being PM, QM. The monopoly price, PM, is higher than the competitive price, PC, and the quantity produced, QM, is less than would be produced in a perfectly competitive market, QC.

13.2.2 Monopoly profits

Measuring the variables discussed above, and assessing the extent of the loss of wealth caused by any one monopoly, is exceptionally difficult. In the UK in particular, but not exclusively, assessments have been made in some cases of the profits made by individual monopolists to determine whether these are 'excessive' and

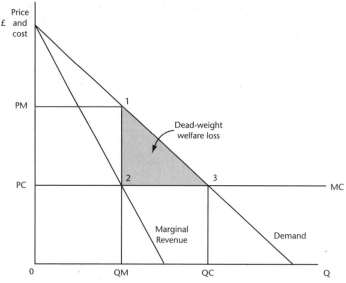

Figure 13.1 Demand and supply curves

Notes: 1. The assumption of constant marginal cost is a simplifying one, and is unlikely to be matched in the real world. However, to relax this assumption does not change the analysis.

2. The rectangle PM, PC, 2, 1, represents a transfer of wealth from consumer to the monopolist. The triangle 1, 2, 3, shows 'dead-weight welfare loss', potential demand that could be supplied efficiently but, under single-price monopoly, is not (see Chapter 1).

indicative of abuse. A report prepared for the OFT's research paper series offers an interesting, although at times very technical, approach (Graham, M., and Steele, A., *The Assessment of Profitability by Competition Authorities*, London, OFT (1997)). A problem with assessing profits, recognized by the authors, is that 'high levels of profit are associated with both competition failure and successful competitive advantage . . . the competition authorities must . . . distinguish high profits due to successful advantage from those due to failures of competition' (para. 1.2). Even where very high profits are identified these may simply be the result of very efficient production and innovation, and not be evidence of market abuse. Similarly, the fact that a monopoly makes low profits does not necessarily mean that it is not abusing its position. It might rather be very inefficient, and be surviving only because it is engaged in perpetrating abuses. See also *The Economics of EC Competition Law*, paras 3.58–3.69, and da Silva, L. C., Neils, G., and Chua, S., 'Assessing Profitability in the Context of Competition Law' [2003/2004] Comp LJ 248.

13.2.3 **Predatory and exclusionary conduct**

Predation may be broadly defined as conduct intended primarily to harm competitors, which is likely to result in a short-term loss in order to allow a long-term gain. It is most generally, although not exclusively, associated with pricing policies, and predatory pricing is considered in some detail in Chapter 14. As Myers emphasizes, there are other categories of anti-competitive conduct involving low prices that are not, strictly, predatory and that may be better described as 'exclusionary' (Myers, G., *Predatory Behaviour in UK Competition Policy*, London, OFT (1994)). Whether predation or exclusionary conduct can be successful is a matter of sharp disagreement, and while economic modelling may be of assistance it is suggested that the issue cannot be resolved simply by reference to abstract analysis. Decisions as to whether to enter any given market are made by entrepreneurs who will to some extent be swayed by their individual assessment of risks. Thus one commentator has evocatively recognized that

A house with a high wall surrounding its property, iron bars on the windows and a moat will be hard to enter without the permission of the owner. It has 'structural' barriers to entry. A second house with a small 'No Trespassing' sign and a two-foot high white picket fence has low structural barriers to entry. It has been pointed out, however, that if the second house has, in addition to the sign and the fence, a lawn strewn with the lifeless corpses of failed entrants, the next entrant may be effectively deterred.   (Rapp, R. T., 'Predatory Pricing Analysis: A Practical Synthesis', NERA, Working Paper No. 2, 1990, pp. 6–7)

It is clear from the case law that the competition authorities recognize reputation effects as playing a significant role in strengthening or maintaining a company's strong position (such an acknowledgement was made by the OFT in its decision *Predation by Aberdeen Journals Ltd* CA98/5/2001 [2001] UKCLR 856, (para. 56)). The EC Commission too has supported a claim of dominance against the largest producer of soda ash in the Community by referring to 'the perception of Solvay by other Community producers as the dominant producer and their reluctance to compete aggressively for Solvay's traditional customers' (*Soda Ash—Solvay* 91/299 (1991) OJ L152/21, para. 45).

13.2.4 Barriers to entry

'The concept of barriers to entry is', as Bork notes, 'crucial to the antitrust debate' (Bork, R. H., *The Antitrust Paradox*, New York, The Free Press (1993), p. 310). The question to be considered is whether economic theory suggests that a monopolist is able to so harm the market structure as to remove or reduce the threat of competition from other companies. It will be immediately apparent that the answer to this question lies at the heart of the Chicago/Harvard debate. A recognition of the role of barriers to entry supports the Structure–Conduct–Performance model advanced by the Harvard School, and discussed in Chapter 1.

Michael Porter, associated with the Harvard Business School, approaches competition issues from the perspective of a company that wishes to strengthen or protect its position, and is not therefore primarily concerned with competition law. The problem for an incumbent is that 'new entrants to an industry bring new capacity, the desire to gain market share, and often substantial resources. Prices can be bid down or incumbents' costs inflated as a result, reducing profitability'. The threat of entry, he argues, depends 'on the barriers to entry that are present, coupled with the reaction from existing competitors that the entrant can expect' (Porter, M. E., *Competitive Strategy*, New York, The Free Press (1980), p. 7). Porter lists five major barriers to entry: economies of scale; product differentiation; capital requirements; switching costs (i.e., the costs to a buyer of switching to a new supplier); and access to distribution channels. By exploiting and reinforcing these barriers it is suggested that incumbents can increase their power to act independently of competition. Whether competition law can be invoked to reduce these barriers will depend on the circumstances of the particular case: notably the law has tackled product differentiation (e.g., *Contraceptive Sheaths* (Cmnd. 8689, 1982 and Cm. 2529, 1994)) and access to distribution channels (e.g., *Films* (Cm. 2673, 1994)). The presence of economies of scale, which is a form of efficiency, or the requirement that entrants must meet the capital costs of entrance, are not matters that should, or can, be addressed by competition law.

The real question to be resolved in any case 'is whether there exist *artificial* entry barriers that are *not forms of superior efficiency*' (Bork, *The Antitrust Paradox*, above, p. 311, emphasis added). Many economists and antitrust commentators would not, in fact, accept that any of the 'barriers' on Porter's list should fall to be resolved by the application of competition law. It is also here that the theoretical debate is at its most intense, and it is not likely to be resolved in the foreseeable future. In practice the competition lawyer may not need to pursue this debate, as many of the cases may be resolved on the basis of observable conduct. Where, for instance, firms have entered and become established in an industry, that in itself will negate the need for debate about barriers in most legal proceedings. This may also be the case where there is clear evidence of failed attempts at entry over time. For further discussion of the role of barriers to entry see *The Economics of EC Competition Law*, paras 3.31 *et seq*.

The issues of vertical integration and vertical restraints which may be associated with both monopolistic and competitive structures are considered in Chapter 8.

13.2.5 Natural monopolies

In one situation a monopoly *is* the efficient market solution. Whether this is the case is determined by the scope of economies of scale: if these are very large in relation to market demand, formally, such that there is no price at which two firms could cover their costs, costs of production are at their lowest level when only one firm is in the market. This will be the case where marginal costs are still falling when the final consumer's demand is satisfied, and will arise in particular where fixed costs are by far the greater component of production, with variable costs being of relatively minor importance. Traditionally such industries have been found to exist where a large and expensive infrastructure is an integral part of that industry (i.e., the utilities, rail transport, and telecommunications). Another type of natural monopoly may also exist under situations of 'network returns'. These arise in industries which are heavily reliant on standards and on product compatibility. A good example is the computing industry. If two operating systems for desktop computers exist, one of which is a superior product (it may even be cheaper) and one of which is already on most computers, it is likely that the requirement that one computer be able to communicate with another will mean that the more popular package will remain dominant, irrespective of other features. The role of such network economies played an important role in the debate about Microsoft's practices and its place in the market.

Developing successful strategies to control these industries has been difficult, and for many years the tendency in 'mixed' economies was to take them into public ownership and therefore direct state control. In the late 1970s and throughout the 1980s the United Kingdom led the way in replacing state ownership with private shareholder ownership, regulating conduct by way of licensing systems that restrict both price rises and the return on capital that can be retained by the company. In some cases this has been achieved by separating the various elements of the infrastructure of what were once highly vertically integrated industries. Typically the approach now is to create strict licence conditions for the elements of the infrastructure that remain natural monopolies, and to encourage competition among the remaining elements, whether downstream or upstream.

13.3 **Social concerns**

Senator Kefauver, author of the United States' Celler–Kefauver Act 1950, argued in support of the Act that 'the history of what has taken place in other nations where . . . economic control [is] in the hands of a very few people is too clear to pass over', thus suggesting that competition law may be employed in the pursuit of socio-political goals. The fact that monopolies redistribute income, generally from the poor to the wealthy (see, e.g., Powell, I., 'The Effect of Reductions in Concentration on Income Distribution' (1987) 69 *Review of Economics and Statistics* 75), may also be used in some quarters to support interventionist arguments. There is no reason why tools of competition law cannot be used in support of wider social objectives, such as income redistribution, but the efficiency of any such move must be doubted. It is unlikely that the application of a sophisticated, and therefore costly, competition law can be more effective in this area than the imposition of, say, a windfall tax on monopoly profits. Fears as to the concentration of power in the hands of the few are also probably better addressed other than by way of competition laws. A well-developed competition law that follows clear economic criteria should, in any event, play its part in raising welfare generally by supporting the competitive process.

13.4 **Conclusion**

The approach taken to monopolies under competition law is determined in part by the recognition accorded to individual rights in the competitive process. When the Chicago economists posit efficiency tests as the only acceptable standard by which to frame legislation, they do so without regard to an individual businessman whose efforts have been stifled by the predatory conduct of a more powerful incumbent and without due recognition of 'reputation' effects. The fact that sooner or later the incumbent will be challenged successfully will be of little concern to the bankrupt entrepreneur who has made the first effort, but the position of the failed business is not, in the overall economy, significant. In both the EC and UK regimes competition enforcement is largely complaint driven. This forces the courts, and therefore economists as expert witnesses, to consider the (anti-)competitive impact of short-run activity that might be expected to have little long-run impact. Whereas in the 1960s and 1970s such analysis might have been considered to be of questionable value, more recent developments in economic modelling have shown that harmful welfare effects may, in fact, flow from such conduct, although the debate is by no means settled.

14

Article 82 EC

Any abuse by one or more undertakings of a dominant position within the common market or in a substantial part of it shall be prohibited as incompatible with the common market in so far as it may affect trade between Member States.

Such abuse may, in particular, consist in:

(a) directly or indirectly imposing unfair purchase or selling prices or other unfair trading conditions;

(b) limiting production, markets or technical development to the prejudice of consumers;

(c) applying dissimilar conditions to equivalent transactions with other trading parties, thereby placing them at a competitive disadvantage;

(d) making the conclusion of contracts subject to acceptance by the other parties of supplementary obligations which, by their nature or according to commercial usage, have no connection with the subject of such contracts.

14.1 Introduction

Article 82 forms the basis of actions far less often than does art. 81—not only does it necessarily apply to fewer undertakings but those to which it does apply, likely to be among the larger organizations, are more likely to be aware of their obligations under competition law. As the guidelines on fines note (see Chapter 6), 'large undertakings usually have legal and economic knowledge and infrastructures which enable them more easily to recognise that their conduct constitutes an infringement and be aware of the consequences stemming from it under competition law'.

Because art. 82 condemns only the 'abuse' of a dominant position the mere holding of such a position, or tactics employed by undertakings to attain a dominant position when they are not yet dominant, is not outlawed. In America, in contrast, s. 2 of the Sherman Act, which condemns 'monopolisation', is designed to control the practices whereby firms *gain* market power (although only where the firm already has a sizeable market share), and in *United States* v *Grinnel Corp.* 384 US 563 (1966) the court sought to attack the 'wilful' acquisition of monopoly power as opposed to the attainment of monopoly through better commercial practices. In

Europemballage Corp. and Continental Can Co. Inc. v *Commission* case 6/72 [1973] CMLR 199, the ECJ made clear the position that the *creation* of a dominant position could not be condemned under art. 82—only its subsequent abuse could be controlled (see para. 26 of the judgment).

The result of the application of art. 82 is that a differential standard of conduct applies to undertakings in a dominant position than to others in the market place. This can be a source of some distress to the managers of an undertaking who may not be able to respond to competitive situations as they would wish, and as perhaps they might have been lawfully able to do when the undertaking was still climbing towards its dominant position. The ECJ has explained the situation thus:

A finding that an undertaking has a dominant position is not in itself a recrimination but simply means that, irrespective of the reasons for which it has such a dominant position, the undertaking concerned has a special responsibility not to allow its conduct to impair genuine undistorted competition on the Common Market. (*Nederlandsche Banden-Industrie Michelin N.V.* v *Commission* case 322/81 [1985] 1 CMLR 282, para. 57)

As an undertaking in a dominant position in a relevant market has greater capacity to distort the market through its actions, it may be reasonable to maintain such a differential standard and to impose this 'special responsibility'. A similar sentiment is clear in *Hoffmann-La Roche & Co. AG* v *Commission* case 85/76 [1979] 3 CMLR 211, where the ECJ held that

The concept of abuse is an objective concept relating to the behaviour of an undertaking in a dominant position which is such as to influence the structure of a market where, as a result of the very presence of the undertaking in question, the degree of competition is weakened. (para. 91)

Once it has been determined that an undertaking is in breach of art. 82, whether that determination is made by the EC Commission or by a national court in the context of an action based on the principle of direct effect (see Chapter 2), there is no opportunity for an exemption to be sought from the application of the prohibition. As Advocate General Lenz stressed in *Ahmed Saeed*, this was a deliberate decision taken by the writers of the Treaty and is implicit in the adoption of the term 'abuse': 'abuses cannot be approved, or at any rate not in a community which recognises the rule of law as its highest principle' (*Ahmed Saeed Flugreisen and Silver Line Reisebüro GmbH* v *Zentrale zur Bekämpfung Unlauteren Wettbewerbs eV* case 66/86 [1990] 4 CMLR 102 at 116). This is not to say, however, that there is no scope for flexibility in the application of the article—the concept of 'abuse' is a flexible one and will usually be determined only after careful analysis of each situation. Another significant difference between art. 82 and art. 81 is that whereas the latter condemns 'anti-competitive' conduct, the prohibition of art. 82 may be extended to situations in which an undertaking exploits its position of dominance purely for its own benefit without reference to the effect that this behaviour may have on competitors. Indeed in some situations exploitative conduct, such as charging 'excessive' prices, may serve as a spur to more effective competition by, for instance, sending a signal to potential entrants as to the high level of profits that may be earned in the market, yet may be condemned as an abuse.

The questions to be asked in relation to the application of art. 82 are:

(a) Is there an undertaking holding a dominant position?

(b) Does this dominant position extend to a substantial part of the common market?

(c) Is the dominant position being abused?

(d) Is the nature of this abuse such as to affect trade between Member States?

These questions will now be dealt with in turn.

14.2 **The meaning of 'dominant position'**

The ECJ has held that

The dominant position referred to in [art. 82] relates to a position of economic strength enjoyed by an undertaking which enables it to prevent effective competition being maintained on the relevant market by giving it the power to behave to an appreciable extent independently of its competitors, customers and ultimately of its consumers.   (*United Brands Co.* v *Commission* case 27/76 [1978] 1 CMLR 429, para. 65)

Dominance does not require that there be *no* competition. In *Hoffmann-La Roche & Co. AG* v *Commission* case 85/76 [1979] 3 CMLR 211, the court held that a finding of dominance 'does not preclude some competition . . . but enables the undertaking which profits by it, if not to determine, at least to have an appreciable influence on the conditions under which that competition will develop, and in any case to act largely in disregard of it' (para. 39).

There is no fixed formula by which the dominance referred to in art. 82 may be established. Rather, by analysis of each case the following matters must be resolved:

(a) the relevant product market within which dominance is alleged;

(b) the relevant geographical market over which the alleged dominance extends;

(c) the relevant time period; and

(d) the relative strength of the alleged dominant undertaking.

The last matter may itself call for an examination of several aspects, most important but not exclusive of which is the market share of the relevant product held by the undertaking. Some care must be taken in defining the 'relevant market', which has a different meaning from the word 'market' in general commerce. The 'relevant market' may not be limited to the undertaking's definition of its sales area or the traditional definition applied by the industry to its sector.

14.2.1 **The relevant product market**

Generally it is in the interests of a defendant undertaking to describe the product market as broadly as possible, and for the Commission to define it narrowly. The more narrowly the market is defined the greater the market share of any one undertaking will be. Thus the manufacturer of the Nissan Micra motor car will have a 100 per cent share of the market, which is to say a total monopoly, if the product market is defined as being 'new Nissan Micras'. If the market is extended to that of small saloon cars the market share will drop to a level that probably remains significant but falls well short of monopoly and if the relevant market is extended to include all motor cars, including perhaps secondhand vehicles, and certain forms of public transport which to some extent compete with new cars, the market share will be insignificant.

The most important factor in defining the relevant product market is that of substitutability (or 'cross-elasticity'). Thus, in *Hoffmann-La Roche*, the ECJ stated that '[t]he concept of the relevant market presupposes that there is a sufficient degree of interchangeability between all the products forming part of the same market'. Substitutability can be analysed from the perspective of both the consumer of the product ('demand substitutability') and the suppliers or potential suppliers of the product ('supply substitutability'). In its notice on market definition (see 14.2.4) the Commission points to the formal test of 'demand substitution arising from small, permanent changes in relative prices', that is to say, to what extent would customers switch to readily available substitutes in response to a hypothetical, small (5–10 per cent) change in price of the product whose market is being assessed? In the United States this is referred to as the 'SSNIP' test, where SSNIP stands for a 'small but significant non-transitory increase in price'. Supply substitution requires that suppliers of other products are able to switch production in the short term in response to small but permanent changes in price. Necessarily, as these postulated changes in price are small and as an effect of the switch in supply is likely to result in smaller market shares for all suppliers, the cost of switching production must be small and the risk not substantial.

One of the more important European cases arose in relation to the market for bananas. In 1975 the Commission adopted a decision relating to certain conduct carried out by United Brands Continental, a subsidiary of an American firm accounting for 35 per cent of world banana exports. After finding that United Brands had engaged in a range of abusive conduct the Commission fined the company, and United Brands brought an action before the ECJ seeking an annulment of the Commission decision (*United Brands Co.* v *Commission* case 27/76 [1978] 1 CMLR 429). In particular the undertaking challenged the definition of the relevant product market adopted by the Commission, which had held that the market in question was that specifically for bananas, as against a more general market for soft fruit or for all fruit. The ECJ defined the problem as being one of whether bananas were 'reasonably interchangeable by consumers with other kinds of fresh fruit' (para. 12). United Brands argued that bananas 'compete with other fresh fruit in the same shops, on the same shelves, at prices which can be compared, satisfying the same needs: consumption as a dessert or between meals' (para. 13), and was able to point to statistics prepared by the United Nations agency, the Food and Agricultural Organization, that showed that consumers switched from buying bananas to buying other types of fruit in the summer months when the alternatives became readily available. The Commission, on the other hand, argued that it was right to treat bananas as being part of a discrete market, and pointed in particular to the fact that 'the banana is a very important part of the diet of certain sections of the community' (para. 19), namely, the very young, the elderly, and the sick, and that the banana possessed unique characteristics: 'appearance, taste, softness, seedlessness [and] easy handling' (para. 31). Further, at that time, bananas were unusual in being available all the year round, and the same statistics relied on by United Brands showed that the demand and price for bananas were generally unresponsive to the supplies of other fruits, with the single exception of grapes and peaches in Germany. In conclusion the Court held that 'a very large number of consumers having a constant need for bananas are not noticeably or even appreciably enticed away' by other fruit and that 'consequently the banana market is a market which is sufficiently distinct from the other fresh fruit market' (para. 35).

It may often be possible to establish that, because of a set of preferences peculiar to that group, particular groups of consumers are insensitive to the price of a given product. However, care should be taken before concluding from this that a separate market exists over which dominance is more easily established. The question is not one of how much the monopolist could in theory charge that group for the product, but one of whether the remaining consumers' behaviour will act as a limit on pricing decisions. Unless a monopolist seller of bananas can isolate the sick and elderly, and force them to pay more, the price can be raised only across the entire supply. This might increase the revenue from that one group, but it is likely to be more than offset by a fall in revenue from other consumers who are able to switch to different products. Market analysis should, if results are to be meaningful, focus on the group of consumers who can switch consumption at the margin, and not on the group who cannot—this is the essence of the SSNIP test.

Similar analysis to that of *United Brands* was conducted in *Nederlandsche Banden-Industrie Michelin N.V.* v *Commission* case 322/81 [1985] 1 CMLR 282. Here the Commission had condemned Michelin, the well-known tyre manufacturer, for, *inter alia*, its policies relating to dealer discounts and bonuses. In challenging the decision Michelin argued that the Commission had incorrectly defined the relevant market and, in so doing, had inflated the market share of Michelin. Had the market been defined correctly, Michelin asserted, the market share would have fallen to 37 per cent, a level which would not support a conclusion of dominance. The market for tyres is a complex one: tyres are supplied both with the original vehicle purchase and as replacements; they are available in different sizes, qualities, and treads, depending in part upon the vehicle to which they are to be attached; old tyres may be given new treads ('retreads') and these compete with new replacement tyres. In taking its decision the Commission defined the relevant market as that for new replacement tyres for lorries, buses, and similar vehicles. For this market Michelin's sales amounted to between 57 per cent and 65 per cent over the period in which the Commission was interested. The Court appeared to be unimpressed with arguments made by Michelin to the effect that the relevant market should include also car and van tyres. While Michelin contended that these should be taken into account as they occupy similar positions on the market, and that suppliers might therefore be able to switch from manufacturing car and van tyres to manufacturing heavy vehicle tyres, the Court made the point that 'there is no interchangeability between car and van tyres on the one hand and heavy-vehicle tyres on the other' (para. 39). Responding to the supply-side substitutability argument, the Court noted that to switch production between tyres for heavy vehicles and those for cars and vans was no easy matter and would require the investment of considerable time and money by manufacturers. Neither did the Court accept that retreads competed directly with new replacement tyres, even though there might be an element of substitution—Michelin had itself conceded that a retread would not always be as safe or reliable as a new tyre. A similar conclusion on market definition was made in *Michelin (II)* 2002/405/EC (2002) OJ L58/25.

It is interesting to note that in 1980 the courts in the United States found, basing their view in part on the existence of a $30 price differential, that separate markets existed in the case of radial and non-radial tyres in the case of *Donald B. Rice Tire Co. v Michelin Tire Corp.* 483 F. Supp. 750 (D. Md. 1980).

While the Commission has usually been successful in defending its market definitions it lost the notable case of *Europemballage Corp. and Continental Can Co. Inc.* v *Commission* case 6/72 [1973] CMLR 199. Here the Court held that the Commission had failed adequately to justify its reasoning in defining the three relevant markets as being those for 'light containers for canned meat products', 'light containers for canned seafood', and 'metal closures for the food packing industry'. The Commission did not give adequate reasons in the contested decision as to why these three areas constituted separate markets or why they stood apart from the wider market for can containers 'for fruit and vegetables, condensed milk, olive oil, fruit juices and chemico-technical products'. It also failed to consider the possibility of food packagers producing their own containers, and the Court was generally dismissive both of the quality of the reasoning in the decision and of the use of inconsistent facts to support arguments.

Demand- and supply-side substitutability may be the most important factor in the determination of the relevant product market, but the Commission and Court have made reference to other factors. In some instances, such as in *AKZO Chemie BV* v *EC Commission* case C–62/86 [1993] 5 CMLR 215 (the discussion of predation in this case is considered in further detail in Chapter 16), the Court has accepted the Commission's view that the action of the allegedly dominant undertaking is itself evidence of the bounds of the product market. It is surely correct that if an undertaking apparently engages in an abusive practice, which would be commercially beneficial only if a dominant position was held, the presumption that it has correctly defined the relevant market, and does indeed have a dominant position, should be raised.

The failure to come to court with a carefully considered market analysis may have fatal consequences for the progress of the case. In *Sockel GmbH v The Body Shop International plc* [2000] UKCLR 262, an action was dismissed largely because the claimant had failed to adequately define the market. In this case the claimant had alleged an abuse of a dominant position on the part of Body Shop, and had depended on the fact that the franchise system itself set out the bounds of the relevant market, without any consideration of competition from other brands and other outlets.

14.2.1.1 *Spare parts and ancillary products*

The issue of spare parts and ancillary products was first dealt with by the EC authorities in some detail in the case of *Hugin* (*Hugin Kassaregister AB and Hugin Cash Registers Ltd v Commission* case 22/78 [1979] 3 CMLR 345). The Commission had taken a decision that the non-dominant supplier of cash machines held a dominant position in the market for spare parts for those machines (78/68, (1978) OJ L22/23). The Court agreed with the Commission that, based on arguments relating to substitutability, the spare parts were not interchangeable with spare parts for other machines, and neither was it reasonable to suggest that a consumer purchase a new cash register from a different supplier as an alternative to fitting a spare part in an existing machine. The case has been followed since (see, e.g., *Volvo AB v Erik Veng (UK) Ltd* case 238/87 [1989] 4 CMLR 122) but it has raised concerns. It may be argued that a consumer choosing an initial purchase (in *Hugin* a cash register, and in *Volvo*, a motor car) must consider, as part of that decision, aspects such as the costs of maintenance and after-sales servicing, of which the availability of spare parts is just one element. In neither of the above cases did the undertaking hold a dominant position in the primary market, and as the consumer is able to make a choice at this stage it is very much to the disadvantage of the undertaking if it has thrust upon it unexpected and unwelcome responsibilities in the secondary market, for which it may not have budgeted, following a finding of dominance in that market. This argument is persuasive as long as the assumption of symmetry of knowledge between consumer and undertaking remains valid, but falls down where the consumer has neither the information nor ready access to it, on which to base such calculations at the point of original purchase.

A similar argument may be made in relation to ancillary products (or 'consumables'/'lock-ins') such as toner cartridges for printers, or semi-manufactured products to work with industrial machinery, and again it might be expected that the consumer, even more so than with spare parts, is in a position to factor in the ancillary items at the time of making the initial purchase. Two major cases, *Hilti* (*Hilti AG v Commission* case T–30/89 [1992] 4 CMLR 16) and *Tetra Pak II* (*Tetra Pak International SA v Commission* case T–83/91 [1992] 4 CMLR 76), dominate the case law. In *Hilti* the Court held that a distinction could be made between three separate markets: a nail-gun used in the construction trade; the cartridge strip in which the nails were placed; and the nails themselves. As with *Hugin*, *Hilti* did not hold a dominant position in the market for fixing systems for use in the construction industry, but did hold such a position in relation to the two ancillary markets. In *Tetra Pak II* the Commission argued that the market for filling machines to package liquid foods into cartons was a different market from that for the cartons themselves into which the foods were placed (92/163 (1992) OJ L72/1). Tetra Pak had argued that it was a supplier of integrated systems, and could not be said to have a dominant position in the market for cartons for its machines as no such separate market existed. On the facts the Court held that there were inconsistencies in the arguments made by Tetra Pak, including the fact that it supplied cartons to users of other manufacturers' machines, and that it would not need to impose restrictive contract terms on its customers for its own cartons if no other manufacturers' cartons could be used. This would be an example of supply-side substitutability where manufacturers making cartons for their own machines could also, with minimal adjustment to production lines, produce cartons for other machines.

In its *25th Report on Competition Policy* (COM (96) 126 final) the Commission accepted that this is a difficult area in which complaints can be resolved only on a case-by-case basis, with the Commission taking into account 'all important factors such as the price and life-time of the primary product, transparency of prices of secondary products, prices of secondary products as a proportion of the primary product value, information costs and other issues' (point 86). Such an approach was taken in *Pelikan/Kyocera* (point 87) where the Commission dealt with a complaint relating to activity in the market for toner cartridges for printers. The Commission was persuaded that Kyocera was not dominant in a secondary market for cartridges to be used with its printers, as consumers 'were well informed about the price charged for consumables and appeared to take this into account in their decision to buy a printer'.

Four factors were set out as being important when making the assessment whether a secondary market existed independently of the primary market:

(1) Would the consumer be in a position to make an informed choice at the point of initial purchase about the life cycle of the product, and the associated costs of any consumables? For example, in the case of a printer and toner cartridges would the consumer be able to 'punish' a company that appeared to abuse its power in the aftermarket by making a different choice in the primary market?

(2) Would the consumer actually make that choice?

(3) Would a sufficient number of consumers respond to apparent abuses in the aftermarket by adjusting their choices in the primary market?

(4) Would the response time of consumers be quick enough to protect those locked in to the aftermarket?

There has been much criticism of the approach taken by the EC Commission in this area, and of the *Hugin* decision in particular, but some support for such a course may be adduced from the American case of *Eastman Kodak Co.* v *Image Technical*

Services Inc. 504 U.S. 451 (1992), where a broadly similar stance was taken in relation to 'locked-in' customers for spare parts where the cost of switching would be high. This has been followed in similar cases in the United States.

14.2.2 **The relevant geographic market**

Having considered what the relevant product market is the Commission must then show the geographic boundaries of that market. In a form of words used frequently in decisions 'this examination enables the Commission to identify the actual and potential competitors of the undertaking in question and other constraints which may exist on the exercise of its supposed market power'. This is an important consideration, because while an undertaking may be dominant in a very small area—the classic example of which is the bus company that is dominant with respect to a single route—art. 82 requires that a dominant position extend to a 'substantial part' of the Community (see 14.3). The close link between these two considerations has been made clear by the ECJ, which has held that for art. 82 to apply 'presupposes the clear delimitation of the substantial part of the [EC] in which it may be able to engage in abuses which hinder effective competition and this is an area where the objective conditions of competition applying to the product in question must be the same for all traders' (*United Brands Co.* v *Commission* case 27/76 [1978] 1 CMLR 429, para. 44). An examination of the geographic market should also take into account the fact that it may be the case that an undertaking may appear to be dominant in one territory, but actually face competition or the threat of competition from outside of that territory that acts as a restraint on its conduct.

In the *United Brands* case, the Commission considered that the geographic market constituted Germany, Denmark, Ireland, and the Benelux countries, but excluded the other three Member States (the UK, Italy, and France) on the grounds that the legacy of history was such that there existed special circumstances relating to the import of bananas in those countries. The undertaking was happy that these countries be excluded, but argued further that the Commission should have held that each Member State constituted a separate market as the conditions of competition were different in each state, with different customs systems and different patterns of consumption. In the three excluded states the Court noted that United Brands would not be in a position to compete on equal terms with other bananas sold in those states, but that while the six other states displayed different characteristics the market in each of them was free, and the conditions of competition were the same for all undertakings trading in them, with the result that 'these six states form[ed] an area which [was] sufficiently homogenous to be considered in its entirety' (at para. 53). It is the conditions of competition, and not the result of that competition, that are important in determining the boundaries of the geographic market. Thus the fact that there are price differences between various areas is not in itself evidence of different markets (see, e.g., *Soda Ash—Solvay* 91/299 (1991) OJ L152/21).

In some instances the identification of the relevant area will be a relatively straightforward matter. There may, for instance, be specific evidence pointing to a clear boundary to the market. Thus in a series of cases relating to television guides and television listings the relevant areas were, in each case, those in which the television programmes themselves were intended primarily to be received (see, e.g., *RTE* v *Commission* case T–69/89 [1991] 4 CMLR 586 (Ireland) and *BBC* v *Commission* case T–70/89 [1991] 4 CMLR 669 (UK)). The action of a state monopoly, or of state regulation, may also define the market strictly, as, for instance, was the situation in *British Leyland plc* v *Commission* case 226/84 [1987] 1 CMLR 185, which related to the system of a national approval certificate for motor cars. The position may be more complicated where there is an apparently national market, as might be the case for any national newspaper, but where there is nevertheless some inter-state trade. If *The Times* is sold on news stands in the major cities in Europe in small numbers, is the relevant geographic market that of the UK or a wider market extending into Europe?

There has been some criticism of the approach taken by the Commission and the ECJ in defining the geographic market in the first *Michelin* case. Although it was recognized that the main tyre companies competed at the global level, the Commission had argued that the actions of each subsidiary were tailored to the specific conditions of each national market and had treated The Netherlands as a separate market from the rest of the Community. The Court agreed that it was 'at that level that the objective conditions of competition [were] alike for traders', and although it accepted that 'in practice dealers established in The Netherlands obtain their supplies only from suppliers operating in The Netherlands' (*Nederlandsche Banden-Industrie Michelin N.V.* v *Commission* case 322/81 [1985] 1 CMLR 282, para. 26), it may be argued that the possibility of consumers going outside The Netherlands for their tyres should have been discussed more fully. It is likely that the competitive conditions in The Netherlands were, at the least, moderately affected by the availability of supplies from elsewhere in the Community.

As a rule of thumb the size of the market is in inverse proportion to the product's transportation costs relative to the value of the product: a product with a high value and a low transportation cost will have a large geographic market; and a product with a low value and a high transportation cost will have a small geographic market. That transport costs may be highly influential in determining the boundaries to the market may be seen in *Napier Brown—British Sugar* 88/518 (1988) OJ L284/41. In finding that British Sugar had abused a dominant position in its market the Commission considered that the UK constituted a geographic market separate from that of the rest of the Community. *Inter alia* the Commission was swayed by the fact that imports into the UK over the period immediately preceding its action had amounted to only 5–10 per cent of consumption, and noted that this was in part the result of 'the natural barrier of the English Channel, which gives rise to additional transport costs' (at para. 44(i)) (a similar conclusion had been reached by the MMC in two reports into mergers in the domestic sugar industry which the Commission in part relied upon). Sugar represents a classic example of a product which has high transport costs in relation to value: it is both bulky and relatively cheap.

In situations where transport costs do not constitute a significant barrier to trade, the relevant geographic market may often be that of the entire Community (see, e.g., *ECS/AKZO* 85/609 (1985) OJ L374/1, para. 66). Thus in *Tetra Pak I (BTG Licence)*, which concerned the market for packaging machines and consumables for liquid foods, of which milk was the most important, the Commission held that 'even if there exist the differing demand conditions between Member States, the [EC] is the relevant geographical market . . . transport costs for both machines and cartons are not significant. In fact carton packaging machinery supplied to dairies in the [EC] comes from producers all over the world' (88/501 (1988) OJ L272/27, para. 41).

14.2.3 **The relevant time period**

Time is a factor that must be considered in order to establish the relevant period:

- (a) over which the dominance is alleged; and
- (b) over which the alleged abuse may have been perpetrated.

However, it is extremely rare for the analysis of the temporal market to be a significant feature of a decision or case. The most notable example arises out of the 1973/74 oil crisis, with the Commission taking a decision holding that one consequence of the crisis was to create a series of temporarily defined separate markets in favour of each supplier as customers were unable to switch to alternative suppliers, supplies being rationed by suppliers and made available only to their traditional customers (*ABG Oil companies operating in the Netherlands* 77/327 (1977) OJ L117/1). While the Commission lost the case on appeal on different grounds, the Court left intact the temporal arguments (*BP v Commission* case 77/77 [1978] 3 CMLR 174). Generally the Commission's determination of the temporal constraints over which the relevant market is defined is not likely to be successfully challenged, but there may well be arguments as to the duration of the alleged abuse as this is a factor in assessing the level of any fines imposed (see Chapter 6).

14.2.4 **The Commission notice on market definition**

In 1997 the Commission published a *notice on the definition of the relevant market for the purpose of Community competition law* ((1997) OJ C372/5). The notice applies equally to analysis conducted for the purposes of applying arts 81 and 82 and Regulation 4064/89 (see Chapter 19), as well as the European Economic Area Agreement. The reason for issuing the notice is made apparent in the introduction:

The definition of the relevant market in both its product and geographic dimensions often has a decisive influence on the assessment of a competition case. By rendering public the procedures the Commission follows when considering market definition and by indicating the criteria and evidence on which it relies to reach a decision, the Commission expects to increase the transparency of its policy and decision making in the area of competition policy.

The notice firmly places the SSNIP test at the heart of market definition. In its decision relating to the *1998 Football World Cup* 2000/12 (2000) OJ L5/55 the Commission was explicit in its application of the notice's SSNIP test to define the relevant market (paras. 66–74), although in *Virgin/British Airways* 2000/74 (2000) OJ L30/1 the Commission indicated that it was not required to perform the SSNIP test, and that the methodology set out in the notice was merely an illustration of the way in which markets operated.

The Commission recognizes that, because the purpose for which competition law is being applied may be different under each legislative head, the methodology outlined above 'might lead to different results depending on the nature of the competition issue being examined', but that certain basic principles apply in all cases. These economic constants are the factors that serve as competitive restraints on the undertaking whose conduct or concentrative transaction is being analysed: demand substitution and supply substitution.

Supply-side substitution, which is a factor in market definition, is to be distinguished from potential competition, which is not. The notice makes clear the fact that the Commission does not consider it appropriate to consider potential competition (see, e.g., *Europemballage Corp. and Continental Can Co. Inc.* v *Commission* case 6/72 [1973] CMLR 199) at the stage of market definition. This is not to say that this factor is disregarded by the Commission, but that 'the conditions under which potential competition will actually represent an effective competitive constraint depend on the analysis of specific factors and circumstances related to the conditions of entry' and that, if required, such analysis will be carried out only *after* the relevant market has been defined. The key distinction between supply-side substitution and potential competition lies in the time period over which each may take place, with potential competition arising only over a longer time frame.

The notice sheds useful light on the practicalities of market analysis and the extent to which the Commission may be able to avoid the sort of analysis undertaken in, for example, the *United Brands* case. It is apparent that in the right circumstances cases will be fairly quickly dealt with where the issue is simply one of 'whether product A and product B belong or do not belong to the same product market', and where the determination that they do will at once eliminate any competition concerns. Where more detailed analysis is called for the Commission may contact main customers, main companies, relevant professional associations, the undertakings directly involved, and where appropriate companies involved in upstream markets, which are defined as those closer to the original source of production or raw input. Not all such contacts will be by way of formal decisions taken under the appropriate secondary legislation, and the Commission may often simply discuss matters with company officers on the telephone, or arrange informal visits to allow it to gain a clearer understanding of the operation of the relevant market. Factors that may serve as evidence to define product markets include: an analysis of the product characteristics; evidence of substitution in the recent past; various econometric and statistical approaches; views of customers and competitors; consumer preferences as perhaps identified by consumer surveys commissioned within the industry in the past; barriers and costs of switching consumption; and the possible existence of different groups of consumers and price discrimination.

A broadly similar approach is taken to the geographic market, the objective being, as indicated above, 'to identify which companies selling the products in the relevant market are actually competing with the parties and constraining their behaviour, with the focus placed on prices'. The evidence that the notice suggests may be used to define the geographic market includes: past evidence of diversion of orders to other areas; basic demand characteristics, including factors such as national preferences; views of customers and competitors; current geographic patterns of purchases; trade flows; and barriers and costs of switching sources.

The notice does not deal with the issue of the temporal definition of the market.

14.2.5 **The relative strength of the alleged dominant undertaking**

Having established the relevant market—product, geographic area, and time period—the next requirement for art. 82 to apply is that dominance in that market be established. Dominance may be attributed to an undertaking by virtue of a variety of factors of which the most important is market share. However, market share may not be the sole determinant of dominance, and situations may arise in which an undertaking commands a large market share yet is not dominant. This might be the case, for example, where there is the serious threat of *potential* competition. Likewise there may be situations where an undertaking has a seemingly innocuous market share yet is still dominant because of the relatively weak positions of its main competitors.

14.2.5.1 *Market share*

The classic statement as to the role of market share in determining dominance is to be found in the case of *Hoffmann-La Roche*. The ECJ held that

although the importance of the market shares may vary from one market to another the view may legitimately be taken that very large shares are in themselves, and save in exceptional circumstances, evidence of the existence of a dominant position. An undertaking which has a very large market share and holds it for some time, by means of the volume of production and the scale of the supply which it stands for—without those having much smaller market shares being able to meet rapidly the demand from those who would like to break away from the undertaking which has the largest market share—is by virtue of that share in a position of strength which makes it an unavoidable trading partner and which already because of this secures for it, at the very least during relatively long periods, that freedom of action which is the special feature of a dominant position. (*Hoffmann-La Roche & Co. Ag* v *Commission* case 85/76 [1979] 3 CMLR 211, para. 41)

In that case the appellant undertaking manufactured various vitamins, each of which was treated as a separate product market, and the analysis of the ECJ is revealing as to the role market shares play and the extent to which a particular share may, by itself, be relied upon in establishing the existence of a dominant position. Where a range of shares is given it is over a three-year period, in which membership of the Community grew from six to nine Member States, and both share by value and share by quantity:

- *Vitamin A*: the market share stood at 47 per cent, and dominance was established, in part by reference to other criteria (paras 50–2).
- *Vitamin B_2*: 75–87 per cent: 'so large that they are in themselves evidence of a dominant position' (para. 56).
- *Vitamin B_3*: 19–51 per cent: 'Market shares of this size either in value or in quantity . . . do not in themselves constitute a factor sufficient to establish a dominant position . . . insufficient evidence of the existence of a dominant position held by Roche for the period in question' (paras 57–8).
- *Vitamin B_6*: 84–90 per cent: 'market shares are . . . so large that they prove the existence of a dominant position' (paras 59–60).
- *Vitamin C*: 63–66 per cent: 'evidence of the existence of a dominant position' but further evidence used to support the conclusion (paras 61–3).
- *Vitamin E*: 50–64 per cent: 'significant', but further evidence used to support the finding of dominance (paras 64–6).
- *Vitamin H*: 93–100 per cent: 'with the result that it in fact has a monopoly' (para. 67).

In *AKZO* the Court, having first cited *Hoffmann-La Roche* to make the point that very large market shares may by themselves be conclusive evidence of dominance, held that a share of 50 per cent: would satisfy this test (*AKZO Chemie BV* v *Commission* case C–62/86 [1993] 5 CMLR 215).

In *Michelin (II)* 2002/405 (2002) OJ L58/25 the Commission relied in part on the fact that 'all the analyses combine to show that Michelin's share of the two relevant markets has exceeded this [50 per cent] threshold consistently for more than 20 years' (para. 175).

The Commission appears on occasion to be more conservative than the Court in its use of market share. In *BBI/Boosey & Hawkes: interim measures* 87/500 (1987) OJ L286/36, Boosey & Hawkes, the leading manufacturer of musical instruments for brass bands, was found to have 'a market share of some 80 per cent to 90 per cent' but the Commission, noting that 'a high market share does however not on its own create a presumption of dominance', pointed also to other evidence. It was significant that the undertaking's own documents claimed that their instruments were 'the automatic first choice of all the top brass bands', and that no other competitor had been able to make a significant impact on the market, in spite of Yamaha making strenuous efforts to do so (para. 18). However, there are clear instances where a finding of dominance is made by exclusive reference to market share. In *Decca* (*Decca Navigator System* 89/113 (1989) OJ L43/27) the undertaking had a legal monopoly in relation to the relevant market for the period during which it held patents in respect of the relevant technology, and thereafter held a market share such as to constitute a de facto monopoly. The Commission did not point to any other evidence to establish its finding of dominance.

 Generally the approach appears to be that a market share of 70 per cent and above will almost certainly constitute a dominant position; a share of 50–70 per cent will raise a presumption of dominance; a share of 40–50 per cent may support a conclusion of dominance; and a share of below 40 per cent is highly unlikely to permit the finding of dominance unless other evidence is overwhelming, although the Commission in its *10th Report on Competition Policy* suggested that an undertaking could still be found to enjoy a dominant position with a market share as low as 20 per cent. In *Virgin/British Airways* 2000/74 (2000) OJ L30/1 the Commission found dominance to exist at a point when BA's market share of the total airline sales in the UK in 1998 amounted to 39.7 per cent (para. 41). This is the lowest figure at which a finding of dominance has been sustained, and even here there were other factors strongly indicative of dominance, including the relatively low market shares of other parties. On appeal to the CFI the Court upheld the findings of the Commission, and rejected BA's assertion that dominance did not exist. At paras 212–14 of its judgment the CFI held that

The economic strength which BA derives from its market share is further reinforced by the world rank it occupies in terms of international scheduled passenger-kilometres flown, the extent of the range of its transport services and its hub network.

 According to BA's own statements, its network operations allow it, in comparison with its five competitors, to offer a wider choice of routes and more frequent flights.

 It is further shown by recital (38) of the contested decision, not challenged by BA, that, in 1995, it operated 92 of the 151 international routes from Heathrow Airport and 43 of the 92 routes in service at Gatwick, that is to say several times the number of routes served by each of its three or four nearest rivals [operating] from those two airports.   (*British Airways plc* v *Commission* case T–219/99, 17 December 2003)

14.2.5.2 *Competitors' positions*

The relative size of the competitors' market shares were determining evidence as to the existence of a dominant position in relation to the vitamins C and E market in *Hoffmann-La Roche* (above) and supporting evidence in relation to the vitamin A market. In the market for vitamin C the Court, for instance, pointed to the fact that 'the gap between Roche's shares (64.8 per cent) and those of its next largest competitors (14.8 per cent and 6.3 per cent) was such as to confirm the conclusion' of dominance (para. 63) and a similar position was found to exist in relation to vitamin E. The comments made in relation to vitamin A, where the market shares were 47 per cent to Roche, and 27 per cent, 18 per cent, 7 per cent, and 1 per cent to the other producers, are more telling:

Since the relevant market thus has the particular features of a narrow oligopolistic market in which the degree of competition by its very nature has already been weakened, Roche's share, which is equal to the aggregate of the shares of its two next largest competitors, proves that it is entirely free to decide what attitude to adopt when confronted by competition. (para. 51)

In *Sabena* (*London European* v *Sabena* 88/589 (1988) OJ L317/47) the Commission found that the market share held by Sabena of the relevant market of computerized airline reservation systems in Belgium was between 40 per cent and 50 per cent. As such a share would not, by itself, support a claim of dominance, the Commission noted that 'the ratio of market shares held by the undertaking concerned to those held by its competitors is also a reliable indicator' (para. 24). In this case the five competing systems were each used by no more than 20 agencies, as compared to the 118 agencies using the Sabena system.

14.2.5.3 *Barriers to entry*

As noted in Chapter 13, the role played by barriers to entry in industrial economics and antitrust analysis is of vital importance. The establishment of the market share of the allegedly dominant undertaking cannot by itself determine the competitive restraints under which the undertaking operates. It is possible, albeit unlikely, that an undertaking could have a 100 per cent market share and yet not be able to reap significant profits if it is constantly aware of the danger of potential competition, which might be triggered by higher prices signalling to entrepreneurs that profits can be made in the market. Barriers to entry are not, however, easily analysed and often require a more dynamic long-term view of market structure than does a straightforward static analysis of current market shares. The situation is further complicated by disagreements between industrial economists as to the meaning of the term 'barrier to entry' and as to those factors that may legitimately be considered to be barriers. It is in the definition of this term that one of the most dramatic differences lies between the Harvard and Chicago schools. In the various decisions taken under art. 82 the Commission has pointed to the existence of identifiable barriers to entry, but has rarely made convincing or detailed arguments and has not developed an entirely satisfactory framework. For example, in *Tetra Pak I* (88/501 (1988) OJ L272/27), as well as relying on the undertaking's 91.8 per cent market share in the relevant market—'machines capable of filling cartons by an aseptic process with UHT-treated liquids'—the Commission considered that the 'barriers to entry to produce aseptic packaging machines are particularly high, which severely limits the entry of new competitors' (para. 44.3). This may be true, but it is not adequately supported by detailed analysis found within the decision itself.

In the absence of a sophisticated analysis the Commission has turned instead to a range of evidence which it considers to be indicative of dominance, and has not always made clear whether these secondary factors are considered also to be evidence of barriers to entry or of dominance per se.

14.2.5.4 *The resources, size, and commercial superiority of the undertaking*

In *British Plasterboard* (*BPB Industries plc* 89/22 (1989) OJ L10/50), once the Commission found that the undertaking's share of the plasterboard market in Great Britain was between 98 per cent and 96 per cent for the relevant period it may seem unnecessary to have referred to other factors to support the argument that the company enjoyed a dominant position. Nevertheless the Commission pointed also to the 'substantial economies in producing on a large scale in integrated industrial complexes' (para. 116) enjoyed by BPB. Further, the extensive product range carried by BPB and the fact that architects were on occasion specific in requiring the use of BPB's products were further points used as evidence of dominance. The failings of a static, snapshot analysis are perhaps demonstrated by this decision. While on these facts it appears the BPB's position would be unassailable, an MMC report in 1990 (*Plasterboard*, Cm. 1224) found that BPB's market share had fallen, in the space of only two years, from 96 per cent to 65 per cent, following the entry of new competition into the market.

Undertakings which have succeeded in developing an efficient and strong distribution system may find that the existence of such a system is one factor that supports a finding of dominance. Thus, for instance, in *Eurofix-Bauco/Hilti* 88/138 (1988) OJ L65/19 one of the factors that the Commission considered to be relevant was Hilti's 'strong and well-organised distribution system—in the EEC it has subsidiaries and independent dealers integrated into its selling network' (para. 69).

In *Soda Ash* (*Soda Ash—Solvay* 91/299 (1991) OJ L152/21) the company's dominant position was established not just by its near-total monopoly in three of the Member States, but also by reference to, *inter alia*, its manufacturing strength with plant in six of the Member States; its upstream integration as the largest producer of salt (a raw material in the manufacture of soda ash) in the Community; and Solvay's 'excellent market coverage as the exclusive or near-exclusive supplier to almost all the major customers in the Community'.

The Commission may turn not only to product ranges, but also to the services offered by the allegedly dominant company, both where these are the primary activity and where they are ancillary to the supply of the primary product. Thus, for example, in a decision taken in respect of shipping services between Zaire and Angola and various North Sea ports (*Cewal* 93/82 (1993) OJ L34/20), the assertion of dominance was supported by reference to the 'network of routes, the capacities of [Cewal's] fleet and the frequency of the services it can provide' (para. 59). The level of technical support that could be provided by Michelin's large number of representatives (*BF BV/NV NBI Michelin* 81/969 (1981) OJ L353/33), which was greater than that of rival manufacturers, was also considered to be indicative of dominance.

14.2.5.5 *Technical superiority and the possession of know-how and intellectual property*

Technical superiority was considered to be a relevant factor by the ECJ in *Hoffmann-La Roche & Co. AG* v *Commission* case 85/76 [1979] 3 CMLR 211, which held that

'Roche's technical lead over its competitors due to the fact that it is the proprietor of several patents relating to vitamin A, even after the expiration of these patents, is a further indication that it occupies a dominant position' (para. 51). Similar considerations were raised in *Eurofix-Bauco/Hilti* 88/138 (1988) OJ L65/19, where Hilti's DX 450 nail-gun, which was central to the issue of market power, was commended for its 'novel technically advantageous features' which were subject to patent protection. The Commission also drew attention to Hilti's 'extremely strong research and development position' which it considered to be a factor in establishing dominance. In *Tetra Pak I* 88/501 (1988) OJ L272/27 this factor was also an issue, with the Commission pointing to Tetra Pak's first-mover advantage: 'it was the first to develop the technology and has vast experience . . . its technology and machines are partially protected by patents' (para. 44.2).

The possession of copyright in published material may also lead to a conclusion of dominance if the relevant market is drawn tightly. The Commission dealt with complaints relating to the practices of the IBA, BBC, and RTE television networks, in relation to programme listings. The undertakings' policy was to reserve to themselves the right to publish advance details of schedules, and they relied in part on their copyright in these listings to obstruct advance publication by magazines that were attempting to compete with the authorized publications. In a short decision, which was subsequently challenged, the Commission held that 'the factual monopoly held by the broadcasting organisations in relation to their . . . listings is strengthened into a legal monopoly' by virtue of the application of copyright laws, and that the companies therefore held a dominant position (*Magill TV Guide/ITP/ BBC and RTE* 89/205 (1989) OJ L78/43).

14.2.5.6 *Super-dominance*

Recent developments in the law of dominance suggest that a refinement to the 'special responsibility' provided for in the *Michelin* case has been created in the case of undertakings which are 'super-dominant'. This follows from the comments of the Advocate General in the case of *Compagnie Maritime Belge SA* v *Commission* joined cases C 395 and 396/96P [2000] 4 CMLR 1076, and may be deduced also from an analysis of the response to abusive conduct in earlier cases. The key statement of Advocate General Fennelly is found in para. 137 of his submission to the Court:

To my mind, art. 82 cannot be interpreted as permitting monopolists or quasi-monopolists to exploit the very significant market power which their superdominance confers so as to preclude the emergence either of a new or additional competitor. Where an undertaking . . . enjoys a position of such overwhelming dominance verging on monopoly, comparable to that which existed in the present case . . . it would not be consonant with the particularly onerous special obligation affecting such a dominant undertaking not to impair further the structure of the feeble existing competition.

The 'particularly onerous special obligation' referred to here may be witnessed at play in some of the 'essential facility' cases discussed in Chapter 16, where the undertakings in question enjoyed total monopoly in some areas of the market, and as a result were able to exclude from other parts of the market potential competition. It had already been recognized by the ECJ in the case of *Tetra Pak* v *Commission (No. 2)* case C–333/94P [1997] 4 CMLR 662 that the scope of the special responsibility provided for in *Michelin* must be considered in the light of the particular facts of each case. The comments of the Advocate General in *Compagnie Maritime Belge* seem to do little more than provide a convenient label for a situation in which the analysis of the particular facts shows that the existing competition to the monopolist is 'feeble' rather than merely 'weakened'.

14.2.5.7 *Joint dominance*

The law relating to joint dominance (also known as 'collective dominance' and 'oligopolistic dominance') is dealt with here in relation to art. 82, and in Chapter 19 in relation to merger control, although it should be recognized that the development of the two threads has been inextricably connected. The economics of what is a difficult area are dealt with in Chapter 18. However, following amendments to the EC merger regulation, discussed in Chapter 19, the link has been broken.

The leading case relating to joint dominance in the context of art. 82 is *Compagnie Maritime Belge SA* v *Commission* joined cases C 395 and 396/96P [2000] 4 CMLR 1076. The case arose by way of an appeal from *Cewal* 93/82 (1993) OJ L34/20 where the Commission had condemned members of a liner conference for attempting, collectively, to eliminate an independent competitor. One of the issues that fell to be dealt with was, following a chain of cases applying the concept in relation to merger control, the extent to which, and the factors conditioning this, a number of undertakings could *collectively* occupy a dominant position. It will be recalled that art. 82 makes reference to a dominant position held by 'one or more' undertakings. The Court held that it was well established that art. 82 could apply to situations in which a dominant position was held by more than one undertaking:

the expression 'one or more undertakings' in art. [82] of the Treaty implies that a dominant position may be held by two or more economic entities legally independent of each other, provided that from an economic point of view they present themselves or act together on a particular market as a collective entity.   (para. 36)

To establish that such a position exists it is necessary, according to the Court, to examine the economic links or factors which give rise to a connection between undertakings. It is not sufficient that the undertakings in question are linked by an agreement or other practice which would fall within art. 81(1) in order to find that a position of joint dominance exists, but such an agreement can result in a position of joint dominance, depending on the way in which the agreement would be implemented. In the present case the way in which the liner conference agreement between the parties operated was such as to place them in the position of presenting 'themselves on that market as a collective entity *vis-à-vis* their competitors, their trading partners and consumers' (para. 44).

Joint dominance was also discussed in the context of art. 82 in *Irish Sugar* 97/624 (1997) OJ L258/1, on appeal *Irish Sugar plc* v *Commission* case T–228/97 [1999]

5 CMLR 1300, paras 38–68. Here it was accepted by all that for joint dominance to exist 'there must be close links between the two entities, and that those links must be such as to be capable of leading to the adoption of the same conduct and policy on the market in question' (para. 45). Here the joint dominance related to a vertical arrangement between a dominant producer of sugar, and the sole bulk distributor of sugar in the same Member State.

14.3 The meaning of 'substantial part'

For art. 82 to apply, the dominant position identified must be found to exist in 'the common market or in a substantial part of it'. Clearly if dominance extends throughout the EC this jurisdictional hurdle is overcome. The meaning of 'substantial part' is, however, open to interpretation, and is likely to be an inconstant factor: an area that would have counted as substantial in a Community of six may no longer be substantial in a Community that has expanded to 25 members, meaning that previous case law may not be a fail-safe guide to future determinations. It has been traditionally argued that a market extending to any single Member State will meet the threshold, but this may no longer be the case. While there are obvious political difficulties in either the Commission, a court in a Member State, or a national authority holding that the relevant state is not 'substantial', the increasing strength of the single market might allow the authorities to argue successfully that, particularly with regard to the smaller states, a state-wide market will not automatically be so classed. However, in *Irish Sugar* 97/624 (1997) OJ L258/1 the Republic of Ireland was found to be a substantial part of the Common Market although it accounted for only 1.2 per cent of the market for the sale of sugar in the EC. The concept also must be related to the specific market for the product in question, and not merely to an examination of the size of the absolute geographic area identified in defining the market boundary, although that is undeniably important.

14.3.1 Examples

While a single Member State may not now automatically be substantial there is no doubt that areas of Member States can be, and that the Community can support several substantial markets in the same product, as long as in each the conditions of competition are different (see the discussion of *United Brands*, above).

The case of *Suiker Unie* (*Cooperatieve Vereniging 'Suiker Unie' UA v Commission* cases 40–48/73, 50/73, 54–56/73, 111/73, 113–114/73 [1976] 1 CMLR 295) remains one of the most important in determining the meaning of 'substantial'. The case itself is exceptionally complicated, with the applicants challenging a Commission decision which imposed fines and cease and desist orders on 16 undertakings (*European Sugar Industry* 73/109 (1973) OJ L140/17), on many different grounds.

One of the applicants (Raffinerie Tirlemontoise) was alleged by the Commission to occupy a dominant position on the sugar market in Belgium and Luxembourg, which the Commission had held to be a substantial part of the Common Market, and claimed before the ECJ that this position was inconsistent with the small level of production of sugar in Belgium relative to the rest of the Community, and with the small number of consumers in the two Member States (it will be recalled that at the time the contested decision was taken the Community's membership was that of the original six Member States). The view taken by the Court was that in determining whether a specific area amounts to a 'substantial part of the common market' it would be necessary to take into account 'the pattern and volume of the production and consumption of the said product as well as the habits and economic opportunities of vendors and purchasers' (para. 371). Also relevant would be the fact that the organization of the sugar market by the Community had tended to reinforce national boundaries. In the year 1971/72 sugar production in the Community as a whole stood at 8,100,000 tonnes, and Belgian production at 770,000 tonnes (9.6 per cent of the total). Consumption in Belgium stood at 350,000 tonnes, compared to 6,500,000 tonnes in the Community (i.e., it was 5.4 per cent of the total). The Court held that these market shares, taken together with the other relevant factors, were such as to mean that the Belgo-Luxembourg market did constitute a substantial part of the Community.

In relation to another applicant, Sudzucker-Verkauf, the question was whether the 'southern part of Germany' constituted a substantial part of the common market. The population of the area in which the undertaking held its position was 22 million at the time the decision was taken, the undertaking's production was about 800,000 tonnes, and the Court held that this market 'is found to be sufficiently large, so far as sugar is concerned, to be considered . . . as a substantial part' of the Community (para. 448).

14.3.2 Infrastructure and facilities

It was noted above that a straightforward comparison of the relative size of the geographic area of the market with that of the Community as a whole will not always be sufficient to establish the meaning of 'substantial part', and in a chain of decisions very small geographic areas have been held to be 'substantial'. These include airports (Brussels Airport) and ports (Holyhead, Rødby, and Roscoff), all of which may be small in themselves but which may be the essential point of access to a market that is itself substantial (see further Chapter 16).

14.4 The concept of abuse

The list of abusive practices set out in art. 82 'merely gives examples, i.e., not an exhaustive list of the kinds of abusive exploitation of a dominant position prohibited by the Treaty' (*Europemballage Corp. and Continental Can Co. Inc.* v *Commission* case 6/72 [1973] CMLR 199, para. 26), and accordingly the Commission and Court have condemned practices not set out in the list. In *Continental Can*, for example, this included the acquisition of shares in a competing undertaking, which had the effect of increasing the power of an *already* dominant position (see the discussion of mergers in Chapter 19). The 'special responsibility' that dominant firms have not to impair or distort competition (*Nederlandsche Banden-Industries Michelin N.V.* v *Commission* case 322/81 [1985] 1 CMLR 282, at 327) suggests that standards of permissible conduct in the EC will be higher than, for example, in the United States. The meaning of abuse might therefore be such as to go beyond the requirement not to act so as to impair the efficient operation of the market place. In *Hoffmann-La Roche & Co. AG* v *Commission* case 85/76 [1979] 3 CMLR 211, the ECJ held that

the concept of abuse is an objective concept relating to the behaviour of an undertaking in a dominant position which is such as to influence the structure of a market where, as a result of the very presence of the undertaking in question, the degree of competition is weakened and which, through recourse to methods different from those which condition normal competition . . . has the effect of hindering the maintenance of the degree of competition still existing in the market.   (para. 91)

The reference to 'normal competition' in this context is questionable. In fact many practices that have been condemned under art. 82 are not abnormal, but their use by undertakings which are already in a position of some strength has an impact that draws the attention of the EC Commission.

The wording of art. 82 does not make reference to the 'object or effect' rubric found in art. 81. It appears, following recent case law, that it is *not* necessary to demonstrate that there is an anti-competitive effect in order to demonstrate that an illegal abuse is taking place. This was most recently confirmed by the CFI in two cases, *Manufacture française des pneumatiques Michelin* v *Commission* case T–219/99, 30 September 2003 and *British Airways* v *Commission* case T–219/99, 17 December 2003. Both of these cases are discussed elsewhere in relation to the abuses considered. At para. 293 of *British Airways* the CFI held that

for the purposes of establishing an infringement of art. 82 EC, it is not necessary to demonstrate that the abuse in question had a concrete effect on the markets concerned. It is sufficient in that respect to demonstrate that the abusive conduct of the undertaking in a dominant position tends to restrict competition, or, in other words, that the conduct is capable of having, or likely to have, such an effect.

And in para. 239 of *Michelin* the court used almost exactly the same words:

For the purposes of establishing an infringement of Article 82 EC, it is sufficient to show that the abusive conduct of the undertaking in a dominant position tends to restrict competition or, in other words, that the conduct is capable of having that effect.

It is only since these two cases that this position has been clear, and the approach of the court has attracted criticism for adopting a standard for the determination of 'abuse' which is too low. For example, it has been argued that the CFI has set a threshold for exclusionary abuse that requires no actual harm, no likelihood of harm, but rather merely the *potential* for harm. This threshold focuses on the restriction on the customer, rather than the effect on the competitor. . . . Aside from the rather conclusory language of object and effect in *Michelin II*, there is no attempt to explain the rationale for these rules in law or competition policy.   (Kallaugher, J., and Sher, B., 'Rebates Revisited: Anti-competitive Effects and Exclusionary Abuse under Article 82', [2004] *ECLR* 263)

Both of these cases deal with exclusionary abuses, and it is to be doubted that the same principle would apply in relation to exploitative abuses, in which the very concept of 'exploitation' is intimately interconnected with the concept of 'abuse'.

14.4.1 Examples of abusive conduct

Abuses arising out of predatory, discriminatory, and excessive prices, and refusals to supply, are considered in some detail in Chapter 16. The remaining examples given here are not a comprehensive listing, but will give some indication of the range of practices that have been condemned and the sort of evidence that is likely to attract the interest of the EC Commission.

14.4.1.1 *Exclusive purchasing and tie-in sales*

There exists a range of purchasing requirements that are sometimes used in order to extend a dominant undertaking's influence or to increase its profits. The most common of these practices are exclusive purchasing requirements, by virtue of which a purchaser agrees not to buy the same product from any other source, and tie-in sales, whereby the purchaser will be supplied with one product only if another is also purchased. In its extreme position, where tie-in sales extend across the complete range of the dominant supplier, such a practice may be termed full-line forcing.

Exclusive purchasing requirements were first dealt with in detail in *Vitamins* 76/642 (1976) OJ L223/27 (on appeal, *Hoffmann-La Roche & Co. AG v Commission* case 85/76 [1979] 3 CMLR 211). Hoffmann's strategy in relation to its bulk sales of synthetic vitamins was to conclude exclusive agreements with customers wherever possible. These 'fidelity agreements' were referred to in a circular issued by the Roche parent company in 1970, which was obtained and quoted by the Commission:

According to the experience of various Roche companies, fidelity contracts provide a very efficient protection against competition, especially as far as BASF are concerned. In our today's Management Information we have therefore made a special provision for such contracts. (para. 12)

In essence the structure of the supply contracts was such that Hoffmann would provide the major part of each customer's requirements at the most favourable price in the relevant market, and at regular intervals, which were usually annual, customers would be given a rebate of between 1 per cent and 20 per cent on their purchases if they had indeed obtained most of their requirements from Hoffmann.

Hoffmann's ability to obtain information about, and to react to, its competitors' practices was enhanced by an 'English clause' in the contracts, which provided that Hoffmann would meet any price offered to a customer by any reputable supplier, or that if it failed to do so it would not remove the benefit of the rebates if the customer bought from the competing supplier. Generally these contracts were concluded for a period of five years, and would thus guarantee to Hoffmann a stable outlet which would potentially exclude other competitors from developing strength in the market.

The Commission found this conduct to be abusive as 'by its nature it hampers the freedom of choice and equality of treatment of purchasers and restricts competition between bulk vitamin manufacturers' (para. 22) and also took the view that the fidelity rebates fell expressly within art. 82(c), 'applying dissimilar conditions to equivalent transactions', because they were not related to objective cost factors.

When the case came before the ECJ it held that

An undertaking which is in a dominant position on a market and ties purchasers—even if it does so at their request—by an obligation or promise on their part to obtain all or most of their requirements exclusively from the said undertaking abuses its dominant position.   (para. 89)

The Court further held that in the absence of exceptional circumstances the granting of rebates designed to support exclusive purchase obligations would be caught by art. 82(c).

In *ICI* (*Soda Ash ICI* 91/300 (1991) OJ L152/40) the Commission found that ICI's strategy in the relevant market was to ensure that its main competitors in the UK, Brenntag and General Chemical, 'at least remained in the United Kingdom market as a presence . . . which met the need of most large customers for a secondary supplier while in fact presenting no real competitive threat' (para. 58). ICI offered its customers a 'top-slice rebate' under which substantial financial incentives were offered to customers purchasing more than their expected regular 'core' supplies from ICI. By tying its customers in this way ICI was able, in effect, to regulate the remainder of the market, and to control both the quantity and the price at which its competitor was able to sell.

Tying and full-line forcing fall within art. 82(d) ('making the conclusion of contracts subject to acceptance by the other parties of supplementary obligations which, by their nature or according to commercial usage, have no connection with the subject of such contracts') unless there are objective reasons to justify the tie. In the *Michelin* decision the primary issue was that of discounts granted to retailers that were considered to be hard for retailers to calculate and that had the effect of encouraging them to switch orders from Michelin's competitors (*BF BV NV NBI Michelin* 81/969 (1981) OJ L353/33). One of the concerns of the Commission was that, for the year 1977, the bonus system operated in such a way as to link the purchases of light tyres to heavy tyres. This is to say that a customer who would ordinarily purchase its heavy tyres from Michelin and its light tyres from another supplier would be encouraged to purchase all its tyres from Michelin in order to earn the bonus. Some do not consider such a practice to have an anti-competitive effect, but it would appear that the parties themselves believe that it is possible to extend monopoly power from one market to another. If Michelin were the only manufacturer of heavy tyres and informed customers that they would not be supplied with such tyres unless also purchasing Michelin's light tyres, the customers would have little option but to refuse to deal with other suppliers.

The Commission examined Michelin's rebate policy again in *Michelin (II)* 2002/405 (2002) OJ L58/25. In essence the scheme was designed to encourage customers to buy more of the Michelin brand in the face of competition from other suppliers of new tyres. Between 1980 and 1998 Michelin operated a complex system of rebates and discounts divided into three main types: quantity rebates, quality rebates based on the dealer's service to users, and rebates dependent on increases in sales ('progress bonuses'). Several aspects of this system that were abusive were identified. Because Michelin paid its rebates up to 13 months after the dealer bought and sold the tyres dealers were often selling initially at a loss, and were never certain as to the amount of the rebate that would be paid. The one-year reference period for the calculation of the rebates encouraged dealers to be loyal to Michelin when they might have had a preference for another manufacturer's product. This element is clearly explained at para. 229 of the decision:

Since it was essential, for the dealer's very survival in certain cases to receive as large as possible an amount of quantity rebates (these being the only means of restoring the dealer's profit margin) and in view of the extremely long period over which Michelin recorded orders, a dealer could not take the risk at any given moment of diversifying his range to any significant extent at Michelin's expense since this could have jeopardised his ability to reach the rebate threshold and could thus have had a major effect on the overall cost price of the Michelin tyres purchased over the year.

The service and progress bonuses were also found to have such-loyalty inducing effects, and to be unfair in the way in which they were applied and paid. A fine of €19.76 million was imposed on Michelin. This included a substantial uplift to take account of the fact that the undertaking had already been punished for substantially similar conduct in the earlier decision.

The Commission decision was upheld in its entirety by the CFI (*Manufacture française des pneumatiques Michelin v Commission* case T–219/99, [2004] 4 CMLR 18). *Inter alia* the CFI was particularly concerned by a rebate system that operated in relation to the entire quantity purchased by the customer, rather than in stepped increments. At para. 88 therefore the Court held that

The incentive to purchase created by a quantity rebate system is therefore much greater where the discounts are calculated on total turnover achieved during a certain period than where they are calculated only tranche by tranche. The longer the reference period, the more loyalty-inducing the quantity rebate system.

The court was also quick to dismiss claims made by Michelin to the effect that the system it operated was economically justified. It appears from the judgment that it is incumbent on the undertaking relying on the scheme to demonstrate that there are genuine efficiencies which justify its operation. At paras 108–9 the CFI held that the applicant provides no specific information in that regard. It merely states that orders for large amounts involve economies and that the customer is entitled to have those economies passed on to him in the price that he pays . . . Far from establishing that the quantity rebates were based on actual cost savings the applicant merely states generally that the quantity rebates were justified by economies of scale in the areas of production costs and distribution. However, such a line of argument is too general and is insufficient to provide economic reasons to explain specifically the discount rates chosen for the various steps in the rebate system in question.

For a critical comment on this decision see RBB Brief 13, February 2004, 'The special responsibility of dominant firms under Article 82: don't compete on price'.

The position in *Hilti* was more obvious than in *Michelin*. In this case (*Eurofix-Bauco/ Hilti* 88/138 (1988) OJ L65/19) the company, which held a dominant position in relation to the market for fastening systems for use in the professional building industry (nail-guns), tied the sales of the two accessories, nails and cartridges, used by them. While there is a clear connection between the three products they may be legitimately viewed as separate markets. Many manufacturers are able to make the cartridges, most of which are in the form of a strip containing usually 10 brass cartridges, that are used to propel the nails, and are also able to make the nails themselves. In several cases Hilti either took, or threatened, legal action, based on its patents, to prevent the manufacture and marketing of cartridges that would be compatible with its nail-guns. The Commission found that Hilti had maintained a policy of only supplying the cartridge strips for use in its guns when the purchaser also took the necessary number of nails, although Hilti had denied this when first asked by the Commission. When carrying out its investigation the Commission came across a letter from Hilti GB to Hilti AG referring to a particular customer who 'has now been advised that an embargo has been placed on cartridge-only sales (only a verbal restriction has been passed to the customer with nothing in writing)'. Other evidence obtained included an internal memo to the sales force relating to another customer who 'wanted a large quantity of Hilti cartridges. These would appear to be required in connection with Profix nails and should in no circumstances be supplied to the customer' (para. 31). In yet other cases the company instituted a policy of reducing discounts given on orders of cartridges if nails were not purchased at the same time. The attempt to restrict competition in the market for the two consumables of which Hilti's behaviour was suggestive was found to constitute an abuse. As regards Hilti's customers, the policies pursued left 'the consumer with no choice over the source of his nails and as such abusively exploit him' (para. 75). As a result of these practices Hilti was fined €6m and ordered to bring the practices to an end.

Similar considerations were to the fore in *Tetra Pak II* (92/163 (1992) OJ L72/1). Tetra Pak's standard supply contracts contained two clauses which had the following effects: (i) the obligation that only Tetra Pak cartons would be used on Tetra Pak machines; and (ii) the obligation to obtain supplies exclusively from Tetra Pak. As the Commission noted, these two clauses would 'make the system airtight: not only is it not possible for the purchaser of a machine to use packaging other than that bearing the Tetra Pak mark, but moreover he may not obtain supplies of packaging from any source other than Tetra Pak' (para. 116). Tetra Pak's defence was that it was not possible to drive a wedge between the two markets (machines and packaging) and that it was the supplier of a totally integrated system, of which many elements were integral components. *Inter alia* the company suggested that: the high-technology machines demand exact packaging that could be supplied only by Tetra Pak; it could offer full servicing only if all components in the process were purchased from it; and only the use of its cartons prevented health problems. As might be expected (particularly in the light of the company's past record) the practice was roundly condemned. Not only did the two clauses highlighted constitute abuses in their own right, they also raised the possibility of further abuse and placed competitors 'who cannot therefore, unlike Tetra Pak itself, subsidise possible losses on a given product through profits made on another product, in an extremely uncomfortable position' (para. 117). The approach of the ECJ and the Commission to this case was criticized by Lord Fraser of Carmyllie in the Lords debate on the Competition Act 1998. He expressed concern at a line of jurisprudence that seems to suggest that dominance in one market creates duties in another (Hansard (HL) 13 November 1997, col. 307).

Bundling of a sort was addressed in the very long decision taken in respect of Microsoft issued by the Commission in March 2004 (*Microsoft*, 24 March 2004). In this case, which covered different ground to the highly publicized and long-running US case against the company, Microsoft was attacked for bundling its Windows Media Player software with its PC operating systems, including Windows 98 and Windows XP. This attack followed a complaint made by Sun Microsystems, which has frequently protested publicly about Microsoft's competitive conduct. The issue of technological bundling is a sensitive one, and it is often pointed out that when the US authorities brought an action against IBM in the 1970s one of their complaints was that the company was bundling hard disc drives with its mainframe computers—a charge that would now seem absurd. In addition to the very large fine imposed on Microsoft the Commission required the company to

within 90 days of the date of notification of this Decision, offer a full-functioning version of the [Windows operating systems] which does not incorporate Windows Media Player; Microsoft Corporation retains the right to offer a bundle of the [Windows operating systems] and Windows Media Player.   (art. 6 of the decision)

It may be reasonable to ask what value this serves. Are many consumers likely to be tempted by a version of Windows *without* an element freely available in another? Microsoft has appealed against this decision.

Monopolies established by law (i.e., by state action) are, unless art. 86(2) applies, subject to the same art. 82 obligations as are privately run enterprises and on many occasions have been treated accordingly. In *Télémarketing (Centre Belge d'Etudes de Marché-Télémarketing SA v Compagnie Luxembourgeoise de Télédiffusion SA* case 311/84 [1986] 2 CMLR 558—an art. 234 reference from the national court) the Luxembourg TV Broadcaster (CLT) operated under a licence issued by the Luxembourg government, and required the plaintiff telemarketing company to have calls placed in response to advertisements screened on the channel routed through an associated company, IPB. CLT argued that this was a matter of pragmatism, as IPB had good notice of changes to schedules and therefore would better be able to anticipate and respond to customers than the complainant's own company. Further, the television channel took the view that customers believed that they were dealing with it, and that it therefore had an obligation to ensure an appropriate level of service. However, for the first year in which it placed advertisements with the broadcaster the complainant had not been required to use IPB and had been able to advertise its own telephone response number. The national court asked the ECJ whether this extension of power over the television broadcasts into an ancillary market, telephone response numbers for advertising, was an abuse of art. 82, and in response the Court held that the action was in breach both of art. 82(a) and of art. 82(d). In insisting that any advertiser buying telephone time did not use its own agency, but instead use that allied to the company, the company had imposed conditions on all other companies that it did not impose on itself. Further, the tie imposed supplementary obligations with no connection with the true subject matter of the contract.

14.4.1.2 *Abusive discounts and rebates*

The use of discounts and rebates in order to facilitate tie-in sales and exclusive purchasing has been considered above. There are other cases in which discounts have been used abusively.

When it began to face emerging competition from France and Spain, British Gypsum, a subsidiary of British Plasterboard Industries, sought ways in which to 'reward the loyalty of merchants who remained exclusively' with them (*BPB Industries plc* 89/22 (1989) OJ L10/50, para. 58). Subsequently a scheme was put in place whereby payments were to be made to selected merchants in the form of contributions to promotional and advertising expenses, and this was later extended to provide added bonuses to those entering exclusive contracts. All these rebates were condemned, and the issue was revisited in 1992 when British Gypsum was encouraged to modify other rebate schemes introduced following the earlier decision. As amended, the rebate schemes, which then related to objectively identifiable savings and could be made available to all customers satisfying the appropriate criteria, were accepted by the Commission (*22nd Report on Competition Policy 1992*, p. 422).

It is now well established that rebate or discount schemes will be acceptable only where they are non-discriminatory and therefore do not fall within art. 82(c). Further illustrations may be found in *Brussels National Airport* 95/364 (1995) OJ L216/8 and in *Irish Sugar* 97/624 (1997) OJ L258/1 (on appeal *Irish Sugar plc* v *Commission* case T–228/97 [1999] 5 CMLR 1300). In the former case British Midland complained that the system of discounts, established by Royal Decree in 1989, was such that only Sabena, its main competitor, could benefit from them. The Commission requested the Belgian authorities to end the system, having found that only the existence of economies of scale could justify such a system, and that that was not the case here. In *Irish Sugar* the company was fined €8.8 m after being found to have abused its dominant position on the Irish sugar market. The company had responded to the threat of imports from France by, *inter alia*, offering various rebate schemes. These extended both to industrial customers making exports of the refined product, and to smaller domestic customers. The rebates were condemned as being ad hoc and without any consistent relationship to objectively identifiable criteria. The effect of the abuse was to maintain prices for sugar in Ireland, and particularly in Northern Ireland, that were significantly higher than in other Member States.

The core allegation made against British Airways, substantiated by the Commission in *Virgin/British Airways* 2000/74 (2000) OJ L30/1 related to the use by BA of the use of commission schemes, in effect discounts, to boost sales of its flights through travel agents at the expense of those of its rivals. The marginal effect of the commission scheme is clearly explained by the Commission in paras 29–30 of the decision. In effect, to combat the offer by BA of a standard commission rate of 7 per cent coupled to a 'performance reward' of 0.5 per cent, at the margin a competing airline would have to offer a commission rate of 17.4 per cent. The Commission accepted that BA would have to offer a marginal rate as high as this to *increase* sales of its own tickets, but noted that 'it is at an advantage over the new entrant who must offer this high rate of commission on all its sales'. Such a scheme was both discriminatory, in that the discounts offered bore no relation to objectively justifiable factors, and exclusionary, at a time when, according to the Commission, BA should have been facing competition in a newly deregulated market.

The Commission's findings in this decision were upheld by the CFI in *British Airways plc* v *Commission* case T–219/99, [2004] 4 CMLR 19. The majority of the judgment was concerned with jurisdictional matters, but in relation to the alleged abuse, as with all other areas, the Court sided with the Commission. In particular the Court dismissed arguments made by BA to the effect that the discount scheme was not discriminatory. At paras 239–40 it held that

BA's arguments based on the importance of the size of the travel agents established in the United Kingdom are irrelevant. The performance reward schemes in dispute were, in themselves, based on a parameter unrelated to the criterion of the size of the undertakings, since they were based on the extent to which travel agents increased their sales of BA tickets in relation to the threshold constituted by the number of BA tickets sold during the previous reference period.

In those circumstances, the Commission was right to hold that BA's performance reward schemes constituted an abuse of BA's dominant position on the United Kingdom market for air travel agency services, in that they produced discriminatory effects within the network of travel agents established in the United Kingdom, thereby inflicting on some of them a competitive disadvantage within the meaning of subparagraph (c) of the second paragraph of Article 82 EC.

14.4.1.3 *The abusive use of intellectual property*

The general position in competition law is that property rights cannot be asserted in such a way as to lead to an anti-competitive outcome (see, e.g., *Flughafen Frankfurt/Main AG* 98/190 (1998) OJ L72/31, para. 89). In relation to intellectual property rights this principle becomes strained, and the relationship between intellectual property and competition law is a difficult one. We have already seen in Chapter 1 that the term 'monopoly' originally referred to a grant from the Crown that was similar to a modern intellectual property right. The modern theory of intellectual property rests on the presumption that the grant of the exclusive right is a reward that is necessary to encourage innovation, and that a monopoly profit is the proper way to achieve this.

The holding of intellectual property does not necessarily confer a dominant position (*Sirena* v *Eda* case 40/70 [1971] ECR 69, para. 16) as it may be the case that the relevant market encompasses products, services, or processes other than the one for which the right is held. There are, however, a number of cases in which it has been found that an intellectual property right acts as a barrier to entry, consolidating the strength of a dominant position (see the discussion of this factor earlier in this chapter). In *Tetra Pak I* 88/501 (1988) OJ L272/27 the EC Commission condemned the acquisition of a licence to intellectual property in an area where the undertaking in question was already dominant.

The leading case, although one that is peculiar on its facts, relating to the abusive use of intellectual property is that of *Magill* (*RTE and Independent Television Productions* v *Commission* cases C 241 and 242/91P [1995] 4 CMLR 418). Here the Commission found that broadcasters in Ireland had abused their dominant position by exploiting the copyright they held in television programme listings to prevent the publication of those listings by third parties. The broadcasters published their own television guides and were able to prevent competition in what was viewed as a separate market from that of the television broadcasting itself. The Court noted that

The appellants—who were, by force of circumstances, the only sources of the basic information on program scheduling which is the indispensable raw material for compiling a weekly television guide—gave viewers wishing to obtain information on the choice of programs for the week ahead no choice but to buy the weekly guides for each station and draw from each of them the information they needed to make comparisons.

The appellants' refusal to provide basic information by relying on national copyright provisions thus prevented the appearance of a new product, a comprehensive weekly guide to television programs, which the appellants did not offer and for which there was a potential consumer demand. Such refusal constitutes an abuse under heading (b) of the second paragraph of art. 82 of the Treaty.

The conclusion of the Court was that the Commission was in a position to remedy an abuse by ordering the compulsory licence of the intellectual property held by the appellants:

In the present case, after finding that the refusal to provide undertakings such as Magill with the basic information contained in television program listings was an abuse of a dominant position, the Commission was entitled under [Regulation 17], in order to ensure that its decision was effective, to require the appellants to provide that information. As the Court of First Instance rightly found, the imposition of that obligation—with the possibility of making authorisation of publication dependent on certain conditions, including payment of royalties—was the only way of bringing infringement to an end.

The *Magill* judgment was heavily criticized by a number of intellectual property and competition lawyers, and it is generally considered to be 'exceptional', although it is not doubted that it remains good law. However, the Commission resorted to a similar approach in the case of *IMS*. Here the Commission took an interim measures decision in relation to the use of intellectual property recognixed under German law. This related to pharmaceutical sales data services, which sprang from a database built around a '1,860 brick structure', in which the country was divided into 'bricks', with each brick containing relevant data about pharmacies, and drug prescription levels. IMS Health Inc held the copyright in this system, and refused to grant a licence to the complainant, National Data Corporation Health Information Services (NDC), an American company expanding sales into Europe. NDC argued that the brick structure was an essential facility, without which it could not compete in providing a rival regional sales service. The Commission agreed, relying on the chain of cases beginning with *Istituto Chemioterapico Italiano and Commercial Solvents* v *Commission* cases 6 & 7/73 [1974] 1 CMLR 309, including *Magill* (see also the discussion of the essential facilities doctrine in Chapter 16), and held that the 'exceptional circumstances' referred to at para. 50 of the *Magill* judgment were present in this case. IMS was required to grant a licence 'without delay to all undertakings currently present on the market for German regional sales data services' (*IMS Health Inc (Interim measures)* (2002/165)). IMS appealed to the CFI, and the Court first held, in August 2001, that the Commission had exceeded its powers under the interim measures procedures by applying a remedy that was so 'far-reaching' (*IMS Health Inc* v *Commission* case T–184/01 R I [2002] 4 CMLR 1. Later, after considering the matter more fully the Court ruled that the Commission Decision be struck down (*IMS Health Inc* v *Commission* case T–184/01 R II [2002] 4 CMLR 2. The CFI was very clear that only rarely would it be appropriate to compulsorily licence intellectual property in response to an alleged breach of art. 82:

It is important to recall that the public interest in respect for property rights in general and for intellectual property rights in particular is expressly reflected in Articles 30 and 295 EC. The mere fact that the applicant has invoked and sought to enforce its copyright in the 1,860 brick structure for economic reasons does not lessen its entitlement to rely upon the exclusive right granted by national law for the very purpose of rewarding innovation.

In the present case, where there is, on the face of it, a clear public interest underlying the applicant's effort to enforce and profit from the specific subject-matter of its copyright in the 1,860 brick structure, the inherently exceptional nature of the power to adopt interim measures would normally require that conduct whose termination or amendment is targeted by such measures fall clearly within the scope of the Treaty competition rules. However, the characterisation of the refusal to licence at issue in the present proceedings as abusive turns, prima facie, on the correctness of the Commission's interpretation of the case law concerning the scope of 'exceptional circumstances'. It is this case law which explains the clearly special situations in which the objective pursued by art. 82 EC may prevail over that underlying the grant of intellectual property rights. In this context, where the abusive nature of the appellant's conduct is not unambiguous having regard to the relevant case law and where there is a tangible risk that it will suffer serious and irreparable harm if forced, in the meantime, to licence its competitors, the balance of interests favours the unimpaired preservation of its copyright until the judgment of the main action.   (paras 143–4)

An appeal to the ECJ by NDC and the Commission was dismissed (*NDC Health Corporation* v *IMS Health Inc and Commission* case C–481/01 P(R) [2002] 5 CMLR 1). A separate proceeding into other aspects of IMS's conduct was closed late in 2002 when the Commission found that the company had, in the face of its investigation, amended its conduct (Commission Press Release IP (02) 1430, 4 October 2002). By decision in 2003 (*IMS Health* 2003/74 (2003) OJ L268/69) the Commission withdrew decision 2002/165.

In a separate development following proceedings in Germany the ECJ was asked questions by the German court via the art. 234 EC referral route. Three questions were asked of the ECJ, the first of which was that of whether it might be an abuse within the meaning of art. 82 were an undertaking with a dominant position to refuse to grant a licence to copyright material in situations in which the claimant company had rejected alternative products not making use of copyright material because their set-up relied upon the copyright material. The Court reiterated the position that, save in exceptional circumstances, the refusal to grant copyright by a dominant undertaking cannot, in itself, be an abuse. Three cumulative conditions had to be met for an abuse to occur: (1) the refusal prevented the emergence of a new product for which there was demand; (2) refusal was unjustified; and (3) refusal would exclude competition on a secondary market. It was the third condition that was most contested in the present case, and the ECJ referred to its judgment in *Oscar Bronner GmbH & Co KG* v *Mediaprint Zeitungs-und Zeitschriftenverlag GmbH & CO KG* case C-7/97 [1999] 4 CMLR 112, following which it was necessary to determine whether the 1860 brick structure constituted an essential upstream factor in the downstream supply of sales data for pharmaceutical products. Whether this was the case was a fact that only the national court could determine (*IMS Health GmbH & Co OHG* v *NDC Health GmbH & Co KG* case C-418/02, judgment of 29 April, 2004).

14.5 **Trade between Member States**

The condemning of an abuse 'in so far as it may affect trade between Member States' is the jurisdictional test of Community involvement, and the same principles apply as for art. 81 (see 3.4). It is the 'abuse', and not the dominant position which must affect trade.

14.6 **The relationship between article 82 and article 81**

Jurisdiction under arts 82 and 81 is not mutually exclusive, and there will be situations where both apply, as for example a case in which a dominant undertaking obliges its customers or smaller competitors to enter into restrictive agreements.

This was acknowledged by the ECJ in *Hoffmann-La Roche* (*Hoffmann-La Roche & Co. AG v Commission* case 85/76 [1979] 3 CMLR 211) where one issue considered under art. 82 related to a contract entered into between Hoffmann and Merck. Under the terms of this contract Merck agreed to purchase exclusively from Hoffmann a considerable quantity of vitamin B_6 for a period of five years. The Court found that the purpose of the contract was to eliminate the risk to Hoffmann of a planned increase in production, and that this constituted an abuse. The Court noted that 'the question might be asked whether the conduct in question does not fall within Article [81] of the Treaty and possibly within its paragraph (3)' (para. 116). It will be recalled that art. 81(3) confers a legal exception to an agreement that falls to be condemned under art. 81(1) where certain criteria are satisfied. Might the potential application of art. 81(3) therefore act as a defence to an action brought under art. 82? The answer is no. The Court went on to hold that art. 82 'is expressly aimed in fact at situations which clearly originate in contractual relations so that in such cases the Commission is entitled . . . to proceed on the basis of Article [81] or Article [82]' (para. 116). The CFI, however, has suggested that this may not be the case where an exemption has been granted on an individual basis. The presumption would be that the Commission would have considered whether art. 82 was in fact relevant, and would not have granted the exemption if that were the case; and in *Tetra Pak* the Advocate General went so far as to say that a practice 'which satisfies the conditions for exception laid down in Article [81(3)] cannot at the same time be regarded as constituting an abuse' (*Tetra Pak Rausing SA v Commission* case T–51/89 [1991] 4 CMLR 334 at 350). In such a case the Commission would be expected to demonstrate either that facts had been withheld from it at the time the exemption was granted, or that there had been a material change in the circumstances in order to succeed with a new claim. Some of the block exemptions (see Chapter 10) expressly state that exemptions granted under their authority do not serve as a defence under art. 82 (e.g., Council Regulation 4056/86 on Maritime Transport (1986) OJ L378/4); and even where no such express provision is made, the general presumption must be that as block exemptions do not require the specific assessment that is needed in the case of art. 81(3) exceptions, they cannot serve as a defence to an art. 82 action.

14.7 Article 82 guidelines

The EC Commission has not, as of May 2004, published guidelines in relation to the application of art. 82 EC. However, in October 2003 a senior Commission official announced that DG Comp was engaged in a review of the policy on abuse of dominance, and that guidelines might follow (Lowe, P., 'DG Competition's Review of the Policy on Abuse of Dominance', Speech to the Fordham Corporate Law Institute, 23 October 2003). The OFT has produced guidance on some aspects of the operation of art. 82 EC alongside the Chapter II Prohibition of the Competition Act 1998.

15

The Chapter II Prohibition

15.1 Introduction

The 'Chapter II Prohibition' is in the following terms:

18.—(1) Subject to section 19, any conduct on the part of one or more undertakings which amounts to the abuse of a dominant position in a market is prohibited if it may affect trade within the United Kingdom.

(2) Conduct may, in particular, constitute such an abuse if it consists in—

(a) directly or indirectly imposing unfair purchase or selling prices or other unfair trading conditions;

(b) limiting production, markets or technical development to the prejudice of consumers;

(c) applying dissimilar conditions to equivalent transactions with other trading parties, thereby placing them at a competitive disadvantage;

(d) making the conclusion of contracts subject to acceptance by the other parties of supplementary obligations which, by their nature or according to commercial usage, have no connection with the subject of the contracts.

(3) In this section—

'dominant position' means a dominant position within the United Kingdom; and 'the United Kingdom' means the United Kingdom or any part of it.

(4) The prohibition imposed by subsection (1) is referred to in this Act as 'the Chapter II prohibition'.

The similarity with art. 82 EC should be immediately evident, and as the Act is to be interpreted and applied so as to achieve results consistent with those that would be achieved under Community law (see the discussion of s. 60 in Chapter 3) guidance as to its application should be sought in the commentary on art. 82. Where conduct is of minor significance (s. 40) fines under s. 36(2) may not be imposed, but other decisions may be taken by the OFT, and private actions may be brought. The appropriate level is set at a turnover of £50m by the Competition Act 1998 (Small Agreements and Conduct of Minor Significance) Regulations 2000, SI 2000/262 (para. 4). This 'safe harbour' does not apply in relation to the application of art. 82 EC by the OFT.

The 2004 amendments to the Competition Act removed sections under which notifications could be made to the OFT in respect of dominant firm conduct. In its guidelines *The major provisions* (OFT 400), the OFT indicates that it will follow EC Commission practice in giving opinions in novel cases. It may also provide confidential guidance to undertakings on the application of the Chapter II Prohibition on an ad hoc basis, although such informal views will not be binding on the OFT. As of May 2004 a number of decisions had been taken in respect of the Chapter II Prohibition by the OFT, concurrent regulators, and the national courts. Most of these cases are discussed in the following chapter. This chapter provides only an outline of the operation of the Chapter II Prohibition.

15.2 The assessment of dominance and abuse

15.2.1 Dominance

Broadly the approach taken to the measurement and control of dominance in the UK will be the same as that in the EC. The key difference is the territorial scope in the application of the Act. The relevant OFT guidelines, which should be read through carefully, are *Article 82 and the Chapter II Prohibition, Assessment of Conduct* (some of the matters raised in this are dealt with in the following chapter), *Assessment of Market Power*, and *Market Definition*. The two basic tests to be applied in relation to the Chapter II Prohibition are whether an undertaking is dominant, and if so, whether it is abusing the dominant position that it holds.

In order to answer the first question it will be necessary to define the relevant market. The relevant guideline 'follows a similar approach to the [EC] Commission's *Notice on Market Definition*' (*Market Definition*, para. 1.2) discussed in the previous chapter. The basic methodology of the EC Commission will be followed, even if it produces a different result because the factual elements are different.

That different results may be reached in different cases, even where similar markets are being investigated, was made clear by the CFI in *Coca-Cola v Commission* case T–125/79 [2000] All ER (EC) 460 where the Court pointed out that market definition must be sensitive to a particular time, and that at other times different conditions might prevail. In the OFT guideline this point is dealt with at paras 5.7–5.8 in the following terms:

In many cases a market may have already been investigated and defined by the OFT or by another competition authority. Sometimes, earlier definitions can be informative when considering the appropriate product or area to use when commencing the hypothetical monopolist test. However, although previous cases can provide useful information, the market definition used may not always be the appropriate one for future cases. First, competitive conditions may change over time. In particular, innovation may make substitution between products easier, or more difficult, and therefore change the market definition. Therefore, the relevant market concerned must be identified according to the particular facts of the case in hand.

Second, a previous product market definition that concerned an area outside the United Kingdom, would not necessarily apply to an area in the United Kingdom if the purchasing behaviour of customers differed significantly between those two areas.

In *Aberdeen Journals* the OFT suffered a heavy defeat when the CAT was highly critical of the approach it took to market definition, and remitted the contested decision to the OFT for further consideration (*Predation by Aberdeen Journals Ltd* CA98/5/2001 [2001] UKCLR 856, on appeal *Aberdeen Journals Ltd* v *The Director General of Fair Trading* [2002] CompAR 167). The CAT set out its most trenchant criticism at paras 146–8 of its judgment:

At this stage of the analysis, we encounter the difficulty that the Decision contains hardly any factual description by the Director of the characteristics of the *Evening Express*, as compared to the *Herald & Post* and *Independent*, nor the extent to which the observable circumstances of the market show that the *Independent* competes not only with the *Herald & Post* but also with the *Evening Express*.

In order to lay the foundation for the definition of the relevant market, we would have expected the Decision to contain a brief factual description, at least in outline, of the objective characteristics of the products concerned—for example the content of each of the three newspapers in question, the kinds of advertisements carried (e.g. display advertisements, recruitment, property, motors, other trade advertisements, classified, notices, etc.), the advertising rates offered by the paid-for and free titles respectively, details of their respective circulations, target audiences and geographical distribution areas.

In our view, such a description of the objective characteristics of the products in question is almost always necessary in cases of disputed market definition, because it is on that foundation that the discussion of the relevant product market must rest.

When the OFT made a new decision its market definition was, in the respects cited above, much more thorough, and the decision withstood the scrutiny of the CAT.

A relevant geographic market does not have to extend to the UK as a whole, but could be regional, or local. In *Predation by Aberdeen Journals Ltd* CA98/5/2001 [2001] UKCLR 856 the relevant geographic market, for example, was Aberdeen.

Once the market has been defined it is necessary to establish whether the undertaking whose conduct is being examined is dominant in this market. Again the factors are the same as under art. 82. The guidelines, *Assessment of Market Power*, refer to the standard definition of dominant position set out by the ECJ in *United Brands Co.* v *Commission* case 27/76 [1978] 1 CMLR 429, discussed in the previous chapter. The guidelines indicate that it is 'unlikely that an undertaking will be individually dominant if its share of the relevant market is below 40 per cent, although dominance could be established below that if other relevant factors (such as the weak position of competitors in that market and entry barriers) provided strong evidence of dominance' (para. 2.12).

The broad framework for assessing market power is set out in Part 3 of the guidelines, the thrust of which in essence is to consider the restraints that would prevent an alleged dominant undertaking from raising its prices. These include existing competitors, potential competitors, and buyer power. In this context the discussion of entry barriers (paras 5.1–5.37) should be examined carefully, as they are likely to play a significant role in the analysis. As the guidelines recognize, 'assessing the effects of entry barriers and the advantages they give to incumbents can be complex' (para. 5.29). Overseas competition will be considered in this assessment as it too can provide an effective constraint on the ability of domestic undertakings to raise prices (para. 5.32). This has been a significant factor in a number of recent merger reports in which mergers have been allowed to proceed on the grounds that anti-competitive effects would be mitigated by the growth in international competition (see, e.g., *Universal Foods Corpn and Pointing Holdings Ltd* (Cm. 4544, December 1999)).

Some evidence of dominance may also be adduced from the performance of the undertaking in question, although such analysis must proceed carefully in order to distinguish an 'excessive' rate of profit (para. 6.5) from profit generated by efficient performance.

15.2.2 Collective dominance

The approach taken to collective dominance should be the same as that taken under art. 82 EC and is discussed at paras 4.23–4.25 of the guideline *Article 82 and the Chapter II Prohibition*. However, the difficulties that are encountered in this approach are one of the major reasons underpinning the provision for market investigation references made in the Enterprise Act 2002 (see Chapter 17).

15.2.3 Abusive conduct

Much of the abusive conduct that has been considered under the Act so far is dealt with in the following chapter in relation to the various abuses. The list of abuses set out in s. 18 of the Act is the same as that for art. 82. The relevant guideline is *Assessment of conduct*, which deals with abuses in terms of the following headings: excessive prices; price discrimination; predation; discounts; margin squeeze; vertical restraints; refusal to supply; and essential facilities. It is perhaps unusual that the first abuse dealt with here is excessive pricing, as this is not an issue in which there has been much case law at the EC level. However, it was addressed in the first infringement decision made in respect of the Chapter II Prohibition by the OFT (*Napp Pharmaceutical Holdings Ltd and Subsidiaries* CA98/2/2001 [2001] UKCLR 597, on appeal *Napp Pharmaceutical Holdings Ltd* v *The Director General of Fair Trading* [2002] CompAR 13). Cases relating to pricing abuses, refusals to supply, and the essential facilities doctrine are dealt with as appropriate in Chapter 16.

15.2.4 Leveraging power from one market to another

Oftel considered a complaint of anti-competitive leveraging made against BT in relation to the promotion of its directory enquiries service on the cover of its telephone book (*BT publishing its 118500 director enquiries number on the front of the BT phonebook* 23 December 2003). In this case a number of providers of directory enquiry services had alleged that BT was leveraging its dominance in the market for phonebook services into the market for telephone directory enquiry services. Without feeling the need to reach a final conclusion on the matter Oftel accepted that BT probably was dominant in the former market, and that the second market was sufficiently closely related to the first for leveraging to take place. However, examination of the effect of the promotion showed that it had no appreciable effect on competition. Survey evidence showed that in areas where the 118500 number was printed on the front of the phonebook calls to that number were only about 1 per cent higher than from other areas. There was in addition compelling evidence that other forms of advertising were more effective, such that competitors could match BT's promotions and were not being unfairly damaged. Of customers surveyed, 82 per cent were aware of the directory enquiries numbers from TV advertising, rather than from any other source. Research also showed that only about 40 per cent of customers kept the phonebook near to the telephone, with 38 per cent keeping it out of sight and a further 10 per cent throwing it away.

16

Abusive practices

16.1 Introduction

Broadly, the approaches taken by different competition authorities to the same forms of dominant-firm anti-competitive conduct are similar, although this is not true in every case. Even before the enactment of the Competition Act 1998 there had been an element of cross-fertilization between the EC and UK in particular. This is more clearly noticeable in the impact Community membership has had on UK law, but domestic actions have been noted, and from time to time cited with approval, at the centre (see, e.g., *Napier Brown* v *British Sugar* 88/518 (1988) OJ L284/41, where the Commission relied in part on a MMC report). With an increasing convergence in Community and national law it is appropriate, therefore, to consider actions taken against specific forms of anti-competitive conduct in each regime alongside each other. Consideration of the practice in the United States and the principles of industrial economics may cast further light on the approaches likely to be taken in the EC and UK. The discussion that follows is focused on a range of pricing practices and refusals to deal, which together constitute the larger part of the anti-competitive and exploitative practices of dominant firms. It does not therefore give examples of all practices that may fall to be condemned in both jurisdictions.

16.2 Pricing policies

Price competition is one of the most visible forms of commercial rivalry and is often of short-term benefit to consumers, who are unlikely to complain about 'price wars'. It is one of the inherent contradictions of competition law that firms may be attacked for pricing too high, which is a matter of exploiting a position of strength and may actually have the effect of promoting competition, for pricing too low, termed 'predatory pricing—an extreme form of price competition, and for setting different prices for different customers. In the appropriate circumstances all of these actions may be of legitimate concern to competition authorities. In the context of art. 82 (see Chapter 14) it is clearly envisaged that the first and last of these are to fall within the meaning of abuse, as the examples set out in the article include: (a) 'directly or indirectly imposing unfair purchase or selling prices' and (b) 'applying dissimilar conditions to equivalent transactions'. Arguably predatory prices are 'unfair' and, as was the case in *ECS/AKZO—interim measures* 83/462 (1983) OJ L252/13, therefore also fall within (a); but even if they are not, their imposition may fall within the more general meaning of 'abuse'.

16.2.1 **Predatory pricing**

'Low prices or price reductions are normally seen as a benefit from and the successful result of the process of competition. Predatory behaviour constitutes a class of anti-competitive behaviour where prices are *too low*, to the extent that the competitive process itself is damaged' (Myers, G., *Predatory Behaviour in UK Competition Policy*, London, OFT (1994), para. 1.1). A good working explanation of the practice of predatory pricing is given by Hay and Morris (Hay, D. A., and Morris, D. J., *Industrial Economics and Organization Theory and Evidence*, Oxford, OUP (1991), p. 580):

A dominant firm reacts to competition in one of its markets, either a geographical or a product market, by cutting price so as to drive the competitor out of business. The competitor in question may be either a new entrant or a small firm that has been a passive 'follower' of the leadership of the dominant firm but has now begun to gain market share. The purpose of the dominant firm's price-cutting is to preserve its long-run monopoly by frightening off potentially serious competition. The dominant firm is therefore quite willing to accept losses in that particular market for the time being—losses which it can absorb since it is earning high profits in other markets. The losses are the price for establishing a tough reputation, which will protect its position in all its markets in the long term.

The primary concerns of competition authorities, then, are that predatory pricing acts either as a barrier to entry, or to drive firms out of a market; that this is achieved by making it unprofitable for entrants to compete with the incumbent, or by sending a false signal to the entrant as to the expected returns from the market; and that the intention behind such predation is to allow the incumbent to raise prices in the long term, once the short-term battle has been won. While any company could, in theory, choose to engage in predatory pricing, only a monopolist with access to significant capital reserves or to the capital market could do so with any hope of success.

Strong arguments are made, in particular by some members of the Chicago school, to the effect that predatory pricing should be of no concern to competition authorities as it can never be a successful strategy and is only ever of benefit to consumers (in particular see Bork, R. H., *The Antitrust Paradox*, New York, The Free Press (1993), pp. 144–55). A leading competition strategist, attempting to discourage firms from taking such action, argues that price competition may be 'highly unstable and quite likely to leave the entire industry worse off from the standpoint of profitability. Price cuts are quickly and easily matched by rivals, and once matched they lower revenues for all firms' (Porter, M. E., *Competitive Strategy*,

New York, The Free Press (1980), p. 17). Following more recent economic developments, and analyses based on game theory, the better view appears to be that predatory pricing can be successful where 'the potential entrant is uncertain about the post-entry [equilibrium] because it does not have precise information about the nature of the incumbent' (Hay, D. A., and Morris, D. J., above, p. 580). In such a situation the entrant is facing the situation where its knowledge does not match that of the incumbent, and it cannot determine whether the action of the price cutter is a result of superior efficiency, in which case the entrant may predict losses following even a successful entrance, or of the desire of the incumbent to gain a reputation as a tough competitor. Further, it is argued by the consultancy firm London Economics that

the presumption that predation is not a rational strategy has been shown to be false in the recent literature . . . Rather, predatory behaviour can be part of a rational strategy under conditions in which there is no differential access to resources and each firm understands perfectly the incentives in the situation at hand.   (London Economics, *Barriers to Entry and Exit in UK Competition Policy*, London, OFT (1994), p. 21)

The first important case to consider the issue in the United States was *Standard Oil Co. of New Jersey* v *US* 221 U.S. 1 (1911), one of the earliest cases based on the Sherman Act 1890, s. 2 to reach the Supreme Court, and the case in which the 'rule of reason' was established (see Chapter 1). Standard Oil had been created in 1870 out of the various companies operating at different levels of the industry owned by, amongst others, the Rockefellers, and was one of the original 'trusts' against which the antitrust legislation had reacted. Within a period of just over 10 years the company controlled some 90 per cent of the oil industry in the United States. The Supreme Court found that one reason for this spectacular growth was that the company had engaged in predatory pricing, its practice having 'necessarily involved the intent to drive others from the field and to exclude them from their right to trade and thus accomplish the mastery which was the end in view'. In an influential analysis which has formed the basis of much of the subsequent literature in this area, McGee has argued that Standard Oil, on the evidence presented, did not act predatorially, and that had it tried to do so it would have failed (McGee, J. S., 'Predatory Price Cutting: The Standard Oil (NJ) Case' (1958) 1 *Journal of Law and Economics*, 137–69). *Standard Oil* was followed very quickly by *US* v *American Tobacco Co.* 221 US 106 (1911), in which the Supreme Court similarly found that the defendant had breached the Sherman Act in fighting price wars with smaller competitors to drive them out of the market.

By the 1970s the attitude of the US antitrust authorities to allegations of predatory pricing was one of varying degrees of scepticism, and the courts too showed an increasing tendency to dismiss private claims alleging predation. In *Matsushita Electric Industrial Co.* v *Zenith Radio Corp.* 475 US 574 (1986), the Supreme Court rejected a complaint made against 21 Japanese manufacturers by two US manufacturers of television sets. The American companies had argued that sets sold by the defendants in the USA were deliberately sold at a low price to weaken the ability of the American firms to compete in the global market. The Court referred with approval to the arguments made by Bork:

As [Bork] shows, the success of such schemes is inherently uncertain: the short-run loss is definite, but the long-run gain depends on successfully neutralising the competition . . . The success of any predatory scheme depends on *maintaining* monopoly power for long enough to recoup predator's losses and to harvest some additional gain. . . . For this reason, there is a consensus among commentators that predatory pricing schemes are rarely tried, and even more rarely successful.   (p. 589)

That the consensus the majority opinion referred to is of doubtful provenance is clear even from the case itself in which four of the judges dissented. Only nine months after *Matsushita* the Supreme Court considered an allegation of predation again in *Cargill Inc.* v *Montfort of Colorado Inc.* 479 US 104 (1986). Here the Court held, by a majority of six to two, that 'there is ample evidence suggesting that the practice does occur' (p. 121). The leading American case is *Brooke Group Ltd* v *Brown & Williamson Tobacco Corp.* 113 S.Ct. 2578 (1993), where the Supreme Court took the opportunity to clarify the law, and in doing so recognized that predation might occur. However, the Court set a two-fold test to be applied that will prove difficult for plaintiffs. For an allegation of predation to be upheld it must now be shown, in the USA, that the prices are below an appropriate measure of cost, and that there exists the likelihood that the investment in predatory prices will be recouped in the future by the defendant.

A major contribution to the debate as to the appropriate standard (or, *per Brooke*, 'cost measure') by which to judge predation was published in 1975 when Areeda and Turner attempted to define a test that could be used by the courts (Areeda, P., and Turner, D. F., 'Predatory Pricing and Related Practices under Section 2 of the Sherman Act' (1975) 88 *Harvard Law Review* 697). Broadly, Areeda and Turner argued that predation occurs when prices are set below marginal cost (see Chapter 1 for definitions of the basic economic terms); but that as marginal cost can be difficult to determine, a proxy measurement of average variable cost, which is easier to ascertain by standard cost-accounting techniques, would produce an acceptably close result. It is difficult to argue that below marginal cost pricing should be acceptable, as it is more profitable to produce nothing than it is to sell below marginal cost. This argument and those made following its publication are analysed in some detail in Scherer, F. M., and Ross, D., *Industrial Market Structure and Economic Performance*, 3rd edn, Boston, Houghton Mifflin (1990), pp. 472–9. While there are problems with what has now become known as the Areeda–Turner rule, it does at least have the benefit of simplicity, and found favour with the US Department of Justice and Federal Trades Commission.

An attempt was made in the leading European case of *ECS/AKZO* to persuade the EC authorities to adopt such a test (85/609 (1985) OJ L374/1; on appeal *AKZO Chemie BV* v *Commission* case C–62/86 [1993] 5 CMLR 215). The Commission had taken swift action following a complaint by an English firm, ECS, that a larger competitor, AKZO, was price cutting predatorially in ECS's traditional market. The product in question was benzoyl peroxide, which has uses both as a bleach in the flour market and as a catalyst in plastics manufacture. ECS had concentrated on the flour additive market in the UK and Ireland, and held a market share of 35 per cent, being heavily reliant on a single customer group, Allied Mills. In 1979 ECS began to expand its sales into the larger plastics markets, dominated by AKZO, and captured one of AKZO's larger customers, BASF, having offered a price significantly lower than that of AKZO. ECS then alleged that AKZO threatened to reduce prices in the UK flour sector, thereby threatening ECS's core operations. A memo prepared by an AKZO executive noted that it had been confirmed to ECS's managing director that 'aggressive commercial action would be taken on the milling side unless he refrained from selling his products to the plastics industry'. The Commission reacted to the complaint initially by ordering interim measures under which AKZO's UK arm was to stay within the profit levels that existed before ECS's competitive move (*ECS/AKZO—interim measures* 83/462 (1983) OJ L252/13). In its final decision in the matter (85/609 (1985) OJ L374/1) the Commission had to consider carefully the argument made by AKZO that its prices 'were not abusive since they always included an element of profit', by which, the Commission notes, AKZO was arguing that they covered average variable costs, and therefore would not fall foul of the Areeda–Turner test (para. 42). Apart from disputing the basis of the accounts on which these figures were derived, the Commission also turned to other evidence, such as the intent underpinning AKZO's conduct, and refused to apply a pure cost-accounting approach to the problem, pointing out that

Article [82] does not prescribe any cost-based legal rule to define the precise stage at which price-cutting by a dominant firm may become abusive and indeed *the broad application of the concept of abuse to different forms of exclusionary behaviour would argue against such a narrow test.* (para. 75, emphasis added)

When the ECJ considered the appeal it appeared to be slightly less sceptical as to the basis of the figures on which AKZO made its arguments, but supported the EC Commission in rejecting the resolution of the issue by the exclusive application of any formal test. The ECJ did suggest, however, that prices below average variable costs would be considered abusive, and that prices set at higher levels than this, but below average total costs, might be considered abusive if other factors suggested a predatory intent.

In the more recent case of *Tetra Pak v Commission (No. 2)* case C–333/94P [1997] 4 CMLR 662, the ECJ indicated that prices set below average variable cost would be automatically held to be abusive, without the need to establish intent. However, it is likely that in such cases the undertaking pricing below average variable cost would be able to rebut the presumption of an abuse in some circumstances, such as where there is obvious over-capacity or over-supply in the market.

Where it can be established that a company is selling at a loss an allegation of predatory conduct will in most cases be sustained, although exceptions might be made where, for example, there has recently been a change in the market structure and the company is still adjusting to this. In *Napier Brown/British Sugar* 88/518

(1988) OJ L284/41, the Commission found that British Sugar was selling retail sugar at a price which did not reflect its own 'transformation costs'. It was making a loss on the retail sales, which it was able to subsidize by profits from its industrial sales. The effect of this, if sustained, would be that any company which could package and market sugar as efficiently as British Sugar, but which did not have its own source of industrial sugar, would leave the market. That being so, the allegation of predatory pricing made by Napier Brown was upheld by the Commission (see para. 66). This conduct would now be characterized as a 'margin squeeze' (see 16.2.4).

In 1997 the Commission considered allegations of predation in *Irish Sugar* 97/624 (1997) OJ L258/1, on appeal *Irish Sugar plc* v *Commission* case t-228/97 [1999] 5 CMLR 1300; upheld on appeal to ECJ, *Irish Sugar plc* v *Commission* case C–497/99 R [2001] 5 CMLR 29. In this case the undertaking targeted price cuts and discounts selectively so as to undermine imports. The case deals with both discriminatory pricing (see below and 16.2.3) and exclusionary pricing, the effect of which may be indistinguishable from predation. In the case itself there is a muddying of the waters between predation and exclusion. The Commission, in condemning prices that lay above average variable cost, indicated that selective reductions would be regarded as strong evidence of intent to predate. The question arose as to the extent to which a company could cut prices in order to meet competition, a matter to which critics of competition policy often point as a failing of the system. The Commission's response was that 'There is no doubt that a firm in a dominant position is entitled to defend that position by competing with other firms in its market. However, the dominant firm must not deliberately attempt to effectively shut out competitors' (para. 134).

Where a smaller competitor would be shut out simply by the fact that the dominant firm is more efficient and has lower costs, it would not be abusive to rely on these advantages as long as the conduct was not introduced so as clearly to target a particular competitor, or was introduced as a specific response to a short-term competitive situation. It would not, for example, be abusive for a company enjoying substantial economies of scale to price consistently, and in a non-discriminatory manner, at a level lower than could be achieved by new entrants into the market.

In essence, the position taken under art. 82 in relation to predation may be summarized as follows:

Price below average variable costs	Predation can be assumed
Price above average variable costs, but below average total costs	Evidence on costs may indicate predation, but the Director General would need to establish evidence that the dominant undertaking intended to eliminate a competitor before predation could be found
Price above average total costs	Evidence does not indicate predation

Even where prices are below average variable costs evidence to justify this may be considered. Such justifications might include: short-run promotions; inefficient entry (a situation where a company mistakenly enters a market in which there is no excess capacity, forcing all firms to cut prices); mistakes; and, the fact that the undertaking is nevertheless making an incremental profit.

Predation is dealt with in Part 4 of the OFT guideline, *Assessement of Conduct.*

In its first two adverse decisions under the Competition Act in relation to the Chapter II Prohibition the OFT condemned predation. In *Napp* the core conduct attacked related to price discrimination, but the undertaking offered prices to one sector of the market place which were substantially below those offered to another sector, and, according to the decision, where it faced competition in the market for its product—sustained release morphine, or MST—Napp's 'prices to hospitals are below direct costs, where direct costs are defined, consistently with Napp's accounting system, as materials and direct labour' (*Napp Pharmaceutical Holdings Limited and Subsidiaries* CA98/2/2001 [2001] UKCLR 597, para. 189). Napp argued that its low prices were justified as sales to hospitals of the drug guaranteed that follow-on sales would be made through prescriptions continued by GPs, and that it was pricing across the entire usage of the drug, and therefore increasing its net revenue by pricing below cost in one sector. On appeal the CAT rejected these arguments, and was scathing of the net revenue argument (*Napp Pharmaceutical Holdings Ltd and Subsidiaries* v *The Director General of Fair Trading* [2002] CompAR 13, paras. 231–66). At para. 225 the CAT held that 'on the uncontested facts the situation that presents itself in this case is therefore that of a virtual monopolist that has been selling at prices well below direct cost'. Following *AKZO* the CAT found that this behaviour would, absent an objective justification, constitute predation. As for the net revenue argument, which had been advanced by the undertaking's economic consultants, the CAT held that it

provides no yardstick for distinguishing between what is legitimate, and what is abusive, behaviour on the part of a dominant undertaking. For instance, a monopolist driving away new entrants by predatory pricing is likely to maximise his net revenue by so doing, for example by avoiding the loss of market share and erosion of prices in the profitable market where he holds a monopoly. Yet plainly such behaviour does not cease to be abusive merely because it is profitable for the monopolist to engage in it.   (para. 259)

In *Predation by Aberdeen Journals Ltd* CA98/5/2001 [2001] UKCLR 856 predation was, as the title of the decision indicates, very much to the fore. In the decision the Director concluded that 'Aberdeen Journals failed to price above average variable costs regarding the *Herald & Post* in March, May and June of 2000' (para. 87). As well as conducting an analysis of the cost structure facing the undertaking, and its revenues, the OFT also relied on significant documentary evidence of intent. The undertaking argued that it was merely meeting competition, and that pricing levels were broadly equivalent between its title and that of the entrant. The OFT, however, found that the only reason for the similarity was that the entrant was being forced to meet the prices set by Aberdeen Journals. Aberdeen Journals, the OFT found, had 'initiated and sustained price cuts, and increased pagination and circulation, rather than simply responded to competition' (para. 79). The undertaking argued that the length of time over which the OFT was analysing the conduct was insufficient to fully take into account the dynamics of the market place, and the OFT accepted that there might well be circumstances in which undertakings 'might inadvertently price below average variable cost for a short period' (para. 109) but it did not accept that this was the situation in the present case. In para. 115 of the decision the Director held that

Even if there were convincing evidence that Aberdeen Journals no longer intended to predate in March 2000 (which the Director is satisfied there is not), Aberdeen Journals' conduct from 1 March to 29 March 2000 would be predatory. These pricing levels were not inadvertent or caused by any external factor. They resulted directly from the sustained predatory campaign pursued by Aberdeen Journals against the *Independent* over the preceding four years, before the Act came into force. Aberdeen Journals' failure to take effective action to cease predating (even though it was subject to investigation by the Office) by reducing its costs or increasing its revenues was, at best, negligent, and continued to have the anticompetitive effect of potentially expelling its only rival from the relevant market. Consequently Aberdeen Journals' failure to cover its average variable costs until 29 March 2000 was not legitimate competitive conduct.

In *Aberdeen Journals Ltd* v *The Director General of Fair Trading* ([2002] CompAR 167) the CAT set this decision aside, remitting it to the Director for reassessment. The CAT did not consider the evidence relating to predation as it found defects in the analysis of the relevant market.

The OFT made a new decision, essentially reaching the same conclusions, but supported by much more thorough market analysis (*Predation by Aberdeen Journals Ltd* CA98/14/2002 [2002] UKCLR 740). The assessment of predation in this decision is set out at paras 150–212, and para. 115 of the original decision was reproduced as new para. 208. This was again appealed to the CAT which gave judgment in June 2003 (*Aberdeen Journals Ltd* v *Office of Fair Trading supported by Aberdeen Independent Ltd* [2003] CompAR 67). This time the CAT upheld the OFT's decision in relation to market definition and dominance, and agreed that the OFT had established that abusive predatory conduct had taken place.

The CAT took the view, consistent with EC case law, that 'pricing below average variable cost is not a normal business practice in normal competitive conditions' (para. 424), and that doing so 'suffices to establish the abuse alleged without it being necessary to examine the question of intention' (ibid.). The evidence brought forward by the OFT was enough to establish on the facts that the undertaking *had* priced below average variable cost, and that over the period in question—albeit a short one—Aberdeen Journals had not attempted to bring the price above variable cost. Economic evidence advanced by the undertaking's expert witness, from the consultancy RBB Economics, was criticized by the Court for not acknowledging that it was the duty of RBB to help the Tribunal, and that 'such duty overrides its obligation to any person from whom RBB has received instructions or by whom RBB is paid' (para. 288).

The topic of predation is covered at some length in the Fall 2003 issue of *Antitrust* (vol. 18, no. 1).

16.2.2 Excessive pricing

The popular, and not entirely accurate, view of monopoly behaviour is that it leads to 'rip-offs' and excessively high prices. As was demonstrated formally in Chapter 13, a monopolist is likely to price higher than a firm in a competitive market. While such situations can be of concern to competition authorities, there is again no standard formula by which excessive pricing may be identified. Excessive pricing is a dangerous strategy as the supernormal profits of which it is indicative are an invitation to other firms to enter the market (see, e.g., the comments made by the MMC in *Cross Solent Ferries*, Cm. 1825, 1992, at para. 7.71). Such a strategy is therefore one that can be pursued successfully in the medium to long term only where there exist strong barriers to entry. These barriers might include a reputation for predation on behalf of the incumbent, so the situation can arise where, in a short space of time, a company prices first predatorially and then excessively.

A further problem in the analysis is to distinguish between excessive prices which lead to supernormal profits, and excessive prices which are the result of X-inefficiency, which might be the case where an incumbent is both inefficient and protected by high barriers to entry.

Where the EC Commission has acted against excessive pricing it often appears to have been on the basis of limited analysis and to have been inspired by concerns about divisions in the internal market. There has not been much case law in this area—a factor highlighted by the CAT in its preliminary hearing in the *Napp* case (*Napp Pharmaceutical Holdings Limited and Subsidiaries* v *The Director General of Fair Trading* [2001] CompAR 1, para. 46).

The first decision to deal with the issue in detail in the EC was that of *General Motors Continental* 75/75 (1975) OJ L29/14. At the time the decision was taken cars sold in Belgium, or imported into Belgium for use, were required to satisfy technical standards laid down in law, and to carry an approval '*plaque d'identification*'. Either the manufacturer or a sole agent had to issue the certificate and confirm that the vehicle met the legal requirements. General Motors Continental was the sole authorized agent for the manufacturers belonging to the General Motors Group (GM). Where the approval certificate was being issued in respect of a car manufactured and sold by a member of GM in Europe a fee of BF1,250 was charged. However, for private customers or dealers who brought cars into Belgium other than through the standard GM distribution channels ('parallel importers') the price for the certificate rose to between BF5,300 and BF30,000, the aim presumably being to encourage such customers to purchase only through approved GM distributors. It appeared to be the case that BF2,500 would be the maximum charged for such certificates by agents authorized in respect of other makes of vehicle. Pointing to the 'extraordinary disparity between actual costs incurred and prices actually charged' the Commission found that GM had 'abused its dominant position within the meaning of [art. 82] and applied unfair prices within the meaning of heading (a)'. Very similar facts arose in the case of *British Leyland* (BL) (84/379 (1984) OJ L207/11) where customers were buying BL-manufactured left-hand drive vehicles in continental Europe at prices substantially lower than the equivalent right-hand drive vehicle in the United Kingdom. BL's UK dealers responded to this situation by putting pressure on BL to curb the trade, and BL at first decided to refuse to grant the necessary 'national type-approval' certificates for the imported vehicles. Then, following public pressure and intervention in the House of Commons, it changed its policy, granting such certificates but at a price of £150. A Commission investigation found that BL was at the same time charging only £25 for the certificate in respect of imported right-hand drive vehicles. Whether a vehicle was right- or left-hand drive made no difference to the legal status of the certificates. BL was then condemned by the Commission for charging a fee that 'was both excessive and discriminatory' (para. 26).

An interesting variant on high pricing was considered in *Sabena* (*London European—Sabena* 88/589 (1988) OJ L317/47), where the primary concern was that pressure was being put on a smaller competitor to raise its prices. Following a complaint made by London European (LE), a small company operating a twice-daily air service on the Luton/Brussels and Luton/Amsterdam routes, the Commission found that Sabena, by refusing to grant LE access to its ticket reservation system, had the intention 'of placing indirect pressure on [LE] to fix a higher level of fares than, as an independent air carrier, it had planned ... an artificial increase in fares [is] totally incompatible with a system of free competition' (para. 29).

In *United Brands* (*United Brands Co.* v *Commission* case 27/76 [1978] 1 CMLR 429, paras 235–68) the ECJ dealt with the Commission arguments to the effect that UB had charged 'unfair' prices 'excessive in relation to the economic value of the product supplied'. The Commission had argued, taking prices charged in Ireland as a base, that a price reduction of some 15 per cent would be appropriate. The Court agreed that 'charging a price which is excessive because it has no reasonable relation to the economic value of the product supplied' is an abuse, and held that the question is one of whether 'the difference between the costs actually incurred and the price actually charged is excessive and, if the answer to this question is in the affirmative, to consider whether a price has been imposed which is either unfair in itself or when compared to competing products'. Unfortunately the Commission had failed to conduct any examination of the cost structures facing UB, and had based its claim of excessive pricing on a superficial comparison of prices based on a single exception to a trend, and on a solitary letter written by UB which was subsequently withdrawn by the undertaking. In respect of this claim, therefore, the Commission decision was in part struck down. Some care must be taken in applying this analysis elsewhere—the concept of 'economic value' is an interesting, but highly subjective one.

In *Duales System Deutschland AG* 2001/463 (2001) OJ L166/1 the Commission condemned what it termed 'unreasonable prices', which it said existed in cases in which 'the price charged for a service is clearly disproportionate to the cost of supplying it' (para. 111). In the case in question the undertaking, DSD, licensed the use of the Green Dot trade mark on packaging, and would in return look after the collection and recycling of such packaging. The Commission first announced that it was inclined to take a favourable view of the arrangement, but then received a number of complaints to the effect that DSD was abusing a dominant position on the German market. However, not all packaging bearing the mark would be dealt with by DSD, even though a licence fee would still be required for this. The Commission found that in these circumstances the fee was 'unfair' (para. 112). The Commission argued that 'as long as DSD makes the licence fee dependent solely on the use of the mark, it is imposing unfair prices and commercial terms on undertakings which do not use the exemption service' (para. 113). Again in Germany, in *Deutsche Post AG* 2001/892 (2001) OJ L331/40, the Commission dealt with a complaint from the British Post Office relating to various practices of its German counterpart. The practices complained of related to DPAG's approach to direct mail sent from the UK to addresses in Germany, but where the originating undertaking (the 'sender') had a connection in Germany. Such mail was on occasion delayed by DPAG, and a higher price was charged to the British Post Office for the onward transmission of this mail, than for deliveries that were entirely domestic in character. At paras 155–67 the Commission dealt with the arguments relating to excessive pricing, concluding that

the tariff charged by DPAG has no sufficient or reasonable relationship to real costs or to the real value of the service provided. Consequently DPAG's pricing exploits customers excessively and should therefore be regarded as an unfair selling price within the meaning of art. 82. In conclusion, the Commission finds that DPAG has abused its dominant position in the German market.

Excessive pricing, which is dealt with in Part 2 of *Assessment of Conduct*, and has been linked by the OFT with discriminatory pricing (see below), was attacked in *Napp Pharmaceutical Holdings Ltd* CA98/2/2001 [2001] UKCLR 597, on appeal *Napp Pharmaceuticals Holdings Ltd* v *The Director General of Fair Trading* [2002] CompAR 16. The Director argued that

The prices charged by Napp for MST in the community are excessive. The Director considers that a price is excessive and an abuse if it is above that which would exist in a competitive market and where it is clear that high profits will not stimulate successful new entry within a reasonable period. Therefore, to show that prices are excessive, it must be demonstrated that (i) prices are higher than would be expected in a competitive market, and (ii) there is no effective competitor pressure to bring them down to competitive levels, nor is there likely to be. (para. 203)

Price comparisons showed that Napp's prices were, to the relevant sector of the market, between 33 per cent and 67 per cent higher than those of the next nearest competitor (table 6). Napp argued that it was justified in charging higher prices because it was the innovator in the industry, and its product had a brand value. The Director however took the view that the product had lost its brand value (para. 211), and that Napp had been rewarded for its invention of the product during the period in which the patent for the product was in existence (para. 209). The Director found that it was inconsistent with normal market processes for Napp to maintain a market share of some 96 per cent at the same time as it charged prices that were so much higher than those of competing products. An analysis of the undertaking's profit margins was also carried out, but this raised problems as the situation in the industry was not symmetrical. Although Napp made a higher margin on sales than its competitors it was also the only undertaking that manufactured the product itself (para. 225). The Director therefore compared the average selling price of Napp's product, which was £15.47, with the average cost of the goods sold by its next most profitable competitor—which it should be emphasized was thought might be *higher* than the cost of production by Napp— which was £3.01. This would lead to a gross margin of 80.5 per cent, and for the next most profitable competitor the margin was less than 70 per cent (para. 228). On appeal the CAT upheld the findings of the Director, and held that the fact that it is difficult to calculate whether a price is higher than that which would exist in a competitive market does not mean that the exercise should not be undertaken (para. 392). The comparisons that could be made in the case all suggested that the Director was correct to find that prices were excessive, and it did not matter that the Director had not specified by exactly how much the prices were excessive (paras 393–405).

16.2.3 Discriminatory pricing

Price discrimination may be defined as the supply of goods or services of the same contract description at different prices at the same time where the difference in price does not reflect cost differences (e.g., in transport or bulk supply). Whereas in a competitive market a producer is able usually to charge only one price for its product, in a monopolistic market the producer may be able to increase income and profits by charging a range of prices. In the extreme case of perfect differentiation the monopolist can charge each customer the maximum the customer is prepared to pay; more likely is the situation where various groups of customers are identified and prices set in relation to each group. The welfare effects of this practice depend on all the circumstances, and in some cases it can be clearly demonstrated that there is greater output as more customers are being satisfied than is the case where a single price maintains. Where there are objections to price discrimination it may be because the one certainty is that it results in a transfer of income from consumers to the monopolist. In the case of perfect differentiation the consumer surplus is transferred completely to the monopolist. Price discrimination can be successful only where the monopolist is able to control resale of the product, otherwise those who could purchase at low prices would resell to those who would be paying the monopolist higher prices; thus price discrimination itself is sometimes taken as evidence of a degree of market power. Price discrimination may also play a part in predatory conduct: where a monopolist funds predatory prices by profits earned elsewhere an element of price discrimination is inevitable, unless the monopolist operates in more than one product or geographic market.

In the United States the Robinson–Patman Act of 1936—'the misshapen progeny of intolerable draftsmanship coupled to wholly mistaken economic theory' (Bork, R. H., *The Antitrust Paradox*, New York, The Free Press (1993), p. 382)—was drafted expressly to deal with the 'problem' of price discrimination. Bork aside, there has been much criticism both of the theory underlying the Act and of its application in practice, and even a report prepared for the US Department of Justice has recommended its repeal.

In the European Community the overriding objective of creating the single market (see Chapter 2) has resulted in greater focus being placed upon price discrimination than would be likely to be the case in purely national jurisdictions. If a monopolist is going to exercise a crude form of price discrimination and set different prices for groups of consumers an obvious division might be between the Member States.

This was the situation in *United Brands* (*United Brands Co.* v *Commission* case 27/76 [1978] 1 CMLR 429). In its decision taken in 1975 (*Chiquita* 76/353 (1976) OJ L95/1) the Commission had attacked United Brands for charging variations in prices for bananas to its customers which were 'not attributable to any differences in customs duties or transport costs, since these [were] borne by the distributor/ripeners'. At one point, according to the Commission's figures, Danish customers were paying 2.38 times the price charged to Irish customers. United Brands was able to achieve this in part by introducing contractual terms that prevented its customers from reselling green bananas to other retailers; once the bananas had ripened their perishability would mean that resale other than to the end consumer was not a practical possibility. The essence of the undertaking's defence was that the price differentials in the final markets were not of its making, being the result of historical factors. Whether United Brands charged these higher prices to some retailers would make little difference to the end consumer, for if United Brands did not take the monopoly profit the retailer would. One of the stronger points made tirelessly by Bork is that a monopoly price can be imposed only once—if there are monopolies at every step of a vertically integrated chain the price does not go on rising indefinitely as at some point the consumer's demand curve must still be faced. After conducting some particularly unconvincing economic analysis the ECJ found in the Commission's favour, in effect holding that United Brands had to bear some of the cost of the creation of the common market. It is unlikely that consumers benefited from the judgment, for if they were able to bear the higher prices these would be imposed by the retailers in place of United Brands.

Recital (c) of art. 82—'applying dissimilar conditions to equivalent transactions with other trading parties, thereby placing them at a competitive disadvantage'— suggests strongly that discriminatory pricing is to be considered an 'abuse', but the Commission does not generally wish to involve itself in pricing decisions. Consider, for instance, its approach in *HOV SVZ/MCN* 94/210 (1994) OJ L104/34. Here the Commission was reacting to a complaint about practices relating to the carriage by rail of sea-borne containers between Belgium, Germany, and The Netherlands. The Commission set out its general position thus:

it is not part of the Commission's duties to assess as such the level of prices charged by an undertaking or to decide which criteria should govern the setting of such prices. On the other hand, where different prices are charged for equivalent transactions, *it is appropriate to assess whether such differences are justified by objective factors.* (paras 158–9, emphasis added)

This is the general case under EC law, the position being that where a supplier can demonstrate that there are 'objective factors' that lead to the price differences, an allegation of abusive behaviour will not be sustained. Accordingly it will be a defence to an action if the supplier can demonstrate that discounts are given for bulk sales because it is cheaper for it to supply in bulk. Thus, for example, in *Tetra Pak II* 92/163 (1992) OJ L72/1—in which the Commission was considering the undertaking's position in relation to packaging machines and the packaging used by the machines—the Commission addressed Tetra Pak's 'selling prices for its cartons which vary considerably from one Member State to another', holding this practice to be 'discriminatory and constitut[ing] an abuse' (para. 154). The Commission was of the view that, particularly as raw materials (the prices of which were determined on the world market and did not therefore vary from Member State to Member State) accounted for 70 per cent of the cost of the cartons, and that given the relevant geographic market for the cartons had been found to be that of the Community as a whole, the 'price differences observed [could not] be explained in economic terms'. The price differences were found to be the result of the 'compartmentalisation policy which Tetra Pak managed artificially to maintain' (para. 154). In relation to the supply of the packaging machines themselves the Commission was even more emphatic, pointing out that 'the transport costs of machines are quite negligible in relation to the market value of the product' (para. 160). One of the requirements imposed on Tetra Pak was that it would 'ensure that any differences between the prices charged for its products in the various Member States result solely from specific market conditions . . . and shall not grant to any customer any form of discount on its products or more favourable payment terms not justified by an objective consideration' (arts 1, 2). Tetra Pak was fined €75 million in respect of the infringements the Commission found.

A number of cases in recent years have dealt with the issue of landing fees at airports. Although these have been based on both art. 82 and art. 86, the issues are the same in either case. A typical case is that of *Portuguese airports* 1999/199 (1999) OJ L69/31, on appeal *Landing fees at Portuguese airports* v *Commission* case C–163/99 [2002] 4 CMLR 31. Here the Commission ruled that differences in landing fees charged, dependent on where the flight originated, were discriminatory and unjustified. The Commission relied on the fact that the services being purchased were the same, wherever the landing plane took off from. The ECJ upheld the Decision, and dismissed the appeal. In *Aeroports de Paris* v *Commission* case C–82/01 [2003] 4 CMLR 609 the ECJ upheld an earlier judgment of the CFI (case t-128/98 [2001] 4 CMLR 38) upholding an EC Commission decision (*Aeroports de Paris*

98/513 (1998) OJ L230/10) in which the Commission had found that Aeroports de Paris had imposed discriminatory rates in relation to licence fees in relation to ground-handling services at its airports.

The second part of art. 82(c)—'thereby placing them at a competitive disadvantage'—is easily dealt with. In part, the use of 'thereby' suggests that it is presumed that a competitive disadvantage flows from the maintenance of 'dissimilar conditions'. On top of this, the ECJ held in *United Brands* that a competitive disadvantage existed 'since compared with what it should have been competition had thereby been distorted' (para. 233). It should be recognized that drawing a comparison with what competition 'should have been' may not be a straightforward matter. It is not necessary therefore to show that any one customer of the discriminating supplier is placed at a competitive disadvantage *vis-à-vis* another.

In the United Kingdom the issue of price discrimination has not been subject to the same scrutiny as it has in the EC and as suggested above, there is a specific reason for the EC Commission to focus on the issue. It is also the case that discrimination will be harder to maintain in a smaller market where customers can more easily respond. Nevertheless, price discrimination was dealt with in the *Napp* case (*Napp Pharmaceutical Holdings Ltd* CA98/2/2001 [2001] UKCLR 597, on appeal *Napp Pharmaceuticals Holdings Ltd* v *The Director General of Fair Trading* [2002] CompAR 13). In the decision price discrimination is dealt with at paras 144–87, para. 144 stating that 'discounts will be an abuse if they serve to strengthen a dominant position in such a way that the degree of dominance reached substantially fetters competition'. Napp produced sustained release morphine tablets (MST), which were distributed to two sectors of the market, hospitals and the community sector. Hospital usage, which accounted for a relatively small share of the overall market, was a trigger for prescription by general practitioners in the community sector. Napp supplied MST to hospitals at a discount of over 90 per cent off the NHS list prices, and the OFT took the view that these discounts were targeted 'specifically at new competitors and hindered competition in the hospital segment of the market' (para. 145). The highest level of discounts was only offered on strengths of its own product line where it faced a direct rival (para. 182). Higher discounts were also offered to hospitals where Napp expected to be awarded a sole contract for a particular region (para. 183). The finding was upheld by the CAT.

It is necessary to consider allegations of price discrimination carefully—as noted by the OFT, 'it is not necessarily the case that price discrimination by a dominant undertaking is an abuse (*Assessment of conduct*, para. 3.3). For example, the Association of British Travel Agents (ABTA) complained to the OFT that British Airways was abusing its dominant position by offering flights over the Internet more cheaply than if they were booked through travel agents. The OFT found that it was reasonable to do so, on the grounds that it was cheaper to sell flights this way (*The Association of British Travel Agents and British Airways Plc* CA98/19/2002 [2003] UKCLR 136).

An allegation of price discrimination made against London Electricity plc (LE) was rejected by Ofgem in September 2003. LE had made an offer to customers who had switched to another supplier to encourage them to return to LE that was greater than that which could be matched by their existing suppliers in order to retain them, and which was out of line with the prices charged to existing LE customers. The authority held that 'price discrimination is only an abuse under the Act if it has an anti-competitive effect' (para. 34). Because there was only 'a severely limited take up of the offer' there was no such effect (*The Gas and Electricity Market Authority's Decision under the Competition Act 1998 that London Electricity plc has not infringed the Prohibition imposed under s. 18(1) of the Act with regard to a 'win back' offer* [2004] UKCLR 239).

16.2.4 **Margin squeezes**

At 16.2.1 the case of *Napier Brown/British Sugar* 88/518 (1988) OJ L288/41 was discussed. In this case a producer of sugar operated in the markets for both industrial sugar and retail sugar. In essence retail sugar is repackaged industrial sugar, and British Sugar was the dominant supplier of industrial sugar in the UK. If another undertaking wished to compete in the market for retail sugar it had first to purchase industrial sugar from British Sugar, and then compete with it in the downstream market. British Sugar was selling this industrial sugar at prices that did not allow a downstream competitor that was equally efficient to it in the retail market to make a sufficient margin on sales to be able to compete effectively. This practice is now known as a 'margin squeeze', and has been identified in a number of industries in which an undertaking operates at different levels of the market, and in the downstream level competes with others to whom it supplies an input at the upstream level. The principles underlying this difficult area can be clearly explained by reference to a hypothetical supplier of a telephone network (A) where the owner of the network also sells telephony services to retail customers. Another undertaking (B) also sells services to retail customers, but is required to do so over the network provided by A. If A charges B a price higher for the network than it charges itself, or charges the same price but in effect operates its own retail services at a paper loss, subsidizing this loss by revenues earned from the network operation, B will not be able to compete even if it is as efficient in relation to retail services as A. Margin squeezes are dealt with in Part 6 of *Assessment of conduct*.

The OFT and Oftel have both considered this area on a number of occasions, but have usually dismissed the complaints. For example, in two decisions the OFT rejected complaints to the effect that British Sky Broadcasting (BSkyB) had engaged in a margin squeeze in relation to the wholesale pay-TV market in the UK (*BSkyB Investigation: Alleged infringement of the Chapter II Prohibition* CA98/20/2002 [2003] UKCLR 240; *Decision of the OFT under s. 47 relating to Decision CA98/20/2002: Alleged infringement of the Chapter II Prohibition by BSkyB* [2003] UKCLR 1075). Complaints were made alleging that the charges BSkyB made to distributors, and the charges BSkyB made to its own subscribers, did not allow distributors to compete with BSkyB in the downstream market. On a first inspection the OFT was concerned, and issued a notice to BSkyB to that effect. Subsequent analysis persuaded it that there was no breach, and when the complainants asked the OFT to vary the decision it stood by its original conclusions. The approach taken by the OFT was to consider whether BSkyB's distribution arm (DisCo) was profitable:

if DisCo is profitable, then distribution rivals as (or more) efficient that DisCo would also be profitable, while less efficient rivals might not be. If DisCo were not profitable then, to remain in business, it must be subsidized by other parts of BSkyB (and any other equally efficient business would also require subsidies.

Whether or not there is an anti-competitive margin squeeze therefore depends on whether or not DisCo is profitable. Since the focus is on DisCo it is not necessary to examine the performance of third parties, which is likely to be affected by various factors. It is also unnecessary to compare the performance of DisCo or third parties to some benchmark of maximum efficiency which would be very difficult. (paras 157–8 of the second decision)

The leading case in the UK as of May 2004 was *Genzyme*. The OFT found that Genzyme Ltd had engaged in exclusionary behaviour in the market for the drug Cerezyme used to treat the rare and debilitating Gaucher disease from which about 180 people suffered in the UK at the time of the decision (*Exclusionary behaviour by Genzyme Ltd* CA98/3/03 [2003] UKCLR 950). Genzyme supplied both the drug, and the care system, including nursing staff, to support those taking the medication. Genzyme supplied the drug to another health care provider, but charged the same price as it did under a previous agreement when it had also supplied the care services. The customer however did not receive any of the ancillary services. This meant that in order to compete with Genzyme it had to incur the additional expense of providing care services. The OFT set out the basic principle in relation to margin squeeze at para. 364 of its decision:

A pricing policy operated by a vertically integrated dominant undertaking may infringe section 18 of the Act. This might occur where a vertically integrated undertaking which is dominant in the upstream market operates a pricing policy which does not allow reasonably efficient competitors in the downstream market a margin sufficient to enable them to survive in the long term. This pricing behaviour is known as 'margin squeeze'.

The effect of the pricing strategy adopted by Genzyme was that its homecare services arm was paying the same price for the entire package that the competitor was paying just for the drug. The OFT found that if Genzyme Homecare was required to pay that price itself it would make no margin on the drug and would make a loss on the homecare services. The conclusion that flowed from this was that 'regardless of how efficient Genzyme Healthcare might be, it is clear that it could not trade profitably on these terms' (para. 375). The OFT found that there was no justification for this pricing policy, and imposed directions requiring Genzyme to alter its pricing structure, and also imposed a penalty of £6.8 million. Genzyme appealed. On 11 March 2004 the CAT upheld the OFT's decision (*Genzyme Limited* v *The OFT* [2004] CAT 4), dealing with the issue of margin squeeze at paras 549–75. The CAT found, *inter alia*, that Genzyme's pricing policy was 'intended to achieve the result of monopolising the supply of homecare services to Gaucher patients in favour of Genzyme Homecare' and that it 'must have appreciated that the inevitable result of its pricing policy would be to force Healthcare [its competitor] to exit the market' (para. 555).

In response to arguments made by Genzyme about the 'objective justifications' advanced for the conduct in question the CAT held first that the concept 'does not fall to be applied in terms of benefits which accrue to the dominant undertaking, but in terms of the general interest' (para. 583), and then proceeded to reject all of the arguments that Genzyme made in support of its practice. However, the CAT reduced the penalty to £3 million, finding in part that the OFT had overstated the length of the infringement.

A complaint against Companies House alleging that it cross-subsidized its commercial activities to the detriment of competitors from the sales of raw bulk data to those competitors was likewise rejected (*Companies House, the Registrar of Companies for England and Wales* [2003] UKCLR 24. For a discussion of these and other cases see Ridyard, D., and Chrysanthou, Y., 'Recent Margin Squeeze Cases under Chapter II and Article 82—An Economic Critique' (2003) *Lawyer's Europe*, Autumn, pp. 12–15), and see also 'The Genzyme Case and the OFT's Margin Squeeze Muddle' (2003) RBB Brief 10, July.

16.3 Refusal to deal or supply, and the essential facilities doctrine

16.3.1 Refusal to supply generally

A general presumption in the commercial world is that companies are free to choose with whom to have dealings. However, there are situations in which a positive obligation is placed on them to supply specific parties. In particular this is likely to be the case where refusals are: imposed to punish a customer who may have traded in more competitive fashion than the retailer wished; the result of the monopolist wishing to exclude others from directly competing with the monopolist in secondary markets; and an attempt to maintain high prices by dampening downstream competition, e.g. cases in which monopolists have refused to supply discount chains. A problem in requiring supplies to be made is that the competition authorities may also have to address issues such as the terms and conditions of supply and be prepared to be involved in an element of ongoing regulation.

In 1984 the Commission stated that '[a]s a general principle an objectively unjustifiable refusal to supply by an undertaking holding a dominant position on a market constitutes an infringement of Article [82]' (*Thirteenth Report on Competition Policy* (1984), point 157). The first case to deal substantially with the issue, *Commercial Solvents*, is one of the least satisfactory of all EC cases (*Istituto Chemioterapico Italiano SpA and Commercial Solvents Corp* v *Commission* cases 6–7/73 [1974] CMLR 309). Here Commercial Solvents (CSC), which manufactured aminobutanol, a raw material in the manufacture of drugs to combat tuberculosis, was required to resume supplies to the complainant Zoja. This followed the decision of CSC to expand into production of the final product itself and to cease supplies of the raw material. Even before that decision had been made Zoja had stopped taking supplies from CSC and had made attempts, which were eventually unsuccessful, to find a source of supplies elsewhere. Supporting the EC Commission the ECJ held that 'an undertaking in a dominant position as regards the production of raw material . . . cannot, just because it decides to start manufacturing [the derivative product] (in competition with its former customers) act in such a way as to eliminate their competition' (para. 25). The analysis of the welfare effects in this case is unsatisfactory. It is, for instance, likely that the vertically integrated CSC would be able to produce the end drug more efficiently than would be achieved by a combination of the two undertakings each engaged in one part of the manufacturing process only.

Similarly, Community law provides that a manufacturer is not allowed to foreclose competition in the market for the repair or service of its product by unreasonably denying spare parts to independent service companies (e.g., *Hugin Kassaregister AB and Hugin Cash Registers Ltd* v *Commission* case 22/78 [1979] 3 CMLR 345, and *Volvo AB* v *Erik Veng* case 238/87 [1989] 4 CMLR 122: see the discussion of both cases at 14.2.1.1).

In *United Brands (United Brands Co.* v *Commission* case 27/76 [1978] 1 CMLR 429) retailers that participated in advertising campaigns promoting rival products, or who resupplied green bananas, were threatened with having supplies cut off. Both actions were condemned by the Commission.

In *Boosey and Hawkes (BBI/Boosey & Hawkes: Interim measures* 87/500 (1987) OJ L286/36) the products in question were musical instruments for brass bands. BBI was established by two companies, GHH, a retailer of brass band instruments, and RCN, a repairer of the instruments, with the intention of manufacturing instruments in competition to Boosey, which was the only British manufacturer of brass instruments. Boosey responded to this move by, *inter alia*, withdrawing supplies of its instruments and spare parts from GHH and RCN. The Commission supported the claimants, holding (at para. 19) that

A dominant undertaking may always take reasonable steps to protect its commercial interests, but such measures must be fair and proportional to the threat. The fact that a customer of a dominant producer becomes associated with a competitor of that manufacturer does not normally entitle the dominant producer to withdraw all supplies immediately or to take reprisals against that customer.

Under the decision adopted Boosey was 'required to meet within seven days of receipt any reasonable order . . . for musical instruments or spare parts' (art. 1).

Refusals to supply may be justified where, for instance, there is a general shortage and the supplier declines to supply new customers in favour of existing arrangements (*ABG Oil companies operating in the Netherlands* 77/327 (1977) OJ L117/1).

There has been little case law in this area under the Competition Act 1998 at the public level. The OFT considered a complaint of refusal to supply relating to a film used in the production of holographic images in *du Pont* but concluded that although the undertaking was dominant it had acted with objective justification. The OFT recognized that 'it is only in exceptional circumstances that competition law should deprive an undertaking of the freedom to determine its trading partners' (para. 28). In the present case the company had moved to a policy of supplying the film only for use in applications relating to security and authentication, and that it would not be able to provide security guarantees to those customers if it was also supplying the film to customers for use in graphic arts applications (*Refusal to supply unprocessed holographic photopolymer film: E I du Pont de Nemours & Company and Op Graphics (Holography) Limited* CA98/07/2003 [2004] UKCLR 253). Oftel has dismissed a number of complaints made against telephone network operators by third parties providing access on to the network via the Internet, or via GSM gateways (banks of SIM cards mounted into a device that provides connectivity between a fixed telephone line and a mobile network), in each case holding that the provider of the network was entitled to do so under the terms of the relevant telecommunications legislation (see, e.g., *Disconnection of VIP Communications Limited's services by T-Mobile Limited*, 22 December 2003).

16.3.2 The essential facilities doctrine

An 'essential facility' is a facility or infrastructure without access to which competitors cannot provide services to their customers. 'The owner of an essential facility which uses its power in one market in order to protect or strengthen its position in another related market . . . imposing a competitive disadvantage on its competitor, infringes Article [82]' (*Sea Containers* v *Stena Sealink* 94/19 (1994) OJ L15/8, at para. 66). To date, in both the EC and the UK, the doctrine has been most prominent in decisions concerned with the operation of transport networks, although it is likely to have an increasing impact on the utilities and telecommunications sectors, especially in the context of deregulation.

Like many aspects of competition law the doctrine has its origins in American practice, and is traced to the case of *United States* v *Terminal Railroad Association* 224 US 383 (1912); USSCR 56 L Ed 810. In *Terminal Railroad* the 38 defendants, owners of a vital network of St Louis transport connections, denied non-owner railroads access to the facilities. Delivering the judgment of the court, Lurton M.J. offered the defendants the option either of restructuring their mutual contracts so as to allow the admission of new firms into the network, or of dissolving the combination. While the court did not make explicit the creation of an essential facilities doctrine, it recognized the threat to competition posed by 'a unified system . . . unless it is the impartial agent of all who [are compelled] to use its facilities' (at 405).

The operation of the doctrine was clarified by the court in *MCI Communications Corporation and MCI Telecommunications Corporation* v *American Telephone and Telegraph Company* 708 F.2d 1081 (1983). Here AT&T, a dominant telecommunications company, refused to interconnect MCI with the local distribution facilities of Bell operating companies, thus limiting the range of services that MCI could offer its customers. The court held that

A monopolist's refusal to deal under these circumstances is governed by the so-called essential facilities doctrine. Such a refusal may be unlawful because a monopolist's control of an essential facility (sometimes called a 'bottleneck') can extend monopoly power from one stage of production to another, and from one market into another. Thus the antitrust laws have imposed on firms controlling an essential facility the obligation to make the facility available on non-discriminatory terms. (para. 31)

A fourfold test was put forward for the doctrine: '(1) control of the essential facility by a monopolist; (2) a competitor's inability practically or reasonably to duplicate the essential facility; (3) the denial of the use of the facility to a competitor; and (4) the feasibility of providing the facility' (para. 32). The focus on the denial of use means that the doctrine is better considered as a specific example of the wider category of cases in which there is a unilateral refusal to supply or deal.

The EC Commission has been keen to embrace the doctrine, which may be applicable under both arts 81 and 82 but is more likely to be of relevance to art. 82 cases as the holding of an essential facility is strong evidence of dominance.

In *British Midland/Aer Lingus* 92/213 (1992) OJ L96/34, the Commission found that those holding dominant positions should not 'withhold facilities which the industry traditionally provides to all other airlines'. Aer Lingus, the dominant undertaking in the market for the London/Dublin air route, was ordered to resume its interline facility with British Midland, having previously withdrawn it. Interlining is based on an agreement under which most of the world's airlines have authorized the others to sell their services, as a result of which travel agents can offer passengers a single ticket providing for transportation by different carriers. The Commission appeared to accept that such a facility could be withdrawn where the dominant airline could give an objective reason for its refusal to continue, such as, *inter alia*, concerns about creditworthiness (para. 26 of the decision), but in the present case no such reason could be advanced. At para. 30 of the decision the Commission's argument is crystallized:

Aer Lingus has not been able to point to efficiencies created by a refusal to interline nor to advance any other persuasive and legitimate business justification for its conduct. Its desire to avoid loss of market share, the circumstance that this is a route of vital importance to the company and that its operating margin is under pressure do not make this a legitimate response to new entry.

Similarities in approach to the American analysis are clear in this decision, as can be seen from a comparative examination of the case of *Otter Tail Power Company* v *United States* 410 US 366 (1973); USSCR 35 L Ed 2d 359.

In its *22nd Annual Report on Competition Policy* (1992, points 216–18) the Commission made it clear that the decision was taken with specific reference to a time period in which air transport was being liberalized, and argued that airlines making use of the new opportunities for competition should be given a fair chance to develop and sustain their challenge to established carriers. However, the duty on

Aer Lingus was to be of a finite duration only, as new entrants should not be able to rely indefinitely on frequencies and services provided by their competitors.

A similar decision was taken by the Commission in *Port of Roscoff* (Commission Press Release IP (95) 492 of 16 May; [1995] 4 CMLR 677). Here the Morlaix Chamber of Commerce, in its capacity as port authority for Roscoff, denied Irish Continental Group (ICG) access to the port. The Commission required the authority to 'take the necessary steps to allow ICG access to the port'. In fact the parties had already reached an agreement subject to the resolution of certain technical requirements, governing access to the port, but the Commission clearly wished to establish strong precedents and guidelines in this area.

A step vital for the development of the essential facilities doctrine was made explicit in *B&I/Sealink, Holyhead* (*22nd Annual Report on Competition Policy* (1992), point 219). It will be recalled that for art. 82 to apply the allegedly dominant position must lie within 'a substantial part' of the EC. Some initial doubts were raised in relation to the doctrine on the grounds that a 'facility' could not constitute the requisite substantial part In *British Midland* the point was skirted, the Commission asserting merely that '[b]oth the UK and Ireland are substantial parts of the common market' (at para. 17). In *B&I* Sealink acted as port authority at Holyhead (the essential facility) in North Wales. The company instituted timetable changes which operated to the detriment of B&I and in favour of Sealink's own services. In particular, the loading and unloading of B&I services had to be interrupted to accommodate Sealink sailings. Indubitably Holyhead is *not* a substantial part of the common market. The Commission, recognizing that this was indeed the case, made clear that (emphasis added) 'it is important to stress that a port, an airport *or any other facility*, even if it is not itself a substantial part of the common market, may be considered as such in so far as reasonable access to the facility is indispensable for the exploitation of a transport route which is substantial'. Recognizing that this argument can extend to any infrastructure, and not merely to transport routes, the Commission stated that '[t]his consequence of Article [82] is of essential importance in the context of deregulation'.

It is important too that in both the American cases, such as *MCI* (above), and *British Midland* it was considered significant that the offender's primary motivation for the exclusionary practice was the long-term detriment of the competitor. In *B&I* it would appear that while such a detriment was a *consequence* of Sealink's action there was little evidence that this was the primary *intention* of Sealink, which was rather to make the best use of its own resources. The requirement imposed in that case, that 'a company which both owns and uses an essential facility . . . should not grant its competitors access on terms less favourable than those which it gives its own services' (*22nd Annual Report on Competition Policy* (1992), point 219), is a stricter test both than that used in the American cases and than that suggested in *British Midland*.

Sealink also came to an arrangement with Sea Containers regarding access to Holyhead following Commission intervention. Subsequently the Commission instituted a formal proceeding, finding in favour of Sea Containers (*Sea Containers/ Stena Sealink* 94/19 (1994) OJ L15/8). The Commission expanded the doctrine further, suggesting that when a company 'is in a position such as that of Sealink in this case, it cannot normally expect to fulfil satisfactorily its duty to provide non-discriminatory access and to resolve its conflicts of interest unless it takes steps to separate its management of the essential facility from its use of it'. The point was not made as strongly as that in *Flughafen Frankfurt/Main AG* 98/190 (1998) OJ L72/31 although the Commission held that an undertaking that owned Frankfurt Airport could not use its property right in that airport and its physical infrastructure to exclude competitors in ancillary services such as baggage loading and cabin cleaning. In *Port of Rødby* 94/119 (1994) OJ L55/52 the principle was applied also to art. 86 EC.

Many of these Community cases could have been dealt with under the more general principles set out in other refusal to deal cases, and it thus appears, particularly in the light of comments in the annual competition reports, that the Commission took a conscious decision, in the face of moves towards deregulation, to introduce the essential facilities doctrine into Community law.

The leading case on the operation of the essential facilities doctrine is now *Oscar Bronner GmbH & Co. KG* v *Mediaprint Zeitungs-und-Zeitschriftenverlag GmbH & Co. KG* (case C–7/97 [1999] 4 CMLR 112). Here Advocate General Jacobs sounded a warning note about the expansion of the doctrine. In this case Bronner was the publisher in Austria of a daily newspaper, *der Standard*, with a market share of 3.6 per cent of circulation. Mediaprint was the publisher of papers with a combined market share of 46.8 per cent. Bronner argued that it could not feasibly develop its own home delivery service in view of its small market share, and that only such a delivery service would allow it to survive. It argued, in effect, that Mediaprint's delivery service constituted an 'essential facility' to which it should have access. Starting from the position that 'the right to choose one's trading partners and freely to dispose of one's property are generally recognised principles in the laws of the Member States' and that 'incursions on those rights require careful justification' (para. 56) the Advocate General argued that 'intervention [under] an application of the essential facilities doctrine . . . can be justified in terms of competition policy only in cases in which the dominant undertaking has a genuine stranglehold on the related market' (para. 65). In this case the Advocate General's view was that Bronner had numerous, albeit less convenient, options open to it, and that to allow it to succeed in this case

would be to lead the Community and national authorities and courts into detailed regulation of the Community markets, entailing the fixing of prices and conditions for supply in large sections of the economy. Intervention on that scale would not only be unworkable but . . . also be anti-competitive in the longer term and indeed would scarcely be compatible with a free market economy.   (para. 69)

The Court followed this opinion in its judgment, holding in particular that 'it does not appear that there are any technical, legal or even economic obstacles capable of making it impossible, or even unreasonably difficult, for any other publishers of daily newspapers to establish, alone or in cooperation with other publishers, its own nationwide home delivery system' (para. 44).

The test that flows from the application of *Oscar Bronner* is in effect that set out by the Advocate General, commenting on a situation where a dominant company has a stranglehold on a related market. Such a situation, he suggested,

might be the case for example where duplication of the facility is impossible or extremely difficult owing to physical, geographical or legal constraints or is highly undesirable for reasons of public policy. It is not sufficient that the undertaking's control over a facility should give it a competitive advantage.

. . . the test in my view must be an objective one: in other words, in order for refusal of access to amount to an abuse, it must be extremely difficult not merely for the undertaking demanding access but for any other undertaking to compete. Thus if the cost of duplicating the facility alone is the barrier to entry, it must be such as to deter any prudent undertaking from entering the market. In that regard it seems to me that it will be necessary to consider all the circumstances, including the extent to which the dominant undertaking, having regard to the degree of amortisation of its investment and the cost of the upkeep must pass on investment or maintenance costs in the prices charged on the relevant market.   (paras 65–6)

The key elements then are that: (i) access to the facility must be genuinely indispensable; (ii) it is not possible practically to replicate the facility; (iii) even by an undertaking of the same size and resources as the holder of the facility. It is not enough that without the facility the putative competitor would find it *difficult* to compete.

In *European Night Services* v *Commission* joined cases t-374/94, etc. [1998] ECR II-3141 the Court ruled that the Commission had taken too restrictive an approach in requiring that parties to a joint venture to 'supply services on their networks on the same technical and financial terms as they allow to [the joint venture]' (see *Night Services* 94/663 (1994) OJ L259/20). In particular the Court took the view that train crews could not constitute an essential facility. One of the more recent cases in which the Commission has been called upon to consider this area arose in 1999 in *Info-Lab/Ricoh* (*Competition Policy Newsletter* (1999) 1:35). Here the Commission, referring to the 'restrictive approach of the ECJ to the doctrine of "essential facilities" in [*Oscar Bronner*]', rejected a complaint by a provider of toner which had asked the Commission to oblige Ricoh to supply it with new empty toner cartridges which it could then fill in order to compete with Ricoh in the market for filled cartridges.

At the time of writing the most recent case to deal with the essential facilities doctrine is *GVG/FS* 2004/33 (2004) OJ L11/17. Here the German railway company Georg Verkehrsoganisation GmbH (GVG) complained that Ferrovie dello Stato SpA (FS), the Italian national railway operator, had refused to grant it access to certain facilities. This prevented GVG from providing an international rail service from various points in Germany to Milan. Although the Commission found that FS was abusing its dominant position FS gave undertakings to the Commission that the abuse would be terminated and not repeated.

There have been few complaints under the Competition Act 1998 in the UK which have relied on the essential facilities doctrine, although the OFT did agree to reopen an investigation (in the process withdrawing an earlier decision) in relation to a crematorium which denied access to its facilities to an independent undertaker (*Harwood Park Crematorium Ltd* CA98/05/03 [2003] UKCLR 772). At the time of writing no final decision had been taken.

17

Market investigation references

17.1 **Introduction**

Market investigations, for which provision is made in Part 4 of the Enterprise Act 2002, are distinctive to the UK, and are one of the strengths of the domestic competition law regime. They sit outside the prohibition framework established in arts 81 and 82 EC and the Chapter I and Chapter II equivalents, and replace provisions in the Fair Trading Act 1973 (FTA 1973) relating to scale and complex monopoly investigation references (see in particular FTA 1973, s. 6). Market investigations are 'not fundamentally different from the 1973 Act, many of the provisions of which are drawn on and modernised in the [Act]' (Mr Alexander, *Hansard*, Standing Committee B, col. 442). However, the discussion of the law of market investigations will be treated here as being entirely new, although reports produced under the earlier regime will be referred to where these shed light on the types of considerations and remedies that may be relevant to market investigations.

The distinctive nature of this part of the domestic regime is clearly set out in the *Explanatory Notes: Enterprise Act 2002* (TSO, 2002). At para. 292 the following introduction to market investigations is given:

The purpose of these investigations is to inquire into markets where it appears that competition has been prevented, restricted or distorted by the structure of a market (or any aspect of its structure), the conduct of persons supplying or acquiring goods or services who operate within it, or the conduct of such persons' customers, but where there has been no obvious breach of the prohibitions on anti-competitive agreements or arrangements or abuse of a dominant position under CA 1998 or Articles 81 or 82 of the EC Treaty. An example of the sort of circumstances in which these provisions might be used would be a situation where a few large firms supplied almost the whole of the market and, without there being any agreement between them (ie a non-collusive oligopoly), they all tended to follow parallel courses of conduct (eg in relation to pricing), while new competitors faced significant barriers to entry into the market, and there was little or no evidence of vigorous competition between the existing players.

In other words, the most important feature of a market investigation is that it focuses, as the name suggests, on the operation of the market as a whole, rather than on the way in which a single firm, or agreement, operates. There is no 'blame' attached to those undertakings which are subject to market investigations. It would be entirely possible for a market investigation to proceed to conclusion, for adverse effects to be identified, and for remedies to be put in place, with no individual firm being condemned. Indeed, there is no procedure for such a condemnation, and firms may only be penalized where they do not confirm to procedural requirements in relation to market investigations, or where they subsequently breach obligations either entered into voluntarily, or imposed upon them, under this Part of the Act. An OFT guideline, *Market Investigation References*, was published in March 2003 (hereinafter 'the Guideline'), and the CC too has published guidance in this area. It is anticipated that there will be approximately two or three market investigations a year, a figure in line with the number of complex monopoly references under the FTA 1973.

17.2 Relationship of market investigations to the Competition Act 1998 and EC law

It surprised a number of commentators that the Government left in place the monopoly provisions of the FTA 1973 at the time when the Chapter II Prohibition of the Competition Act 1998 (CA 98) was introduced into domestic law. In practice, however, the scale monopoly provisions of the FTA 1973, which applied to single firm conduct, were never used after the entry into force of the Chapter II Prohibition, although the complex monopoly provisions were. During the committee discussions about the Enterprise Bill the Government indicated that

In general we would expect the OFT to use the Competition Act in cases in which it suspects that the Act's prohibitions on anti-competitive agreements or abuse of dominance are being infringed, and market investigation powers in cases in which the Act is not applicable. Whenever the choice is less straightforward, the decision about which powers to use will be at the OFT's discretion, on examination of all the facts of the case in question. (Hansard, Standing Committee B, 1 May 2002, col. 427).

The OFT has made the position more emphatic in its Guideline, stating that it will only proceed to a market investigation where either: (1) there are reasonable grounds to suspect that market features prevent, restrict, or distort competition, but are not actionable under the CA 98; or (2) action is possible under the CA 98 but it is likely to be ineffective in dealing with the adverse effects on competition (para. 2.3). The circumstances in which this might be the case are broadly considered in para. 2.8 where it is argued that there may be situations in which anti-competitive conduct by a single firm is 'associated with structural features of the market, for example by barriers to entry or regulation'. In such a situation, it is suggested that a market investigation may be a more appropriate solution than a CA 98 action. However, in this respect it should be noted also that the market investigation provisions were brought forward before the final shape of Regulation 1/2003 became clear. Under the older Regulation 17 structural remedies were not available to the competition authorities to resolve breaches of arts 81 and 82 EC (and by implication via s. 60, CA 98 breaches of the Chapter I Prohibition and the Chapter II Prohibition) save in the most exceptional circumstances. However, under Regulation 1/2003 structural remedies are expressly provided for at art. 7 (see Chapter 6). While these are only to be employed in restricted circumstances, it is likely that these would encompass precisely the concerns mooted by the OFT at para. 2.8. In other words, the presence of structural remedies under the CA 98 eliminate the need for market investigations in respect of single firm conduct falling within the Chapter II Prohibition. Thus situations such as the one examined in relation to the supply of raw unprocessed milk in 2000, in which the CC, using its FTA 1973 powers, recommended the break-up of Milk Marque, the dominant undertaking in this market, might not proceed to a market investigation reference in future (*Milk: A report on the supply in Great Britain of raw cows' milk*, Cm. 4286, 2000).

Most market investigations are likely therefore to relate to situations of non-collusive oligopoly, typically markets with a relatively small number of participants (although this has not always been the case in the past), recognizing a degree of interdependence, but nevertheless taking decisions unilaterally, and tending to act in the same, or similar, way. Such situations are not caught by art. 81 EC unless there is at least a 'concerted practice' (see Chapter 9), as the essential requirement of art. 81 is that there be some coordination between the undertakings in question. However, the concept of dominance may, as we have seen in Chapter 14, be applicable to situations of 'collective dominance', in which more than one undertaking enjoys a dominant position by virtue of the structure of the market, or links between the undertakings falling short of collusion (see in particular *Airtours plc v Commission* case T–342/99 [2002] 5 CMLR 7 at para. 62—discussed at 19.2.2.4.1). It will be remembered that it is a requirement of Regulation 1/2003 that Member States applying their own competition law to situations falling within arts 81 and 82 must first apply the relevant EC article, and may not subsequently in the application of their domestic law reach a situation which is in conflict with the result obtained under EC law (Regulation 1/2003, art. 3(1)—see generally Chapter 3). At the same time art. 3(2) expressly provides that 'Member States shall not under this Regulation be precluded from adopting and applying on their territory stricter national laws which prohibit or sanction unilateral conduct engaged in by undertakings'. In the OFT Guideline it is recognized that the relevant law in respect of collective dominance is 'underdeveloped' (para. 2.5), and it is likely that in the vast majority of situations in which market investigations will be carried out a collective dominant position subject to the application of art. 82 EC would not be found to exist. It is possible that anti-competitive agreements, and in particular vertical agreements, might be identified to exist in the course of a market investigation, in which case these would need to be dealt with by way of the application of art. 81 EC.

17.3 **The making of market investigation references**

Section 131(1) of the Enterprise Act 2002 is in the following terms:

The OFT may, subject to subsection (4), make a reference to the Commission if the OFT has reasonable grounds for suspecting that any feature, or combination of features, of a market in the United Kingdom for goods or services prevents, restricts or distorts competition in connection with the supply or acquisition of any goods or services in the United Kingdom or a part of the United Kingdom.

In addition to the OFT the relevant sector regulators (see Chapter 2), as a consequence of amendments to the relevant pieces of legislation, also have the power to make references in respect of the industries for which they are responsible, as does the Minister in limited circumstances (s. 132(3)). The reference to the 'Commission' here is to the CC. Section 131(2) goes on further to state that

For the purposes of this Part any reference to a feature of a market in the United Kingdom for goods or services shall be construed as a reference to—

- (a) the structure of the market concerned or any aspect of that structure;
- (b) any conduct (whether or not in the market concerned) of one or more than one person who supplies or acquires goods or services in the market concerned; or
- (c) any conduct relating to the market concerned of customers of any person who supplies or acquires goods or services.

For the purposes of these provisions 'conduct' includes not only positive actions, but also failures to act, and any unintentional conduct (s. 131(3)). Thus, for example, conduct could include a failure to supply certain categories of customers, or a failure to compete on price where price competition might be expected and/or desirable.

In the Guideline the OFT has set out its basic position in relation to the making of references at para. 2.1:

The OFT will only make references to the CC when the reference test set out in section 131 and, in its view, each of the following criteria have been met:

- — it would not be more appropriate to deal with the competition issues identified by applying CA98 or using other powers available to the OFT or, where appropriate, to sectoral regulators
- — it would not be more appropriate to address the problem identified by means of undertakings in lieu of a reference
- — the scale of the suspected problem, in terms of its adverse effect on competition, is such that a reference would be an appropriate response to it
- — there is a reasonable chance that the appropriate remedies will be available.

It appears therefore to be the case that a market investigation is seen as a measure of last resort, to be employed only when other powers are not suitable to the task.

Before making a reference the OFT is obliged to consult any person on whom the decision is 'likely to have a substantial impact' (s. 169(1)), and when it gives its decisions is required to state the reason for the making of the reference (see the discussion of the store cards reference at 17.7 below). Persons who are aggrieved by a decision to make a reference may apply to the CAT for a review of that decision (s. 179(1)). Any such application must be brought within three months of the date of the making of the contested decision. The standard of review in this respect is that of judicial review, i.e., *Wednesbury* unreasonableness (*Associated Provincial Picture Houses Ltd* v *Wednesbury Corpn* [1948] 1 KB 223), and it is hard to envisage the circumstances in which the OFT would leave itself open to a successful application. A further appeal, on matters of law only, may be made against decisions of the CAT to the Court of Appeal or in Scotland, the Court of Session (s. 179(6)). The OFT has been given the power to conduct necessary investigations in s. 174. The powers in this respect are not as strong as those available under the CA 98, and do not confer on the OFT the ability to conduct 'dawn raids' or searches of company premises. The OFT can compel the attendance of witnesses and the presentation of documents.

Once a reference has been made, it may be varied subsequently although there is a duty to consult the CC before this is done. In some cases the CC itself might ask that a reference be varied. Such a scenario is discussed in para. 3.13 of the Guideline, where the OFT raises the possibility that the CC might identify markets affected by the reference which differ from those identified by the OFT (e.g., the CC might find that a market not recognized as being affected in fact is, or it might conclude that a market considered by the OFT to be a single market is in fact two or more separate markets). Where the CC asks the OFT to vary the reference so as to permit the CC to carry out further investigations the OFT has indicated that 'it is very likely that [it] would respond positively'.

17.3.1 Undertakings in lieu of references

Section 154 permits the OFT to accept undertakings in lieu of making a reference, and s. 154(2) is in the following terms:

The OFT may, instead of making such a reference and for the purpose of remedying, mitigating or preventing—

  (a) the adverse effect on competition concerned; or

  (b) any detrimental effect on customers so far as it has resulted from, or may be expected to result from, the adverse effect on competition;

accept, from such persons as it considers appropriate, undertakings to take such action as it considers appropriate.

It is not likely that such undertakings will be commonly made. First, the OFT may not be convinced, in the light of its own analysis of the situation, which would be less rigorous than that of the CC following a reference, that any undertakings offered would properly remedy the situation. Secondly:

trying to negotiate undertakings with several parties, in circumstances in which possible adverse effects on competition have not been comprehensively analysed, is likely to pose serious practical difficulties. By contrast, where an adverse effect on competition arises from the conduct of a very few firms there may be more scope for accepting undertakings in lieu, provided that the OFT is confident that they will achieve a comprehensive solution. (Guideline, para. 2.21)

17.4 **Market investigations and the CC**

Any reference made by the OFT, other regulator, or Minister, is made to the CC. Once a reference is made the CC it has up to two years in which to make its report on the matters referred (s. 137(1)), although it is hoped that the majority of investigations will be completed in a shorter period than this. The first reference made under these provisions, in relation to store cards, is discussed at 17.7 below. Section 134 of the Enterprise Act 2002 (EA 02) states that the primary role of the CC is to determine whether there is an adverse effect on competition in relation to the referred matter. Section 134(2) provides that

For the purposes of this Part, in relation to a market investigation reference, there is an adverse effect on competition if any feature, or combination of features, of a market in the United Kingdom for relevant goods or services prevents, restricts or distorts competition in connection with the supply or acquisition of any goods or services in the United Kingdom or a part of the United Kingdom.

The reference here to 'features' of a market is deliberately broad, and relates to both the structure of a market, and the behaviour of firms on that market. It could also encompass matters such as the flow of information, or government regulation. For the purposes of carrying out a market investigation the CC has been given the necessary investigative powers (s. 176—under which powers from other parts of the Act are brought into play to govern the conduct of market investigation references). The CC may compel the attendance of witnesses and the production of documents and other necessary information, and penalties may be imposed if obligations imposed under these powers are not met.

Where the CC finds that there is an adverse effect on competition, or 'any detrimental effect on customers' (s. 134(4)(a)), it is required to determine what action should be taken, either by it or by other relevant parties, to remedy this effect. The meaning of the term 'detrimental effect on customers' is further clarified in s. 134(5) as being

(a) higher prices, lower quality or less choice of goods or services in any market in the United Kingdom (whether or not the market to which the feature or features concerned relate); or

(b) less innovation in relation to goods or services.

At this point the CC may balance the harms that arise from the conduct or structure with any claimed countervailing benefits. This is not a 'legal exception' and it does not mirror art. 81 EC, but in practice the same considerations are likely to be considered. In essence the countervailing consumer benefits are those to customers which are the mirror of the detriments referred to in s. 134(5) (s. 134(7)).

In undertaking its analysis the CC is free to set its own methodology. In its own guidelines published in relation to market investigations (*Market Investigation References: Competition Commission Guidelines*, CC3), the CC breaks the process of evaluation into two key areas: market definition; and the assessment of competition.

17.4.1 The market

Following on from the equivalent provision in the FTA 1973 the 'relevant goods or services' referred to in s. 134(1) and (2) EA 02 means 'goods or services of a description to be specified in the reference'. It is possible therefore, but unlikely, that the OFT could make a reference based on an erroneous understanding of the relevant market. In such a case it would be open to the CC to request that the reference be appropriately varied following its initial examination of the facts. The CC Guidelines *inter alia* set out the now standard approach to market definition of the SSNIP test when determining the relevant product and geographic market. The discussion in this section of the document is particularly sensitive to the problems of obtaining necessary information, and the 'cellophane fallacy'.

17.4.2 The assessment of competition

The assessment of conditions of competition on the market will include a large number of factors. At para. 3.3 of its Guidelines the CC indicates that its analysis in the first instance 'will typically include a consideration of rivalry from other firms within the market, the threat of entry and/or countervailing power of customers, but need not be restricted to these'. Inter-firm rivalry may be conditioned by factors such as market shares and concentrations. Where the potential for competition within the market is not strong, other factors need to be considered, in particular barriers to entry, expansion, and exit. Other factors influencing competition within a market where the structure is not conducive to competition might include countervailing buyer power, supplier power, the extent of vertical integration, switching costs facing customers who wish to change their supplier (i.e., the expense of actually moving from one supplier to another), and information problems.

The primary distinguishing feature of market investigations, noted above, is the ability of the OFT and CC to deal with non-collusive coordinated conduct. This cannot be tackled via a prohibition on illegal agreements or other forms of active coordination, as there is no active behaviour to condemn. Neither can it be dealt with on the basis of the application of art. 82 EC or the Chapter II Prohibition, unless the relevant markets are characterized by at most three firms (although not impossible it is highly unlikely that the law of 'collective dominance' could be applied to four or more firms; the EC Commission indicated as much in the case of *Price Waterhouse/Coopers and Lybrand* 1999/152 (1999) OJ L50/27, when it held that collective dominance involving more than three or four suppliers would be unlikely because of the complexity of the interrelationships involved, and the consequent temptation to deviate (see paras 94–119). The basic dynamics of such a situation are explained at para. 3.58 of the CC Guidelines:

Where markets are sufficiently concentrated, the actions of individual firms can have identifiable effects on their competitors, such that firms recognise their interdependence. The interdependence of oligopolistic firms may lead them to anticipate competitors' responses to their own actions and take this into account in their own decisions. If, as will often be the case, this interdependence persists through time in such markets, the repeated nature of such decisions can have significant effects on business strategies and on competition. In particular, under certain conditions discussed below, it can become rational to refrain from initiating price cuts which would be unavoidable in more competitive circumstances.

A further possible outcome in such markets is that 'price increases by one firm to levels that might otherwise have been uncompetitive may well prove profitable' (para. 3.60). Markets with these features were regularly investigated under the complex monopoly provisions of the FTA 1973. The problem of coordinated effects, as the CC refers to this position, may also be dealt with under the EC merger regulation (see Chapter 19), but the law in this respect has yet to develop to maturity. The CC Guidelines provide a clear discussion of the factors which may underpin such markets, and a large part of this section is reproduced here:

3.62 A number of conditions are necessary for such behaviour to occur and be sustainable through time. First, the market has to be sufficiently concentrated for firms to be aware of the behaviour of their competitors, and for any significant deviation from the prevailing behaviour by a firm to be observed by other firms in the market. Where prices are transparent any deviation from the prevailing behaviour will be clear. However, even where they are not transparent, as is often the case in intermediate markets, any deviation from the prevailing behaviour by a competitor may nonetheless be readily apparent, because the essence of interdependence is that price cuts by one firm will have a significant impact on others' volumes.

3.63 Secondly, it must be clear that it will be costly for firms to deviate from the prevailing behaviour; so costly that it will be in a firm's interests to go along with the prevailing behaviour rather than seek to deviate from it. In many cases, the mere fact of the interdependence and hence the strong likelihood of a matching price cut may be enough to create such a disincentive. Timing will, however, be significant here. If prices can be adjusted quickly then such a response is very likely, but in markets where prices can only be set infrequently, the short-term gains from lower prices until a response is possible could outweigh the long-term gains of higher oligopolistic prices. If price setting is very infrequent then the basic perception of interdependence may cease to hold at all.

3.64 Thirdly, this type of parallelism can only be sustained in markets where there are relatively weak competitive constraints. If barriers to entry are low, then the threat of entry will tend to undermine such conduct. Alternatively, if there is a fringe of other firms in a market outside the core oligopolists, and if the competitive fringe firms have both the incentive to undercut and scope to attract significant volume away from the core oligopolists, then an uncompetitive price level is unlikely to be sustainable.

A number of factors are set out which might tend to reinforce the tendency of a market towards the production of coordinated effects. These include most obviously the degree of concentration in the market, and the presence of entry barriers protecting the incumbent firms from the disruption new entrants would bring with them. Other factors include the degree of transparency in the market (the more information that flows the more likely it is that firms will tend to move towards a common position), and the homogeneity of the product(s) in question.

It will not always be the case that a simple examination of the conditions of competition will produce a clear picture of the actual way in which competition is working in practice, and in particular whether there are the adverse effects the CC is directed to consider. The outcomes of competition can be as important in this respect as the conditions of competition, and the CC will examine evidence in this respect as part of its overall investigation. The most obvious factor to consider in this respect is that of prices. While a straightforward assessment of whether prices are 'high' or 'low' may appear superficially attractive, any such consideration would be subject to value judgements as to what constitutes a high or low price. More useful is consideration of the movements of prices over time. Typically price fluctuations between firms may be indicative of price competition, as firms vie with each other to win customers, whereas price stability might be indicative of a coordinated effect (see para. 3.79 of the Guidelines). Another indication of the state of competition might be the amount of profits being made by participants in that market. However, this analysis can be fraught with difficulty. The essence of the position taken by the CC is explained in the Guidelines in the following terms:

3.81 Profitability is the crucial incentive and signal in a market economy and high profits by individual companies at various times are fully consistent with competitive markets. More generally, a competitive market is likely to generate significant variations in profit levels between firms as supply and demand conditions change, but with an overall tendency towards levels commensurate with the cost of capital of the firms involved. At points in time, the profits of some firms may exceed what might be termed the 'normal' level. Reasons for this could include, for instance, cyclical factors, transitory price or other initiatives, the fact that some firms may be more efficient than others and, the fact that some firms may be earning profits gained as a result of past innovation. However, in nearly all cases competition should result in pressure on profit levels towards the cost of capital in the medium to long run.

3.82 However, a situation where, persistently, profits are substantially in excess of the cost of capital for firms that represent a substantial part of the market could be an indication of limitations in the competitive process. For instance, in some cases a high level of profitability could be indicative of significantly coordinated behaviour.

It must also be recognized that low profits may also be indicative of ineffective competition, if they are suggestive of inefficiencies that can be maintained because firms lack the discipline imposed by effective competition.

International price comparisons may also be invoked, although the CC is aware that the scope to use them as an indication of a lack of competition is limited, and that a number of factors need to be considered in order to be able to make a useful comparison. Such comparisons have been made in the past however, perhaps most significantly in the FTA 1973 report *New Cars* (discussed at 17.8.5 below).

17.5 **Remedies**

Where the CC identifies adverse effects s. 138 of the Enterprise Act 2002 creates an obligation on it to

take such action under section 159 or 160 as it considers to be reasonable and practicable—

(a) to remedy, mitigate or prevent the adverse effect on competition concerned; and

(b) to remedy, mitigate or prevent any detrimental effects on customers so far as they have resulted from, or may be expected to result from, the adverse effect on competition.

Section 134(6) further requires the CC

in particular to have regard to the need to achieve as comprehensive a solution as is reasonable and practicable to the adverse effect on competition and any detrimental effects on customers so far as resulting from the adverse effect on competition.

Part 4 of the CC Guidelines deals with the remedying of the adverse effects. The general position is that it is unlikely that the CC would identify an adverse effect and not at the same time impose a remedy for this. However, there could be some circumstances where no remedies will be put forward. This could include situations where any remedy would be ineffective due to international factors (remedies cannot be imposed outside the UK). Apart from some statutory limits there are virtually no restrictions on the remedies which the CC may seek to impose in market investigation reference cases. Remedies set out in the Guidelines include: divestment; the reduction of barriers to entry; behavioural orders; price caps; and monitoring remedies (which might include, e.g., the imposition of a requirement to report regularly to the OFT with certain information).

Under investigations carried out under the FTA 1973 a great many different remedies have at different times been set, although the procedure for their implementation was very different. Price controls were, for example, imposed on British Telecommunications plc in respect of its advertising rates for its *Yellow Pages* publications in July 1996 following the publication of the MMC report, *Classified Directory Advertising Services* (Cm. 3171, March 1996). In 2001 the operation of the undertaking given by BT in relation to prices was reviewed by the OFT (*Classified Directory Advertising Services; Review of undertakings given by BT to the Secretary of State in July 1996*, OFT 332, May 2001 [2001] UKCLR 1140). At this time the OFT recommended that the price cap be tightened, BT's profits from publishing the *Yellow Pages* directories having remained exceptionally high, but along with this greater restriction it also recommended that a number of other undertakings be relaxed. A further survey of some of the more recent FTA cases is provided later in this chapter.

17.5.1 **Undertakings and orders**

There are two main mechanisms by which remedies required under this Part of the Act may be created. These are by way of undertakings, and by orders. Undertakings are entered into voluntarily by the parties, and orders are imposed upon them. However, once undertakings are entered into they become binding and are enforceable before the courts.

The possibility for the OFT to accept undertakings in lieu of making a market investigation reference to the CC has already been noted above at 17.3.1. Interim and final undertakings may be sought by the CC or, in the case where a public interest consideration is invoked (see below), by the Secretary of State. In all cases the party requiring the undertaking may subsequently release the parties from it if it is appropriate to do so. Orders may be made at both the interim and final stage in the proceedings, and may contain anything set out in Schedule 8 to the Act. The list here is very wide indeed. Where orders and undertakings are not complied with they may be enforced by way of civil proceedings brought against the wrongdoers by the OFT for an injunction, interdict, or any other appropriate remedy or relief (s. 167(6)). Third parties who are harmed by non-compliance are also able to take action, and can seek damages or other relief as appropriate (s. 167(4)).

17.6 Public interest cases

In exceptional cases the Secretary of State for Trade and Industry can become involved in market investigations. This situation can arise only where a public interest issue, as provided for in s. 152, has been raised. At the time of Royal Assent the only such interest was specified to be that of public security, although the power was left open to add to this list. Where a public interest issue arises the Secretary of State may issue an intervention notice (s. 140). Where any such notice is in force the CC is required to determine, in addition to the competition questions, whether further action is required in light of the public interest consideration. It is then up to the Secretary of State, within 90 days of the delivery of the report, to publish a decision as to the matters raised.

17.7 Store card services

The first market investigation reference made by the OFT to the CC was on 18 March 2004 and related to the supply of store card services (OFT press release 47/04, 18 March 2004). Concerns in relation to the transparency of credit card terms were raised by the Treasury Select Committee, and the OFT launched a store cards study in response (published as OFT 706 *Store Cards*, March 2004). This study was undertaken on the basis of the broad power in s. 5 of the Enterprise Act 2002 under which '[t]he OFT has the function of obtaining, compiling and keeping under review information about matters relating to the carrying out of its functions'. The OFT found that in 2002 store card new business was worth £4.8 bn, and accounted for 2.5 per cent of total consumer credit gross lending. Recognizing that store card use was a relatively small part of the total credit business the OFT nevertheless noted that the overall sums of money involved were large, and that there was a substantial disparity between the interest rates charged on credit cards, and those levied on store cards. The OFT found a number of features which appeared to prevent, restrict, or distort competition in the market for the supply of store card credit services to retailers, and also in connection with the provision of consumer credit through store cards. While progress was being made in relation to the lack of transparency in the way in which store cards were offered and used the OFT remained concerned that not enough was being done in this respect. A survey carried out as a 'mystery shopping exercise' found, for example, that only 23 per cent of shoppers were offered the opportunity to take copies of agreements away and read them at leisure before signing up to the card, and 75 per cent of the remaining customers were refused the opportunity to do so when they asked. This was contrary to information given to the OFT by the card providers themselves. Other problems identified included: a limited ability of card providers to expand their share of supply of store card services to retailers due to substantial barriers to entry and switching; and the fact that users of store cards were not readily able to assess the costs and benefits associated with their use. The broad conclusion of the OFT in this respect was that 'there is insufficient competition to ensure that consumers get good value, and that retailers . . . may be able to increase their profits by the lack of transparency as to the value for money from using store cards' (OFT 706, para. 1.11). Following the necessary consultations under s. 169, EA 02, the OFT took the view that a full CC investigation would establish whether there were adverse effects on competition and made the reference accordingly. It should be noted that the burdens imposed by this process must presumably be considerable. The OFT's report of its own inquiry, which lasted some six months, runs to 108 pages, and the investigation before the CC is likely to be lengthy and expensive. The terms of reference to the CC are given here in full:

The OFT, in exercise of its powers under section 131 of the Enterprise Act 2002, hereby makes a reference to the Competition Commission for an investigation into the supply of the following services (the reference services) in the United Kingdom:

(a) store card credit services to retailers and services related thereto (store card credit services); and

(b) consumer credit through store cards.

The OFT has reasonable grounds for suspecting that a feature or a combination of features of the markets in which the reference services are supplied prevent, restrict or distort competition in connection with the supply of the reference services in the United Kingdom. For the purposes of this reference:

'Store card' means a payment card issued with respect to the purchase of the goods, services or facilities of only one retailer or of retailers who are members of a single group of interconnected bodies corporate or who trade under a common name and which permits the holder of the payment card under his contract with the issuer of the card to discharge less than the whole of any outstanding balance on his payment card account on or before the expiry of a specified period (subject to any contractual requirements with respect to minimum or fixed amounts of payment).

'Payment card' means a card, the use of which enables the person to whom it is issued ('the holder') to discharge his obligation to a supplier in respect of payment for the acquisition of goods, services or facilities.

'Issuer' means a person who contracts or proposes to contract with a consumer for the issue of a store card.

17.8 Conduct against the public interest considered under the FTA 1973

It will take a number of years before a pattern emerges in the approach taken by the OFT and CC to conduct which prevents, restricts, or distorts competition. However, although the wording of the test under the FTA 1973 was very different, a consideration of the application of the FTA 1973 to both scale and complex monopoly situations may be instructive as to the sorts of issues that may be raised in market investigation references, and the remedies that might be imposed. The test set out in the FTA 1973 was a 'public interest' test (which bears no relation to public interest considerations that may be raised by the Secretary of State in relation to market investigation references), and this was heavily and often criticized as being imprecise. Section 84(1) of the Act required the CC (or in the case of the majority of these investigations, the MMC) to have regard to a number of matters, of which the first was 'the desirability (a) of maintaining and promoting effective competition between persons supplying goods and services in the United Kingdom'. Subsection (b) required the CC to consider the interests of consumers, purchasers, and other users of goods and services, and subsection (c) made reference to the reduction of costs, technological development, and the entry of new competitors through competition. Although other matters could be considered, in practice the CC focused very much on competition, and in its later reports under these provisions referred almost exclusively to competition considerations. It is probably the case that all the conclusions reached in CC reports under scale and complex monopoly investigations would equally be reached were the same situations to be referred as market investigations. The discussion below is a relatively short survey of what is in fact a vast area. Although only a small number of reports were published each year, each one tended to be large, and often dealt with a number of different patterns of conduct which raised concerns.

17.8.1 Vertical restraints

Although the law on vertical restraints under art. 81 EC and the Chapter I Prohibition has now been aligned, we have seen in Chapter 8 that there has been intense debate amongst industrial economists and regulators as to the stance to be taken towards vertical restraints. On a number of occasions the MMC/CC considered the extent to which vertically integrated industries operated against the public interest. One of the more interesting reports was published in 1997 when the MMC examined the retail travel industry (*Foreign Package Holidays*, Cm. 3813, 1997). Here the MMC examined in particular the links between tour operators and the high street travel agents, the larger chains of which were owned by tour operators whose packages they sell in preference to those of other operators. It was feared by some in the industry that the MMC would demand that these vertical links be broken, perhaps by requiring divestiture. Instead the MMC required that the links between the retail and the operational arms be made more transparent to allow the consumer to be aware of the tie at the time of making the booking or purchase.

The impact of long-term supply contracts creating a vertical link between cinema chains and cinema advertising services was examined in *Cinema Advertising Services* (Cm. 1080, 1990). Here an investigation was launched following a complaint by the advertising agency Pearl & Dean Ltd to the effect that it had suffered as a result of various unfair practices engaged in by Rank Screen Advertising (RSA). The latter had exclusive access to the Odeon cinema chain, which accounted for 17 per cent of the market, and the Rank Organisation as a whole had a strong involvement in distribution. Contracts with the Cannon chain, accounting for 30 per cent of the market, extended for as long as 14 years. The OFT was concerned that these factors would exclude Pearl & Dean from large parts of the market, and that independent cinemas, dependent to a substantial degree on films released through the Rank Organisation, would be inhibited from going outside Rank for advertising services. The MMC however found that the contracts were won as the result 'of competition and [RSA] has no reason to expect criticism for this achievement', the length of the contracts arising at the request of Cannon (paras 9.36–9.42). In this case therefore the MMC found that 'neither the practice of negotiating long-term contracts nor RSA's relationship with Odeon are facts which operate, or may be expected to operate, against the public interest' (para. 9.45).

Competition authorities have given a considerable amount of attention to the issue of 'freezer exclusivity' (the supply of freezer cabinets to retailers of impulse ice cream on condition that only the supplier's ice cream be stocked in the cabinets). The MMC first considered this issue in 1994 (*Ice Cream*, Cm. 2524, 1994), and the EC Commission examined the issue over a long period of time before issuing an infringement decision in the case of *Van den Bergh Foods Ltd* 98/351 (1998) OJ L246/1. The conclusions reached by the MMC in 1994, which largely exonerated the practice, were heavily criticized and in 1999 it reconsidered the issue following a new reference by the OFT. In 2000 the CC recommended that Birds Eye Walls (BEW), the largest undertaking operating in this market in the UK, be prevented from entering into any agreement for capacity in relation to any freezer used for storage and/or the display of wrapped impulse ice cream in any outlet in Great Britain, unless it made available 50 per cent of the display space, and the full storage space, to competing manufacturers of impulse ice cream products (*The Supply of Impulse Ice Cream*, Cm. 4510, 2000). Undertakings were accepted from BEW in April 2000 (DTI press release P/2000/260, 7 April 2000). The treatment of the distribution channel operated by BEW in this case in effect recognized it as an 'essential facility', and followed the approach suggested by the ECJ in *Oscar Bronner GmbH* v *Mediaprint Zeitungs GmbH* case C–7/97 [1999] 4 CMLR 112, although some commentators have doubted that a distribution network could constitute an essential facility in the light of this judgment. It should also be noted that this case was treated as a scale monopoly (BEW holding more than 25 per cent of the relevant market). It is possible that were the situation to arise today it would be dealt with under the application of the CA 98.

17.8.2 Full-line forcing, tie-in sales, and line discounts

Full-line forcing requires a customer to accept all of a supplier's range of products, denying the customer the opportunity to purchase selectively. This may serve as a barrier to entry to a competitor competing on only a limited range of options. Tie-in sales tie the supply of one product to supply of another. The MMC considered both practices in a subject-specific report, *Full-line Forcing and Tie-in Sales* (HC 212, 1981). The general view taken by the MMC was that these practices are neither 'consistently harmful, beneficial or neutral but [depend] on the circumstances' (see *Tambrands Ltd*, Cm. 3168, 1996, para. 2.35). In the Tambrands report the MMC investigation (under the now-defunct Competition Act 1980) was triggered by a complaint from a supermarket chain, which argued that the monopoly supplier of tampons was structuring incentives to retailers in such a way that the stocking of competing brands of tampons was impeded. Tambrands accepted that its policy was to 'get the broadest possible distribution of its product range . . . and that the range-stocking requirement could be expected to benefit new products' (para. 2.29). The MMC found that, in the context of the case, such a requirement was not anti-competitive. Similar conclusions were reached in respect of perfumes (*Fine Fragrances*, Cm. 2380, 1993). On the other hand, in *Carbonated Drinks* (Cm. 1625, 1991) the MMC concluded that the operation of minimum-stock requirements and exclusivity by Coca-Cola & Schweppes Beverages Ltd contributed to the already significant barriers to entry in the market for carbonated drinks, and fell to be condemned.

On two occasions the MMC examined the practice of tying sales of toner to the supply of photocopiers. Following the first such report (HC 47, 1976–77) Rank Xerox gave undertakings to the Secretary of State, which included an obligation to permit all customers, before entering into an agreement, to buy toner independently of the supply of the photocopier, and commitments to transparent pricing. When Rank Xerox sought to be released from this undertaking in 1983 the MMC partially accepted that manufacturers had 'a legitimate interest in seeking to ensure that suitable toner is used in their machines' (Cm. 1963, 1991, para. 9.118) and found the market at the level of the supply of photocopiers themselves to be competitive, such that a supplier seeking to impose a tie faced competitive pressures. In conclusion the MMC did not object to Rank Xerox being released from the earlier undertakings, although in 1997 the OFT indicated that it still considered that some problems remained ('Photocopier Industry Cleans up its Selling Practices', OFT press release 9/97, 20 March 1997). In *Matches and Disposable Lighters* (Cm. 1854, 1992), the MMC found that the existence of range-stocking requirements imposed by Bryant & May in relation to its matches and lighters operated against the public interest, on the grounds that 'customers are likely to buy less matches and disposable lighters from Bryant & May's competitors than they would do otherwise' (para. 7.50).

17.8.3 Anti-competitive use of property rights

On a number of occasions the MMC (and the OFT) considered whether property rights—whether in real or intellectual property—were being exploited in such a way as to be contrary to the public interest. The OFT had made the basic position clear in *The Southern Vectis Omnibus Company Limited: refusal to allow access to Newport Bus Station, Isle of Wight* (1988), when it stated that

it has been established that where the effect is to restrict, distort or prevent competition, the manner in which property rights are exercised may amount to an anti-competitive practice as defined in the Competition Act 1980.   (para. 7.4)

The argument is more controversial when made in respect of intellectual property, which is in essence the grant of a legalized monopoly by the state as a reward for the invention or creation. The MMC expressed concerns about the potential exploitation of intellectual property in *Ford Motor Company Ltd* (Cmnd. 9437, 1985). In this case the MMC found that the practice of Ford in refusing to grant licences to any person to manufacture or sell spare parts for its cars, reinforced through reliance on copyright, was against the public interest. At the time the MMC did not have the power to compel the compulsory licensing of intellectual property, and subsequently changes were made to the law in the Copyright, Designs and Patents Act 1988, at s. 144, which provides in part:

144 Powers exercisable in consequence of report of Competition Commission

(1) Subsection (1A) applies where whatever needs to be remedied, mitigated or prevented by the Secretary of State, the Office of Fair Trading or (as the case may be) the Competition Commission under section 12(5) of the Competition Act 1980 or section 41(2), 55(2), 66(6), 75(2), 83(2), 138(2), 147(2) or 160(2) of, or paragraph 5(2) or 10(2) of Schedule 7 to, the Enterprise Act 2002 (powers to take remedial action following references to the Commission in connection with public bodies and certain other persons, mergers or market investigations) consists of or includes—

(a) conditions in licences granted by the owner of copyright in a work restricting the use of the work by the licensee or the right of the copyright owner to grant other licences; or

(b) a refusal of a copyright owner to grant licences on reasonable terms.

(1A) The powers conferred by Schedule 8 to the Enterprise Act 2002 include power to cancel or modify those conditions and, instead or in addition, to provide that licences in respect of the copyright shall be available as of right.

The reference here to the Enterprise Act means that where the CC feels the need to compel that copyright be licensed in order to remedy an adverse situation under a market investigation it has the power to do so.

17.8.4 Advertising issues

In a number of reports in 1976 the MMC looked at restrictions on the advertising of professional services (professions examined included accountants, solicitors in England and Wales, and separately in Scotland, barristers, and veterinary surgeons). In these reports the MMC took a sceptical stance towards claims that restrictions on advertising were necessary to ensure the reputation of the industry. Later, in *Osteopaths* (Cm. 583, 1989) the MMC recommended that advertising restrictions be lifted, noting that the British Code of Advertising Practice would provide some safeguards to consumers. A good discussion of issues relating to such advertising may be found in 'Advertising restrictions in professional services' in Amato, G., and Laudati, L. L., *The Anti-competitive Impact of Regulation* Cheltenham, Edward Elgar (2001).

17.8.5 Recent FTA 1973 investigations

More recent FTA 1973 complex monopoly investigations include the 2000 report *New Cars: A report on the supply of new motor cars within the UK* (Cm. 4660, 2000) in which the CC found that 'prices paid by UK private customers are currently likely to be, on average, about 10 per cent too high' (para. 1.17). Following the report the DTI entered into a consultation process with the industry designed to even the balance between individual and fleet purchasers. In *Supermarkets: A report on the supply of groceries from multiple stores in the UK* (Cm. 4842, 2000), the CC found that the industry was 'currently overall broadly competitive and that, overall, excessive prices are not being charged, nor excessive profits earned' (para. 1.13). However, the CC did accept that some problems were raised in certain areas of the UK by virtue of a limited choice for end consumers of supermarkets, and noted that these problems were exacerbated by a shortage of suitable land on which to build new outlets. In an unusually prescriptive recommendation the CC suggested that 'in certain clearly defined circumstances, the [OFT's] approval should be required for particular parties to be allowed to acquire or develop large new stores' (para. 1.1.3) and that the OFT should develop a specialist, albeit small, unit to deal with these cases. Other recommendations were also made, and in December 2001 a 'behaviour code for supermarkets and suppliers' was accepted by the supermarket chains (DTI press release P/201/725, 18 December 2001).

A substantial report was published in 2002 into *The supply of banking services by clearing banks to small and medium-sized enterprises within the UK* (Cm. 5319, March 2002) in which the CC identified a number of problems in the industry, and made several recommendations designed to alleviate them. These included a suggestion that the eight main clearing banks make it easier for customers to move between them, that they provide better information on alternative suppliers, and make banking statements clearer. It was also recommended that the four main clearing banks offer to all small and medium-sized enterprises an account that paid interest at the Bank of England base rate less 2.5 per cent, or one on which there were no charges, or a choice of the two (para. 2.609). Each of the banks agreed to implement this latter remedy by no later than 1 January 2003 (DTI press release P/2002/469, 18 July 2002). In April 2003 the CC made ten recommendations in relation to the supply of veterinary services. *Inter alia* these included a recommendation to the effect that all vets should display a large and prominent sign notifying customers of the charges made by vets for medicines, along with information relating to other sources of supply (*Veterinary medicines: A report on the supply within the United Kingdom of prescription-only veterinary medicines*, Cm. 5781, April 2003). At the time of writing the most recently published report was the voluminous *Extended warranties on domestic electrical goods: A report on the supply of extended warranties on domestic electrical goods within the UK* (Cm. 6089, December 2003). Here the CC identified a number of factors which were harmful. Amongst other concerns, the CC found that 'providers limited the choice of product, and limited the provision of relevant information about that product and alternatives (including price information)' (para. 1.16). In part as a result of this the larger retailers and manufacturers were able to charge excessive prices, and were making very significant profits. Two packages of possible remedies were advanced by the CC, with the majority of the reference panel finding in favour of 'package two' which consisted of four main features: (1) a requirement preventing retailers from selling extended warranties of longer than one year's duration; (2) a requirement to display the extended warranty price alongside the display price of the product itself; (3) a right on the part of a customer to cancel extended warranties, and to obtain a pro-rata money refund; and (4) the provision of a full standard information leaflet setting out information on statutory rights, and on the availability of other extended warranties.

17.9 Conclusion

While market investigation references have not received the attention that has fallen on the cartel offence—for perhaps understandable reasons—the weapon is potentially very useful indeed. There are likely to be two or three such references a year, and these are most likely to be focused on oligopolistic markets. These markets defy analysis under either the 'agreements' route, or the 'dominance' route, and the power to impose remedies under the Act is virtually unfettered. Under the Fair Trading Act 1973 a similar procedure led to sometimes impressive results (as we have seen above). It remains to be seen how effective market investigation references will be in the future.

18

An introduction to the economics
of merger control

18.1 Introduction

Even those commentators and analysts who would argue that competition law
should be greatly curtailed on the grounds that its application causes more harm
than good would in most cases support the existence of some form of merger
control. However the economics of merger control is not a matter that has been
subject to a great deal of scrutiny until recently. For a fuller discussion of the issues
dealt with here see Bishop, S., and Walker, M., *The Economics of EC Competition Law*,
London, Sweet & Maxwell (2nd edn, 2002), ch. 7.

In this brief chapter we will deal with the key arguments that underpin the policy
goals behind merger control. In essence these relate to two factors: first, the
creation or extension of monopoly power, including the raising of barriers to entry
for potential competitors; and secondly, increasing the scope for collusion in a
market which, post-merger, will be more oligopolistic and less competitive than
was the market pre-merger. It will be noted that the first of these two factors is
related to the control of dominant firm conduct, and that, as we have already
seen, dominance itself is not condemned in either the EC or the UK. Nevertheless
in merger control we find a situation where the attainment or extension of
dominance may be condemned.

The greatest procedural difference between merger control and the control of
dominance post-merger is that any analysis of a merger will usually be undertaken
ex ante, and any assessment of dominant firm behaviour will always be made
ex post. The assessment of individual mergers may therefore be particularly contentious as the undertakings concerned and the authorities are arguing on the basis of
anticipated, rather than *actual*, results, and the scope of the transactions concerned
is sometimes very substantial.

For the present purposes the term 'merger' will be taken to refer to any situation
in which the ownership of two or more undertakings is joined together. In the
world of business the process that may lead to this joining of ownership may take
many different forms, and may be either amicable and consensual, or unwelcome
and hostile. In Community law the term used in preference to 'merger' is 'concentration' and a concentration is deemed to arise where there is a merger of 'two or
more previously independent undertakings or parts of undertakings' (Regulation

139/2004, art. 3(1)(a)), or where an undertaking or person controlling an undertaking acquires control of another undertaking (art. 3(1)(b)). The law relating to these tests is dealt with in Chapter 19.

Mergers may take place either vertically or horizontally. The latter case, which will typically be of more concern to the competition authorities, arises where firms in the same industry, dealing in the same goods or services in the same geographic market, merge. A third type of merger, a conglomerate merger, may also be identified. A conglomerate merger is one in which firms produce products which are not in the same market, but which may to a greater or lesser extent be substitutes for each other. Although merger activity tends to fluctuate depending on the state of the economy and of the structure of particular industries the statistics show that the majority of mergers are horizontal ones, although in the 1960s there was in the United States a wave of conglomerate mergers in response to the harsh line being taken towards horizontal mergers by the antitrust authorities.

Mergers take place, like most business moves, primarily in order to increase profits. This may come about either because the effect of the merger is to reduce competition between the participants to the merger, or where the merger leads to cost savings through the gaining of efficiencies as a result of the joining of assets and fixed factors of production, allowing prices to be reduced and market shares to be increased. Increased concentration however will not inevitably lead to increased profits, and in some situations it may be demonstrated that the combined profits of a merged entity might be lower than the profits of the two independent undertakings were pre-merger. The argument whereby this result is achieved is a technical one.

A merger might have advantages over other forms of expansion (internal growth is an alternative to a merger). If an undertaking is seeking to increase its market share, the alternative to a merger is to expand production unilaterally. The result of this will be to lead to lower prices across the industry, and lower profit margins, and the ultimate impact on market shares will be uncertain *ex ante*. A merger may have particular advantages when an undertaking wishes to diversify into a market in which it is not presently based, overcoming barriers to entry, and again avoiding intense competition should the incumbent choose to defend its territory. Mergers also allow a much quicker, and a more certain response than does a strategy of internal growth. It might take only three months for a significant merger to yield results, but several years for the same results to be achieved by way of a 'competitive' process.

Mergers may also be undertaken for other reasons than merely to increase profits. In uncertain markets a merger may reflect differing views on future market performance among differing entrepreneurs. One owner may take a dim view of long-term market prospects, and another may anticipate brighter prospects. This might lead the former to be susceptible to offers from the latter. In some cases mergers might be driven by the desire of business leaders to manage a larger entity, and perhaps to operate at a global, rather than local, level. Even in this case however the rational entrepreneur would be presumed still to be making profit-maximizing decisions.

The fact that mergers take place for diverse reasons, and that the outcomes cannot be certain, suggests that a per se rule prohibiting mergers should be rejected, and that mergers should be assessed on a case-by-case basis. This is the process that exists in the EC and the UK, as well as the USA, although in the case of horizontal mergers there are some presumptions relating to the size of market shares pre- and post-merger which may come into play.

18.2 Horizontal mergers

Horizontal mergers may be substitutable for cartels, and Neumann points to the fact that 'in the US, after cartels were declared illegal by the Sherman Act, they were replaced by mergers which could more effectively be defended by invoking the rule of reason' (Neumann, M., *Competition Policy: History, Theory and Practice*, Cheltenham, Edward Elgar (2001), p. 113). The very fact that this is true suggests that horizontal mergers should be treated with some suspicion. However, the position is not a straightforward one. Cartels may self-destruct, but will in most cases be less efficient than mergers. Mergers are likely to be more efficient than cartels as they may generate economies of scale and of scope, but they are structurally embedded in a way that cartels are not. The key issue with horizontal mergers is that they may allow market power to be wielded, either by single-firm monopolists, or by collusive oligopolies. The EC Commission has produced a *Notice on the appraisal of horizontal mergers* (2004) OJ C31/5, which should be referred to for further discussion.

18.2.1 The creation of a monopoly

The situation in which a merger creates a single-firm monopoly, or adds to the power of a single-firm monopoly, is relatively straightforward, and follows the relevant economic processes concerning monopoly conduct. Where the effect of a merger is to substantially lessen competition, or to create or strengthen a dominant position as a result of which competition will be impaired, the merger is likely to be blocked. As we have seen in relation to monopolies, harm may be presumed to flow from the mere fact of the existence of a monopoly. However, as there are substantial harms in misapplying regulation or competition-law solutions to what may be later shown to have been efficient conduct, and as most monopolies will over time be eroded, the existence of monopoly itself is not condemned. Nevertheless, in the case where it can be clearly demonstrated that a single, preventable, transaction will lead to the creation of a monopoly there are strong policy reasons why that transaction should be prevented. Of course the analysis needed to demonstrate that a monopoly will be created is not always straightforward, and the concept of market definition was first developed by the competition authorities to deal with the issue of whether a 'relevant market' was being monopolized as a result of a merger. These issues are best left to economics, and whilst the role of a legal team is likely to be of paramount importance in the process of any substantial merger, the role in relation to the substantive test of the merger's effect is likely to be less so.

18.2.2 Oligopolies and oligopolistic coordination

The Commission, in its *Notice on the appraisal of horizontal mergers*, identifies two aspects in which concerns may be raised in respect of oligopoly markets. The first of these relates to competitive oligopolies in which competitive constraints may be weakened by the fact of the merger. In these situations the Commission will pay strong attention to measures of market concentration, and will be concerned about the ability and the incentive of the merging firms to increase prices (a unilateral effect independant of any collusion).

The second area of concern, that a merger will lead to a more concentrated market in which oligopolistic collusion will be facilitated, is both theoretically and practically a difficult one. The basic danger is noted in the US DOJ *Horizontal Merger Guidelines* of 1992, s. 2.1:

A merger may diminish competition by enabling firms in the relevant market more likely, more successfully, or more completely to engage in coordinated interaction that harms consumers. Coordinated interaction is comprised of actions by a group of firms that are profitable for each of them only as a result of the accommodating reactions of the others. This behaviour includes tacit or express collusion, and may or may not be lawful in and of itself.

The Commission approach is similar, emphasizing that a change in the market structure may be such that firms would consider it possible, rational, and therefore preferable , to coordinate activity on the market such that prices would be set above competitive levels, but without any agreement to this effect being necessary.

The economic issues that arise in these cases have been examined in a number of decisions taken in the EC. These are considered in the section on 'joint dominance' at 19.2.2.4.1. The EC Commission has developed a 'checklist' of factors that it considers to be relevant to a finding of a situation in which an oligopoly can successfully coordinate action. In these cases, if the factors arise only following a merger, that merger is likely to be blocked. The factors highlighted are: concentration (probably up to a maximum of three firms), product homogeneity, symmetry of market shares and costs, transparency in pricing, the ease with which a firm may retaliate to another's competitive action, barriers to entry, inelastic demand, and absence of buyer power. It is also important that the market be relatively stable and mature. However, each of these factors should be considered carefully, as any industry is likely to show some of these features, and even if the majority of these factors are present an analysis sensitive to the particular conditions of the relevant market is necessary to determine if collusive conduct is likely to follow.

The collusion itself may take various forms. Most typically it would take the form of increasing prices, as was feared would be the case in the *Gencor/Lonhro* merger (97/26 (1997) OJ L11/30). Alternatively, as in *Airtours/First Choice* 2000/276 (2000) OJ L93/1 it may take the form of reducing capacity, or production, with the end result of increasing prices albeit in a competitive structure where price competition still existed; or it may take the form of market sharing. In each case different conditions must exist in order for such collusion to be effective. When analysing the possibility for collusion it is necessary to consider the problem in four stages. First, a plausible mechanism whereby collusion can take place must be identified. Secondly, the market must be analysed to determine whether it has within it characteristics or features which would support the suggested collusive mechanism. The third step is to identify whether those particular features exist in the particular case under consideration. The fourth step is to consider whether evidence of past conduct is suggestive that a collusive outcome might emerge in the new market situation. For example, in *Gencor/Lonhro* the Commission was concerned that there was evidence of previous collusive activity in the South African mining industry.

18.2.3 **The failing firm defence**

An argument is sometimes made that a merger which 'saves' a failing firm should not be blocked, on the grounds that were it not for the merger the market would also be more concentrated following the exit of the failing firm, and there would be social costs to this failure. Thus in the US DOJ *Horizontal Merger Guidelines* of 1992, s. 5.0 we find:

A merger is not likely to create or enhance market power or to facilitate its exercise, if imminent failure . . . of one of the merging firms would cause the assets of that firm to exit the relevant market. In such circumstances, post-merger performance in the relevant market may be no worse than market performance had the merger been blocked and the assets left the market.

This argument underlay the Competition Commission inquiry into the Air Canada and Canadian Airlines Corporation merger (Cm. 4838, August 2000). Here the Canadian Airlines Corporation would 'sooner or later run out of money' (report, para. 2.13) were it not saved by the merger. Although the Competition Commission was concerned about the reduction in competition on transatlantic routes from the UK to Canada following the merger it accepted that these were the result not directly of the merger, but of the fact that one of the parties was going out of business.

The failing firm defence was dismissed in the CC report into the Safeway merger (*Safeway plc and Asda Group Limited (owned by Wal-Mart Stores Inc); Wm Morrison Supermarkets PLC; J Sainsbury plc; and Tesco plc: A report on the mergers in contemplation* Commission, 5950, September 2003)) in which the CC considered a number of prospective mergers in what was viewed as a socially sensitive market. The CC here noted that in order to 'conclude that Safeway was failing, we would need to be satisfied that it was unable to meet its financial obligations in the near future and that in this respect it was unable to restructure itself successfully' (para 2.182). In fact, in this case, Safeway was still competing effectively, albeit not on the basis of the scale economics achieved by its larger rivals.

In the *Notice on the appraisal of horizontal mergers* the Commission stressed that it would be for the notifying parties to demonstrate that there was indeed a failing firm defence, and indicated that three criteria were relevant:

First, the allegedly failing firm would in the near future be forced out of the market because of financial difficulties if not taken over by another undertaking. Second, there is no less anti-competitive alternative purchase than the notified merger. Third, in the absence of a merger the assets of the failing firm would inevitably exit the market.

18.3 Vertical mergers

Vertical mergers generally give rise to less economic concern than do horizontal mergers, although

Vertical mergers can make entry more difficult by foreclosing rivals from previously independent firms at either the vertical level, by increasing capital requirements associated with entry and by promoting product differentiation. A vertically integrated oligopoly is insulated from competitive pressures that come from vertically related, competitive levels. This makes oligopolistic output coordination easier. (Martin, S., *Industrial Economics*, New York, Macmillan (2nd edn, 1994), p. 309)

Vertical mergers will not further concentrate a market, and the danger most often identified is that, as Martin suggests, they might foreclose a market to competition. For example, if a television broadcast network were to merge with a film production studio competing networks might find it more difficult to obtain product to transmit, and might therefore find it harder to compete for viewers. Where both of the relevant vertical markets are competitive there is likely to be no competitive harm from a vertical merger, and the presumption should instead be that the firms are merging as they have identified efficiencies of doing so that competition will force them to pass on to the consumer.

The process whereby oligopolistic collusion might be facilitated by vertical mergers is not immediately intuitive. However, the problem may be explained clearly by way of an example. Consider the situation where a four-firm oligopoly packages 85 per cent of the budget short-haul foreign package holidays sold to holidaymakers in a particular territory, but that these holidays are marketed by 20 independent chains of retailers, some of which have very large customer bases. Competition between these chains for custom, and the buying power that some of them are able to exercise, should compel the four firms producing the product to compete for their patronage, and should therefore dampen the adverse effects of there being a narrow oligopoly. If on the other hand each of the four firms bought four retail chains the position would be somewhat different, and it is likely that the oligopoly would be able more effectively to coordinate at all levels of the chain, raising prices to end consumers. Vertical integration may therefore be an essential condition for an oligopoly successfully to exploit its market power. However, such concerns will normally arise only where both markets, upstream and downstream, are concentrated, and where entry barriers are significant. The fact remains that the great majority of vertical mergers are not seriously challenged by the application of merger control procedures.

19

The EC merger control regime and the treatment of joint ventures

19.1 Introduction

This is the first of two chapters providing an outline of the application of competition law to mergers—the UK law is dealt with in the following chapter, and the basis for further study of this complex area (the subject is too vast to be dealt with completely in an introductory textbook). The majority of competition law regimes give a prominent place to the control of mergers, which cannot be treated in the same way as other anti-competitive practices. Anti-competitive agreements, and dominant firm conduct, are in most cases, although not exclusively, investigated and analysed after the event (although of course the parties to an agreement or conduct may themselves evaluate this prior to going ahead, and in some circumstances notifications may be made to the relevant authority). Mergers are better dealt with prior to their being implemented—or 'consummated'—as it can be both very difficult and exceptionally costly to disentangle a merger which has already taken place. This prior assessment is necessarily undertaken without the benefit of hindsight. In the case of the EC regime only the very largest mergers fall to be reviewed. This means inevitably that the stakes are high, both for the EC Commission, which, subject to certain express provisions, has exclusive competence to rule on mergers falling within its jurisdiction, and for the merging undertakings, who may have invested heavily in the merger process, and for whom much may ride on a successful outcome.

Certain key questions may be asked of any merger regime: over what mergers is jurisdiction to be asserted; is notification compulsory or voluntary; what is the subjective test by which mergers are evaluated; and what procedures are in place to ensure the efficacy of the merger regime? In the case of the EC merger control regime the answers to these questions are found primarily in Council Regulation (EC) 139/2004 on the control of concentrations between undertakings (the EC Merger Regulation) (2004) OJ L24/1. Hereinafter this regulation will be referred to as the ECMR. As is the case with the application of arts 81 and 82 EC the approach taken to merger control in the EC has changed to some extent over time. The single market considerations that were so important in determining some of the key principles of the application of art. 81 have also played a role in the shaping of the merger regime, and the response taken to the assessment of mergers, as has the need of industry to adapt to this change in market conditions. Thus in the ECMR at recitals (3) to (5) it is provided that

(3) The completion of the internal market and of economic and monetary union, the enlargement of the European Union and the lowering of international barriers to trade and investment will continue to result in major corporate reorganisations, particularly in the form of concentrations.

(4) Such reorganisations are to be welcomed to the extent that they are in line with the requirements of dynamic competition and capable of increasing the competitiveness of European industry, improving the conditions of growth and raising the standard of living in the Community.

(5) However, it should be ensured that the process of reorganisation does not result in lasting damage to competition; Community law must therefore include provisions governing those concentrations which may significantly impede effective competition in the common market or in a substantial part of it.

Changing responses to the role and importance of merger control, and to the assertion of jurisdiction by the EC at the expense of the Member States, has been reflected too in the development of the ECMR itself. The ECMR was first enacted as Regulation 4064/89 (consolidated version with corrections published at (1990) OJ L257/13), and this in turn was amended by Regulation 1310/97 (1997) OJ L180/1. The 2004 version of the ECMR represents a significant development, although not as significant as some would have hoped, of the EC merger regime, the examination of which will occupy most of the remainder of this chapter.

Joint ventures will also be considered here. A joint venture is a form of arrangement between undertakings which is usually designed to facilitate long-term cooperation (although some joint ventures may be of deliberately short duration). Joint ventures are dealt with in this chapter because, at Community level, they are closely related to merger control. At Community level a distinction is drawn between joint ventures which are 'concentrative', and which fall to be dealt with under the ECMR, and those which fall within the direct framework of art. 81 EC. This symmetry does not exist in the case of the UK, where there is no specific legal entity recognized as a joint venture, although various vehicles are available to companies seeking to implement such an arrangement.

19.2 Merger control in the European Community

19.2.1 The application of arts 81 and 82 and the development of the Merger Regulation

Articles 81 and 82 do not, explicitly, provide for the control of mergers, and for some time the general consensus was that they could not be applied to merger situations. This view was given added support by the fact that the older European Coal and Steel Community (ECSC) Treaty expressly dealt with merger control at art. 66. The fact that such an express provision had been omitted from the EEC Treaty suggested that the control of mergers was not to be encompassed within the EEC competition law regime. However, the application by the Commission of first art. 82 and then art. 81 to merger situations, and the approval of this action by the ECJ, confirmed that Community competition law could be applied to mergers in certain circumstances.

The first such action, taken under art. 82, was in the *Continental Can* case (*Europemballage Corp. and Continental Can Co.* v *Commission* case 6/72 [1973] CMLR 199. By way of a decision taken in 1972 (*Re Continental Can Co. Inc*, 72/71 (1972) OJ L7/25) the EC Commission had found a breach of art. 82 in a situation in which a takeover bid was made by a dominant undertaking for a smaller competitor. The Commission first intervened in the deal, which took the form of a takeover bid made for Thomassen & Drijver Verblifa (TDV) by Europemballage, itself a subsidiary of a much larger American company, Continental Can, with large interests in Europe. The Commission indicated that such an arrangement might be an abuse of art. 82 (see Chapter 14) in that it would adversely affect the structure of competition in a situation where competition was already weakened by the presence of the allegedly dominant undertaking. The takeover nevertheless went ahead, whereupon the Commission found that an abuse had indeed occurred, and ordered that steps be taken to bring the infringement to an end. On appeal the case was rejected by the ECJ on the grounds, largely, that the Commission had failed adequately to identify the relevant market, and had therefore not established that Continental Can was dominant within the meaning of art. 82. However, the Court did confirm that the article could be applied to situations in which a dominant undertaking sought to reduce further competition by the takeover of another undertaking, even in situations in which the transaction was in no way coerced. In particular the Court was not persuaded that the inclusion of a merger control provision in the ECSC Treaty meant that no such powers were to be available under the EEC Treaty. By expressly considering not only the wording of arts 81 and 82, but also the more expansive wording of art. 3(g) EC, to the effect that competition in the common market should not be distorted, the Court adopted a wide interpretation of the relevant provisions. Given that the Commission had been given the power by the Court, although again not expressly in the relevant legislation, to adopt interim measures (*Camera Care Ltd* v *Commission* case 792/79R [1980] 1 CMLR 334), the spectre was raised of the Commission using its authority to order that contemplated mergers not be consummated where they involved an undertaking in a dominant position. Such uncertainty could be damaging to merger plans, which are often highly sensitive, and in the course of which terms may be inserted to the effect that any regulatory intervention will see the abandonment of the plans.

In *BAT Ltd and RJ Reynolds Industries Inc* v *Commission* cases 142 and 156/84 [1988] 4 CMLR 24, the Commission considered the application of art. 81 to an agreement between cigarette manufacturers including Rembrandt Group, which had a controlling interest in Rothmans, and Philip Morris which would have given Philip

Morris a strong degree of control over the Rembrandt tobacco division. The two parties notified their agreement to the Commission, and, following negotiations between the parties, the agreement was given the approval of the Commission. However, the very fact that the parties had chosen to notify the agreement, and the fact that the Commission chose to consider it, was evidence of the possibility of the application of art. 81 to agreements leading to mergers. BAT and Reynolds, two large undertakings competing with the notifying parties, brought an action before the ECJ on the basis of art. 230 EC to challenge the clearance decision of the Commission. The Court rejected the applicants' argument holding that it could not be demonstrated that the notified agreements actually had the object or effect of preventing, restricting, or distorting competition. At the same time the Court, supporting the stance taken by the Commission, held that agreements which lead to concentrations in the market could be reviewed in the light of art. 81 and could fall within the prohibition of art. 81(1).

These two strands of administrative and judicial development led to a degree of uncertainty for mergers taking place within the Community, and raised the prospect that a clearance by a national authority examining the transaction on the basis of an application of a domestic merger regime could subsequently be followed by a condemnation under EC competition law. The spectre was also raised of third parties, or, for example, aggrieved shareholders, bringing actions on the basis of the application of either art. 81 or art. 82 in national courts. In particular it was recognized that the application of art. 81(2) to a fully consummated merger could have disastrous and unpredictable consequences. Further, the application of arts 81 or 82 would depend on their individual jurisdictional bases, and might fail to catch other mergers which were equally harmful. This is recognized in recital (7) of the ECMR:

Articles 81 and 82, while applicable, according to the case-law of the Court of Justice, to certain concentrations, are not sufficient to control all operations which may prove to be incompatible with the system of undistorted competition envisaged in the Treaty.

Accordingly the EC Commission brought forward proposals to introduce a measure to clarify the position, on the basis not only of art. 83, but also of art. 308, under which the Community may give itself powers to perform tasks necessary for the attainment of the objectives of the EC, in situations where an express power has not been made available. This proposal resulted, after intense negotiations with the Member States, in the enactment of Regulation 4064/89 on the Control of Concentrations Between Undertakings (1989) OJ L395/1—as a result of a substantial number of textual errors in the first publication this was republished at (1990) OJ L257/13). This Regulation entered into force on 21 September 1990. Fundamental to the new regime was the fact that, save with certain defined exceptions, the EC would have exclusive competence in relation to mergers falling within the thresholds set out. In 1997 the Regulation was subject to some significant amendment by the introduction of Regulation 1310/97 (1997) OJ L180/1. These amendments, which particularly affected the thresholds at which the EC merger regime would apply, were not as substantial as had been hoped for by the EC Commission, and at the end of 2001 the Commission launched a major review of the mergers regime (*Green Paper on the Review of Council Regulation (EEC) No. 4064/89* COM(2001) 745/6 final, 11 December 2001). This was designed in part to open up a discussion as to the extent to which the regime should align itself more closely with that of the USA in an effort to avoid conflict (in this respect see also Chapter 4). As discussed below, the test of a merger's acceptance under Regulation 4064/89 was strongly linked to the concept of dominance set out in art. 82 EC. The USA, on the other hand—along with a number of other jurisdictions, including the UK—employs a different test, that of whether the merger under examination would tend to 'substantially lessen competition' (hereinafter the SLC test). As the Green Paper recognized, this would

Facilitate merger parties' global assessment of possible competition issues arising from contemplated transactions, by obviating the need to argue their case according to differently formulated tests. This would in turn provide competition agencies with a better basis on which to build effective cooperation in cases that are notified in several jurisdictions. (para. 160)

The response to this argument, and the nature of the evaluative test embedded in the ECMR are discussed below in some detail.

At the same time as raising discussion about the test itself, the Commission sought to reduce the very high threshold at which Regulation 4064/89 applied. This the Commission had also attempted at the time of the 1997 revisions, in an effort to allow more mergers to be considered under a single 'one-stop shop' procedure. This is an issue that, with the enlargement of the EC in May 2004, has become more important over time. In essence the mergers considered at the Community level are only the very largest ones, and at this level of transaction undertakings face the risk of having their mergers considered by the authorities of a number of jurisdictions, both inside and outside the EC, with the financial and legal risks to which that gives rise. From the outset of the regime the thresholds have been higher than the Commission would have liked, and there has been constant pressure placed on the Member States to revise these in a downward direction. The Commission was not successful in this regard, although there is a commitment in the present ECMR to report on the thresholds by 1 July 2009, and the Commission *may* present proposals to have these amended (ECMR, art. 1(4) and (5)).

19.2.2 The application of the ECMR

19.2.2.1 *The meaning of 'concentration'*

Although the ECMR is subtitled ('the EC Merger Regulation') the control extends to 'concentrations', which may take many forms. The definition of 'concentration' for the purposes of the ECMR is given in art. 3 of the Regulation. In essence the test is one of whether there is a 'change of control on a lasting basis' (art. 3(1)). This follows recital (20) which makes reference to a definition applying to a situation in which there is 'a lasting change in control of the undertakings concerned and therefore in the structure of the market'. Such a change may occur through the merger of previously independent undertakings, or the acquisition by a controller of one undertaking of control of another. 'Acquisition' is given a wide meaning, to include a direct financial purchase by contract, a purchase of shares or securities, or any other means. Control may be direct or indirect, and

shall be constituted by rights, contracts or any other means which, either separately or in combination and having regard to the considerations of fact or of law involved, confer the possibility of exercising decisive influence on an undertaking'. (art. 3(2))

Both ownership, and rights, may give rise to control. For example, a minority shareholder may exercise rights on the basis of particular rights attached to their shares, effectively giving them a 'decisive influence' over the affairs of the undertaking in question. The question of whether control exists is to be determined pragmatically, the essential ingredient being that of an influence over the business strategy of the undertaking(s) concerned. For example, the right of a minority shareholder to veto certain decisions might not be found to constitute control for the purposes of the ECMR.

The term 'decisive influence' is not defined in the ECMR, and it is not entirely clear where the boundaries of this concept lie. Only in the most exceptional circumstances has the Commission found that a decisive influence has existed where less than 25 per cent of the share capital of an undertaking has been held by a single person. However, in the case of *CCIE/GTE* (1992) OJ C225/14 a share of 19 per cent was found to trigger control. In this instance all remaining shares were held by an investment bank, whose approval was not necessary for significant decisions. In essence the determination of whether there is a 'decisive influence' is a fact to be determined in the light of all the relevant circumstances (see, for example, *Gencor Ltd* v *Commission* case T–102/96 [1999] 4 CMLR 971, at paras 167—94).

For the purposes of the ECMR concentrations must take place between undertakings (the meaning of which term has been dealt with above (see Chapter 2), and the Regulation refers also to 'persons'. Where an individual acquires an undertaking they may, by virtue of other commercial interests, be considered to be an undertaking for the purposes of the Regulation. This was the case, for example, in *Asko/Jacobs/Adia* (1993) in which a private investor, holding interests in a number of undertakings, was himself considered to be an undertaking. Member States, even though they are not for the purposes of competition law considered to be undertakings, may be 'persons' for the purposes of the Regulation, and public bodies are certainly encompassed within the terms of the ECMR. In *Air France/Sabena* [1994] 5 CMLR M1, the Commission noted that their determination that the Regulation applied 'cannot be called into question by the fact that the Belgian state is not an undertaking' (para. 11). The fact that state involvement in industry and potentially in mergers is intended to be caught by the ECMR is further evidenced in recital (22) which makes reference to a general 'principle of non-discrimination between the public and the private sectors'. There is also specific reference, here, to the calculation of the turnover of an undertaking operating in the public sector. This rule does not apply, however, where the state is exercising its role as a public authority, rather than as a commercial actor.

19.2.2.2 'Community dimension'

Where a concentration has a Community dimension the EC Commission has, subject to specific exceptions set out on the face of the ECMR, exclusive jurisdiction within the EC to review that concentration. Article 21(3) provides therefore that 'no Member State shall apply its national legislation on competition to any concentration that has a Community dimension'. This provision therefore encapsulates the 'one-stop shop' underpinning EC merger control. For the purposes of the ECMR mergers have a Community dimension where

(a) the combined aggregate worldwide turnover of all the undertakings concerned is more than EUR 5,000 million; and

(b) the aggregate Community-wide turnover of each of at least two of the undertakings concerned is more than EUR 250 million,

unless each of the undertakings concerned achieves more than two-thirds of its aggregate Community-wide turnover within one and the same member state. (art. 1(2))

This basic threshold criterion is significantly higher than that which was sought by the Commission, both at the time of the introduction of the regime in 1989, and at the time of the 1997 revisions. In 1996 the Commission produced a Green Paper proposing that the thresholds be reduced to a worldwide turnover of €2bn, and a Community level of €100m. This proposal was rebuffed in 1997, when the Council adopted a compromise, leaving the basic requirement of art. 1(2) intact, but adding to it a new layer of jurisdiction now set out in art. 1(3). This is in the following terms:

A concentration that does not meet the thresholds laid down in paragraph 2 has a Community dimension where:

(a) the combined aggregate worldwide turnover of all the undertakings concerned is more than EUR 2,500 million;

(b) in each of at least three Member States, the combined aggregate turnover of all the undertakings concerned is more than EUR 100 million;

(c) in each of at least three Member States included for the purpose of point (b), the aggregate turnover of each of at least two of the undertakings concerned is more than EUR 25 million; and

(d) the aggregate Community-wide turnover of each of at least two of the undertakings concerned is more than EUR 100 million,

unless each of the undertakings concerned achieves more than two-thirds of its aggregate Community-wide turnover within one and the same Member State.

This test, while not going as far as the Commission sought, was designed to bring within its ambit mergers that would have faced multiple notifications in the individual Member States, although the Commission's own research indicated that only around 10 extra mergers would be caught a year under this rubric. As indicated above, the Commission is required to report on the operation of these criteria by the end of 1 July 2009. Article 5 of the ECMR sets out more detailed rules relating to the way in which the turnover of the relevant parties is to be calculated, and this is supported by further clarification published by the Commission.

Although it does not form part of the definition of a concentration having a Community dimension a further jurisdictional test may be mentioned here. This is provided for in art. 4(5) which relates to situations in which a concentration 'is capable of being reviewed under the laws of at least three Member States'. In such a case the parties may notify the concentration to the Commission, indicating that they would prefer it to exercise exclusive jurisdiction. This is not an obligation on the parties, but is subject to their own assessment as to which route is preferable. In these circumstances the Commission is then required to transmit this submission to the Member States, and will assert jurisdiction unless any of the states express their disagreement within 15 working days.

Because the formula set out in art. 1 is not an obviously easy one to apply, a simple example of its application is given here (Figure 19.1). Many other

Figure 19.1 Application of operation of Regulation 4064/89, as amended

Turnover (€ m)	A	B
Worldwide	3,500	2,000
Community-Wide	1,500	200
Germany	75	100
France	110	15
Italy	100	30
United Kingdom	1,200	30
Netherlands	15	25
Two-thirds earned in one MS	Yes, UK	No

The acquisition of undertaking B by undertaking A (the two undertakings concerned) would not fall within the original jurisdiction of the Commission because B does not earn 250 million euro turnover in the Community. The acquisition would, however, be caught by the additional thresholds since:

(a) A and B each earns more than 100 million euro from sales in the Community (art. 1(3)(d) is satisfied);

(b) the combined aggregate turnover of A and B exceeds 100 million euro in four Member States (France, Germany, Italy, and the United Kingdom) (art. 1(3)(b) is satisfied);

(c) the aggregate turnover of each of A and B is more than 25 million euro in Germany, Italy, and the United Kingdom (art. 1(3)(c) is satisfied); and

(d) the two-thirds proviso does not apply since B does not earn more than two-thirds of the Community turnover in the United Kingdom (or, indeed, any Member State) even though the acquirer A does.

Source: C. J. Cook and C. S. Kerse, *EC Merger Control*, London, Sweet & Maxwell (3rd edn, 2000), p. 63. Reproduced with permission.

permutations are of course possible, and the most effective way to understand the operation of this article is to work through some of these. The example given is taken, with kind permission, from Cook, C. J, and Kerse, C. S., *EC Merger Control*, London, Sweet & Maxwell (3rd edn, 2000), p. 63. This is one of the leading practitioner texts in this area, and a new edition is anticipated.

The two-thirds rule set out at the end of both art. 1(2) and art. 1(3) is designed to leave to Member States control over those mergers in which the effects will be very substantially felt within that state, even though these may also be situations in which the Community as a whole is affected. This test can produce unwelcome results. For example, in 1992 two undertakings, Lloyds, and the Hong Kong and Shanghai Banking Corporation (HSBC) were bidding for Midland Bank in the UK. The proposed takeover between Lloyds and Midland fell outside the terms of the regulation as both companies had more than two-thirds of their turnover in the UK. HSBC, on the other hand, did not have two-thirds of its turnover in the UK, and accordingly its bid fell to be considered by the EC Commission. When the Lloyds bid was referred to the UK regulator (the Monopolies and Mergers Commission, now the CC) it collapsed. In effect the Community consideration of the HSBC bid gave it a substantial advantage; having satisfied the Commission as to the nature of the concentration, and its effects, this bid was successful.

There is no explicit territorial limit placed on the application of the criteria set out in relation to the Community dimension of a concentration. In recital (9) it is recognized that

The scope of application of this Regulation should be defined according to the geographical area of activity of the undertakings concerned and be limited by quantitative thresholds in order to cover those concentrations which have a Community dimension.

And in recital (10) there is an express recognition of the fact that this should apply 'irrespective of whether or not the undertakings effecting the concentration have their seat or their principal fields of activity in the Community'. The effect of this is that a merger between two undertakings based outside the EC will fall within the terms of the ECMR as long as the relevant thresholds are met. This was the case, for example, in respect of the merger between Boeing and McDonnell Douglas in the USA (97/816 (1997) OJ L336/16), and between Gencor and Lonhro in South Africa (see *Gencor/Lonhro* 97/26 (1997) OJ L11/30; see also Chapter 4). In *General Electric/Honeywell* (Decision of 3 July 2001), the Commission blocked a merger between two American undertakings that had been approved by the relevant authorities in the USA. Article 7 of the Decision published on the Commission web site makes clear the rigidity that follows the application of these straightforward turnover criteria:

The undertakings concerned have a combined aggregate worldwide turnover of more than EUR 5,000 million . . . Both GE and Honeywell have a Community-wide turnover in excess of EUR 250 million . . . , but they do not achieve more than two-thirds of their aggregate Community-wide turnover within one and the same Member State. The notified operation therefore has a Community dimension.

While the assertion of jurisdiction over 'foreign' mergers is sometimes treated with hostility by the home states of the merging undertakings it is not unusual for extra-territorial jurisdiction to be asserted in the case of large mergers. The USA in particular has reviewed a number of mergers entered into by parties based primarily in the EC.

19.2.2.3 *Notification*

Undertakings engaged in a merger with a Community dimension are required to pre-notify that merger to the Commission. This obligation, according to recital (34) arises 'following the conclusion of the agreement, the announcement of the public bid or the acquisition of a controlling interest'. No concentration with a Community dimension may lawfully be consummated until the Commission has taken a final decision as to the compatibility of that concentration with the ECMR. Notifications to the Commission are dealt with in the ECMR, art. 4.

Along with the obligation to notify in the circumstances specified in recital (34), which is given full legal effect in art. 4(1), notifications may also be made in situations in which parties are contemplating a merger and seek the security of regulatory clearance prior to going ahead. This represents a change to the position in Regulation 4064/89, and brings the procedures in the EC into line in this respect with those in the USA. However, the Commission will only accept such notifications where the parties demonstrate 'a good faith intention to conclude the agreement' or where they have announced their intention to make a public bid. This is to prevent the Commission having to consider numbers of speculative applications that would clog up its already overstretched resources. Notifications are to be made either by the parties jointly, or by the party acquiring control (art. 4(2)). Once a notification of a merger with a Community dimension is made the Commission is required to publish the fact of the notification, although in doing so it must 'take account of the legitimate interests of undertakings in the protection of their business secrets' (art. 4(3)).

Further provisions relate to instances in which the parties notifying the concentration consider that it may, in parts, fall within the jurisdiction of a Member State on the grounds considered at 19.2.2.6. In addition, where the concentration does not fall within the ECMR thresholds, but where the merger would fall to be considered by at least three Member States, the parties may make a 'reasoned submission' to the Commission informing it that the concentration should be examined by it (art. 4(5)). In these circumstances the Commission is required to liaise with the relevant Member States in accordance with the rules set out in art. 4.

19.2.2.4 *The substantive test*

The most important difference between the current ECMR and the earlier version lies in the substantive test under which the concentration in question is to be evaluated. The test set out in Regulation 4064/89 was one exclusively related to dominance (discussed further below). As noted in 19.2.1 the EC Commission mooted, in the Green Paper, a move to the SLC test. The position in the ECMR is now a hybrid of the two tests. The central difficulty with the operation of the dominance test, as it stood, disregarding international convergence, lay in the application of the ECMR to situations in which mergers were taking place in oligopolistic markets, where single-firm dominance was not being created, but where the argument was made that a position of collective dominance (also known as 'joint dominance' and 'oligopolistic dominance') was being created. The difficulties of analysing such situations, and applying the law of dominance to them, are considered further below.

In recitals (25) and (26) of the ECMR the rationale for expanding the evaluative test, and the links between this and the dominance test, is made clearly, in the following terms:

(25) In view of the consequences that concentrations in oligopolistic market structures may have, it is all the more necessary to maintain effective competition in such markets. Many oligopolistic markets exhibit a healthy degree of competition. However, under certain circumstances, concentrations involving the elimination of important competitive constraints that the merging parties had exerted upon each other, as well as a reduction of competitive pressure on the remaining competitors, may, even in the absence of a likelihood of coordination between the members of the oligopoly, result in a significant impediment to effective competition. The Community courts have, however, not to date expressly interpreted Regulation (EEC) No 4064/89 as requiring concentrations giving rise to such non-coordinated effects to be declared incompatible with the common market. Therefore, in the interests of legal certainty, it should be made clear that this Regulation permits effective control of all such concentrations by providing that any concentration which would significantly impede effective competition, in the common market or in a substantial part of it, should be declared incompatible with the common market. The notion of 'significant impediment to effective competition' in Article 2(2) and (3) should be interpreted as extending, beyond the concept of dominance, only to the anti-competitive effects of a concentration resulting from the non-coordinated behaviour of undertakings which would not have a dominant position on the market concerned.

(26) A significant impediment to effective competition generally results from the creation or strengthening of a dominant position. With a view to preserving the guidance that may be drawn from past judgments of the European courts and Commission decisions pursuant to Regulation (EEC) No 4064/89, while at the same time maintaining consistency with the standards of competitive harm which have been applied by the Commission and the Community courts regarding the compatibility of a concentration with the common market, this Regulation should accordingly establish the principle that a concentration with a Community dimension which would significantly impede effective competition, in the common market, or in a substantial part thereof, in particular as a result of the creation or strengthening of a dominant position, is to be declared incompatible with the common market.

The test of significantly impeding effective competition will hereinafter be abbreviated as 'SIEC'. To encapsulate the principle underlying the new test more succinctly

[it] is intended to deal with situations of non-collusive oligopoly [i.e., situations lying outside the application of art. 81(1)] where the effect of the merger may still impede competition, although the merged entity's market share falls below the traditional dominance threshold.

The new SIEC formula is likely to enhance the Commission's power to block transactions particularly in cases of 'unilateral effects' where a merger may reduce competition even though it does not lead to joint or single firm dominance.   (Clifford Chance, *The New EC Merger Regulation: What has changed?* Client Briefing, December 2003)

The legal test to be applied to any concentration with a Community dimension is set out at art. 2 of the ECMR. Article 2(2) provides that

A concentration which would not significantly impede effective competition in the common market or in a substantial part of it, in particular as a result of the creation or strengthening of a dominant position, shall be declared compatible with the common market.

The reverse of this is that a concentration which does significantly impede effective competition to the extent set out here, shall be declared to be incompatible with the common market (ECMR, art. 2(3)).

19.2.2.4.1 *Collective dominance under the ECMR*

It has been noted above that the test of a concentration's acceptance is a hybrid of that of whether the merger tended to create or strengthen a dominant position, and SIEC. Until the revision of the ECMR the sole test lay in the first plank of this rubric. There was a clear linkage between the wording adopted in Regulation 4064/89, and art. 82, which makes explicit reference to a dominant position held by 'one or more undertakings'. The EC Commission, supported to varying degrees by the Court, has developed the law of 'joint' dominance, in the context of both art. 82 and the ECMR, to deal with situations in which dominance could be considered to be held by more than one party (in the context of merger control the economics of this situation is considered briefly at 18.2.2).

While the relevant law in this respect developed in tandem under art. 82 and Regulation 4064/89, from the operation of the current ECMR it is anticipated that there will be a separation between arguments made under art. 82 and those made under the ECMR. As critics of the Commission's approach have pointed out, this has in fact always partly been the case. An analysis that is taken prospectively anticipating future conduct is to some extent necessarily sundered from an analysis taking place with full knowledge (if not always with full understanding) of an observable market situation.

The starting point for the collective dominance case law was *Kali und Salz* case IV/M080 (1994) OJ L186/38 (on appeal *France* v *Commission* case C–68/94 and *Société Commercial des Potasses et de L'Azote (SCPA) and Entreprise Miniére et Chimique (EMC)* v *Commission* case C–30/95 [1998] 4 CMLR 829) in which a proposed joint venture was blocked on the grounds that it 'would lead to a situation of oligopolistic dominance'. This decision was affected by the fact that the products concerned—potash and rock salt—were homogenous (i.e., not subject to consumer differentiation), and that the joint venture would be matched by only one other Community producer in the geographic market. There were already close links between the undertakings concerned. The decision was overturned by the CFI, but the Court accepted the basic argument that Regulation 4064/89 could be applied to positions of collective dominance. This case left some difficulties in its wake. In the course of the decision the Commission had made reference to 'economic links' between the undertakings, and it was unclear whether these links were an essential ingredient of collective dominance. Collective dominance is also sometimes referred to as 'oligopolistic dominance', and although this term is not preferred it gives some indication of the problems that may be encountered in markets in which there are few players, and which tend towards parallel conduct, even if this falls short of a concerted practice (it will be remembered that undertakings are permitted to align their conduct to other undertakings if this is a truly independent action—see 'Concerted practices' at 9.2.3). If the number of undertakings in a con-centrated market is reduced by a merger between two or more of them, a possible effect is that such parallel action is more likely. This will be the case in particular where the product is homogenous, the market is highly concentrated, the market is transparent in the sense that there is a strong flow of information, and the market is relatively stable.

The problems left by *Kali und Salz* were tackled further by the EC Commission in *Gencor/Lonhro* 97/26 (1997) OJ L11/30 (on appeal *Gencor Ltd v Commission* case T–102/96 [1999] 4 CMLR 971). Here the Commission made clearer its view of collective dominance, holding that

[it] can occur where a mere adaptation by members of the oligopoly to market conditions causes anti-competitive parallel behaviour whereby the oligopoly becomes dominant. Active collusion would therefore not be required for members of the oligopoly to become dominant and to behave to an appreciable extent independently of their remaining competitors, their customers and, ultimately, their consumers. (para 140)

In *Gencor* the relevant market was that for precious metals, platinum and rhodium, worldwide, and there were only three significant competitors, all based in South Africa. The merger would reduce the number of competitors to two, and there was also a history of parallel behaviour in the South African market. The CFI agreed with the Commission that the concept of economic links could be drawn widely to include economic interdependence, irrespective of the mechanisms by which this situation came about. Thus the CFI held that

there is no reason whatsoever in legal or economic terms to exclude from the notion of economic links the relationship of interdependence existing between the parties to a tight oligopoly within which, in a market with the appropriate characteristics in particular in terms of market concentration, transparency and product homogeneity, those parties are in a strong position to anticipate one another's behaviour and are therefore strongly encouraged to align their conduct in the market, in particular in such a way as to maximise their joint profits by restricting production with a view to increasing prices. In such a context each trader is aware that highly competitive action on its part designed to increase its market share (for example, a price cut) would provoke identical action by the others, so that it would derive no benefit from its initiative. (paras 104–5)

In another mergers decision, *Price Waterhouse/Coopers and Lybrand* 1999/152 (1999) OJ L50/27, the Commission recognized that some of the elements that had been mentioned in *Gencor* were also factors in the accountancy market. However, after the merger there were to be five competitors in the market and here the

Commission held that 'collective dominance involving more than three or four suppliers is unlikely because of the complexity of the interrelationships involved, and the consequent temptation to deviate' (see paras 94–119).

The clearest statement of these principles to date, and in light of the amended test in the ECMR perhaps the final statement, is that in *Airtours/First Choice* 2000/276 (2000) OJ L93/1 in which the Commission blocked a merger between two companies in the UK market for short-haul foreign package holidays, travel agency services, and the supply to tour operators of seats on charter flights to short-haul destinations. At para. 87 of its decision the Commission set out the conditions that it felt needed to be in place for a finding of collective dominance to be sustained. These included: product homogeneity; low demand growth; low price sensitivity of demand; similar cost structure of the main suppliers; substantial entry barriers; and insignificant countervailing buyer power. The Commission expressly held that collective dominance did not require that there be any collusion between the parties, stating in response to concerns raised by Airtours that 'active collusive conduct of any kind is not a prerequisite for collective dominance to occur. It is sufficient that adaptation to market conditions causes an anti-competitive outcome' (para. 53). The decision came as a surprise to many, given that the market would appear to be very dynamic. The economic consultancy NERA argued, in its regular newsletter, that 'package holidays are differentiated, branded consumer products' and that the market was one in which 'there has been a huge variability in supplier shares and profitability and in which high profile exits . . . have been counterbalanced by instances of equally dramatic entry and growth'. On appeal to the CFI the Commission decision was overturned (*Airtours plc* v *Commission* case T–342/99 [2002] 5 CMLR 7). At para. 62 of its judgment the CFI stated that three conditions were necessary for a finding of collective dominance. This part of the judgment is of such importance that it is worth quoting at length:

—first, each member of the dominant oligopoly must have the ability to know how the other members are behaving in order to monitor whether or not they are adopting the common policy. As the Commission specifically acknowledges, it is not enough for each member of the dominant oligopoly to be aware that interdependent market conduct is profitable for all of them but each member must also have a means of knowing whether the other operators are adopting the same strategy and whether they are maintaining it. There must, therefore, be sufficient market transparency for all members of the dominant oligopoly to be aware, sufficiently precisely and quickly, of the way in which the other Members' market conduct is evolving;

—secondly, the situation of tacit co-ordination must be sustainable over time, that is to say, there must be an incentive not to depart from the common policy on the market. As the Commission observes, it is only if all the members of the dominant oligopoly maintain the parallel conduct that all can benefit. The notion of retaliation in respect of conduct deviating from the common policy is thus inherent in this condition. In this instance, the parties concur that, for a situation of collective dominance to be viable, there must be adequate deterrents to ensure that there is a long-term incentive in not departing from the common policy, which means that each member of the dominant oligopoly must be aware that highly competitive action on its part designed to increase its market share would provoke identical action by the others, so that it would derive no benefit from its initiative . . . ;

—thirdly, to prove the existence of a collective dominant position to the requisite legal standard, the Commission must also establish that the foreseeable reaction of current and future competitors, as well as of consumers, would not jeopardise the results expected from the common policy.

In the present case the CFI found that the Commission had made 'a series of errors of assessment as to factors fundamental to any assessment of whether a collective dominant position might be created' (para. 294). The decision was annulled.

In the future it is to be hoped that arguments as to the existence or otherwise of a collective dominant position can be avoided by reference instead to the SIEC part of the test of art. 2 ECMR, rather than by shoe-horning such cases into a dominance analysis.

19.2.2.4.2 *The consideration of countervailing efficiencies*
As with art. 82 EC, the ECMR is a unitary instrument—and any balancing of the good arising out of a concentration, with the harm that is anticipated to flow, is to be undertaken by the Commission. This is recognized in recital (29), as is the obligation of the Commission to publish guidance in this respect:

(29) In order to determine the impact of a concentration on competition in the common market, it is appropriate to take account of any substantiated and likely efficiencies put forward by the undertakings concerned. It is possible that the efficiencies brought about by the concentration counteract the potential harm to consumers, that it might otherwise have and that, as a consequence, the concentration would not significantly impede effective competition, in the common market or in a substantial part of it . . .

This is reflected in art. 2(1)(b) which makes reference to the Commission's ability to take into account, *inter alia*, 'the development of technical and economic progress provided that it is to consumers' advantage and does not form an obstacle to competition' (this is the same wording as in Regulation 4064/89).

The position as set out in recital (29) is somewhat different from that of Regulation 4064/89, under which it was argued that the Commission was not in a position explicitly to consider efficiency claims, an early provision to this effect having been removed from the draft of that Regulation. (This subject is well dealt with in Lindsay, A., *The EC Merger Regulation: Substantive Issues*, London, Sweet & Maxwell, 2003 at heading 8.2.) The Commission argued that the Regulation did not permit such claims to be taken into account, either because such arguments were not well made, or because art. 2(1)(b) of Regulation 4064/89 did not allow them to be. There are, however, a number of cases in which it has been argued that such efficiencies have played a role in allowing the Commission to clear mergers that might otherwise have been problematic (see Camesasca, P. D., 'The Explicit Efficiency Defence in Merger Control: Does it Make the Difference?' [1999] ECLR 14). Camesasca accepts that 'the wording of the [Regulation] legally does not leave scope for taking dynamic efficiencies into account once dominance is concluded upon' (at pp. 24–5). However, in *Aerospatiale-Alenia/de Havilland* (91/619 (1991) OJ L334/42), the first merger to be blocked under Regulation 4064/89, the Commission addressed the argument that the merger would reduce costs of production.

The Commission, at para. 64, argued that any such savings would be 'negligible' and could, in any event, be achieved by other means. The mere fact, however, that such arguments were debated by the Commission, in the terms which were adopted, suggested that, in the words of Camesasca, 'the Commission requires efficiencies to be substantial and merger specific' (at p. 25). This position is reflected in the 2004 guidelines prepared by the Commission, which require any such efficiencies now claimed to be substantial, verifiable, timely, and of direct benefit to consumers.

Even allowing for the consideration of countervailing efficiencies it would appear that not all matters claimed as countervailing benefits will be accepted by the Commission. For example, in an appeal against the *Nestlé/Perrier* decision (92/553 (1992) OJ L356/1), in which the merger was cleared, trade unions argued that as a result of the concentration employment interests would be damaged. The Commission argued before the CFI that it did not have any positive obligation to take such considerations into account, although the CFI appeared to suggest that the Commission was, to a limited extent, required to consider the general aims and objectives of the EC as set out in, for example, art. 2 EC. The CFI rejected the unions' argument on the grounds that the workers' rights were protected under other EC instruments, and were not directly harmed by the Commission decision to permit the merger (*Comité Central d'Entreprise de la Société Anonyme Vittel* v *Commission* case T–12/93 [1995] ECR II-1247).

19.2.2.4.3 *The economic assessment of concentrations*
DG Comp encompasses within it a Merger Task Force which operates alongside the other enforcement activities of the Directorate, with its own staff and procedures. The Commission has also appointed a Chief Competition Economist to oversee the Commission's work generally in this area, and has set up an internal panel to assess the conclusions of the investigating team with a 'pair of fresh eyes'. It has been noted by commentators that the quality of analysis undertaken in merger cases is more sophisticated than in standard art. 81 and art. 82 cases, and is having the effect of improving the standard of economic analysis overall. Initiatives such as the notice on market definition (see Chapter 14) have emerged in response to the experience gained in merger cases. In that notice it was recognized not only that the approach overall could be made more transparent, but that mergers and joint ventures required special consideration.

The Commission is committed to the publication of guidelines relating to horizontal, non-horizontal, and conglomerate mergers.

19.2.2.5 *Procedures under the ECMR*

19.2.2.5.1 *Phase I proceedings*
One of the defining characteristics of the ECMR, in contrast to arts 81 and 82, is that its operation imposes strict timetables on all the relevant parties, including the EC Commission, at all stages of the proceedings. Proceedings under the ECMR may be broken down into two main stages: Phase I and Phase II. Phase I applies

to the procedures leading to a first decision, and Phase II to the procedures which apply when a more substantial review of the notified concentration is necessary.

Article 6 provides that the Commission is obliged to 'examine the notification as soon as it is received' (art. 6(1)), and the Commission has 25 working days to take a decision under art. 6(1) (art. 10(1)—although this time period may be extended where a request from a Member State is received under art. 9(2) (see below)). Three decisions are possible at this stage. The first is that the concentration does not have a Community dimension. In this case the procedures are terminated at this stage, the Commission recording that fact by a decision. The second scenario is that the concentration does have a Community dimension, but 'does not raise serious doubts as to its compatibility with the common market' (art. 6(1)(b)). In this case the Commission shall declare that the concentration is compatible with the common market. Any decision taken in this respect is also deemed to cover 'restrictions directly related and necessary to the concentration'. This is to say that any terms of the transaction which might fall within either art. 81, or national competition law, are cleared at the same time as long as they bear a sufficiently close relation to the concentration itself. At this stage the undertakings also have the opportunity to offer 'modifications' to the transaction, which might include, for example, divestitures of certain elements of the package, or conduct remedies, designed to allay the serious doubts. Where such commitments are offered the strict time limit of 25 days for the making of a decision can be increased by 10 days to allow the Commission time to review these commitments. The Commission may also, when making such a decision, attach to it conditions and obligations necessary to ensure that any commitments entered into by the undertakings are adhered to. Where any decision made under art. 6(1)(a) or (b) is based on incorrect information provided by the undertakings concerned, or where it has been made as a result of deceit by those undertakings, the decision may subsequently be revoked. Decisions may also be revoked if the parties breach any obligation attached to such a decision (art. 6(3)).

The third possibility is that the concentration both has a Community dimension, and 'raises serious doubts as to its compatibility with the common market' (art. 6(1)(c)). In this case the Commission will initiate proceedings under Phase II.

Where a concentration is notified to the EC Commission in accordance with art. 4, and indeed even where a concentration with a Community dimension has not been notified, 'it shall not be implemented either before its notification or until it has been declared compatible with the common market' (ECMR, art. 7(1)). A derogation from these suspensory, or standstill, provisions may be granted by the Commission on receipt of a reasoned request (art. 7(3)).

19.2.2.5.2 *Phase II proceedings*
The central substantive powers of the Commission under the ECMR are set out in art. 8, which makes provision for the key decisions that the EC Commission can take. Article 8(1) provides for the making of a decision to the effect that the notified

concentration is compatible with the common market. Under para. 2 of the article the Commission may find that a concentration is compatible following the offer of modifications by the undertakings making the notification. It may also 'attach to its decision conditions and obligations intended to ensure that the undertakings concerned comply with the commitments they have entered into'. Decisions taken pursuant to arts 8(1) or (2) 'shall be taken as soon as it appears that the serious doubts referred to in art. 6(1)(c) have been removed', and at the latest within 90 working days from the date at which the Phase II proceedings are initiated (art. 10(2)).

Paragraphs 3 and 4 of art. 8 relate to decisions made to the effect that concentrations are incompatible with the common market. Here it is provided in particular at art. 8(3) that

Where the Commission finds that a concentration fulfils the criterion defined in Article 2(3) or, in the cases referred to in Article 2(4), does not fulfil the criteria laid down in Article 81(3) of the Treaty, it shall issue a decision declaring that the concentration is incompatible with the common market.

Decisions taken in respect of art. 8(3) shall be made within 90 working days from the date on which the Phase II proceedings are opened, although this period may be increased to 105 working days where the undertakings offer commitments, unless these are offered within the first 55 days, or where the notifying parties ask for an extension (art. 10(3)). All timetable conditions set out in art. 10(1)–(3) may be extended where the Commission, as a result of action by one or more of the notifying parties, needs to resort to the information gathering-powers set out in the ECMR.

Where a concentration has been wrongly implemented the Commission has substantial powers to require that the situation be remedied. Article 8(4) therefore provides that:

Where the Commission finds that a concentration:

(a) has already been implemented and that concentration has been declared incompatible with the common market, or

(b) has been implemented in contravention of a condition attached to a decision taken under paragraph 2, which has found that, in the absence of the condition, the concentration would fulfil the criterion laid down in Article 2(3) or, in the cases referred to in Article 2(4), would not fulfil the criteria laid down in Article 81(3) of the Treaty,

the Commission may:

— require the undertakings concerned to dissolve the concentration, in particular through the dissolution of the merger or the disposal of all the shares or assets acquired, so as to restore the situation prevailing prior to the implementation of the concentration; in circumstances where restoration of the situation prevailing before the implementation of the concentration is not possible through dissolution of the concentration, the Commission may take any other measure appropriate to achieve such restoration as far as possible,

— order any other appropriate measure to ensure that the undertakings concerned dissolve the concentration or take other restorative measures as required in its decision.

The Commission may also take interim measures where a concentration has been implemented, and no final decision has yet been taken, or a condition of implementation has been disregarded, or where a merger declared incompatible with the common market has been implemented (art. 8(5)). In 2001 the Commission published its *Merger Remedies Guidelines* (2001) OJ C68/3, which should be referred to for more detail about the types of remedies that may be employed and relevant procedures.

19.2.2.5.3 *Investigation and enforcement*

Regulation 1/2003 (see Chapters 5 and 6) sets out rules on investigations and procedures in respect of the application of arts 81 and 82 EC and not in respect of concentrations with a Community dimension. Instead the ECMR sets out its own rules relating to investigation and enforcement in this respect. The powers in the ECMR are stronger than those set out in Regulation 4064/89, and are substantially in line with those of Regulation 1/2003. Article 11 makes provision for requests for information. Article 11(2) allows the Commission to send a 'simple request for information' to a person or undertaking, and art. 11(3) allows the Commission to proceed by way of a formal decision. In both instances penalties are available if information provided is incorrect or misleading, or in the case of art. 11(3) is not supplied within the appropriate time limit. The Commission may also interview any natural or legal person, but only with their consent (art. 11(7)). Governments and competent authorities of the Member States are required to supply all necessary information to the Commission to allow it to carry out its duties (art. 11(6)). The Commission also has the power to conduct 'all necessary inspections of undertakings and associations of undertakings' (art. 13), and may ask Member States to carry out inspections on its behalf (art. 12). Under art. 13 the powers of the Commission are comparable to those of Regulation 1/2003, giving it the power to enter premises, examine books and records, take copies or extracts of these, seal business premises for the period of the inspection, and to ask any representative or member of staff of the undertaking for explanations (art. 13(2)).

Under art. 14 the Commission may impose financial penalties in a number of situations. Fines of 1 per cent of turnover of the undertaking or undertakings may be imposed in relation to procedural breaches, and fines of 10 per cent of turnover may be imposed in situations in which substantive breaches of the ECMR occur. As with Regulation 1/2003, 'in fixing the amount of the fine, regard shall be had to the nature, gravity and duration of the infringement' (art. 14(4)). There are no guidelines specifically relating to the imposition of penalties under the ECMR. Article 15 provides for the imposition of periodic penalty payments of up to 5 per cent of the average daily aggregate turnover of the undertaking concerned for each working day of delay from the deadline given in a decision to compel an undertaking to supply information, comply with an investigation, or comply with any decision imposing an obligation in relation to a concentration's consummation. As with all matters over which the Commission exercises jurisdiction, the Court of Justice has the power to review decisions taken by the Commission imposing a fine or periodic penalty (art. 16).

Before taking the decisions specified in art. 6(3) (revocation of a decision not to proceed to Phase II), art. 8(2)–(6) (Phase II decisions), and art. 14 and 15 the Commission must give the undertakings concerned the opportunity to make their views known (art. 18). Decisions of the Commission are to be published (art. 20), but in doing so the Commission is to have regard to the obligation not to disclose 'information they have acquired through the application [of the ECMR] of the kind covered by the obligation of professional secrecy' (art. 17).

19.2.2.6 *The role of Member States*

Subject to certain specified situations the ECMR gives the Commission exclusive competence over concentrations with a Community dimension. There is a general obligation on the Commission to 'act in close and constant liaison with the competent authorities of the Member States' (recital (13)). The principle of subsidiarity underpins the ECMR. The operation of this principle in the context of merger review is set out in recital (8) which indicates that mergers 'the impact of which on the market goes beyond the national borders of any one Member State' should be reviewed at Community level. In fact this is not the case as is clear from the definition of Community dimension. Many mergers not falling within this threshold of jurisdiction will still have effects beyond the borders of a single Member State. At the same time some mergers having a Community dimension will have effects which are particularly pronounced in a single Member State, or in more than one Member State. In the appropriate circumstances, defined in the ECMR, such mergers may be referred back to the Member States, either in whole or in part. Equally, a Member State may request that the EC Commission take over jurisdiction in the case of a concentration which does *not* have a Community dimension, but which falls within the jurisdiction of the requesting Member State.

In the ECMR itself are to be found two exceptions to the principle of exclusive Commission competence. Article 9 makes provision for the referral of concentrations to the competent authorities of the Member States. Article 9(2) (sometimes called 'the German clause') provides that any Member State, either on its own initiative, or at the suggestion of the Commission, may inform the Commission that the Member State should be granted the right to assert jurisdiction where

(a) a concentration threatens to affect significantly competition in a market within that Member State, which presents all the characteristics of a distinct market, or

(b) a concentration affects competition in a market within that Member State, which presents all the characteristics of a distinct market and which does not constitute a substantial part of the common market.

Once these criteria are met, the Commission may, under art. 9(3), either deal with the case itself taking into account the concerns of the Member State, or refer all or part of the case back to the relevant national authority. A number of requests have been made on the basis of art. 9(3) of the ECMR. One such request was made by the UK authorities in the case of *Exxon Corpn/Mobil Corpn* (EC Case No IV/M. 1383; DTI press release P/99/780, 29 September 1999). Here the DTI welcomed the EC Commission's 'resolution of competition detriments in the North West of Scotland, following which the Commission did not need to refer the case to the UK authorities as had been requested'. In 2000 the EC Commission referred back to the UK authorities several proposed mergers, including Anglo American plc/Tarmac plc (DTI press release P/2000/19, 13 January 2000), Hanson plc/Pioneer International Ltd (DTI press release P/2000/212, 18 April 2000), Nabisco Group Holdings Corp/ United Biscuits (Holdings) plc/The Horizon Biscuit Co (DTI press release P/2000/ 280, 18 April 2000), Interbrew SA/Bass Holdings Ltd (DTI press release P/2000/585, 22 August 2000), and Go-Ahead Group plc/Caisse des Dépôts Développement SA (C3D)/Rhône Capital LLC (DTI press release P/2000/695, 20 October 2000). In 2003 however, only one such referral was reported, Arla/Express Dairies (OFT press release PN 74/03, 11 June 2003). In this latter case the UK argued that the market for the supply of fresh processed milk fell under art. 9(2)(b), and that the market for the supply of fresh non-bulk cream (cream for retail supply in small pots, or to caterers in larger pots) fell within art. 9(2)(a). This merger was subsequently approved by the UK authorities on 15 October 2003. This was the fifteenth such request made to the EC Commission under art. 9 by the UK authorities.

Article 21(4) of the ECMR allows for referral of a concentration with a Community dimension back to a Member State in the event of there being the need to 'take appropriate measures to protect legitimate interests other than those taken into account by [the ECMR]'. These legitimate interests expressly include 'public security, plurality of the media and prudential rules'. These provisions are rarely invoked, but in June 2000, for example, the UK authorities asserted jurisdiction over the public security aspects of Thomson CSF's proposed acquisition of Racal Electronics plc (DTI press release P/2000/401, 12 June 2000). This provision was also invoked in November 2002, in the case of BAE System/Astrim/EADS (DTI press release P/2002/732, 22 November 2002).

Under the terms of art. 22 ('the Dutch clause'), Member States may refer a concentration to the Commission where it does not have a Community dimension, but 'affects trade between Member States and threatens to significantly affect competition within the territory of the Member State or States making the request' (art. 22(1)). This provision is rarely used, although in 2002 the DTI asked the Commission to consider the competition aspects of the proposed merger between GE Engine Services and Unison Industries (DTI press release P/2002/134, 28 February 2002). Once art. 22 is invoked the national authorities referring the matter to the Commission lose control over the process, and cannot determine the scope of the Commission's review (*Endemol Entertainment Holding NV* v *Commission* case T–221/95 [1999] 5 CMLR 611, paras 37–47).

A final exception to the principle of subsidiarity is found in the Treaty itself, at art. 296. This is in the following terms:

Any Member State may take such measures as it considers necessary for the protection of the essential interests of its security which are connected with the production of or trade in arms, munitions and war material; such measures shall not adversely affect the conditions of competition in the common market regarding products which are not intended for specifically military purposes.

19.2.2.7 *Mergers blocked*

As of April 2004, the EC Commission has made public details of 18 cases in which mergers falling within its jurisdiction have been blocked under art. 8(3) of Regulation 4064/89. These are the following (dates are given due to the sometimes long delay between the making and the publication of the decisions):

- *Tetra Laval/Sidel* (30 October 2001)
- *CVC/Lenzing* (17 October 2001)
- *Schneider/Legrand* (10 October 2001)
- *General Electric/Honeywell* (3 July 2001, 2004/134 (2004) OJ L48/1)
- *SCA/Metsa Tissue* (31 January 2001, 2002/156 (2002) OJ L57/1)
- *MCI Worldcom/Sprint* (28 June 2000)
- *Volvo/Scania* (15 March 2000, 2001/403 (2001) OJ L143/74)
- *Airtours/First Choice* (22 September 1999, 2000/276 (2000) OJ L93/1)
- *Deutsche Telekom/Beta Research*; and *Bertelsmann/Kirch/Premiére* (27 May 1998, 1999/153 (1999) OJ L53/1)
- *Blokker/Toys "Я" Us (II)* (26 June 1997, 98/663 (1998) OJ L316/1)
- *Saint Gobain/Wacker Chemie/NOM* (4 December 1996, 97/610 (1996) OJ L247/1)
- *Kesko/Tuko* (20 November 1996, 97/277 (1997) OJ L110/53)
- *Gencor/Lonhro* (24 April 1996, (1997) OJ L11/30)
- *RTL/Veronica/Endemol* ('HMG') (20 September 1995, 96/346 (1996) OJ L134/21)
- *Nordic Satellite Distribution* (19 July 1995, 96/177 (1996) OJ L53/20)
- *MSG Media Service* (9 November 1994, 94/922 (1994) OJ L364/1)
- *Aérospatiale/Alenia/De Havilland* (2 October 1991, 91/619 (1991) OJ L334/42)

Some of these decisions are set out in more detail below, and it is notable that in three cases, *Tetra Laval/Sidel*, *Schneider/Legrand*, and *Airtours/First Choice* the Commission lost on appeal to the CFI.

19.2.2.7.1 *Tetra Laval/Sidel*

In *Tetra Laval/Sidel* the undertakings had already put into effect a concentration at the time at which it was blocked by the Commission. The notification was received on 18 May 2001, and the Commission found that there were three main horizontal overlaps in the relevant markets which lay in packaging systems for various foodstuffs and liquids. The undertakings offered commitments to the Commission to alleviate the concerns raised, but the Commission rejected these as being insufficient. At the time at which the Commission made its decision pursuant to art. 8(3) of Regulation 4064/89 (30 October 2001) Tetra Laval had acquired just over 95 per cent of Sidel's shares by virtue of a public bid. By virtue of art. 8(4) of the Regulation the Commission presented to the parties proposals to remedy the harm, which required the divestiture of the two undertakings in a very short space of time. Tetra did not object to the divestiture, but did argue that there was no necessity to do this as a matter of urgency, and argued that there was 'virtually no competition at present between the two businesses'. The Commission did not agree, and expressed strongly its concerns about the effect of current investment and product development decisions on future competition between the parties. The Commission insisted that:

An effective and final divestiture should consist of the sale of Sidel as a going concern without any change in its status, or in the scope or current range of its activities, which might weaken its viability and effectiveness as a competitor on the markets in question. (para. 22 of the Decision of 30 January 2002, DG Comp web site)

Tetra Laval would have the choice of the method of divestiture as long as this basic objective was met, and the Commission made an order to that effect. Tetra Laval was also banned from maintaining any minority shareholding or other financial interest in Sidel which might have the effect of impeding the restoration of competition.

The undertakings appealed both decisions to the CFI, which annulled the art. 8(3) decision and found as a consequence that the divestiture decision was also invalid (*Tetra Laval BV* v *Commission (I)* case T–5/02 [2002] 5 CMLR 28; *Tetra Laval BV* v *Commission (II)* case T–80/02 [2002] 5 CMLR 29). The CFI rejected arguments to the effect that the Commission had breached procedural requirements, but did find that the Commission had 'committed manifest errors of assessment in relying on the horizontal and vertical effects of the modified merger to support its analysis of the creation of a dominant position' (para. 141). Further, the Commission had overstated the conglomerate effects of the merger, and had wrongly disregarded the commitments offered by Tetra Laval. On 13 January 2003 the Commission lodged its appeal against the CFI judgments as cases C–12 and 13/03 P *Commission* v *Tetra Laval BV*.

19.2.2.7.2 *Schneider/Legrand*
In this case the Commission blocked a merger between two French electrical equipment manufacturers who were both active worldwide, holding that the merger would create or strengthen a dominant position in various sectors of the market, and that commitments proposed by Schneider were not sufficient (Commission decision of 10 October 2001). A number of relevant product markets were identified in the general area of individual components, or of particular types of switchboard, and other built products, and the Commission found that the geographic markets were national in scope. Brand loyalty was a strong feature of the market, with some electricians working with the same brands for their entire careers, with the effect that branding was very important, and that manufacturers

sought to develop as wide a range of products as possible. This in turn raised a substantial barrier to entry, as any new entrant would have to build a brand from scratch. Further, there was a lack of price sensitivity. Prior to the merger both parties had very wide ranges of products and following the merger there would be only two countries in the EEA in which the combined entity would not occupy a leading position. The Commission also found that there was little countervailing buyer power, as given the fragmented nature of the market at the purchaser level, and the nature of brand loyalty, no buyers would be in a position to exercise a significant competitive constraint on the producer. In conclusion the Commission found that the merged entity would be able to raise the price of its products for its own benefit, and declared the merger to be incompatible with the common market.

Schneider launched a successful appeal against the decision (*Schneider Electric SA v Commission* case T–310/01 [2003] 4 CMLR 17). The CFI found that the Commission had failed properly to evaluate the geographic market, noting that there were different national geographic markets, but referring to the Europe-wide coverage of the merged entity to show that a dominant position would be created (paras 176–7). While the Court did not rule that the Commission could not undertake such an exercise it did require that were the Commission to do so it was obliged to demonstrate clearly the link between the two different geographic situations, and had failed in this case to do so. The Court further found that the Commission had failed adequately to consider the role of wholesalers and had not clearly demonstrated that they would be unable to exercise a restraint on the merged entity. The decision was annulled.

19.2.2.7.3 *General Electric/Honeywell*
The blocking of the GE/Honeywell merger was particularly contentious, given that the US authorities had expressly consented to the same merger proceeding (see above, at 4.1 and 4.2.2). The relevant parties entered into an agreement on 22 October 2000 under which Honeywell would become a wholly owned subsidiary of GE. The primary markets affected were parts of the aerospace and power systems industries, and the Commission found that 'in these sectors the transaction brings about significant horizontal, vertical and conglomerate effects' (art. 8—in all cases here references are to the version of the Decision published on the DG Comp web site). In the market for the supply of jet engines for large commercial aircraft the Commission found that GE enjoyed several of the features of a dominant undertaking, and that the effect of the transaction would be to transmute this position of dominance into one of monopoly (para. 86). In the market for large regional jet engines there existed various factors which contributed to GE's dominance, including its considerable financial strength, and its ability to buy large quantities of aircraft and to offer comprehensive packaged solutions to airlines (para. 163). In particular, 'no other engine competitor has the size, financial strength or vertical integration to replicate such offers' (para. 173). In the market for avionics (products relating to the range of equipment used for the control of the aircraft and for navigation, communication, and the assessment of flying

conditions) and for some non-avionics products Honeywell was found to be the leading supplier, and no competitor was able independently to replicate its range of products (para. 330). In the case of engine controls the merger would have led to vertical foreclosure effects, eliminating Honeywell as an independent supplier of engine controls to jet engine manufacturers competing with GE (para. 340). Finding that the proposed merger would bring about anti-competitive effects, and that suggested solutions advanced by the parties would not be sufficient to remedy these, the Commission blocked the merger.

19.2.2.7.4 *Airtours/First Choice* and *Gencor/Lonhro*
The approach of both the EC Commission and the CFI to these mergers has already been discussed above at 19.2.2.4.1.

19.2.3 Joint ventures and the ECMR

Joint ventures (JVs) are expressly encompassed within the definition of 'concentration' at art. 3(4) of the ECMR. This provides that 'the creation of a joint venture performing on a lasting basis all the functions of an autonomous economic entity shall constitute a concentration'. The two key elements here are those of the JV being 'lasting' and 'autonomous'. In 1998 the Commission published its *Notice on the concept of full-function joint ventures under Council Regulation (EEC) No 4064/89 on the control of concentrations between undertakings* (1998) OJ C66/1. Recognizing that JVs cover a wide range of activities, 'from merger-like operations to cooperation for particular functions such as R&D, production or distribution' (para. 3) the purpose of the notice is to draw a distinction between those JVs to which the ECMR applies, and those which fall to be analysed under art. 81.

The essential characteristic of a full-function (or 'concentrative') JV is that

[it] must operate on a market, performing the functions normally carried out by undertakings operating on the same market. In order to do so the joint venture must have a management dedicated to its day-to-day operations and access to sufficient resources including finance, staff, and assets (tangible and intangible) in order to conduct on a lasting basis its business activities within the area provided for in the joint-venture agreement.   (para. 12)

A JV will not therefore fall within the terms of the ECMR if it performs only a single limited function on behalf of its parents. This would include, for example, a JV limited to fulfilling a R&D activity, or producing goods on behalf of the parents, or principally acting as a sales agency merely distributing the goods of its parents.

Where a JV is found to be full function, and therefore subject to the ECMR (assuming the relevant thresholds are met) it may also serve as a means of coordinating the activity of the parent companies. If this is the case any such coordination is to be considered at the same time as the evaluation of the JV under the terms of the ECMR, although this analysis will be carried out through the application of art. 81.

19.2.4 **Joint ventures and art. 81 EC**

Cooperative joint ventures are horizontal agreements which fall to be considered within the terms of art. 81(3) where they do not have the concentrative aspects that bring them within the terms of the ECMR. The EC Commission *Guidelines on the Applicability of Article 81 to Horizontal Cooperation Agreements* are the most complete statement on the position. There is a welcome recognition in the new guidelines, in response to criticism made over the years from a number of quarters, that it is the fact of horizontal cooperation, and not its form, that should form the basis of analysis within the competition rules. Thus the guidelines recognize, at para. 7, that there is an 'enormous variety in types and combinations of horizontal co-operation and market circumstances in which they operate'. In effect, therefore, the separate treatment accorded to horizontal joint ventures under the old Notice has been replaced by a more economically driven and less formalistic approach. Research and development agreements, and specialization agreements which take the form of cooperative joint ventures, are to be analysed in accordance with the terms of the block exemptions discussed above where the market thresholds are below the levels required of the regulations. Other cooperative joint ventures should be analysed in accordance with the principles set out in Chapter 9, and the guidelines are discussed there in relation to horizontal cooperation.

20

The UK merger control regime and the treatment of joint ventures

20.1 Introduction

The operation of the EC merger control regime was dealt with in the preceding chapter, where it was seen that, subject to only a small number of exceptions, where EC law applies to a merger it does so to the exclusion of relevant Member State law. The merger control regime of any Member State therefore remains very much a matter of national law, in which jurisdiction may be asserted over any merger that is not reserved to the EC. The UK merger regime is set out in the Enterprise Act 2002, which replaced in this respect the regime of the Fair Trading Act 1973. The discussion here relates to mainstream merger control and does not include, for example, discussion of mergers in the newspaper industry, which have their own special regime. At the time of writing there have been few reviews of mergers under these provisions, so most of the discussion here is necessarily based on the words of the legislation and the relevant guidance.

Part 3 of the Enterprise Act 2002 made several key reforms to the merger control process in the UK. Thus in the White Paper *A World Class Competition Regime* (Cm. 5233, DTI, July 2000) the DTI stated its position in the following terms at para. 5.2:

Government policy in recent years has been to take merger decisions primarily on competition grounds. Practice has also been for the Government to follow the advice of the competition authorities in most cases. The reform proposals build on these developments. They have two central elements. Firstly, decisions on the vast majority of mergers will be transferred from Ministers to the OFT and the Competition Commission. Secondly, the test against which mergers are assessed will be changed from a broad-based 'public interest' test to a new competition-based test. The Government is also committed to procedural and other improvements, such as the introduction of maximum statutory timetables for investigations, and building more transparency into the process.

It was the shift towards an economic approach that drew most comment. In fact, however, this merely reflected a policy change that had already taken place in practice. A new test for a merger's acceptance, the 'substantial lessening of competition' (SLC) test was adopted, which is therefore not the same as the test in the EC regime, although again differences may be less noticed than the similarities in practice. Perhaps the most important change, however, lay in the redefining of the roles of the OFT and the Competition Commission (CC), with merger control now being largely a two-stage process—as is the case in the EC. In the UK the first hurdle the merger has to clear is that of the OFT, which may decide to refer a merger to the CC, or to try and negotiate a solution where it considers that there may be an SLC (the 'stage one procedure'). The CC has the role of evaluating a merger more fully following a reference by the OFT, and where it finds that the merger is to be blocked or condemned is responsible for imposing its own remedies (the 'stage two procedure'). In some special public interest cases the relevant Secretary of State may become involved. Both the OFT and the CC have published guidance in relation to merger control.

20.2 Stage One

20.2.1 Notifications and references

Unlike the position under the EC merger regime (ECMR) there is no requirement in the UK to notify mergers to the OFT. At the same time the OFT has a legal duty to refer certain completed mergers to the CC. This is the case where a relevant merger situation has been created which has resulted, or may be expected to result, in an SLC (s. 21(1)). The OFT publication, *Mergers: Substantive Assessment Guidance*, gives indications as to the situations in which the OFT is likely, or not likely, to refer mergers to the CC.

There are two major qualifications to the general rule set out in s. 21(1). The first is that where the merger does not affect a sufficiently important market no reference is necessary. In the view of the OFT this is likely to be the case only rarely. Section 22(2) provides that a reference need not be made where

any relevant customer benefits in relation to the creation of the relevant merger situation concerned outweigh the substantial lessening of competition concerned and any adverse effects of the substantial lessening of competition concerned.

The concept of relevant customer benefit is set out at length in s. 30 of the Act. Section 30 provides that a relevant customer benefit exists if it provides customers with 'lower prices, higher quality or greater choice', or 'greater innovation'. The benefit must accrue within a reasonable period of time, and must be unlikely to accrue without the creation of the merger situation, and the SLC.

20.2.2 Merger situations falling within the Act

In order to qualify as a merger falling within the terms of the Act the requirements are that:

— two or more enterprises (defined in s. 129) cease to be distinct; *and*
— the value of the turnover in the UK of the enterprise being taken over exceeds £70m; *or*

— in relation to the supply of goods or services of any description, at least one-quarter of all the goods or services of that description which are supplied in the UK are supplied by or to one and the same person (s. 23(1), (2), (3), and (4)).

These criteria, while being substantial, nevertheless caught a merger early in 2004 between Tesco plc and a Co-op store in Uxbridge Road, Slough (OFT press release 14/04, 2 February 2004).

20.2.2.1 *Cease to be distinct*

Enterprises 'cease to be distinct' where 'they are brought under common ownership or common control' (s. 26(1)). Three levels of control may be discerned: material influence over policy; control over policy; and a controlling interest in the relevant enterprise. Section 26(4)(a), for example, would cover the situation in which there was a change from 'material influence' to 'control'. Section 29 provides that in situations where control is obtained by 'a series of transactions', these may be treated as having occurred simultaneously on the date on which the last of them occurred, thus obviating the need to examine the transactions individually, consolidating the examination of all into a single reference. This applies only over any two-year period. Section 27 deals with the time when enterprises cease to become distinct. The effect of the section is to allow the authorities to treat any incremental changes in control achieved through a series of transactions ('successive events') as having all taken effect on the date of the last transaction, and there is no need to determine which precise transaction led to the increase in control necessary to qualify as a merger situation. The difference between this section and s. 29 is that s. 27 applies to what might be deemed a single transaction, whereas s. 29 applies to a series of discrete transactions.

There are various ways in which 'common control' may be found to exist. Section 26(2) provides that enterprises may be treated as being under common control if they are:

(a) enterprises of interconnected bodies corporate;

(b) enterprises carried on by two or more bodies corporate, of which one and the same person has control; and

(c) an enterprise carried on by a body corporate and an enterprise carried on by a person or group of persons having control of that body corporate.

A controlling interest in an enterprise will normally be found to exist where the shareholding reaches the point where more than 50 per cent of the voting rights have been acquired. The question is one of fact, and the most important single factor is probably the ability of the shareholder (who will have a minority holding, albeit possibly the largest single holding) to appoint directors to the board.

20.2.2.2 *Turnover exceeds £70m*

The turnover test, set out in s. 23(1)(b), and expanded on in s. 28, represents a compromise between the Government, which had insisted on a figure of £45m up to Third Reading, and the House of Lords, which was insisting on a figure of £100m. The effect of the move from £45m to £70m is estimated to be that 50 per cent fewer mergers would be caught by the provisions. The value of the turnover, which must be turnover in the UK, of the enterprise being taken over is to be determined in accordance with rules made by the Secretary of State. The OFT has published guidance on turnover and its calculation.

20.2.2.3 *Twenty-five per cent of relevant goods or services*

A relevant merger situation is created where the merger creates or enhances a share of the market, however defined, of 25 per cent or above. Section 23 allows the person making the reference to determine what the reference framework in terms of the relevant goods or services is, as well as the appropriate benchmark by which the 25 per cent figure is determined. The OFT has indicated, in its guideline *Mergers: Substantive Assessment Guidance*, that

[it] will have regard to the narrowest reasonable description of a set of goods or services to determine whether the share of supply test is met. In so doing the OFT may have regard to the value, cost, price, quantity, capacity, number of workers employed or any other criterion in determining whether the 25 per cent test is met. This practice is intended to make it easier for companies and their advisers to determine whether the Act applies to a particular merger situation. (para. 2.24)

It is very hard to see how having regard to 'any other criterion' can 'make it easier for companies' to determine whether or not they are caught by the provisions of the Act.

20.2.3 **Time limits**

References must be made to the CC within four months of their completion, or within four months of the notice of material facts being made public or given to the OFT, where this is later (s. 24). There has been no reported case in which the issue of 'being made public' was a key factor, and it has been suggested that 'the filing of documents at Companies House should be sufficient to place the information in the public domain and make it readily ascertainable' (Livingston, D., *Competition Law and Practice*, London, FT Law and Tax (1995), para. 33.52). Section 31 gives the OFT the power to request information in relation to mergers from any person carrying on an enterprise which has ceased to be distinct. The time limits provided for may be extended by a further 20 days by agreement between the OFT and the relevant parties, or by notice by the OFT where it has not been given requested information, where undertakings are being sought, or where the UK has made a request to the EC Commission under art. 22(3) of the EC Merger Regulation (see 19.2.2.6).

20.2.4 Anticipated mergers

In addition to being able to make references in cases where a relevant merger situation has arisen, the OFT may also make references in respect of anticipated mergers (s. 33). In recent years, the majority of references have been in relation to anticipated mergers. Exactly the same provisions are made in respect of such references as apply to consummated mergers, save that in the case of anticipated mergers these operate prospectively rather than reactively.

20.2.5 The substantial lessening of competition test

Both the OFT and the CC must carry out SLC analysis. For the OFT the question is whether, in light of potential or actual SLC, the merger should be referred to the CC. For the CC the analysis is that of whether the merger should be blocked, or condoned, or if some remedy may be imposed that will render the merger acceptable. The broad approach to the SLC test is set out at para. 133 of the DTI *Explanatory Notes to the Enterprise Act 2002* in the following terms:

The concept of a substantial lessening of competition and its application to the context of a reference inquiry will be for the CC to explain in detail in its guidance. Similar language is used in the legislation controlling mergers in a number of other major jurisdictions, including the US, Canada, Australia, and New Zealand. The concept is an economic one, best understood by reference to the question of whether a merger will increase or facilitate the exercise of market power (whether unilateral, or through coordinated behaviour), leading to reduced output, higher prices, less innovation or lower quality of choice. A number of matters may be potentially relevant to the assessment of whether a merger will result in a substantial lessening of competition. The matters may include, but are not limited to:

- market shares and concentration;
- extent of effective competition before and after the merger;
- efficiency and financial performance of firms in the market;
- barriers to entry and expansion in the relevant market;
- availability of substitute products and the scope for supply- or demand-side substitution;
- extent of change and innovation in a market;
- whether in the absence of the merger one of the firms would fail and, if so, whether its failure would cause the assets of that firm to exit the market;
- the conduct of customers or of suppliers to those in the market.

Although the SLC test is not the same test as that adopted in the EC, it must be stressed that the SLC test does not replace a test similar to the one operated in the EC. Rather, the test of the Fair Trading Act 1973 was that of whether a merger might operate, or be expected to operate, against the public interest. In this context the SLC test is to be greatly preferred for its economic coherence. The general concerns raised about mergers have been discussed in Chapter 18.

For the OFT to make a reference to the CC on the basis of an actual or anticipated SLC it is required that it 'has a reasonably held belief that, on the basis of the evidence available to it, there is at least a significant prospect that a merger may be expected to lessen competition substantially' (*Mergers: Substantive Assessment Guidance*, para. 3.2). The broad approach that the OFT will take to the SLC test is set out at paras 3.5–3.24 of the guidance. For the CC the approach is set out, in more detail, at part 3 of its guideline, *Merger References: Competition Commission Guidelines*, June 2003.

One useful indicator of competition in the market place may be found in a concentration ratio, of which the most commonly used is the Herfindahl–Hirschman Index (HHI) (see 9.3.2.1). The OFT places some weight on this measure, and it has indicated that it

is likely to regard any market with a post-merger HHI in excess of 1,800 as highly concentrated, and any market with a post-merger HHI in excess of 1,000 as concentrated. In a highly concentrated market, a merger with a delta ['Delta' is the change in the HHI achieved by subtracting the pre-merger HHI from the post-merger HHI] in excess of 50 may give rise to potential competition concerns. In a concentrated market, a merger with a delta in excess of 100 may give rise to potential competition concerns.   (OFT guideline, para. 4.3)

For the CC, on the other hand, less weight is likely to be placed on these measures. It is not involved in the process of determining whether to refer a merger, and is more sensitive to a wider range of factors. Thus the CC notes that reference to concentration thresholds will be used 'only as one factor in its wider assessment of competition' (para. 3.10).

Where efficiencies are claimed for any mergers the OFT requires these to be demonstrable, merger specific, and likely to be passed on to consumers (para. 4.34). This follows the approach taken to consumer benefit in s. 30 of the Act, although efficiencies and consumer benefits are not exactly the same thing. This follows the response of the Irish Delegation to the EC Commission's suggestion that an efficiency defence be explicitly recognized in EC merger control:

The Green Paper seems to us to be inherently correct in expressing scepticism about efficiencies arising from mergers.

- Empirical studies indicate that, on aggregate, the *ex post* performance of merged companies is, at best, mixed, suggesting that efficiencies may systematically fall below the parties' genuine expectations.

- From an economic theory perspective, there is a fundamental doubt about efficiencies in mergers where market power increases. If we believe that competition is fundamental to driving cost reductions, then efficiencies are less likely to be attained precisely in the case where a merger creates market power . . .

- It is not always obvious that a merger (involving market power) is necessary to achieve many efficiency benefits.

- If an efficiency defence is allowed, then firms will have a strong incentive to exaggerate the efficiencies and it can be extremely difficult for a competition authority to verify them in advance. For this reason, the burden should likely lie on the parties to show the efficiencies, and a high standard of proof should be required.

20.2.6 *IBA Health Limited* v *The OFT*

At the end of 2003 a decision by the OFT not to refer a merger to the CC was appealed by a competitor of the merged entity to the CAT (see 20.5 for appeals). The case led to a substantial amount of litigation and clarified the criteria to be taken into account by the OFT when deciding whether or not to refer a merger. By an application dated 21 November 2003 IBA Health Limited (IBA), an Australian public company and a global supplier of IT solutions to the healthcare industry, applied pursuant to s. 120 of the Enterprise Act 2002 ('EA 02') to a review of the decision of the OFT not to make a merger reference to the CC on an anticipated acquisition by iSOFT Group plc of Torex plc, both providers of IT applications to the health sector.

The OFT found that by any measure the market shares of the parties post-merger would be substantial, being either 39 per cent of contracts awarded over the past five years, or 44 per cent of the installed base of systems on a historic basis. However, the OFT was swayed by the fact that a new procurement system for healthcare IT in the public sector in England was being launched, and the OFT took the view that this would alter the pattern of future purchases such that past market shares were no indication of likely success in the future. It was primarily on this basis that the decision was taken not to refer the merger. IBA argued, *inter alia*, that it would take many years for the new system to come fully on line, and that in the interim period the installed base would continue to be significant, particularly as regards contracting activity at lower levels in the health service.

The CAT held that the first question to be considered was whether the OFT was confronted with a real question as to whether or not it was, or might have been, the case that the iSOFT/Torex merger might be expected to lead to a substantial lessening of competition (*IBA Health Limited* v *The OFT* [2003] CAT 27). The CAT suggested that in 'grey area' cases where real issues as to the substantial lessening of competition potentially arise, there was a two-part test. The OFT must satisfy itself that (1) there is no significant prospect of a substantial lessening of competition; and (2) there is no significant prospect of an alternative view being taken in the context of a fuller investigation by the CC (para 197). The CAT held that where there is a real issue as to whether there is an SLC it is only in the exceptional case that the OFT should seek to resolve the matter itself rather than make a reference to the CC (para. 199). In 'grey area' cases it is inherently difficult for the OFT to explore the matter in sufficient depth to be able to decide *not* to make a reference with the necessary degree of certainty.

The broad question the CAT had to ask itself in the course of such a proceeding as in the present case was whether it was satisfied that the OFT's decision was not erroneous in law, and was one which it was reasonably open to the OFT to take, giving the word 'reasonably' its ordinary and natural meaning (para. 225). The Tribunal was unable, on the basis of the evidence before it, to be satisfied that the OFT had asked itself the right question, namely whether the OFT was satisfied *not only* that there was no significant prospect of an SLC *but also* that there was no significant prospect of the CC reaching an alternative view after a fuller investigation (para. 232). The CAT quashed the decision, and the OFT appealed to the Court of Appeal (*OFT and others* v *IBA Health Limited* [2004] EWCA Civ 142).

The Court of Appeal held that the two-part test formulated by the CAT was not the right test to apply, and that the right test was that stated in s. 33(1). It was necessary for the OFT to form the relevant belief which must be reasonable and objectively justified by the relevant facts. The test for the OFT was whether the anticipated merger 'may result in a relevant merger situation or not'. The CAT did, however, apply the proper standards for judicial review. It did not reverse the burden of proof on the applicant, but was entitled and bound to examine with care why adverse hypotheses were rejected by the OFT in so short a time, and whether that rejection was justified, particularly in view of the statutory requirement on the OFT to give reasons (para. 57). The Court held that the OFT applied too high a test of likelihood when forming their belief, or failed to adequately justify the belief that they formed in accordance with the proper test. Notwithstanding the fact that the CAT adopted a wrong test as to likelihood, their ultimate conclusion was right and should be upheld (para. 75).

20.2.7 Initial and interim measures, and undertakings in lieu of references

Where the OFT is considering whether to make a reference under s. 22, it may, for the purpose of preventing pre-emptive action, that is to say action taken by the companies which might thwart the OFT or the CC, accept undertakings from the relevant parties to take such action(s) as it considers to be appropriate (s. 71). The OFT's guidance points to the sorts of situations in which such undertakings may be appropriate:

undertakings in lieu have typically been used in merger cases in the past where a substantial lessening of competition arises from an overlap that is relatively small in the context of the merger (e.g. a few local markets affected by a national merger.   (para. 8.3)

There have been a number of cases already in which the OFT has sought undertakings in lieu of references. These are always notified on the OFT web site. For example, in relation to the acquisition of the Wales and Borders rail franchise by Arriva plc the latter company indicated that it would be willing to offer an undertaking opening up integrated ticketing arrangements to bus companies. This dealt with the OFT concern that competition from rival bus companies could be harmed if Arriva introduced integrated ticketing only in relation to its own services (OFT press release 44/04, 16 March 2004). Undertakings were also accepted from Tesco plc in relation to its purchase of the Slough Co-op store, which it agreed to sell (OFT press release 14/04, 2 February 2004).

As an alternative to accepting undertakings under s. 71, the OFT may make initial enforcement orders under s. 72. For such an order to be made, the OFT has to believe not only that a relevant merger situation has been created, but also that pre-emptive action is either in progress or in contemplation.

Since the concern raised by mergers is a structural one, the OFT has indicated that it is more likely to accept structural than behavioural undertakings (guideline, paras 8.6–8.9). Once an undertaking has been accepted, the OFT is prevented from making a reference in relation to the merger situation, unless material facts have not been notified to the OFT or made public before the undertaking concerned was accepted (s. 73(2)).

Where an undertaking made under s. 73 is not being fulfilled, or where information given to the OFT or made public, which informed the undertaking, was false or misleading, the OFT may make an order compelling performance, or anything permitted by Sch. 8 (s. 75, see below).

Standstill provisions are enshrined in ss. 77 and 78. In the first case, once a completed merger has been referred to the CC, the parties are prevented from completing any arrangements which have resulted in the merger, or making further arrangements in consequence of that result, or transferring the ownership or control of any enterprises to which the reference relates (s. 77(2)). The consent of the CC may be given to such transactions, however. These provisions apply also to a person's conduct outside the UK, but only if he is: (a) a UK national; or (b) a body incorporated under the law of the UK, or any part of the UK; or (c) a person carrying on business in the UK. Section 78 operates in relation to anticipated mergers, and imposes a prohibition on the acquisition or transfer of shares (directly or indirectly) in a company in any enterprise to which the merger reference relates during the relevant period.

Section 80 gives the CC the power to accept interim undertakings once a reference has been made to it. These undertakings may be, in addition to any initial undertakings, accepted by the OFT, or may be a re-adoption of OFT undertakings in the appropriate circumstances.

20.3 Stage Two

20.3.1 Questions to be decided by the CC

In addition to determining whether there is a relevant merger, and whether it may result in an SLC, the CC is required to consider what actions it should take in order to prevent, mitigate, or remedy the SLC. It is required in this respect

to have regard to the need to achieve as comprehensive a solution as is reasonable and practicable to the substantial lessening of competition and any adverse effects arising from it. (s. 35(4))

This provision is elaborated on in the *Explanatory Notes* at para. 134:

The reference to a 'comprehensive solution' will require the CC to consider remedies that address the substantial lessening of competition itself (e.g. the features arising from the merger that give rise to the creation of market power) because it is generally more effective to tackle the cause of any problems at their source rather than by tackling the symptoms or adverse effects.

This appears to be suggesting that structural remedies—either blocking an anticipated merger, or requiring divestiture post-merger—are to be generally preferred to conduct remedies where the CC has found that there is SLC flowing from the merger. The application of remedies by the CC is considered in Part 4 of its merger guidelines.

The CC is also required to take into account any relevant customer benefits that flow from the merger, and to balance these against the SLC. Where the CC identifies that a merger has an anti-competitive outcome, it is under a duty, imposed on it by s. 41, so far as it is practicable and reasonable to do so, to remedy, mitigate, or prevent the adverse effects in relation both to the SLC itself and from any effects of the SLC. In doing so, it is given the discretion to take into account any relevant customer benefits, and has scope

if it considers that customer benefits are of sufficient importance, to impose a lesser competition remedy or no remedy at all if the only steps that the CC could take to remedy the competition problem are steps that would mean that the customer benefits could not be realised.   (*Explanatory Notes*, para. 149)

The CC itself has indicated that it would be likely that remedial action would be required in situations in which it determined that a merger would be likely to result in an SLC, unless it did identify the existence of customer benefits. There might also be some other rare cases, such as where any remedial action lay outside the jurisdiction of the UK, where it would be outside the power of the CC to impose a remedy.

The CC will also consider the cost of any remedy when considering whether to impose it. However, the CC has indicated that in the case of completed mergers, it will not consider the costs of divestment to the parties, as the parties would have had the opportunity to seek a clearance of the merger prior to its consummation. Nor will the CC consider costs outside the competitive structure, such as environmental costs, or the social costs of unemployment, unless it is required to do so by the Secretary of State through the imposition of a specified public interest consideration (see below).

Remedies should also be proportional to the harm identified as arising out of the merger. This means that where two remedies are being considered, each of which is equally effective, the cheaper should be the one chosen.

The types of remedies that are available to the CC are set out at para. 4.17 of its guidelines as follows:

The CC will consider any of the following types of remedies:

(a) remedies that are intended to restore all or part of the status quo ante market structure, for example:

- — prohibition of a proposed merger;
- — divestment of a completed acquisition;
- — partial prohibition or divestment;

(b) remedies that are intended to increase the competition that will be faced by the merged firm (whether from existing competitors or new entrants), for example
- — requiring access to essential inputs/facilities;
- — licensing know-how or IPRs;
- — dismantling exclusive distribution arrangements;
- — removing no-competition clauses in customer contracts;

(c) remedies aimed at excluding or limiting the possibility that the merged firm will take advantage of the increased market power resulting from the merger to behave anti-competitively or to exploit its customers or suppliers, for example:
- — a price cap or other restraint on prices;
- — a commitment to non-discriminatory behaviour;
- — an obligation to increase the transparency of prices;
- — an obligation to refrain from conduct, the main purpose of which is to inhibit entry.

The starting point for the CC when considering its approach to the remedy, if one is considered necessary, will be to choose the action that is most likely to restore the competition that has been damaged by the merger (para. 4.23). This is to say that, like the OFT, it is more likely to favour structural remedies than behavioural remedies. An additional factor in favour of structural remedies is that they do not require on-going policing. The CC may also recommend that action be taken by others, for example, by way of legislation, where regulations exist that limit entry, or to amend licence conditions in the case of regulated undertakings.

20.3.2 Merger reports

The CC is required to publish a report on a merger reference within a period of 24 weeks from the date of the reference concerned (ss. 38(1) and 39(1)), although, in exceptional circumstances, this period may be extended by up to a further eight weeks (s. 39(3)). The period may also be extended where a relevant person has failed to comply with the requirements of s. 109, which relates to the attendance of witnesses and the production of documents. This report is to contain its decision, the reasons for its decision, and any information necessary to understand the decision. It has the power to carry out necessary investigations in order to prepare the report (s. 38(2)).

20.3.4 Powers of investigation

Sections 109–17 deal with the power of the CC to require the presentation of evidence and documents needed for the purposes of a merger inquiry. Section 109 confers on the CC the power to compel the attendance of witnesses and the production of documents. A notice may be given to any person requiring them to attend a specified hearing, and to give evidence to the CC or a person nominated by the CC (s. 109(1)). A similar power exists in relation to the presentation of documents. The CC may also require the supply of 'estimates, forecasts returns or other information' (s. 109(3)). The CC may take evidence on oath (s. 109(5)). No material may be required where the production of such could not be compelled in civil proceedings before a court. This preserves the right against self-incrimination, and a protection in respect of legally privileged material. In the context of a wide-ranging mergers investigation, it is unlikely that these limitations would be often invoked.

Where the CC finds that a person has, without reasonable cause, failed to comply with an obligation imposed by way of s. 109, it may directly impose a penalty on that person, subject to an appeal to the CAT (s. 110(1)). Any penalty imposed under this section 'shall be of such an amount as the Commission considers appropriate' (s. 111(1)). The amount may be fixed, or may be calculated on a daily rate until such time as compliance is ensured. An offence is committed if any person intentionally alters, suppresses, or destroys any document which he has been required to produce, and, on conviction, he may face a fine not exceeding the statutory maximum, or a term of imprisonment not exceeding two years, or a combination of the two. However, no offence may be deemed to have been committed if the CC has acted under s. 110(1) and imposed its own penalty. The maximum penalty that may be imposed in the case of a fixed amount is £30,000, and, in the case of a daily penalty, the maximum amount per day is £15,000 (s. 111(7)). Where it imposes a penalty, the CC is required, as soon as is practicable, to give a notice relating to the penalty. The person to whom the notice is addressed may, within 14 days, apply to the CC for it to specify a different rate, or different dates for payment of the penalty. The CC has published its *Statement of Policy on Penalties* (June 2003) which deals in particular with the assessment of situations in which there has been a failure to comply with the requirement to supply information, and the imposition of penalties in relation to this. In relation to the failure to supply information, the CC will consider 'whether there is any reasonable excuse for the failure to comply, and, in particular, 'the extent to which the failure arose from circumstances outside the control of the person who has failed to comply' (para. 12). Five factors are set out as being likely to increase the prospect of a penalty being imposed (para. 13):

(i) the failure affected the efficient carrying out of the CC's functions;

(ii) other persons were adversely affected;

(iii) deterrence of future non-compliance;

(iv) the absence of good reason; and

(v) whether the person failing to comply sought to gain, or did gain, by so doing.

Appeals against penalties may be made to the CAT. Appeals may be made against the imposition or nature of the penalty, the amount of the penalty, and the date on which the penalty is to be paid (s. 114). The CAT may not substitute its own assessment of the penalty unless the substituted figure is lower than the figure that would be required by the CC. A further appeal may be made to the Court of Appeal against the judgment of the CAT (s. 114(10)).

An offence is committed in any case if a person supplies the OFT or the CC or the Secretary of State with information that is false or misleading in a material respect, knowing that to be the case, or recklessly to that effect (s. 117).

20.3.5 Final powers of the CC

The CC has the power to accept final undertakings from parties in order to remedy concerns raised in its reports (s. 82). It also has the power to make orders where any such final undertakings are not fulfilled, or where information which was false or misleading in a material respect was given to it or to the OFT. If an order is made under this section, it may not be varied or revoked unless the OFT advises that such a change is appropriate in the light of changed circumstances. Final orders may also be made by the CC, in accordance with s. 41 (s. 84). Any order made under this section may contain anything permitted by Sch. 8. No order shall be made under this section if an undertaking has been accepted and is being complied with under s. 82. An undertaking made under s. 82 may contain matters *not* set out in Sch. 8 (s. 89).

Schedule 8 contains the list of matters that may be imposed in orders for the purpose of remedying any adverse effects of mergers identified by the CC in its report. Most of the items set out in the Schedule are self-explanatory. The most significant of the new items included on the list is that at para. 10, under which an order may require any relevant person to supply goods or services 'to a particular standard or in a particular manner'. An example of the way in which this provision might be applied is given in the *Explanatory Notes* and relates to the fact that it would be possible to tell a bus company to maintain a certain frequency of service (para. 238).

20.4 Public interest cases

20.4.1 Intervention by the Secretary of State

The OFT has a duty to notify the Secretary of State in any case where it is considering making a reference under ss. 22 or 33 of any matter which it believes to relate to public interest considerations (s. 57(1)). The CC has a duty to bring to the attention of the Secretary of State any representations made about the exercise of his powers under s. 57(2). Section 44 gives the Secretary of State the power to intervene in cases where a relevant merger situation raises public interest issues which are specified in s. 58. This is to say that the Secretary of State should have the power to refer a case that qualifies for investigation if he or she believes that the merger may operate against the public interest. The result will be that the Secretary of State will refer cases to the Competition Commission. The public interest test that the Secretary of State will apply under the new regime will be more limited than that in the [FTA 1973]. The Secretary of State will be limited to taking account of the relevant public interest considerations and any substantial lessening of competition. (Hansard, Standing Committee B, col. 347)

At the time of writing the only such consideration is that of national security, although the power exists for the Secretary of State to add to this list.

Intervention notices may be issued by the Secretary of State only where the OFT has not yet made a decision in respect of a merger situation. However, a notice may be issued where the OFT has made a decision to accept undertakings under s. 71 as an alternative to making a reference (see below). The details that must be included in intervention notices are set out in s. 43. They come into force when they are given, and cease to be in force at the point when the matter is finally determined. Where an intervention notice has been given, the OFT is required to give to the Secretary of State a report containing its advice on the considerations relevant to the making of a standard reference under ss. 22 or 33. In essence, the report is to be the summary of the position that the OFT would take in relation to the making of a merger reference, and may also 'include advice and recommendations on any public interest consideration mentioned in the intervention notice concerned' (s. 44(6)).

Following the receipt of the OFT's report, it is for the Secretary of State to refer the matter to the Commission if he or she is minded to do so. References may be made in two circumstances, either where the Secretary of State believes at the time of the receipt of the OFT report that there is, or there is not, SLC as a result of the merger, as long as he or she believes that 'the situation operates or may be expected to operate against the public interest' or where the Secretary of State decides, having received the report of the OFT, that there is no public interest consideration to which he or she is able to have regard. In the former situation, the Secretary of State is bound by the views of the OFT as regards the competition matters, but not as regards matters relating to the public interest consideration. Section 45(6) therefore provides that *any* anti-competitive outcome identified by the OFT shall be treated as being against the public interest, unless it is out-weighed by the relevant public interest consideration. Some qualifications on the power to refer are set out in s. 46. These mirror those which limit the OFT's power to make references set out in ss. 22 and 33. In the second situation, the Secretary of State does not make a reference, and therefore the matter is to be remitted to the OFT for it to deal with as it considers appropriate under the normal merger rules (s. 56(1)).

The requirements of reports made by the CC in response to a reference made by the Secretary of State are at first the same as for those in the case of references made by the OFT. However, the CC must also consider whether, taking account only of any substantial lessening of competition and the admissible public interest consideration or considerations concerned, the creation of that situation operates or may be expected to operate against the public interest. (s. 47(2)(b))

As with references made by the OFT, the CC also has a duty to determine what action should be taken to remedy the situation, the difference being that in this case, the recommendation will be for action to be taken by the Secretary of State under s. 55. Where the relevant intervention notice has ceased to be in force, the CC will revert to an analysis of the merger as if the reference had been made under s. 22 or s. 33, as appropriate. In this case, it will have an extra 20 days in which to produce its report from the date set by the Secretary of State (s. 56(3)–(5)).

20.4.2 Decisions of the Secretary of State

Where the Secretary of State has received a report from the CC, he or she 'shall decide whether to make an adverse public interest finding in relation to a relevant merger situation or whether to make no finding in the matter at all' (s. 54(2)). No finding shall be made in situations in which the Secretary of State decides that there is no public interest consideration which is relevant to the consideration of the merger situation (s. 54(4)). An adverse decision may be made in any case in which the Secretary of State, taking into account the public interest consideration, finds that the merger may be expected to operate against the public interest. The Secretary of State is bound by any decision taken by the CC in relation to the competitive effects of the merger. Any decision shall be made within 30 days of the receipt of the CC's report (s. 54(5)). Where the Secretary of State makes an adverse finding, he or she may take such action under Sch. 7, para. 9 or para. 11 as he or she considers reasonable in order to remedy, mitigate, or prevent any of the adverse effects of the merger on the public interest.

20.5 Appeals

Any decision of the OFT or the Secretary of State in connection with a merger reference may be appealed to the CAT within three months (s. 120). The standard for appeals is that of judicial review, meaning that the focus will be on the procedures adopted rather than the substance of the decision taken. As noted in the *Explanatory Notes*:

Case law suggests such grounds could include: (i) that an error of law was made; (ii) that there was a material procedural error; such as a material failure of an inquiry panel to comply with the Chairman's procedural rules; (iii) that a material error as to the facts has been made; and (iv) that there was some other material illegality (such as unreasonableness or lack of proportionality). Judicial review evolves over time and the approach in subsection (6) has been taken to ensure the grounds of review continue to mirror any such developments. (para. 284)

When it reviews any decision, the CAT may quash the whole decision, or only a part of that decision. Further appeals on points of law only may be made to the Court of Appeal or the Court of Session, with the leave of the CAT.

This right to appeal is available to third parties (for an example see 20.2.6), as well as to those subject to the reference. Schedule 3 provides for tribunal rules that may, *inter alia*, permit the CAT to reject proceedings if it appears to it that the persons bringing them do not have sufficient interest in a decision, or where it believes that the appeal is vexatious.

20.6 Third party rights

Apart from the third party rights to appeal decisions made in relation to merger references, ss. 94 and 95 ensure that those injured by the breach of enforcement undertakings, orders, and statutory restrictions may bring actions before the courts. A duty is owed 'to any person who may be affected by a contravention of the undertaking or (as the case may be) order' (s. 94(3)). Any breach which results in loss or damage is actionable. It is a defence, however, for the defendant 'to show that he took all reasonable steps and exercised all due diligence to avoid contravening the undertaking or order' (s. 94(5)).

20.7 Joint ventures in the UK

There is no specific recognition in UK domestic law of the concept of a 'joint venture'. Instead there is a variety of ways by which companies can put into place mechanisms to facilitate long-term cooperation. These can include the creation of a third company, legally separate, in which the two partners play a joint role in terms of management and ownership, and putting into place contractual arrangements. The consideration of any such scheme will fall to be considered under the general competition law applicable in the UK.

21

The common law and competition

21.1 Introduction

While there is not a common law of competition as such, there are areas in which the operation of the common law impacts upon issues that are closely related to the public regulation of competition. As was seen in Chapter 1, the common law was originally important in this area, and at the time of its enactment the Sherman Act was viewed within the United States largely as a codification of existing common-law principles. The fact that common law now occupies only a residual role in relation to competition law generally may be attributed to several factors. One may be the apparent success of forms of public regulation, which have reduced the need for reliance on a common law. Another lies in the reluctance of the judiciary to venture into what is seen as a difficult and technical area; it was Fry LJ who commented in *Mogul Steamship* v *McGregor* (1889) 28 QBD 598 at 625, that 'to draw a line between fair and unfair competition . . . passes the power of the courts'. A related reason may be found in the reluctance of the judiciary to distinguish economic interests from those of personal liberty. The comment of Lord Atkinson in *H. Morris Ltd* v *Saxelby* [1916] 1 AC 688 at 700, HL is typical: 'no person has an abstract right to be protected against competition *per se* in his trade or business'. The most important area in which the common law continues to have relevance is the contract-based restraint of trade doctrine. Other areas where the common law may play a role are in the statutory tort lying in relation to breaches of arts 81 and 82, conspiracy, and a bundle of related 'economic torts'.

21.2 The restraint of trade doctrine

21.2.1 The development of the doctrine

The roots of the doctrine of restraint of trade are obscure. In *Chitty on Contracts* it is stated that 'cases go back to the second half of the sixteenth century' (Guest, A. G. (ed.), *Chitty on Contracts*, London, Sweet & Maxwell (27th edn, 1994), para. 16–066), although the first reported case appears to be *John Dyer's* case (1414) YB 2

Hen 5, fo. 5, pl. 26. In this case, the defendant, a dyer, had given a bond to the plaintiff not to exercise his trade in the same town for six months. The bond was declared void by Hull J in no uncertain terms (technically the case was not one of 'restraint of trade', which was unknown then as a cause of action, but the case may be appropriately categorized as such at this distance).

The essence of the restraint of trade doctrine is that it is contrary to public policy to enforce contracts that are in unreasonable restraint of trade. It is generally considered to be the case that a contract in restraint of trade is void, unless that restraint can be shown to be a reasonable one. However, in *A. Schroeder Music Publishing Co. Ltd* v *Macaulay* [1974] 3 All ER 617, HL Lord Reid suggested that the contract in this case was 'unenforceable' (at 623), i.e., voidable, and whether such contracts are in fact void or voidable remains unclear. Whether a restraint is 'reasonable' is to be considered both in relation to the parties themselves, and in relation to the public interest.

Restraint of trade thus relates primarily to situations in which 'a party (the covenantor) agrees with any other party (the covenantee) to restrict his liberty in the future to carry on trade with other persons not parties to the contract in such manner as he chooses' (*Petrofina (Great Britain) Ltd* v *Martin* [1966] Ch 146, *per* Diplock LJ at 180).

All contracts restrain trade: if A agrees with B to sell B a car, then A cannot, without breaking that contract, sell that car to C. Clearly restraints of this nature are the essence of contractual relationships and will not, save in exceptional circumstances, be struck down. The difficulty with restraint of trade is to identify those situations in which the doctrine will apply, which is to say those in which the restraint is both unreasonable between the parties and against the public interest.

As is the case today, the doctrine, even in its earliest development, was determined by reference to the 'public interest', and public policy will also have an impact on the way in which the private interests of the parties are to be determined. This flexible criterion has meant that 'the law as to contracts in restraint of trade had, more than any other class of contracts, been moulded by changing ideas of public policy' (Holdsworth, W., *A History of English Law*, London, Methuen (1937), vol. 7, p. 6). The development of the doctrine became for a time inextricably linked with the resistance to the grants of monopoly by the Crown (see Chapter 1). In the reign of Elizabeth I, for example, all restraints were likely to be condemned as being contrary to public policy (*Colgate* v *Bacheler* (1602) Cro Eliz 872). By 1711, in the case of *Mitchell* v *Reynolds* (1711) 1 P. Wms 181, the courts had begun to distinguish between restraints which operated at the local level and those which purported to be countrywide. In *Mitchell* a countrywide restraint was criticized in the following terms: 'what does it signify to a tradesman in London what another does in Newcastle?' Even in the twentieth century *Mitchell* was referred to as 'among all the decisions, the most outstanding and helpful authority' (*H. Morris Ltd* v *Saxelby* [1916] 1 AC 688, HL, *per* Lord Shaw at 717). Public policy now recognizes that there is a broad interest in encouraging the sale and transfer of businesses, and mobility of employment. If an employer could not to a certain extent restrain the activities of an employee once he or she leaves the employment there might be less incentive to employ the worker in the first place. The same may be true of someone buying a business, who would be less attracted were the vendor immediately able to set up in competition to the new purchaser (see, e.g., Lord Watson in *Nordenfelt* v *Maxim Nordenfelt Guns and Ammunition Co. Ltd* [1984] AC 535 at 552).

The concept of 'reasonableness' appears to have entered into the application of the doctrine in the seventeenth century, and is usually traced to *Rogers* v *Parrey* (1613) 80 ER 1012. Here the judges, including Coke CJ, were called upon to determine the validity of a restraint under which the defendant had promised not to exercise his trade as a joiner 'in a shop, parcel of a house, to him demised in London, for 21 years'. Croke J expressed his concern as to the effect of the restraint: 'The doubt which at first troubled me, was, for the binding of one, that he should not use and exercise his trade, being his livelihood'. However, the fact that this was not the case here swayed the court, which unanimously agreed with Coke CJ that 'as this case here is, for a time certain, and in a place certain, a man may be well bound, and restrained from using his trade'. In *Broad* v *Jolyffe* (1620) Cro Jac 596, the court considered a case in which a trader selling his old stock to another had promised as part of the bargain that he would not trade in competition with the purchaser by keeping a shop in a particular place. When the plaintiff brought an action to enforce this term, the court was of the view that this was sustainable:

upon a valuable consideration one may restrain himself that he shall not use his trade in such a particular place; for he who gives that consideration expects the benefit of his customers; and it is usual here in London for one to let his shop and wares to his servant when he is out of his apprenticeship; as also to covenant that he shall not use his trade in such a shop or in such a street; so for a valuable consideration and voluntarily one may agree that he will not use his trade.

The extent to which the test of reasonableness could be reduced to clear criteria continued to exercise the courts through the eighteenth and nineteenth centuries. A problem facing the courts during this period was the rapid development in the patterns of commerce, and in particular the growth in transport and communications that would quickly render obsolete restrictive interpretations of the doctrine. In *Horner* v *Graves* (1831) 131 ER 284, the court refused to adopt a strict definition, holding instead (at 743) that

we do not see how a better test can be applied to the question whether reasonable or not, than by considering whether the restraint is such only as to afford a fair protection to the interests of the party in favour of whom it is given, and not so large as to interfere with the interests of the public. Whatever restraint is larger than the necessary protection of the party, can be of no benefit to either, it can only be oppressive; and if oppressive, it is, in the eyes of the law, unreasonable. Whatever is injurious to the interests of the public is void, on the grounds of public policy.

The test of reasonableness became the overriding consideration in *Nordenfelt* v *Maxim Nordenfelt Guns and Ammunition Co. Ltd* [1894] AC 535, and it was here that the modern test for determining the validity of any restraining contract was formulated by Lord Macnaghten, where he held (at 565):

The true view at the present time I think, is this: The public have an interest in every person's carrying on his trade freely: so has the individual. All interference with individual liberty of action in trading, and all restraints of trade of themselves, if there is nothing more, are contrary to public policy, and therefore void. That is the general rule. But there are exceptions: restraints of trade and interference with individual liberty of action may be justified by the special circumstances of a particular case. It is a sufficient justification, and indeed it is the only justification, if the restriction is reasonable—reasonable, that is, in reference to the interests of the parties concerned and reasonable in reference to the interests of the public, so framed and so guarded as to afford adequate protection to the party in whose favour it is imposed, while at the same time it is in no way injurious to the public.

In this case the flexibility of approach that Lord Macnaghten's summary of the position called for meant that a restriction unlimited geographically, and lasting for 25 years, was upheld. The restriction had been accepted by a manufacturer of guns who had sold his business and all the patents associated with it, and who had accepted a worldwide restriction on setting up a competing business. Given the nature of the arms trade, the court found that such a worldwide restriction served to protect the genuine commercial interest of the purchaser of the business and did not contain unreasonable restrictions. *Nordenfelt* may be contrasted with *Mason* v *Provident Clothing and Supply Co. Ltd* [1913] AC 724, in which a restriction on a salesman working for a cloth company, to the effect that he could not work within 25 miles of London for three years after leaving his job, was held to be too restrictive in relation to the interest being protected and the relevant circumstances. While it appears that the extent to which restraints are 'purchased' may be persuasive, the general principle is that the courts will not allow a party to 'buy' a restraint, and will not, in assessing whether a restraint is reasonable, consider the 'reward' given to the plaintiff in return for the acceptance of the restraint. To do so would raise the spectre of the courts assessing the adequacy of consideration, in this case for a single term in the contract, which is a matter that the courts generally avoid.

It has been suggested by Lever that

Any idea that courts are inherently ill equipped to apply *any* sort of economic regulatory rules is readily dispelled when it is recalled that it was the English courts themselves that developed, without legislative assistance, the doctrine. (Lever, J., 'UK Economic Regulation: Use and Abuse of the Law' [1992] *ECLR* 55)

However, the interpretation given to 'reasonable', and in particular the restricted role assigned to the 'public interest', means that the doctrine serves a limited function, and the courts have very obviously rejected any scope for extending it so as to provide a more general protection to the competitive process itself.

21.2.2 The current operation of the doctrine

Restraint of trade concerns will not, save in exceptional circumstances, be raised in standard commercial contracts. There are two situations where the doctrine remains vibrant, both of which have obvious implications for the competitive market. The first concerns post-contract employment considerations, where an employee accepts restrictions on future conduct if he or she leaves that employment. Typically such restrictions might include a limitation on the time that must elapse before the employee works for a competing company, or sets up in direct competition himself. It is also common for a geographical area to be identified, within which the employee is, for a set period, not permitted to compete. The second common situation relates to the sale of businesses and the goodwill attached thereto, where the seller will agree to restrictions on its liberty to maintain a similar business. This was the position in *Broad* v *Jolyffe* (above), where the court recognized that there were often benefits accruing to the seller in accepting such a restriction, if, by doing so, the value of the business it is selling increases: a business is worth less if purchasers know that they are shortly going to be facing competition from the very person selling them that business. Both of these situations have important consequences for competition. For example, if a pop star covenants with his recording label not to record for another label for a certain period after the termination of his contract, that may reduce the ability of labels to compete with each other. If a business owner covenants not to set up in competition to the purchaser of his business, that may reduce the consumer choice in that area.

The position remains that there are three requirements for the operation of the doctrine:

(a) the restraint must protect a legitimate interest of the party in whose favour it operates;

(b) the restraint must be no wider than is necessary to protect this interest; and

(c) the restraint must be reasonable in relation to the public interest.

These last two requirements appear to be often conflated into an overall balancing act undertaken by the courts. Whether a restraint is reasonable or not is to be considered in the light of the circumstances at the time when the restraint was imposed (see, e.g., *Watson* v *Prager* [1991] 3 All ER 487).

It is for the party claiming the benefit of the restraint to show that it is reasonable and that there is a legitimate interest to protect. This was made clear in *H. Morris Ltd* v *Saxelby* [1916] 1 AC 688, HL, where Lord Atkinson held (at 700) that

the onus of establishing to the satisfaction of the judge who tries the case facts and circumstances which show that the restraint is of the reasonable character [between the parties] [rests] upon the person alleging that it is of that character, and the onus of showing that, notwithstanding that it is of that character, it is nevertheless injurious to the public and therefore void, [rests], in like manner, on the party alleging the latter.

This *dictum* has been used in support of the contention that the test of whether a restraint is reasonable between the parties is a private matter between them, and that only if the restriction is found to be reasonable should the public interest then be considered. However, such a clear division between the two factors is difficult to sustain. The point was made by Lord Pearce in *Esso Petroleum Co. Ltd* v *Harper's Garage (Stourport) Ltd* ([1968] AC 269 at 324:

There is not, as some cases seem to suggest, a separation between what is reasonable on grounds of public policy and what is reasonable as between the parties. There is one broad question: is it in the interests of the community that this restraint should, as between the parties, be held to be reasonable and enforceable?

In the same case Lord Hodson gave further credence to the notion that the two factors tend to become conflated, when he noted (at 319) that 'the interests of the individual are much discussed in the cases on restraint of trade which seldom, if ever, have been expressly decided on public grounds'.

If the case does revolve around the public interest consideration, it is for the party claiming that the restriction is unreasonable to demonstrate that it is against the public interest (*Morris* v *Saxelby*, above). However, although this places a significant burden on the party challenging the restraint, the court is entitled to consider all surrounding aspects, and will be expected to achieve a balance between the private and public interest. There may be situations in which the defendant is expected to explain why a particular restraint is justifiable when, on the face of it, the restraint appears to be contrary to the public or private interest.

The consideration of public interest has caused some problems for the judiciary. The application of the doctrine to the economically important area of exclusive distribution contracts (or 'solus agreements' as they are sometimes referred to in the English cases) shows both the problems with applying a public interest test, and the application of the doctrine to areas central to competition law.

Esso Petroleum (above) was the first important case to consider this issue, and the case remains of fundamental importance to this area. This concerned a vertical distribution agreement under which the respondents agreed to buy petrol only from the appellant. The respondents owned two garages. In relation to the first the exclusive agreement was to last four years and five months, in return for which commitment the respondents were to be entitled to a discount on the petrol they obtained from the wholesaler. In relation to the second garage the respondents had accepted a £7,000 loan from the appellant, which was to be repaid as a mortgage over 21 years. The obligation to obtain petrol exclusively from the appellant was to continue for as long as the loan continued to be owed. Having decided that such a tie could fall to be considered within the restraint of trade doctrine, the court proceeded to consider whether either tie was in unreasonable restraint of trade. The first tie was considered to be in the interests of both the parties and was not found to be against the public interest. The longer tie was considered to be excessive in relation to the interest being protected, and was thus rendered unenforceable. The factors that were considered to be legitimate interests of the parties included the maintenance of the distribution system and the benefit of a stable flow of petrol to the market.

Their Lordships gave different reasons for the application of the doctrine to this situation, but the majority agreed on the formulation of what has been labelled the 'opening the door' test. Lord Reid set this out (at 298):

Restraint of trade appears to me to imply that a man contracts to give up some freedom which otherwise he would have had. A person buying or leasing land had no previous right to be there at all, let alone to trade there, and when he takes possession of that land subject to a negative restrictive covenant he gives up no right or freedom which he previously had.

Rightly, this formulation has come in for some criticism, notably, but not exclusively, by Valentine Korah ('Solus Agreements and Restraint of Trade' (1969) 32 *MLR* 323). While the approach has formal attractions, carrying as it does a degree of certainty, it takes little account of the realities of situations. The application of the test presumes that the surrendering of an existing freedom is somehow worse than entering a market for a first time carrying a restriction on freedom. In practice there may be little distinction between the two, particularly if it becomes apparent that the restricted entrant could have found much better terms and conditions elsewhere which would equally have facilitated entrance. Although the House devoted a lot of discussion to the concept of the public interest in the case, there is no point at which the public interest in the particular facts of the case itself are adequately resolved or discussed. It was also not made clear to what types of vertical restraints the doctrine would be applied. It was suggested, for example, that the traditional ties between landlords and breweries would not fall within the application of the doctrine as these were so much a part of accepted commercial practice (see too the comments of Lord Denning in *Petrofina (Great Britain) Ltd* v *Martin* [1966] Ch 146). If this is indeed the case, then it may be that over time the acceptance of solus ties will see a reduction in the scope of the application of the doctrine to these.

An example following *Esso* is *Texaco Ltd* v *Mulberry Filling Station Ltd* [1972] 1 All ER 513. The defendant, owner of a petrol filling station, had borrowed £36,000 from the plaintiff's agent, and accepted an obligation to buy petrol only from that supplier for a period of four years and seven months. The defendant subsequently broke this tie, and when he was sued under the contract sought to avoid the obligations on the basis of the restraint of trade doctrine. Ungoed-Thomas J accepted Lord Macnaghten's formulation of the doctrine from *Nordenfelt* (above), but was concerned that 'the doctrine has been much considered since, and has been the subject of observations which are by no means easy to reconcile' (at 521). In an effort to reconcile the authorities the judge took a very restricted view of the meaning of public interest, so as to exclude 'the interests of the public at large'. The judge's view (at 526) was that restraint of trade

is part of the doctrine of the common law and not of economics . . . if it refers to interests of the public at large, it might . . . involve balancing a mass of conflicting economic, social and other interests which a court of law might be ill-adapted to achieve; but, more important, interests of the public at large would lack sufficiently specific formulation to be capable of judicial as contrasted with unregulated personal decision and application—a decision varying, as Lord Eldon LC put it, like the length of the chancellor's foot.

Such a restrictive approach has not been taken since, but it is established law that the interests of the competitive economy are not part of the doctrine.

A final limitation of the doctrine arises from its place in contract law: the doctrine of privity means that only parties to the contract may invoke the doctrine, and third parties may not recover damages under it. There has, however, been a sprinkling of cases in which a more flexible approach has been taken, the most significant of which is *Eastham v Newcastle United Football Club Ltd* [1964] Ch 413. George Eastham was a distinguished inside forward for Newcastle United, but wished to transfer to another club. He was prevented from doing so by the rules of the Football Association (FA) and the League. These were binding on all the 92 league clubs. Under these rules a player could be retained by a club for the following season by the offer of a minimum wage acceptable to the League, which in this case was £418. Until the offer was accepted the player would not actually be under contract to the club and would not be playing. Only if players were able to persuade the FA that there were special grounds for allowing them to change their clubs could they move; and without such approval it would be virtually impossible to play professional football anywhere in the world, with the notable exception of Australia. That the agreement between the clubs and the FA operated in restraint of trade was evidently clear, and the justifications advanced for its continuance were rejected by the court. The fact that Eastham was not himself a party to the agreements was not held to be a bar to his action, given that his interests were so immediately affected by the agreement (see also *Greig v Insole* [1978] 1 WLR 302, relating to Test- and county-match bans on cricketers who had played for Kerry Packer, and *Watson v Prager* [1993] EMLR 275, relating to contracts between professional boxers and their managers). A similar approach was taken in *Pharmaceutical Society of Great Britain v Dickson* [1970] AC 403, where an individual chemist outlet was able to challenge a rule of the Pharmaceutical Society restricting the types of goods in which their members might deal; and in *Nagle v Feilden* [1966] 2 QB 633, the court held invalid a rule of the Jockey Club that prevented a woman from holding a trainer's licence. The issue of the 'right to work' considered in both this latter case and others raises further complexities that lie beyond the scope of this text.

The restraint of trade doctrine, for all its longevity, continues to play a vibrant part in domestic contract law, and to impact on competitive situations. For example, in *Hollis & Co v Mark Richard Stocks* [2000] UKCLR 658, the appellant was a solicitor employed by the respondent. A restraint in his contract of employment restricting him from working within a 10-mile radius of the respondent's office from the termination of his employment was found to be a reasonable one when it was challenged as being in restraint of trade. In *Lapthorne v Eurofi Ltd* [2001] UKCLR 996, on the other hand, the respondent was successful in challenging a post-termination clause in his contract which restricted his future employment. The relevant clause was too widely drawn, and hence fell within the restraint of trade doctrine and was unenforceable. Restraint of trade was a central argument in the case of *WWF—World Wide Fund for Nature (formerly World Wildlife Fund) and World Wildlife Fund Inc v World Wrestling Federation* ([2002] UKCLR 388) which related to the use of the initials 'WWF' by the defendant. In 1994 after a number of disputes the parties had entered into a contract under which the defendant would limit its use of the initials. In 1997 the Wrestling Federation set up a web site making extensive use of the initials, and in 1998 it altered its logo so as to make it more obviously constitute the letters WWF. The fund objected, relying on the contract, and the defendant argued this was in restraint of trade. The court found that the federation 'gains no assistance . . . from the doctrine of restraint of trade' (para. 66), holding that where parties enter into a contract to avoid litigation and settle a dispute 'the presumption is that the restraints, having been agreed between the two parties most involved, represent a reasonable division of their interests' (para. 48).

21.2.3 The restraint of trade doctrine and EC law

In a recent case the restraint of trade doctrine was pleaded alongside the operation of art. 81 by a defendant seeking to avoid contractual obligations entered into in relation to a vertical distribution system for scooters for the mobility challenged manufactured by the defendant (*Days Medical Aids Limited* v *Pihsiang Machinery Manufacturing Co Ltd* [2004] EWHC 44 (Comm)). Following a disagreement with the distributor, a company based in Wales, the defendant, based in Taiwan, had repudiated the contract, and then faced an action for damages, which were eventually awarded in substantial amounts. At paras 265–6 of the judgment Langley MJ, referring to cases such as *WWF* (above) held that the restraint of trade doctrine did not 'predominantly pursue an objective different from articles 81 and 82', and therefore held that he was precluded from applying the doctrine in situations in which art. 81 was applicable by virtue of the operation of Regulation 1/2003, art. 3, and the general principles governing the relationship between national and Community competition law. If this is held to be the case in future, and it is by no means certain that this judgment will be followed, this is a remarkable recognition of the extent to which the doctrine has moved from being a matter of individual liberty, and become one of economic regulation.

21.2.4 Conclusion

The fact that restraint of trade can be applied to vertical commercial arrangements, and to the rules of professional associations, as well as to the classic sale of business or employee/employer relationships means that it continues to be relevant to competition law. In some situations the doctrine has been able to fill in gaps left by the statutory regulation. It is also becoming increasingly important in relation to ties between recording artists and their record companies, and to those between sportsmen and sportswomen and their managers or teams (see, e.g., Greenfield, S., and Osborn, G., *Contract and Control in the Entertainment Industry*, Dartmouth, Ashgate (1998)). The doctrine may also be examined as part of the wider class of illegal or unenforceable contracts, and may in particular be relevant to situations in which there are inequalities of bargaining power. Those interested in these aspects of restraint of trade should refer to a more detailed contract law text.

21.3 Economic torts

As early as 1410 it was clear that the mere act of competition could not be classed as tortious, even though the competition might have harmful effects for some parties (*The Schoolmasters of Gloucester Case* (1410) YB 11 Hen IV, fo 47, pl. 21). While the view persisted through the nineteenth century that it might be unlawful in some circumstances to deliberately act in such a way as to harm another's economic interests, judicial acceptance of this principle diminished, and the general position in English law was summed up by Bowen LJ in *Mogul Steamship* v *McGregor* (1889) 23 QBD 598, CA:

> The substance of my view is this: that competition, however severe and egotistical, if unattended by circumstances of dishonesty, intimidation, molestation [or other illegalities] gives rise to no cause of action at common law. I myself should deem it to be a misfortune, if we were to attempt to prescribe to the business world how honest and peaceable trade was to be carried on in a case where no such illegal elements as I have mentioned exist, or were to adopt some standard of judicial 'reasonableness' or of 'normal' prices or 'fair freights' to which commercial adventurers, otherwise innocent, were bound to conform.

This view informs the various torts which relate to matters of competition. In each case, whether it be conspiracy, or inducement to break a contract, or interference with economic interests, the general rule is that an action which by itself is lawful does not become actionable if it results in adverse consequences for any particular trader. The courts are not well equipped to regulate competition, and in recognition of this fact will generally intervene only following an act that is itself recognized as unlawful. For a thorough discussion of the following torts see Carty, H., *An Analysis of the Economic Torts*, Oxford, OUP (2001).

21.3.1 Conspiracy

If there is an exception to the general principle set out above, and it has been recognized that 'the tensions in this history have, however, left their mark . . . there remains a penumbra of doubt' (Brazier, M. (ed.), *Clerk & Lindsell on Torts*, London, Sweet & Maxwell (17th edn, 1995), para. 23–04), it lies in the tort of 'conspiracy to injure'. Conspiracy in relation to economic torts has two arms, and a tort may also lie in situations in which there is a conspiracy to use unlawful means, which is related to the crime of conspiracy, although the unlawful means need not be criminal ones. The tort of conspiracy to injure may exist in situations in which there is a combination to harm another for no legitimate reason (see *Crofter Hand Woven Harris Tweed* v *Veitch* [1942] AC 435, HL).

The general proposition may be expressed thus:

(1) A combination of two or more persons wilfully to injure a man in his trade is unlawful and, if it results in damage to him is actionable. (2) If the real purpose of the combination is not to injure another, but to forward or defend the trade of those who enter into it, then no wrong is committed and no action will lie, although damage to another ensues. (*Sorrell* v *Smith* [1925] AC 700, *per* Lord Cave CJ)

Mogul Steamship v *McGregor* (1889) 23 QBD 598, CA; [1892] AC 25, HL is further authority for the proposition that it is quite legitimate, at common law, to conspire with others to improve a business position, even if harm to another is a direct consequence of this. In this case a group of shipowners formed an association to restrict access to routes, to raise prices, and thence to increase the profits made. When the plaintiff company attempted to enter the market by undercutting the group's prices, the group acted in concert and reduced prices so as to drive out the entrant. The action was brought on the basis of both restraint of trade and conspiracy. Even had it been established that there was a restraint of trade issue, privity of contract would have prevented the plaintiff from recovering under this head.

There have been cases where the plaintiff has been successful in an action for damages following conspiracy. One such is *Quinn* v *Leathem* [1901] AC 495, in which a butcher employing a non-unionized workforce lost custom when the union persuaded one of those being supplied meat by Leathem to cease to do business with him. Here there was no legitimate benefit to the union or to the customer in agreeing that the customer should cease to trade with Leathem, and the real object of the 'conspiracy' was to injure the plaintiff. In this, and other similar cases, it is necessary to establish, on the facts, that it is the intention to injure which is paramount. The House of Lords has labelled this tort 'anomalous' as A is able to recover following B's otherwise lawful act that is made tortious only because it is committed as part of an agreement with C. However, the tort is 'too well established to be discarded, however anomalous it may seem' (*Lonhro Ltd* v *Shell Petroleum Co. (No. 2)* [1982] AC 173 at 189).

Although these principles remain good law, they have largely fallen into disuse, and it is unlikely that competition practitioners will have much recourse to the conspiracy doctrine now that art. 81 EC and the Chapter I Prohibition of the Competition Act 1998 are better able to provide a remedy in similar situations.

Where a conspiracy employs unlawful means and causes injury to a party a claim may also be upheld. This principle may extend to situations where the act complained of is not a criminal one, and in one case conspiracy was raised success-fully when it was argued that the arrangement would, under the terms of the Restrictive Trade Practices Act 1956, be against the public interest (*Daily Mirror Newspapers Ltd* v *Gardner* [1968] 2 QB 762). It appeared briefly to be the case that intention to injure was also to be a determining factor in cases based on conspiracy using unlawful means, at which point the distinction between the two heads of conspiracy would be eroded. This was suggested in *Lonhro Ltd* v *Shell Petroleum Co. (No. 2)* [1982] AC 173, HL. In *Lonhro plc* v *Fayed* [1992] 1 AC 448, HL, the House of Lords retreated from this position, holding that it was necessary only to show that there had been an intent to injure, and not that this was to be the purpose of the conspiracy.

21.3.2 **Unlawful interference with economic interests**

Unlawful interference with economic interests will arise in situations in which a defendant commits an actionable wrong with the intention of harming the plaintiff. The tort is an independent one that is not dependent on conspiracy (see above), or inducement to breach a contract (see below).

In *Lonhro plc* v *Fayed* [1990] 2 QB 479, the plaintiff alleged that it had been tortiously deprived of the chance to bid for the share capital in the House of Fraser, which amongst other things owned Harrods, by virtue of the defendants mis-representing their financial status. The plaintiff relied, in part, on the speech of Lord Watson in *Allen* v *Flood* [1898] AC 1, in which may be found the basis of a tort of *unlawful* interference with economic interests. This tort may apply where A intends damage to B, and achieves this by wrongful behaviour towards C (in *Lonhro*, a deceit), so that C's behaviour will damage B. A may then be liable to B. The Court accepted that such a tort existed, but, Dillon LJ argued, 'the detailed limits of [the tort] have yet to be refined' (at 489). It may be the case that there is little to distinguish *Allen* v *Flood* from *Mogul Steamship*, with the difference being that *Allen* v *Flood* relates to the actions of a single person and *Mogul Steamship* to conspiracy. Dillon LJ suggested, however, that it need not necessarily be the case that it was the predominant purpose of the tortfeasor to injure the victim rather than to pursue their own benefit (at 488–9), and that an action might lie on the basis merely that there had been wrongful conduct with respect to a third party, such as wrongful interference with a third party's contract, which caused harm to the plaintiff. The action complained of *must* be unlawful, and it was stressed in *Allen* v *Flood* that a lawfully exercised right cannot, in this context, become unlawful whatever the motive of the party.

21.3.3 **Unlawful interference with contractual relations and inducing a breach of contract**

It is a tort for C to induce B to breach a contract with A, to the detriment of A, without there being a reasonable justification. For example, in *Greig* v *Insole* [1978] 1 WLR 302 promoters of a cricket tournament brought an action against the English cricket authorities when the latter induced players contracted with the promoter to break those contracts. The application of this doctrine may be par-ticularly pertinent to competitive situations, as it means that it may be tortious for one party to acquire another's customers by unlawfully inducing those customers to break contracts, or where existing contractual relationships are otherwise unlawfully interfered with (*DC Thomson and Co. Ltd* v *Deakin* [1952] Ch 646). It will not apply to situations in which A merely tries to persuade B's customers that A offers a better deal; B must show that A both knew of the existing contract and intended to interfere with it.

Although there have been some suggestions to the effect that a simple interference with a contract will lie within the tort (see, e.g., Lord Denning in *Torquay Hotel Co. Ltd* v *Cousins* [1969] 2 Ch 106), the better view remains that no action lies unless a full breach is induced.

21.3.4 **The tort of unfair competition**

The Paris Convention for the Protection of Industrial Property, art. 10*bis* requires that:

(1) The countries of the Union are bound to assure to nationals of such countries effective protection against unfair competition.
(2) Any act of competition contrary to honest practices in industrial or commercial matters constitutes an act of unfair competition.

The United Kingdom has not introduced specific instruments to ensure compliance with this principle, which relates primarily to intellectual property, and it is generally accepted that the obligations imposed by this article are met by the torts of passing off and injurious falsehood, and by the Trade Descriptions Act 1968. While these laws may indeed be invoked to protect economic interests 'it may be safely asserted that there is no tort of unfair competition in this country' (Adams, J., 'Is there a Tort of Unfair Competition?' [1985] *Journal of Business Law* 26, at p. 32). Because of its close relationship with intellectual property law, consideration of these issues belongs more properly to a text on intellectual property law. For a clear summary of the present position the reader is referred to Robertson, A., and Horton, A., 'Does the United Kingdom or the European Community Need an Unfair Competition Law?' [1995] *EIPR* 568.

21.3.5 **Statutory torts**

Because of the close relationship between the statutory torts based on breaches of arts 81 and 82, and those to be based on the Chapter I and II Prohibitions of the Competition Act 1998, and the public regulation of competition the doctrine of statutory torts is dealt with in Chapter 7.

INDEX